HYPATIA'S
DAUGHTERS

A **Hypatia** BOOK

HYPATIA'S DAUGHTERS

Fifteen Hundred Years of Women Philosophers

EDITED BY
LINDA LOPEZ McALISTER

INDIANA UNIVERSITY PRESS
Bloomington and Indianapolis

Manufactured in the United States of America

Library of Congress Cataloging-in-Publication Data

Hypatia's daughters : fifteen hundred years of women philosophers /
edited by Linda Lopez McAlister.
    p. cm. — (A Hypatia book)
    Includes index.
    ISBN 0-253-33057-2 (alk. paper). — ISBN 0-253-21060-7 (pbk. :
alk. paper)
    1. Women philosophers. I. McAlister, Linda L. II. Series.
B105.W6H97   1996
108'.2—dc20   95-45598

1 2 3 4 5 01 00 99 98 97 96

CONTENTS

INTRODUCTION

LINDA LOPEZ McALISTER

It was ten years ago when editor Margaret Simons published a short notice in volume I, number 2, of *Hypatia: A Journal of Feminist Philosophy* inviting proposals for a special issue on the history of women in philosophy. When I responded to her call and was invited by the *Hypatia* editorial board to guest edit that issue, the "state of the art" in the study of the history of women in philosophy was vastly different than it is a decade later. At that time, like many of us who were working on the history of women in philosophy, I was largely fueled in my efforts by the combination of surprise, delight, and anger I felt when I had learned, only recently, that *there had been* women philosophers in the past after all, despite the fact that not a word about them had been included in either my graduate or my undergraduate philosophy curricula. The reason for a feminist to be surprised and delighted at this is obvious enough, but reasons for anger were, perhaps, somewhat more complex. It came first from a sense that an injustice had been done to these women philosophers. For, as I then thought, even if they weren't very good philosophers (and I naively assumed that they must not have been very good or they *would have* appeared in the histories) they deserve at least to be mentioned in the histories of philosophy, just as many quite insignificant-seeming male philosophers are at least alluded to in these works. Another reason for anger was that, since the traces of these women philosophers had been effectively removed from the histories of philosophy, women philosophers of my generation, i.e., those who studied philosophy in the 1950s and 1960s, had been, as feminist historian Gerda Lerner puts it, "denied the opportunity to stand on the shoulders of our foremothers."[1] If you think no woman has traveled this road before you, and it is a road, as Lerner also points out, that runs contrary to thousands of years of negative gender indoctrination around the question of women's rational and philosophical capabilities, it is very hard to persevere in thinking of yourself as philosophical material, so to speak. So the anger was not just at the injustice done to these women by erasing them from history; it was also at the injustice done to us in depriving us of knowledge of possible models and foremothers.

The first organized modern effort to identify and retrieve earlier women philosophers from the historical black hole to which they had been consigned by nineteenth- and twentieth-century historians of philosophy had been started by Mary Ellen Waithe only in 1981.[2] Her Project on the History of Women in Philosophy was joined by approximately forty scholars from many different countries, who worked for a dozen years researching, translating, and writing biographical and philosophical essays about more than 150 women philosophers.[3] But a decade ago the results of the project had not yet appeared in print.

Few journal articles had as yet been published on women in the history of philosophy, and, aside from the occasional "big name," e.g., Hypatia or Wollstonecraft, there was little information among philosophers even about who they were. As I pointed out in my introduction to the special issue of *Hypatia* (McAlister 1989), the eight-volume *Encyclopedia of Philosophy* (Edwards 1967) didn't contain a single article about a woman, making it clear that even the "big names" weren't considered important as philosophers. In this atmosphere it seemed to be striking a blow for feminism merely to identify these women philosophers and tell the world that they had existed. So, when I put forth the call for papers for that special issue it was very broadly written, seeking papers on "any aspect" of the history of women in philosophy, including "expository, biographical, and bibliographical pieces" as well as "feminist analyses of the works of women philosophers," "discussions of ways to 'mainstream' the works of women philosophers into history of philosophy curricula," "assessments of the contributions of women to philosophy," and "items for an Archives section." It felt as if we were starting at the beginning, and in many ways we were. Even with such a broad call for papers, the number of submissions we received was relatively low, and after the review process was concluded, we did not have quite enough accepted papers to make a complete issue of the journal, so Margaret Simons filled out the issue with an unrelated paper.

If someone wanted to include women philosophers in their history of philosophy courses in the 1980s, it was extremely difficult to do so. Not only were there, as yet, few secondary sources available; there were also virtually no primary sources. Selections of philosophical writings by women were seldom, if ever, included in history of philosophy textbooks, and full works by women philosophers were mostly long out of print and only accessible in rare book collections of major libraries. Some whose work was becoming available thanks to the more general feminist movement, e.g., Sor Juana de la Cruz or Christine de Pisan or Charlotte Perkins Gilman, were not generally thought of as philosophers (an assessment that is called into question by the chapters in this volume about them).

Where has the study of the history of women in philosophy come in the intervening decade? A long way. First, Mary Ellen Waithe's Project on the History of Women in Philosophy began to bear fruit. The volumes of *A History of Women Philosophers* that contained the results of the project began slowly to appear—volume one covering the period between 600 B.C. and A.D. 500 came out in 1987. That was followed in 1989 by volume two (500–1600), with volume three (1600–1900) appearing in 1991 and volume four (1900–today) in 1995.[4]

Also in 1987 at the Eastern Division meetings of the American Philosophical Association, Veda Cobb Stevens announced the founding of an organization dedicated to the history of women in philosophy, the Society for the Study of Women Philosophers. She presided over the inaugural meeting, which included a program of speakers reflecting the society's broadly inclusive view of who counts as a woman philosopher.[5] This organization has flourished and now typically sponsors two sessions at each Eastern Division annual meeting, during which half a dozen or more papers on women philosophers are presented. The annual calls for papers for the society reach people who are already engaged in writing about women philosophers and encourage people who are not yet doing such research to start doing it.

The *Hypatia* special issue on the history of women in philosophy appeared in spring 1989. Despite the lack of availability of the primary texts of the women philosophers written about in that issue, I received reports that it had been used as a supplement to mainstream history of philosophy courses.

In the intervening years, as might have been expected, *Hypatia: A Journal of Feminist Philosophy,* of which I became general editor in 1990, has continued to publish articles about women philosophers. But now other journals, both feminist and mainstream, also are willing to publish such articles. This volume includes chapters reprinted not only from *Hypatia* but also *Women's Studies International Forum, Philosophical Quarterly,* and the *Journal of the History of Philosophy.*

The problem of the accessibility of the writings of women philosophers from the past is also, gradually, being addressed. Margaret Atherton has edited a small selection of excerpts suitable for use in undergraduate history of philosophy classes titled *Women Philosophers of the Early Modern Period* (Atherton 1994), and Eileen O'Neill is preparing a more comprehensive two-volume collection, *Women Philosophers of the Seventeenth and Eighteenth Centuries: A Collection of Primary Sources* (O'Neill, n.d.). More and more new philosophy textbooks that come across my desk include selections by women philosophers.

In the mid-1990s there is a major movement by publishers of English-language books to bring out a whole raft of new or revised philosophical encyclopedias. The *Encyclopedia of Philosophy* is producing an addendum or appendix that will actually include articles on women philosophers. Various other more specialized encyclopedias and "companions," in such areas as the history of philosophy, feminist theory, and twentieth-century philosophy are in the works, all of which are using women philosophers as writers, editors, etc., and are, therefore, almost certain to contain information about women philosophers.

To my knowledge this volume is the first book-length collection of articles about women in the history of philosophy.[6] Articles that appeared in the original *Hypatia* special issue on women in the history of philosophy (now out of print) make up about one-third of the chapters.[7] Roughly another third are reprinted from later issues of *Hypatia*.[8] And, finally, a third are either reprinted from other journals[9] or are published for the first time in this volume.[10]

Why is this book called *Hypatia's Daughters*? Hypatia, after all, wasn't the first woman philosopher. The Project on the History of Women in Philosophy amply documented that there were many women philosophers before Hypatia; she didn't come along until the fourth century A.D. Among those who preceded her were numbers of Pythagorean women philosophers from the sixth to the third or second century B.C. and others—Aspasia of Miletus (died circa 401 B.C.), Diotima of Mantinea (supposing she was an actual person and not merely a fictional character invented by Plato, she would have lived in the fourth century B.C.), Roman empress Julia Domna (A.D. 170–217), and Makrina (died A.D. 380), to name a few (Waithe 1987). Yet I have chosen to call this book *Hypatia's Daughters* and to include in it articles by contemporary philosophers about women philosophers from Hypatia's time until the present for several reasons, both practical and symbolic. First, it's fair to say that the historical woman Hypatia is among the best known and remembered of ancient women philosophers. She is recognized not so much for her work itself, which for many centuries was believed, erroneously, to have been entirely lost, though in fact, as Mary Ellen Waithe argues in her chapter, some of it has survived but was misplaced, catalogued under the names of others. Rather, it is Hypatia's reputation as learned woman and teacher, passed on to us from antiquity by her students, and the dramatic nature of her horrible death at the hands of the Christians that have kept her memory alive and provided the grist for many dramatizations and fictional recreations of the event over the centuries. We begin this volume with one such contemporary reimagining of Hypatia's murder, by Ursule Molinaro. Second, most of the recent writing concerning women in the history of philosophy has been about those who lived and worked in the fifteen hundred years since Hypatia lived.

And, of course, as I've already mentioned, the basis for this volume is the special issue that *Hypatia: A Journal of Feminist Philosophy,* named in honor of Hypatia, published on women in the history of philosophy in 1989, so the title alludes to the origin of the collection it names.

Among the chapters in this collection the reader may be able to discern several strata of work. Among the earliest pieces, those dating from the 1989 special issue, for example, you are likely to find chapters that are more expository in nature, simply trying to say who the woman philosopher was and what her views were on a specific set of philosophical issues without attempting to give a particularly feminist slant to the analysis or to look for ways in which being a woman philosopher with a particular social location and at a particular juncture in history might have made a difference to her philosophizing. As time went on, however, and we got over the newness of the rediscovery that there had been women in the history of philosophy, approaches to writing this history began to change. Perhaps the most important change is that we no longer naively assume that these women probably weren't really that important or that good as philosophers. For one thing, we have learned that many of them were very well known for their philosophical pursuits in their own day. And it was not unusual, for example, that women philosophers were treated with a great deal of respect by their male contemporaries in the sixteenth through eighteenth centuries, as chapters on Princess Elisabeth, Anne Conway, Sor Juana, Damaris Cudworth Masham, Catharine Trotter, and Belle van Zuylen suggest. We have learned a lot, too, in the last decade about canon building and the kind of factors that might have an influence on who belongs in the canon of worthies and who does not. It no longer looks quite so much like a pure meritocracy as it used to. As historians of philosophy have shed their naive ideas about who gets recognized as a philosopher and who does not, we have been more likely to engage the work of early women philosophers *as philosophy* with a new respect for their ideas and contributions. We have moved from reportage, through a stage of defending their right to be considered philosophers (even if they are not in the histories of philosophy and didn't write in the genres of choice for philosophical writing in their time and place), into a phase in which we are more likely to be willing to engage their ideas seriously and see them in relation to the issues that are of concern to us at the end of the twentieth century.

Furthermore, it is an inescapable fact that feminist philosophy, as it has been developing over recent decades, itself has implications for the historiography of philosophy. These implications demand that a feminist history of philosophy be written in a manner quite different from previous histories of philosophy. When I first studied the history of philosophy, it consisted (apart, perhaps, from very brief biographical sketches of the philosophers that were deemed to be largely irrelevant to their philosophy) of a long linear narrative, stretching from the Pre-Socratics to the present, of philosophical ideas and logical argumentation. As this narrative unfolds, the prevailing position is repeatedly attacked and vanquished by a new one which, in turn, becomes the position of the moment—something like a vast, unending intellectual chess tournament in which the leader is forever being deposed by a new leader. A few philosophers may have had different views of the matter, e.g., Hegelians or Franz Brentano in the nineteenth century. But even Brentano, who ventured the idea that this history of philosophy was not a *linear* but a *cyclical* progression, still believed that in writing the history of philosophy the only thing that counts is the play of pure, rational, disembodied, ahistorical, apolitical, disinterested, universally valid thought that forms the true and definitive story of how Western philosophy has developed.

Feminist philosophy as it has emerged in recent years contests many of the assumptions underlying this traditional way of conceiving of philosophy. It calls into question the "innocence" of philosophy by calling into question the notion that philosophical thought is, or could be, ungendered, unaffected by the political, social, psychological, and other positions philosophers occupy. These critiques demand that the feminist history of philosophy approach its subject in a new and multifaceted way. It will, of course, still be a narrative of philosophical positions and arguments, but any narrative that is constructed will recognize that it is but one of many possible narratives. This history will be written in the belief that philosophers' lives and experience are not irrelevant but, rather, essential to the philosophical views they hold, and, further, that their experience itself is not appropriately viewed as unimpeachable first-person testimony but as something that stands in need of interpretation in light of the social forces that underlie it.

The chapters in *Hypatia's Daughters* constitute a diverse group of approaches and methodologies to the history of women in philosophy, and reflect the changes just described. The history of women in philosophy is a rapidly developing and fascinating subfield, and this book can be seen as a kind of record of where it has been and where it is going at the end of the twentieth century.

I would like to thank Joan Catapano at Indiana University Press for her enthusiasm for this project from the moment I suggested it and for her encouragement. Each of the anonymous readers of my original proposal wrote extremely thoughtful and helpful comments, and they will recognize when they see the book how much it has been improved by their ideas. Thanks, too, to *Hypatia*'s graduate assistant, Eileen Kahl, whose broken arm kept her from doing *Hypatia* work but, luckily for this book, did not keep her from putting in innumerable hours in the library tracking down articles from other sources to be considered for inclusion. Her good judgment and recommendations were invaluable to me. Thanks go, as well, to Laura Sells and other *Hypatia* staff members who cheerfully put up with a second project setting up shop in our small office in the Department of Women's Studies at University of South Florida. In the final stages of preparing the manuscript I was provided with research facilities at the Alice Paul Center for the Study of Women at the University of Pennsylvania by Carroll Smith-Rosenberg and Demie Kurz, co-directors of the Penn Women's Studies Program, and with a loving home in Philadelphia by Sharon Bode, whose support over the years deserves the most thanks of all.

NOTES

1. See Lerner (1992) and McAlister (1994).

2. As she mentions in her introduction to the series of books that ensued, there were earlier compilations of women in the history of philosophy and it was one of these, Gilles Menage's 1690 work *Historia Mulierum Philosopharum* that first made her aware there had been women in the history of philosophy and started her on her modern-day efforts to find them again.

3. The results of that project began appearing in late 1987, when volume 1 of *A History of Women Philosophers* was published. The fourth and final volume of the work did not appear until 1995. See Waithe (1987, ix–xxi) for an account of how and why the Project on Women in the History of Philosophy got started.

4. There is a discrepancy between the volume itself, which gives a publication date of 1995, and the Library of Congress catalogue listing, which gives it as 1994.

5. The statement of purpose of the Society for the Study of Women Philosophers reflects the generosity of the late Veda Cobb Stevens's vision:

1. The first purpose of the Society for the Study of Women Philosophers is to create and sustain a "Republic of Letters," in which women are both citizens and sovereigns. To that end, we shall commemorate women philosophers of the past as well as of the present by engaging their texts, whether critically or appreciatively, in a dialogical interchange. In this way, both we and our sisters from the past can also become interlocutors for our sisters in the future.
2. The second purpose of our Society is to examine the nature of philosophy, specifically in light of women's contributions to the discipline. Thus, papers are welcome which reflect on the methodology and style of women

philosophers themselves, or which compare the texts of women with those of men.

3. Furthermore, since philosophical method may be distinguished from philosophical understanding, it is possible that philosophical understanding could be reached in a variety of ways. The Society, therefore, will also explore the nature of philosophy by comparing the works of women philosophers with those of women thinkers of other types, such as poets, mystics, novelists or biographers. We thus hope to enlarge and enrich the resources of everyone who is concerned with the central and most basic questions of human life.

The first meeting of the society reflected this third point by including a paper on philosophical aspects of a Virginia Woolf novel and a reading of some of her philosophical poems by the poet Amy Clampitt.

6. A book-length collection of selected papers presented at sessions of the Society for the Study of Women Philosophers over the years is being prepared under the editorship of Cecile Tougas and Sara Ebenreck.

7. They are the chapters by Molinaro, Duran, Frankel, McFadden, Egan, and Baseheart. I have omitted Beatrice Zedler's fascinating and admirable scholarly piece on "The Three Princesses" because its focus is more biographical than philosophical, because two of the three princesses, while important to the history of philosophy for their support of philosophers and philosophical institutions, did not themselves write philosophy, and because Andrea Nye's new paper on Princess Elisabeth is an admirable example of the way in which women philosophers are now being paid attention to, not just because they are some previously unknown phenomenon but on the basis of the philosophical views they have developed. I have also omitted Joan Gibson's article "Educating for Silence: Renaissance Women and the Language Arts" because, although it does a wonderful job of providing background information on the kind of education sixteenth- and seventeenth-century women philosophers would have had, it does not deal with any specific woman philosopher. Finally, I have omitted Mary Ellen Waithe's piece on incorporating women into history of philosophy curricula, "On Not Teaching the History of Philosophy."

8. They are the chapters by John, Nye (Heloise), Cutting-Gray, Mackenzie, Jacobs.

9. These are the chapters by Green, Bolton, and Hermsen.

10. The new chapters are Nye (Princess Elisabeth), Waithe, Beggs, and Green and Radford Curry.

A CHRISTIAN MARTYR IN REVERSE
HYPATIA: 370–415 A.D.

URSULE MOLINARO

The screams of a 45-year-old Greek philosopher being dismembered[1] by early-5th-century Christians, in their early-5th-century church of Caesareum, in Alexandria, center of early-5th-century civilization, reverberated between the moon gate & the sun gate of that civilized Egyptian city.

Before the philosopher's broken body was thrown into the civilized Alexandrian gutter, for public burning.

& smoke signals rose from the disorderly chunks of her charring flesh, warning future centuries of reformers & healers that they must hush their knowledge if they wished to avoid burning as heretics, or witches. If they wished to stay alive.

In a world run by a new brand of Christians, politicians of faith, who outlawed independent thought. Especially when thought by women. Whom they offered a new role model of depleasurized submission as they converted the great & lusty earthmother goddess into a chaste mother of a martyred god.

Whose teachings they converted into an orthodox church.

Which converted heresy—a word that used to mean: choice; of a view of life other than the norm—into the crime of otherness. Punishable by torture.

—The sudden heresy of astrology.

Which St. Augustine repudiated   together with the suddenly heretic Christianity of the Manichees, & the pagan philosophy of the Greeks after the repudiated stars warned him of the sudden heresy of all his former beliefs. & sources of knowledge.

As they warned Theron, Alexandria's foremost Greek astrologer & mathematician, of the impending martyrdom of his only daughter. The 45-year-old Greek philosopher Hypatia.

Hypatia vol. 4, no. 1 (Spring 1989) © by Ursule Molinaro

Whose chart Theron had cast at the moment of her birth. Taking pride in her strong Mercury that promised eloquent intelligence in fortunate aspect to her Jupiter. That gave her early recognition; a renown greater than his own. Rejoicing at her Moon exalted in the sign of the Bull, that made her clear strong voice turn logic into music. Shaking his head at her Venus in the sign of the Ram, which made her willful in matters of emotion & aesthetics.

Although he had to smile when he recognized that willful Venus in his 4-year-old daughter's request to wear golden sandals on her feet.

& when the 12-year-old started to bind her thick red hair in golden nets.

He was still smiling though with thinner lips when the already renowned young philosopher started to have lovers.

Whose charts he also cast.

& when she married the philosopher Isidore. Whose charted philosophical acquiescence to his willful wife's many amorous friendships made Theron shake his head. & wonder if his brilliant daughter was perhaps abusing the power over men seemingly granted to her by the stars.

Which seemed to turn against her, suddenly, as she approached her 45th year. When the lined-up planets foreshadowed an event of such horror that Theron's civilized early-5th-century mind refused to believe what he saw in her progressions.

Which he recast & recast, until belief in his science outweighed his belief in civilized early-5th-century humanity. & he warned his daughter. Urging her to slip out of the city. To travel to Sicily, perhaps, where earlier Greek philosophers had lived out disgraced lives in quiet meditation, & discreet teaching.

But Hypatia refused to listen to her father.

Or perhaps she did listen, but refused to leave a city that used to sit at her feet, listening to her learning. That seemed to be the only city in her civilized world. Where her current lover lived also.

Or perhaps Hypatia was sensing the end of an era, beyond which she had no desire to live.

Her era, that had allowed her to be learned. More learned than her learned astrologer/mathematician father Theron. Than her philosopher husband Isidore.

& to share her learning. With students as illustrious as Synesius of Cyrene. The only Christian she knew to laugh a hearty laugh. Who had just recently become Bishop of Ptolemais. Who was writing her many affectionate, admiring letters.

An era that had allowed a woman to think. & to become known because of her thoughts.

That allowed the known thinking woman to have lovers, besides having a philosophical philosopher husband.

Powerful lovers, like Orestes, the pagan prefect of Egypt. Her current lover, whom she refused to leave behind in Alexandria.

Whom the Christian gossip of that city had taking orders from his known philosopher-mistress. Whom gossip suspected of being behind the pagan prefect's opposition to Alexandria's Christian patriarch St. Cyril.

Who denied having expressed the unchristian wish to see the accursed woman dead. To his reader Peter.

Who denied having repeated the Christian patriarch's unexpressed unchristian wish   casually, after a mass   to a group of lingering clergy.

Who denied having mentioned the known 45-year-old philosopher by name, in various exhortations

—about the adulterous conduct of pagan wives   the insidious influence of adulterous sex on the minds of pagan politicians; which had led to the martyrdom of earlier Christians in the past—

addressed to various gatherings of their faithful.

Who stopped the unmentioned known 45-year-old philosopher's carriage on its way to her lecture hall. & forced it to go instead to their Christian church of Caesareum.

Where the gathered faithful pulled the philosopher from her carriage.

By the long red hair. In its habitual net of fine gold, that instantly disappeared beneath a faithful cloak.

& by the feet   with their polished toe nails   in their habitual golden leather sandals. That instantly disappeared.

& by her tunic. Which tore. & left her nude.

Standing for another instant   staring wide-eyed across a sea of bodies that were pausing briefly, getting ready to charge   into the new Christian era in which she had no desire to live.

Until she realized how long it took a healthy 45-year-old woman's body to be torn fingers from hands from wrists from elbows from shoulders toes from feet from ankles from knees from thighs. For the 45-year-old heart to stop beating. For her brain to lose its exceptional consciousness.

NOTE

1. According to *The Women's Encyclopedia of Myths and Secrets* (1983): the martyring Christians scraped the flesh off Hypatia's bones with oyster shells.

REFERENCE

Walker, Barbara. 1983. *The woman's encyclopedia of myths and secrets*. New York: Harper & Row.

FINDING BITS AND PIECES OF HYPATIA

MARY ELLEN WAITHE

When *Hypatia: A Journal of Feminist Philosophy* was founded in 1983 and the decision was made to name it after a famous ancient woman philosopher, the received wisdom was that *none of Hypatia's writings survived*. As it turned out, the conventional wisdom was false. In the present chapter I will describe what we can surmise about Hypatia's life, her students, her teaching and her writing.[1]

Hypatia was probably born *circa* 370–375, although some scholars claim (on questionable grounds) a much earlier date.[2] Hypatia was already teaching in Alexandria and was sufficiently well known throughout northern Africa by the year 390, when Synesius came from Cyrene to become her student. Accounts of outrageous tactics that Hypatia used to counter a male student's sexual harassment by throwing the fifth-century equivalent of a used sanitary napkin at him may be apocryphal (Toland 1720; Lewis 1921). Nevertheless they provide insight into the personality of a woman philosopher who was determined to be an outstanding teacher and scholar in a brutally misogynist environment. A traditional middle platonist, Hypatia was sympathetic to Plotinian and Porphyryian metaphysics and to stoicism. In 415, she was savagely murdered, allegedly by a gang of monks. According to the Suda[3] *Lexicon,* her corpse was then hacked into pieces and burned.

The converse of what happened to her corpse happened to the *corpus* of her works. Scholars have been finding and analyzing bits and pieces of scattered mathematical and astronomical writings deriving from the time and place she lived. Like forensic experts who have found scattered body parts, they have independently and in some cases, tentatively, identified these remains as hers.

To date, the best analysis of Hypatia the teacher has come from a study of one of Hypatia's students, Synesius of Cyrene. After studying with Hypatia, Synesius converted to Christianity and soon became Bishop of Ptolemais. His letters to Hypatia have survived, and were translated and analyzed during the nineteenth and twentieth centuries (Lapatz 1870; Fitzgerald 1926). Letters from Hypatia to Synesius probably have not survived. Synesius' letters are full of clues: names of persons who may have been her students and to whom some copy of Hypatia's works might have been loaned, names of cities to which her works might have been sent.

Hypatia of Alexandria by the Polish scholar Maria Dzielska (1995) pieces together a magnificent analysis of Hypatia's teachings and personality based almost exclusively on Synesius' letters. Apparently unknown to Dzielska her analysis of Hypatia's personality and teachings corresponds nicely with that given by the historian of science and mathematics, Wilbur Knorr (1989). And while Dzielska may be accused of somewhat overstating the case by attributing almost every view of Synesius' to Hypatia, Knorr is scrupulous to a fault (if such a thing is possible) when it comes to reserving judgment about identifying particular works as originating with Hypatia.

The connection between philosophic analysis with religious practice may seem a strange one to contemporary secular philosophers. *Our* philosophical views about metaphysics and epistemology have little to do with how we act. But it is impossible to understand and appreciate Hypatia's without understanding two basic things. One is that the philosophical *is* the personal. Holding certain philosophical views about metaphysics implies seeing the world in a particular way. Two, mathematics and astronomy are sciences that apply particular metaphysical views and are the key to achieving personal ethical and religious knowledge. For Hypatia and for her students, the Plotinian interpretation of Plato's metaphysics implied a way of life. Philosophy was not just a job, the teaching of its content was not mere academic exercise, having nothing to do with daily life. Philosophy *was* life. Dzielska brings that point home in a clear and convincing way. For Hypatia, mathematics and astronomy were ways of applying or verifying metaphysical and epistemological features of neo-Platonic Plotinian philosophy. Most mathematicians and astronomers of fourth-century Alexandria, including Hypatia's father, Theon, were not philosophers. Their interests were more technical than philosophical. But Hypatia sought for greater meaning, so the truths of mathematics and astronomy needed to fit into a greater cosmological and ethical framework. This was consistent with the ancient traditions in philosophy from Pythagorean times when philosophy implied a way of life. It is the Pythagoreans with whom *harmonia* was first identified as a mathematical, musical *and* ethical principle. Dzielska reminds us that Synesius called mathematics:

"divine geometry," and its "holy" principles, we remember were applied to the achievement of reciprocal friendly relationships. (*Ep.* 93).

> Of all mathematical sciences auxiliary to metaphysical knowledge,
> Hypatia regarded astronomy as the highest. . . . Synesius preserves her
> view that "astronomy is itself a divine form of knowledge." (Dzielska
> 1995, 54)

Dzielska identifies as disciples of Hypatia not only Synesius, but also
Herculianus, Olympius, and Euoptius who was Synesius' younger brother.
There are others: Ision, Hesychius, an Alexander who was Synesius'
uncle, Athanasius, Theodosius, and Gaius. In addition, Dzielska names
some as possible students: Herculianus' brother Cyrus, Syrus, Petrus,
Paeonius, and Auxentius. These are names mentioned by Synesius as
"companions," those regarding whom exists a connection to "Alexandria," "our Mother, Hypatia," "sacred/holy philosophy/mysteries," or to
"time spent profitably in our youth," "in study," "in contemplation," etc.
Dzielska may cast Hypatia's net too far on the basis of Synesius' "evidence." Synesius seems to have been a blowhard, a braggart, and a self-
aggrandizing name-dropper. But Dzielska's conjecture is plausible and
warrants further scrutiny. In addition to the regular students, Dzielska
says that notable public figures may have been occasional attendees at
quasi-public lectures given by Hypatia. On this list Dzielska includes
Orestes, the augustal prefect of Alexandria, and possibly Pendadius and
Heliodorus, the archontes, Ammonius the curialis, Isidore of Pelusium
(later, St. Isidore), Simplicius the military commander, and other un-
named officials. On Dzielska's view, (and, assuming that she's got Hypatia's roster correct, I'm tempted to agree, here) Hypatia taught only
wealthy young male aristocrats from politically powerful families. On that
account Hypatia is described by Dzielska as an elitist who did nothing to
advance the education of women. But while Synesius appeared to study
geometry and metaphysics with Hypatia, it is clear that other students
studied much more. You have only to look at the works attributed to
Hypatia to get a sense of her scholarship and her teaching activities.

Hypatia of Alexandria was a deeply committed educator and scholar. At
Alexandria during Hypatia's time, the practical applications of mathematics and astronomy were often to be found in the works of the geographers,
the architects, the observational astronomers, and the astrologers. The
technical and theoretical aspects of mathematics and astronomy were
still taught in the schools, often as applied philosophy; i.e., as applied
metaphysics. Hypatia was a philosopher of this stripe. A work by the historian of mathematics, Montluca (1960) mentioned that Hypatia's father,
Theon had "ascribed" one of the books (Book III) of his *Commentary
on Ptolemy's Syntaxis Mathematica* to the authorship of Hypatia. The
Belgian astronomer, Rome, located the only two copies of that *Commentary* that contained Book III in the Vatican collection early this century. During and following the time Rome was establishing the text he

published a number of articles describing various parts of the commentary, but always describing it either as by Theon or as by Theon and Hypatia. Rome's final, established text (Rome 1943) summarized the idiosyncrasies of style (didactic, very terse, formal language) and content (greater mathematical precision) found within Book III (and some later books, too).

Paul Tannery, a French engineer by training, but a historian of science and mathematics by profession, identified a set of problems in the surviving editions of Diophantus' *Arithmetica*[4] as deriving from Hypatia (Tannery 1893–1895). Those problems were also noted by the mathematician Thomas Heath (1960) and translated from Tannery in my *History of Women Philosophers* (Waithe 1987).

The writings Hypatia prepared were for the teaching of students and ancient copies succumbed to the vagaries of time and happenstance (including the burning of the Library at Alexandria). Hypatia's work has a character not unlike that which philosophy has today vis-à-vis medicine. Today, philosophy of medicine and bioethics use philosophy as a tool with which to impose rigor on the science of medicine and with which to analyze ethical issues arising in medical practice. In order to do this well, bioethicists must learn in some depth (but limited breadth) the relevant content areas within the medical sciences. I think that Hypatia used philosophy in exactly the same way when teaching mathematics and astronomy.

In addition to philosophy, Hypatia taught algebra, geometry, and astronomy, preparing for her students critical editions of the texts of her predecessors (Diophantus, Apollonius Pergaeus, Ptolemy, Euclid, Archimedes, Pappus, Zenodorus, etc.). But she is always a philosopher, and so she corrects these texts. Unlike texts by her father and by some of her predecessors, she doesn't play the role of the brilliant scholar who is too knowledgeable to have to complete her proofs. Unlike her father Theon, she is satisfied with approximations and rounding-off. Sometimes she improves the rigor of theorems by finding and then filling in gaps to achieve greater completeness. Sometimes she plays with the theories, extending computations to many additional place values, thereby achieving greater accuracy which improves the predictability of astronomical calculations. Sometimes she pushes the classical proofs to improve their soundness by devising direct proofs where only indirect proofs existed before. Sometimes she connects geometrical theorems to their astronomical applications and to Platonic metaphysics and cosmology. One of the hallmarks of Hypatia's *corpus* (to the extent that we can guarantee that the works are hers) is the symmetry with which she lays out the elements of her proofs, following each with related alternative cases. When possible, she comes up with two seemingly competing hypotheses and works the proof twice, as if to show that no matter how you reasonably might conceptualize the problem, you can get the correct result. The impression here is of a teacher taking into account different students' different learning styles, and their different intuitions. She is not the officious professor full of a sense of her own importance. She doesn't force her students into her mode of thinking about things. She nurtures them, she cultivates diversity. She sees the larger picture, beyond the narrow proof. Hypatia makes no attempt at rhetorical innovation so characteristic of philosophical writing that would appear during the 11th and 12th centuries; her language is terse, precise, repetitive, methodical. It's the beauty of the logic of the proofs, not the aesthetics of the prose that Hypatia cares about. Knorr (1989, esp. ch. 11 and 12) has given an argument that is more compelling than he himself seems willing to believe concerning a group of works ascribable to Hypatia.[5] When we piece together the old evidence I assembled from Halley, Heath, Rome, and Tannery with new evidence from Knorr, the following may tentatively be attributed to Hypatia:

(1) **A***, an edition of Diophantus' *Arithmetica* including new lemmas and other original problems. (Tannery 1893–1895; Heath 1960)

(2) **CS***, the lost prototype based on Archimedes' *Sphere and Cylinder* surviving only as CS: John of Tynemouth's *De curvis superficibus*. (Knorr 1989)

(3) **AI***, the anonymous (lost) prototype that relied heavily on Zenodorus' text on isoperimetric figures, but is now incorporated into *Introduction to the Almagest* by an anonymous author. (Knorr 1989)

(4) **DC***, the lost prototype commentary edition of Archimedes' *Dimension of the Circle*. (Knorr 1989)

(5) **C***, a commentary edition of Apollonius Pergaeus' *Conics* that formed the basis for later commentary editions. (Waithe 1987)[6]

(6) **SM**, an edition (partly concordance, partly revision) of work begun by Theon in Book III (and perhaps other books) of Theon's *Commentary of Ptolemy's Syntaxis Mathematica*. (Rome 1943)

In each case, except **SM**, it is important to remember that we do not have Hypatia's original writings extant; nor do we have a faithful copy seasoned only with obvious corrections and *marginalia*. We are identifying within the context of a surviving later work, an earlier edition or a prototype (indicated by *). This earlier edition or prototype differs from the larger work within which it is found in some one or more ways. It may use a different style of writing, betray a higher level of sophistication, etc. That is how it is possible to mark out Hypatia's material subsequently incorporated (without citation!) by later writers.

On my reading of Knorr's findings, we can supplement the Suda's description of three works by Hypatia[7] with three additional works. I elsewhere suggest (Waithe n.d.) evaluating the entire *corpus* for the respective levels of complexity of technical knowledge required to prepare each work. When we do so, the above ordering I think, suggests the possible order of their composition by Hypatia.

It is my hypothesis that work requiring the least technical knowledge such as algebra and plane geometry may be assumed to have been composed earlier than works requiring the additional mastery of astronomy. On this theory, **A*** on Diophantus' algebra, would be an early work.[8]

CS*, **AI*** and **DC***, however are works on Archimedean geometry. According to Knorr (1990), the Latin CS appears to translate and incorporate an earlier Greek document, **CS***, by Hypatia. Hypatia's **CS*** differs from what is known about the original *Sphere and Cylinder* by Archimedes in several ways:

    (a) it gives a condensed account of Archimedes' chief results on the surface area and volume of the sphere;

    (b) it is lacking entirely Archimedes' results on spherical sectors and segments;

    (c) it contains other results not attributable to Archimedes' own writings;

    (d) it adopts forms of proof not recognizably Archimedean, including citations to Euclidean theorems (from *Elements*) in each proposition.

These differences between the Hypatian prototype and Archimedes' *Sphere and Cylinder* reflect Hypatia's purely pedagogical interests in condensing Archimedes' material from the form in which it then existed, and focussing it on special topics. It also reflects her scholarly interests in incorporating her own cases, reporting her own results, demonstrating her improved methodology, and providing broader theoretical foundations for the proofs from Euclid, from the commentary literature on Hero's *Metrica* and *Stereometrica*, from her father's *Commentary on Ptolemy's Syntaxis Mathematica Book I.*

An identifying feature of Hypatia's work in **CS*** and also in **AI*** perhaps is that she prefers Euclidean methodology over the Archimedean in formulating the results of certain problems. Where the identical problems are treated in other tracts by Pappus, by *his* student Theon, and by others, only Hypatia interjects the philosophically preferable direct proof in favor of what for Pappus and Theon was the traditional standard: Archimedean indirect proof.

AI* is a brief but condensed passage applying the insights of Zenodorus in his *On Isoperimetric Figures* to Archimedean spherical geometry. It is very much like similar tracts by Pappus and Theon, but the differences betray a philosopher's touch (Knorr 1989, 689–751 and 774–80). Some language alludes to Plato's argument in *Timeaus* regarding the shape of the universe. Hypatia's tract explores mathematical explanations for the perfect creation of the universe as a circle moving within a circle. Her reasoning here is that such a construction would be more spacious than any other isoperimetric configuration of the universe and therefore would be able to contain more intelligible beings than would a universe of any other shape. This tract is really no more than a paraphrase of **CS*** (see above). Although it is a separate document in summary form, it would be stretching the point to denote this as a genuinely separate work.

The lost prototype **DC*** is a Commentary on Archimedes' *Dimension of the Circle*. Hypatia is believed to be responsible for preparing an adaptation of Theon's Commentary edition of Archimedes' *Dimension of the Circle*. It is a loosely adapted account of Archimedes' original work, but not based directly on the original. Hypatia introduces and partly deconstructs the substance and results of *Dimension of the Circle*, and adds relevant secondary source materials on plane geometry, including clarifications and amplifications from Pappus and Theon, and Hypatia's own improvements to these. The original Archimedean work is not itself highly technical, but requires understanding of Euclid's *Elements XII*, and Hypatia's apparent penchant for doing long computations, something we see later, in **SM**.

If we trace the paths that this single work **DC***, has taken since Hypatia's death, we get a glimpse of the kind of influence her works had, and the seriousness with which later scholars took her contributions, albeit, in time, without her name attached to the documents. A copy of this particular work **DC***, went to Baghdad, and during the 9th century was translated into Arabic at the Baghdad court of caliph al-Ma'mun by Qusta ibn Luqa. Adaptations were produced by the Banu Musa (sons of Musa: Muhammad, Ahmad and Hassan— 9th century) who included the substance of **DC*** in their *On the measurement of plane and curved figures* (which also contained their adaptation of **CS*** *supra*.) Other versions derived from that of Qusta ibn Luqa were produced by Abu 'l-Rashid ʿAbd al-Hadi (*circa* 12th century), and by Nasir al-Tusi (13th century). It surfaced in two 12th-century Latin versions (by Plato of Tivoli and by Gerard of Cremona), and also in a Hebrew version likely by Kalonymos ben Kalonymos,[9] (sometimes Qalonymous, etc.) a 14th century Jewish philosopher who was born in Provence but lived mostly in Rome.

Let me return to the issue of the development of Hypatia's work. CS*, AI*, and DC* bear textual affinities to each other, according to Knorr (1989, 805ff). It is my conjecture that due to their similarities, they may have been written closely together in what we might call Hypatia's middle period. C*, on Apollonian geometry, is more sophisticated than CS*, AI* and DC* in part because it adopts Pappus' results and improves upon them (Knorr 1982, 1–24). C* and SM may, therefore, represent Hypatia's late period.

A decade ago it was noted that:

> The Suda *Lexicon*, Fabricus in *Bibliotheca Graecorum* and Socrates Scholasticus in *Historiae Ecclesiasticae* all mention that Hypatia authored a commentary on Apollonius of Perga's *Conic Sections*. This Commentary appears to be the only one of the three Hypatian writings reported lost which has actually failed to survive. Edmund Halley, the 17th century British astronomer, collected the ancient Latin and Arabic versions of *Conic Sections* in an attempt to reconstruct the original and to separate scholia and commentary from the original text. This was apparently an insurmountable task, at least with respect to identifying the Hypatian commentary, for although Halley's text lists Hypatia's commentary among its contents, there exists only a title page without additional text. I have not been successful in locating the materials that Halley was working from, but there appears to be little reason to hope that Hypatia's commentary on Apollonius' *Conic Sections* has in fact survived. (Waithe 1987, 191)

Subsequently Professor Knorr[10] mentioned a tantalizing alternative reading of Halley, namely, that Halley intended readers to understand that the collected commentary editions in his volume were based on Hypatia's commentary. The *Commentary on Apollonius Pergaeus' Conics* (C*), to my knowledge does not exist as a separate document, but if I understand Knorr's comment correctly, it may be imbedded in the surviving Halley edition. C*, if indeed it can be teased out from the successor commentary editions, would be the least securely attributed work by Hypatia. C*, whatever it is, presumably formed the basis for other accounts of Apollonius' work, including the Commentary by Eutocius of Askalon on Books I–IV for which he acknowledges his indebtedness to "the copies." Knorr (1982 and 1989) suggests that Eutocius' reference is to commentaries including that (which, for Eutocius would have been the most recent) by Hypatia. In the (unlikely?) event that all differences between the Eutocius and Apollonian texts were to be attributed solely to Hypatia (and not to any other intermediary commentators and scholiasts), we could hazard the following wild guess regarding her possible contribution. By demonstrating connections between remarks by Pappus and her own adaptation of Euclid's theorems on the circle, Hypatia sketches a proof of two original theorems that had been hypothesized, but not demonstrated by Pappus. C* shows that Hypatia was no mere authority on Pappus. She contributes a small but significant improvement to mathematical theory on the projection of the cone: an essential geometric feature of every earth-bound astronomical observation. This is the work of no merely competent professor. Hypatia is an innovative scholar contributing to the theory of her disciplines. I suggest therefore, that C* is likely to be a later work than the Archimedean tracts, CS*, AI* and DC*.

Theon attributes to Hypatia the preparation of at least Book III, "On the Motions of the Sun," in his *Commentary on Syntaxis Mathematica* (SM). Rome (1943) and Knorr (1989) suggest that Hypatia possibly had a hand in Books IV and IX as well. Theon's identification at the beginning of Book III of Hypatia as "the Philosopher" indicates that she had already risen to the top of her career and was a well-established senior scholar with an independent reputation as a philosopher. That Hypatia is acknowledged by her father to have revised what was then and would remain (until Copernicus) the most influential work on mathematical astronomy, is clear evidence of her reputation as a mathematician and theoretical (perhaps not an observational) astronomer. The preparation of C* would have made that reputation indisputable. This view accords with my hypothesis that Hypatia's algebraic and geometrical writings preceded SM. SM is a lengthy work of significant complexity and the only astronomical work of Hypatia's *corpus*. In part because it is on Ptolemaic astronomy as derived through Pappus, I am inclined to view it as a more mature work which relied, nevertheless, on the prior development of C*. The expertise required to produce SM would need to build upon precisely the kinds of expertise demonstrated in all of the prior works. Theon was probably very old by the time of the preparation of the written *Commentary on Syntaxis Mathematica*, and ready to prepare a final edition of the lectures he (and Hypatia?) had given to students. In this work, Hypatia modelled a particular didactic innovation on that of Pappus. To enable students to make quicker and more accurate calculations, Hypatia introduced a system of long division in the sexagesimal system utilizing a table of divisors and dividends. The tables facilitate quicker and more accurate calculations, carrying the results to more integer places than generally recommended by Theon and Pappus. Why is this significant? It is significant because one of the difficulties with the works of the ancient astronomers was that predictability of astronomical events became less precise the further in time they were projected from that of the original observation. One method Hypatia employed to correct for this was to refine and redefine original calculations and to provide resources with which to carry out the results to greater accuracy. In addition, numerous examples are proved twice, employing competing hypotheses. Hypatia noticed some errors in Ptolemy's geocentric model that caused her to be concerned whether it always accurately predicted the position of the sun. I am not sure whether anything should be made of her cryptic comment, but it would be interesting to see whether later astronomers noticed it, and whether it influenced reconsideration of the heliocentric model.

Scholars have often wondered at the identification of Hypatia as a philosopher, and at the curiosity that the titles of her works mentioned by her late contemporary Suidas were scientific and mathematical. Where were her philosophical writings? Clearly, her writings themselves provide significant evidence that what in the modern era are identified as mathematical and astronomical theories needed the touch of a philosopher's conceptual analysis and methodology. And just as bioethics is now considered part of philosophy, so in early 5th-century Alexandria, were the problems of mathematics and astronomy considered to fit squarely within the sphere of philosophy.

When we consider the characteristics of her writings and the description of her philosophical views decipherable through the writings of Synesius of Cyrene, the Hypatian fingerprint begins to emerge. It is the mark of a philosopher who introduces beginning students to Platonic metaphysics, addressing moral and cosmological concerns fleshed out in Plotinian mysteries, tinged with the deep personal religious awe and quasi-mystical contemplation of the One. But the truths of mathematics, especially "divine geometry" prepare one for consideration of higher philosophy. Developing technical expertise in astronomy is part and parcel of testing cosmological theories. For Hypatia, doing so involves filling in significant gaps in the logic of geometrical and astronomical theory. As a scholar, she becomes adept at doing so. But she is also an educator who delights in honing students' abilities to become philosophers. She is a dedicated teacher who prepares for her student a careful, symmetrical exposition of elements of mathematical and astronomical proofs with the introduction of a series of related alternative cases, all expressed in extremely precise application of technical terminology. But all along, her efforts are philosophically motivated: she is on and takes her students along on a quest for completeness, instilling in them a desire to consider all possibilities. She was a model for us all.

NOTES

1. See also Waithe (1987).

2. Notably Dzielska (1995). See below.

3. The conventional wisdom on this changes with the wind. Traditionally, the author has been referred to as "Suidas." Then it was considered an erroneous appellation and the Suda were revealed to be a committee or group of authors who composed the *Lexicon*. More recently, I am again seeing references to "Suidas." I use the names interchangeably.

4. Not *Arithmeticorum* as I originally cited it.

5. I make this paradoxical comment because the original articles by Knorr on the separate documents considered in his book are generally silent about his conjecture that Hypatia is the common source of the prototypes **CS***, **AI***, and **DC***, e.g., "Archimedes and the Measurement of the Circle: A New Interpretation," (1976), "Ancient Versions of Two Trigonometric Lemmas," (1985), "Archimedes' *Dimension of the Circle:* A View of the Genesis of the Extant Text," (1986). And although these works have understandably been somewhat revised by the later interpretations made in Knorr's book, the absence of mention of his hypothesis that Hypatia is the author of the prototype **CS*** from which is derived Johannes de Tinnemue's Latin translation in Knorr's 1990 paper "John of Tynemouth *alias* John of London: emerging portrait of a singular medieval mathematician," *BHJS*, (1990), 23: 293–330 leaves me worried that Knorr has abandoned his hypothesis (for which I admit a bias).

6. I made reference to this in my original chapter (Waithe, 1987) on Hypatia. Knorr wrote to me suggesting that what I may not have understood was that the entire edition Halley prepared may be based on the Hypatian edition of Apollonius. Halley, 1710.

7. Knorr (1989) assumes (p. 755–6) that Suidas' mention of an "Astronomical Table" as one of the three works by Hypatia refers to something other than the tables that are part of the *Syntaxis*. I am inclined to agree with Tannery's conjecture here ". . . that Hypatia commented on the *Astronomical Tables* that are part of the *Almagest*, just as her father Theon commented on the manual tables [*Canones Procheiroi*] of Ptolemy that formed a separate {part of that} work. (Tannery, "L'Article de Suidas Sur Hypatia," *Annales de la Faculte des Letters de Bordeaux*, (1880), p. 199, translation and material in {brackets} mine.

8. Hypatia's introduction of new problems and of alternative solutions to original problems helps illustrate the abstractness and generalizability of algebraic theory. Diophantus' original problems often appeared to be mere puzzles rather than illustrations of general theorems, corollaries, etc. Hypatia demonstrated the generality and indeterminateness of a problem by substituting for assumed unknowns numeric values which themselves are unrelated (e.g., not surds, multiples, powers, fractions, or square roots) to the original value. Therefore, although algebraic, the purpose of **A*** fits squarely within the tradition of philosophy of mathematics.

9. Kalonymos ben Kalonymos also translated treatises on Euclid, Apollonius, Ptolemy and Averroes.

10. Professor Knorr to Professor Waithe, personal communication, November, 1987.

REFERENCES

Dzielska, Maria. 1995. *Hypatia of Alexandria*. Cambridge: Harvard University Press.

Fitzgerald, A. 1926. *The letters of Synesius*. London: Oxford University Press.

Halley, Edmund. 1710. *Apollonius Pergaeus conic sections*. Oxford.

Heath, Thomas. 1960. *Diophantus of Alexandria*. New York: Dolphin.

Knorr, Wilbur. 1982. Observations on the early history of the conics. *Centaurus* 26:1–24.

————. 1989. *Textual studies in Ancient and Medieval geometry*. Boston: Birkhauser.

————. 1990. John of Tynemmouth *alias* John of London: Emerging portrait of a singular Medieval mathematician. *BHJS*.

Lapatz, F. 1870. *Lettres des Synesius. Traduit pur la premier fois et suivies d'etudes sur les derniers moments de l'Hellenisme*. Paris.

Lewis, Thomas. 1921. *The history of Hypatia, a most impudent schoolmistress of Alexandria*. London: Bickerton.

Montluca, J. 1960. *Histoire des mathematiques*. Paris: Librarie Scientifique et Technique.

Rome, A. 1943. *Commentaires de Pappus et de Theon d'Alexandrie sur l'Almageste, Tome III., Theon d'Alexandrie Commentaire sur les Livres 3 et 4 d l'Almageste, Studi e Testi*. Citta del Vaticano; Biblioteca Apostolica Vaticana.

Tannery, Paul. 1880. L'article de Suidas sur Hypatia. *Annales de la Faculte des Lettres de Bordeaux*.

————. [1893–95]. 1974. *Diophanti Alexandrini opera omnia*. Two volumes. Stutgardiae: Teubner.

Toland, John. [1720]. 1921. Hypatia; or, The history of a most beautiful, most virtuous, most learned, and every way accomplish'd lady; who was torn to pieces by the clergy of Alexandria, to gratify the pride, emulation, and cruelty of their Archbishop Cyril. In *Tetradymus*. London: J. Brotherton.

Waithe, Mary Ellen. 1987. *A history of women philosophers, Volume 1: Ancient women philosophers*. Dordrecht: Kluwer Academic Publishers.

HILDEGARD OF BINGEN

A NEW TWELFTH-CENTURY WOMAN PHILOSOPHER?

HELEN J. JOHN, S.N.D.

"Any questions?" I ask my weekend philosophy class.

"The question is, Why haven't we heard of Hildegard before? Why isn't she in *everyone's* philosophy courses?"

Very good questions, with two answers—one simple and one complicated. The simple answer is that up until now, we haven't had the source materials. The complicated answer to the question why Hildegard has not been studied *in philosophy*, I'll save for the end of this essay.

The three books chosen for review here, taken together, provide a solid foundation for introducing Hildegard into philosophy classes. Barbara Newman, in *Sister of Wisdom: St. Hildegard's Theology of the Feminine,* makes clear *why* Hildegard deserves our attention. Newman demonstrates how feminine images of divine power, nurturance, fecundity, and freshness pervade Hildegard's metaphysics, cosmology, and anthropology.

Hildegard's own *Scivias*, now published unabridged in English in Paulist Press's Classics of Western Spirituality, provides us with a substantial portion of *what* Hildegard had to say, in the great first volume of her visionary trilogy.

Sabina Flanagan's biography, *Hildegard of Bingen 1098–1179: A Visionary Life,* gives us a broad introduction to Hildegard's writings and other activities, together with sociological and psychological explanations of *how* she could do what she did.

Newman's *Sister of Wisdom* gives us a captivating account of Hildegard's relevance for feminists. Newman boldly claims Hildegard "as the first Christian thinker to deal seriously and positively with the feminine as such, not merely with the challenges posed by and for women in a male-dominated world" (Newman 1987, xvii). She situates Hildegard in the sapiential tradition, which seeks out and celebrates divine Wisdom indwelling in all creation (Newman 1987, xvii).

Hildegard's method of teaching moves within the rich and complex world of Christian symbolism; in this regard she is profoundly at home in the thought and art of her time. Her visions portray reality in ideal Forms: divine Wisdom and heavenly Love; Eve and Mary as archetypes of fallen and redeemed humanity; Ecclesia, Mother Church, as the graced and vulnerable people of God. From contemplation of these figures, Hildegard draws a rich and nuanced "theology of the feminine." Accordingly, Newman explains, much of her own book consists of "interpretation of highly symbolic texts, together with the manuscript paintings that illustrate them" (Newman 1987, xviii).

For Hildegard (as for her male contemporaries, Bernard Silvestris and Alan of Lille), feminine symbolic figures give expression to a "Platonizing cosmology," whose themes are "the divine ideas, eternal in the mind of God and bodied forth in creatures; the world soul; the deep resonance of macrocosm with microcosm; the fervent hope of access to God through human rationality and virtue" (Newman 1987, 44–45). Newman points out that for Hildegard the ideal symbolic forms of her visions seemed more *real* than the actual people she encountered. "She was a Platonist not only by virtue of this or that opinion, but in her most fundamental habits of thought and perception" (Newman 1987, 247).

Hildegard presents an all-encompassing vision of reality pervaded by the imagery and the experience of her own womanly existence: "Where the feminine presides, God stoops to humanity and humanity aspires to God." The world of our experience appears to Hildegard metaphysically, as coming forth from God in creation and returning to God in self-realization; salvation history unfolds in divine revelation and human response. "Hildegard herself perceived [reality], in her last vision, as the endless circulation of the energy of love" (Newman 1987, 45).

This overarching design is not unique to Hildegard. It is in essence the Pseudo-Dionysian theme of creation's coming forth from God and returning to God—the design that Aquinas chose to structure his *Summa Theologiae*. Nor does Hildegard reject the customary masculine images of God, or even the established male prerogatives, of medieval Christendom. Newman gives full weight to Hildegard's use of masculine names of God, as Father, Son, King, Redeemer, and Judge; and she confronts directly and repeatedly the paradoxical character of Hildegard's acceptance of her own womanly weakness as the condition of God's wondrous power at work in her life (Newman 1987, 45; 2–4; 248–49).

But the originality and fascination of Hildegard's thought, as Newman presents it, grows from Hildegard's elaboration of distinctively feminine themes and images. The principle of all life, of all reality, in Hildegard's thought is named *viriditas*; the fresh green of new leaves is emblematic of growth and fertility in all the aspects of nature, and in all the manifestations of grace (Newman 1987, 102). Divine Love, Caritas, in the guise of the *anima mundi*, the world soul, embraces the universe, with the human being at its heart (Newman 1987, 64–71). For each human being is a microcosm, a little world through whom the great world, the universe as macrocosm, comes to self-awareness: "Nothing in the macrocosm lacksi"ts correlative in the microcosm; nothing in the world is mortal or meaningless" (Newman 1987, 70).

In her medical notes (for which she claimed no special inspiration), Hildegard writes as "a woman who, virgin though she was, had clearly come to terms with her own sensuality, and in all likelihood talked with other women about theirs" (Newman 1987, 131); she relies less upon classical humor theory than upon her own observations of women (Newman 1987, 132). Prudence Allen, R.S.M., found in the medical writings grounds for naming Hildegard foundress of a "philosophy of sex complementarity" (Allen 1985, 292–315). Newman goes much further, arguing that Hildegard saw her own womanhood as archetypal at once of the human and of the divine:

> So when she envisaged the Church as woman, developing ancient typological motifs into a portrait of unprecedented liveliness and complexity, she was testifying that humankind in its totality—women and men in history, in community, in relation with God—had a feminine face. (Newman 1987, 249)

As we have seen, Newman traces the grand themes of Hildegard's vision to their completion in meaningful details. She writes with clarity and warmth, and in so doing, demonstrates and dramatizes the importance of Hildegard's contribution to our understanding of Christianity, of medieval culture, and—especially—of the meaning and value of women's existence and experience.

Hildegard's *Scivias*, the first volume of her visionary trilogy, is a kind of audiovisual *Summa Theologiae*, encompassing the whole of reality: God, created nature, the incarnation of God's Word, redemption, and salvation history. *Scivias* is shortened Latin for "Know the ways [of the Lord]"; the overall plan of the book is the grand three-part design of creation, redemption, and sanctification.

Hildegard begins with an account of her own prophetic calling, in language strongly reminiscent of Isaiah, or of John on Patmos; she then fills in her vast outline with a series of visions—each described in vivid color, with words of comment from on high, followed by explanations and reflections on each of the symbolic details.

The architectonic design of *Scivias*, like that of Dante's *Commedia*, cries out for visual illustration. Fortunately, a manuscript prepared in Hildegard's lifetime, and under her supervision, provided gorgeously colored illuminations for each of the visions. This original manuscript was lost during World War II, but an exact copy of text and illuminations, made from the original by the nuns of Hildegard's daughter-monastery at Eibingen, has survived. This copy is the source for colored plates in the Latin critical text (Hildegard 1978) and for black-and-white drawings in the Paulist Press translation.

In the final vision of *Scivias*, following the revelation of the new heaven and the new earth, after the last judgment, Hildegard bursts into song in the "Symphony of the Blessed"—first in a concert of hymns in honor of Mary, the angels, and all the saints; then in the earliest known morality play, the *Ordo Virtutum*, a musical drama in which the pilgrim Soul is challenged and encouraged by a melodious chorus of (feminine) Virtues, in her struggle against the Devil. In keeping with Hildegard's conviction that earthly music is symbol and manifestation of divine order in the world, the Devil, having rejected the heavenly harmony, cannot sing; he can only shout.

The complete translation of *Scivias* provides a fine starting point for first-hand acquaintance with Hildegard. If the whole (close to five hundred pages of text) should seem intimidating, feminist readers might choose to start with selected passages.

For example, in Book One, Vision II (Creation and the Fall), Eve, symbolized by *"a white cloud, which had come forth from a beautiful human form and contained within itself many and many stars"* is described as "bearing in her body the whole multitude of the human race, shining with God's preordination" (Hildegard, 1990, 77, chap. 10). In the reflections that follow, on original sin and on marriage, Hildegard flatly contradicts St. Paul (1 Cor 11), insisting that "woman was created for the sake of man, and *man for the sake of woman*" (Hildegard 1990, 78, chap. 12, my emphasis). She also rejects the idea that a woman should remain away from church while she is menstruating (Hildegard 1990, 83, chap. 20).

In her vision of human reproduction (Book 1, Vision 4), Hildegard describes men *and* women alike as bearing in their bodies human seed for procreation (Hildegard 1990, 107 (plate), 118 (text), chap. 13). Apart from this clear rejection of the view of woman as impotent male, Hildegard's description of pregnancy and childbirth seems Aristotelian rather than Platonic:

> after a woman has conceived by human semen, an infant with all its
> members whole is formed in the secret chamber of her womb! . . . by
> God's secret and hidden command and will, fitly and rightly at the

divinely appointed time the infant in the maternal womb receives a
spirit, and shows by the movements of its body that it lives, just as the
earth opens and brings forth the flowers of its use when the dew falls on it.
(Hildegard 1990, 119, chap. 16)

Here Hildegard introduces a favorite theme: that each human being as
microcosm corresponds both in structure and in life cycle to the whole
created universe:

> . . . the soul, burning with a fire of profound knowledge, which discerns
> whatever is within the circle of its understanding, and, without the form
> of human members, since it is not corporeal or transitory like a human
> body, gives strength to the heart and rules the whole body as its founda-
> tion, as the firmament of Heaven contains the lower regions and touches
> the higher. . . . it gives vitality to the marrow and veins and members of
> the whole body, as the tree from its root gives sap and greenness to all the
> branches. (Hildegard 1990, 120, chap. 16)

Here Hildegard's writing reflects a fresh sensitivity to nature and to womanly experience.

The first unabridged English translation of *Scivias* appears in the
Paulist Press series, Classics of Western Spirituality. The series aims
at providing reliable translations, with helpful backgrounding. In the case
of *Scivias*, the sheer size of the text and the need for illustrations place
severe limits on introductory materials; nonetheless, Caroline Walker
Bynum's preface and Barbara Newman's introduction serve well to situate
Hildegard's text in its medieval context and to point up its continuing relevance. The translators have made a difficult Latin text readable in English;
moreover, their retention of numbers for the short chapters will enable
readers, even those with very little Latin, to make use of the critical Latin
edition, with its colored illustrations and its exhaustive index (practically
a concordance), for the study of Hildegard's vocabulary and imagery
(Hildegard 1978).

Sabina Flanagan's intention in *Hildegard of Bingen, 1098–1179: A
Visionary Life* is "to provide a comprehensive introduction to Hildegard,
in the light of current scholarship." This account of Hildegard's achievements is incorporated into a sociological "argument about how Hildegard
was able to enter domains generally seen as the preserve of men"
(Flanagan 1989, xiii). Flanagan's work stays close to the primary
sources—no mean scholarly task, given the range and bulk of Hildegard's
own writings and the abundant documentation of her life by her contemporaries. Of Flanagan's ten chapters, four describe the contents of
Hildegard's writings. In the remaining chapters, while recounting the
major events of Hildegard's life, Flanagan answers the question "How did

she do it?" with reflections on the formation and function of Hildegard's prophetic persona.

According to Flanagan, Hildegard saw herself "as the mouthpiece of the Lord, merely conveying his messages to her hearers and readers." Since the prophet's message came directly from God, "to be a female prophet was to confirm women's inferiority, rather than to deny it" (Flanagan 1989, 14–15). By claiming the role of prophet, Hildegard could escape from her situation as a "frustrated writer" (Flanagan 1989, 44). In the conflict situations of her life—when she decided to remove her sisters from Disibodenberg to a new monastery; when she protested and mourned the decision of her favorite younger nun, Richardis von Stade, to accept appointment as abbess of another monastery; when her community was placed under interdict because a young nobleman, who, it was claimed, had died excommunicate, had been buried in the convent cemetery—Hildegard relied with unshakable certainty on her own insight into God's will (Flanagan 1989, 179–192).

Flanagan devotes her concluding chapter to the relationship between Hildegard's achievements and her health, following up the suggestions of Charles Singer and Oliver Sacks that certain aspects of Hildegard's visionary experience can be explained by her suffering from migraine (Flanagan 1989, 199–206). Flanagan describes Hildegard's migraine experience as a "wonderfully adaptable instrument" in support of her prophetic role (Flanagan 1989, 209–211).

Flanagan's book provides a useful overview of Hildegard's life and work. But her stress on sociological, psychological, and physiological explanations seems to play down the significance of her heroine's accomplishments. In attributing Hildegard's impulse to write to "her own particular neuro-physiological profile," Flanagan distances herself from the religious context of Hildegard's life and teaching (Flanagan 1989, 208). Flanagan implies that Hildegard's claim to a prophetic role was a more or less conscious strategy for advancing her "hidden agenda" of joining "the male literary and theological elite" (Flanagan 1989, 44). Disturbingly, she raises, but never clearly resolves, the question as to whether "Hildegard's appeal to her privileged source of authority could be seen as cynically manipulative in her personal dealings and intellectually dishonest in her writings" (Flanagan 1989, 193).

The sharp line that Flanagan draws between "acting as God's mouthpiece" and "expressing her own thoughts and opinions" (Flanagan 1989, 193) seems to reflect a perspective quite remote from Hildegard's own world. As Flanagan notes in her preface, "To provide a general account of twelfth-century natural history, cosmology, or theology is beyond the scope of my book" (Flanagan 1989, xiii). But Christian authors generally recognize God as source of *all* truth *and* recognize too that all teachings must be tested and validated in the light both of Christian faith and of human reason and experience. Male authors of Hildegard's time typically held positions of authority in the teaching church; women who realized they had something important to say must, by that very conviction, have seen themselves as divinely empowered and mandated to say it. For Hildegard, who seems to have known no woman author before herself, the prophetic calling served to energize her own natural gifts of symbolic imagination, analogical reasoning, understanding of what she read, and observation of nature and human experience. Certainly, physiology and psychology played a role in shaping her thought (as they do for all of us), but she herself sought and found validation for her visions and her message in the affirmation of the church community, which she secured early in her career and valued throughout her life (Newman 1987, 8–14).

Elizabeth Petroff has described both the personal and the public impact of visionary experience for medieval women, in words that could serve as a portrait of Hildegard:

> Visions led women to the acquisition of power in the world while affirm-
> ing their knowledge of themselves as women. Visions were a socially
> sanctioned activity that freed a woman from conventional female roles
> by identifying her as a genuine religious figure. . . . Her visions gave her
> the strength to grow internally and to change the world, to build con-
> vents, found hospitals, preach, attack injustice and greed, even within
> the church. (Petroff 1986, 6)

Consideration of visionary experience from this perspective recognizes both its religious meaning and its creative power. Flanagan's approach, while interesting and informative, tends to detach Hildegard from her experiential and intellectual context in medieval Christendom; in so doing, it implicitly deprives her teaching of continuing vitality and relevance.

We come back, then, to the question we started with: Why haven't we—as women working in philosophy—heard of Hildegard before? We can see from our sampling of recent Hildegardian scholarship—theological, spiritual, and historical—that her work has importance for us today. But we still lack an answer to a more complicated version of our question—that is, Why hasn't she been studied *as a philosopher*, that is, as an interpreter of human experience?

The writings of Newman and Flanagan suggest two explanations, complementary to each other.

Newman's designation of Hildegard's achievement as "theology" bypasses (understandably) academic controversies regarding the interplay of theology and philosophy in medieval thought. Authors of the twentieth-century "scholastic renaissance" (such as Etienne Gilson, Jacques Maritain, and Frederick Copleston) argued that medieval Christian thinkers should be counted as philosophers *insofar as* they relied upon human reason and experience (as distinct from divine revelation) in their search for understanding—even for understanding of God and the things of God. (So, for example, the philosophical concept of *person* was elaborated in early Christian debates upon the correct meaning of the Holy Trinity and of the Incarnation of Jesus.) As one trained in the context of "Christian philosophy" (at Louvain around 1960), I find in Hildegard—as in Augustine, Abelard, or Aquinas—a religious thinker who draws on both cultural heritage and personal experience in her search for wisdom. The great Hildegardian themes traced by Newman—the verdant freshness pervading creation; the human microcosm as mirror image and speaking voice of the universe; the personified virtues embodying divine grace and human achievements; Wisdom and Love as emblems of the divine, immanent in human beings and in all created nature—all rely for their meaning and relevance to us on the ways in which they speak to our own experience and insight. Their religious value cannot be separated from their human and womanly significance; Hildegard's human wisdom—like all medieval philosophy—provides essential life-support to her explication of revealed truth. Newman presents in detail the philosophical wealth of Hildegard's thought but does not situate it explicitly within the tradition of "faith seeking understanding" in which it lives and moves.

Flanagan's focus on Hildegard's "prophetic persona" as "strategy" exemplifies another approach which has served to justify the exclusion of women from consideration in medieval philosophy: it marks a quite unmedieval separation of mystic vision from human (and womanly) insight. In point of fact, medieval Christian authors generally—from Augustine through Abelard and Aquinas to Dante—lived and moved, like Hildegard, in a world pervaded with lucid human intelligence and with mystical experience—both gifts of the one Spirit of Wisdom.

Their medieval world vision was structured with a complexity mirrored in the architecture of the cathedrals. Faith in revelation, deductive and inductive reasoning, delighted experience of the natural world and of human life, symbolic imagination and the yearning for transcendent union with God—all were interwoven in the teaching and writing, music and art of medieval Christendom. To situate Hildegard's approach to wisdom—in its methods and content—within its religious *and* its philosophical context is a task that lies before us, promising both effort and delight.

REFERENCES

Allen, Prudence, R.S.M. 1985. *The concept of woman: The Aristotelian revolution 750 BC–AD 1250*. Montreal: Eden Press.

Flanagan, Sabina. 1989. *Hildegard of Bingen 1098–1179: A visionary life.* New York: Routledge.

Hildegard of Bingen. 1978. *Scivias.* Edited by A. Fuehrkoetter and A. Carlevaris. Corpus Christianorum Continuatio Medievalis 43, 43A. Turnhout, Antwerp, Belgium: Brepols.

———. 1990. *Scivias.* Translated by Mother Columba Hart and Jane Bishop. Introduced by Barbara J. Newman. Preface by Caroline Walker Bynum. New York: Paulist Press.

Newman, Barbara. 1987. *Sister of Wisdom: St. Hildegard's theology of the feminine.* Berkeley and Los Angeles: University of California Press.

Petroff, Elizabeth Alvilda. 1986. *Medieval women's visionary literature.* Oxford: Oxford University Press.

A WOMAN'S THOUGHT OR A MAN'S DISCIPLINE?

THE LETTERS OF ABELARD AND HELOISE

ANDREA NYE

The nature and the existence of philosophy have never been more in question than at the present moment. The distances between British linguistic analysis and Continental hermeneutics, scientific empiricism and African-American liberatory pragmatism, logical semantics and feminist critique often seem unnegotiable. Any common ground called philosophy on which debate could be carried out among such diverse schools and movements has eroded away. In each of these cases there is the same underlying and perhaps unresolvable difference: either philosophy is a professional discipline independent of political or social concerns or it is an ongoing critical and cultural discourse deeply rooted in lived experience, dependent on interpersonal understanding, and prophetic of future action.

In what follows I consider this macroquestion of the nature and possible future of philosophy by way of microstudy of a disagreement between a woman student and her male philosophy teacher, a disagreement that occurred at the very beginnings of philosophy as an academic discipline. The woman is the twelfth-century abbess Heloise. Her teacher is the famous Peter Abelard, originator of many of the attitudes and practices of academic philosophy as we know it today. At issue between them were conflicting ideals of goodness and love but also differences regarding thought and language. It is my hope that a careful reading of their dispute will show that the personal nature of their disagreement is not irrelevant to the question of the nature of philosophy.

The story of Heloise and Abelard is celebrated in history and legend as follows:

Hypatia vol. 7, no. 3 (Summer 1992) © by Andrea Nye

Abelard, at the peak of his fame as a philosopher and dialectician, jaded with his many triumphs in intellectual combat, decides to turn his attention to the conquest of a woman. Hearing of the beauty and intelligence of Heloise, then a young girl, he convinces her uncle, a canon, to hire him as her tutor with the plan of seducing her. They become lovers, are discovered by the uncle, and flee his anger. Eventually Heloise bears a child and a secret marriage is contracted, apparently with the uncle's consent. When the uncle insists on making the marriage known, however, Abelard refuses and removes Heloise to the convent where she had been educated. Enraged that Heloise can now never live a normal life and afraid that Abelard is confining her to be rid of her, the uncle sends a band of men to castrate Abelard. After the deed has been done, Heloise takes religious orders on Abelard's command.

Nine years after these unhappy events, Heloise read Abelard's confessionary autobiography *Historia calamitatum (The Story of my Misfortunes;* Abelard 1933).[1] Distressed by what she took as a distorted account of what happened between them, she initiated a correspondence in which she disputed his teaching on the religious vocation, love, and morality. She was not the only one to do so. Abelard was already under attack for his interjection of logic into matters of faith. Concerned that the hundreds of inconsistencies in Christian teaching Abelard listed in his tour de force, *Sic et Non,* might not be resolved, powerful monastics like Bernard of Clairvaux accused Abelard of heresy. Regardless of clerical resistance, however, Abelard's philosophy became the new intellectual fashion. His brilliant expositions of classical authorities, especially Aristotle, his subtle reformulations of logic, his slashing refutations of rivals, his insistence that rational understanding could never tolerate inconsistency had begun to detach learning from revelation and establish a style of disputation that would become the accepted form of academic learning.

Like many male philosophers throughout history, Abelard was willing, with some ulterior motives, to take on a woman student. Heloise had proven her aptitude; even as a young girl she was known for her learning and her intelligence. As Peter the Venerable wrote praising her:

> I used to hear at that time of the woman, who although still caught up in the obligation of the world, devoted all her application to knowledge of letters. . . . And at a time when nearly all the whole world is indifferent and deplorably apathetic toward such occupations, and wisdom can scarcely get a foothold . . . you have surpassed all women in wisdom, and have gone further even than almost every man. (Heloise and Abelard 1974, 277)

Heloise had a superior early education in the nunnery of Argenteuil and had heard of the great philosopher Peter Abelard well before he approached her. Abelard, with an ego that was secure if not overweening, was willing to treat Heloise's reputation for learning as an attraction and not a deficit. Her literacy, he reasoned, would be an advantage. Not only did it afford a pretext for them to be together as teacher and student, but it would also expand the field of erotic exchange. When they were not together they could correspond; when together, philosophical discussion would provide added intimacy. With no doubt of his eventual success, he began her education.

By the time of Heloise's letters to Abelard, however, it was clear that she had greatly disappointed her teacher. Abelard answers her letters reluctantly, tired of her "continual complaint" and her lack of "rationality." He makes it clear how unphilosophical and sinful he finds what she says on the subjects of love, ethics, personal obligation, and the church. Heloise confesses her failure to discipline her thought as her teacher wished:

> For nothing is less under our control than the spirit,[2] which we are more forced to obey than we are able to command; when its agitations move us, none of us can hold back their sudden impulse and they easily break through, and even more easily overflow into words which are expressions of the passion of the spirit. (Heloise and Abelard 1950–56, MS XV, 94; 159)

In his answer, Abelard refers her inability to discipline her mind to a special weakness of the female sex for loose, undisciplined speech. In a diatribe against the dangers of "idle talk," Abelard liberally quotes the Bible: "If anyone thinks he is religious, while not restraining his tongue, he is deceiving himself and his religion is worthless" (James 1:26; quoted in MS XVIII, 245; 188). Or, "Like a city that is exposed and unprotected by walls is a man who in speaking cannot restrain his speech" (Proverbs 25: 28; ibid.) We must "tether" our tongue to the truth, he tells his troublesome ex-student, lest it "run all over the whole world in its thoughts." "We must direct our thought to what can be understood and adhere to it by thinking" (ibid.).

It is Heloise's "woman's" tongue, her feminine way of speaking, that particularly disables her in philosophy, according to Abelard.

> The more subtle [the tongue] is in you (vobis), and the more flexible because of the softness of your body, the more mobile and prone to words it is, and exhibits itself as the seedbed of all evil. This defect in you is noted by the Apostle when he forbids women to speak in church; not even on matters pertaining to God does he permit them to speak unless they question their husbands at home. In discoursing of such things or whatever things are to be done, he particularly subjects them to silence, writing on this to Timothy: A woman must learn in silence and with

complete submission. I do not permit a woman to teach, nor to rule over a man, but to be silent. (MS XVIII, 245–46; 188–89)

This unruliness of speech on Heloise's part required an especially vigilant discipline on the part of her teacher. With the institutionalized punishments of low grades, failed theses, and refusal of tenure or promotion not yet available, Abelard used more direct methods. Encouraged by her uncle, for whose credulity he had only contempt, Abelard used physical punishment as he saw fit to ensure Heloise's intellectual as well as erotic submission. Abelard explains:

In giving her to me not only to teach but to punish with force, what else was [her uncle] doing but offering me complete license, and providing the opportunity, whether I wished it or not, for me to make her manageable with threats and blows if persuasion did not work. (MS XII, 183; 67)[3]

The aggressive military style of this pedagogical discipline is consistent with the style of Abelard's new philosophical logic. In his autobiography Abelard describes logic in martial terms. Like his soldier father, he is a professional fighter, a fighter with words. He "sallies out" on the field of conquest to defeat his enemies. He gives them fatal blows with the sharpness of his arguments. He forces them to retreat, wounded and dishonored, from the field of battle.

But Abelard's discipline, successful as it may have been in defeating academic rivals and bringing about Heloise's sexual submission, was not sufficient to make her a philosopher on his terms. By the time of her letters, it is clear that Heloise does not accept either the content or the style of the arguments urged on her by Abelard, arguments that were to prove decisively that owing to his castration love must be over between them, that monasticism provides a more virtuous life than lay devotion, and that the remedy for earthly disappointment is surrender to God. Some commentators have found Heloise's refusal to agree with his logic so unbelievable in a respected abbess that they have denied the authenticity of her letters.[4]

When Heloise's authentic voice has been recognized, commentators have typically praised the philosopher's reason over the woman's "hysteria." According to the editor of Abelard's and Heloise's letters, J. T. Muckle, Abelard gives a "reasoned reply" to Heloise's "impassioned reproaches, reflections and entreaties," and "it is quite evident that Abelard in his two replies tries to raise Heloise up to a truer love of God." Muckle expresses surprise that Abelard, the philosopher, is as patient as he is. Commenting on Abelard's refusal to respond to some of Heloise's complaints, he says: "One would expect that Abelard would have chided her

and tried to set her right in regard to such extravagant and sinful dispositions."[5] Heloise's problem, according to Muckle, is that she is irrevocably
trapped in her situation and in her emotions, which, although admirable
to romantics, are not relevant to philosophy. Other commentators have
been more harsh, arguing that Heloise's position is "ludicrous" or "pa-
thetic."[6]

Even sympathetic readers of the letters, regularly cited by feminist
commentators,[7] have stressed the lack of originality of Heloise's thought.
Nowhere is this more evident than in Etienne Gilson's anxious explanation of Heloise's arguments against marriage (Gilson 1960). Heloise argues
as follows:

> God knows I required nothing from you but yourself, purely you, not
> anything of yours, no marriage contract, no dowry, nor did I study how
> to gratify my own desires, but rather yours, as you know. And if the title
> of wife seems more saintly or respectable, sweeter for me always is the
> name of friend, or, if you won't take offense, even concubine or whore,
> because it seemed to me that the more I was humble the more I would
> win your favor, and also the less harm I would do to your fame and repu-
> tation. You yourself did not completely forget this in your own account;
> in the letter of consolation I have spoken of above [Abelard's autobiog-
> raphy] you did not think it unworthy to set out some of the arguments
> by which I tried to dissuade you from joining us in an ill-fated marriage,
> but you remained silent about my preference for a love that is free over
> a marriage that is chains. . . . Neither wealth nor power, which depends
> on fortune, makes a person better, but rather virtue. Not any less, if
> someone more willingly marries a rich man than a poor one, and covets
> in her husband not himself what belongs to him, she weighs herself as
> an object for sale. Certainly, such a person, drawn into marriage by
> such desires, is owed wages, not favor. (MS XV, 70–71; 113–14)

This radical critique of the institution of arranged medieval marriages, in
which alliances were made for material wealth and social status, is not interpreted by Gilson as a philosophical position but is explained away as a
misguided strategy of seduction on Heloise's part. Heloise, he argues, ignoring the sensuality of her descriptions of physical passion, was essentially
chaste. Her foremost desire was for celibacy for both her and Abelard.
Because Abelard would not accept this, the next best thing was fornication
which preserved Abelard's reputation. To accomplish this end, Heloise
uses a "piece of sophistry." By appealing to what is base in Abelard, she encourages him to live a lie.

Following Abelard's lead, Gilson acknowledges "some" of Heloise's
argument but fails to mention her "preference" for love over opportunis-
tic marriage. Just as Abelard did, he stresses her concern that nothing

irrevocable be done to prevent Abelard from returning to the celibacy necessary for advancement in the church. She goes so far as to pose as a whore to entice Abelard to what is "base" (Gilson 1960, 51–53). Gilson makes clear the mythic underpinning of his understanding of Heloise's situation: Eve, using specious arguments, tempted Adam to his downfall. "The devil knows well that the woman is always a ready made cause of man's destruction" (Gilson 1960, 63–64).

Insofar as Heloise has a philosophy of love and an ethics, Gilson continues, these are derivative, borrowed from Abelard's ethics of intention and, via Abelard, from Cicero's view of disinterested friendship. The conflict between Abelard and Heloise, in Gilson's view, is not between two philosophers but between theory and practice. Heloise is more intent on practicing what Abelard preaches than is Abelard. To this end, in order to trick Abelard into correct practice on his terms, she foolishly embarks on an "endless road of moral casuistry," making out "fornication" to be a means to Abelard's eventual honor rather than a sin against God's law (Gilson 1960, 58–59). The deep source of her challenge to Abelard, Gilson concludes, is neither morality nor the defense of behavior in accordance with morality, but an attempt to exonerate herself from guilt. She borrows Abelard's "morality of intention" because it allows her to argue that what she did was innocent in motive and so not culpable. Heloise, concludes Gilson, realized in horror that she had again repeated the original sin of Eve and brought about the "downfall" of a man. She was "guilty even before the marriage when she yielded to the attractions of the flesh" (Gilson 1960, 64). In order to defend herself, she grasps onto Abelard's morality of intention. Now she can claim that she brought about evil but did not intend it and so is not culpable.

Although it may be understandable coming from a Catholic philosopher reacting to the scandal of a nun's open defense of sexual love, this interpretation, which has been adopted by many commentators and which makes Heloise's position derivative and reactive, is consistent neither with what Heloise says in her letters nor with her position of authority. Although as a young girl Heloise had been Abelard's student, at the time of the letters she was no powerless dependent either intellectually or materially. As a nun and abbess, she wrote from the one situation in which medieval women lived relatively free from men's control. Although Heloise bowed to the official ruling that convents be supervised by monks as well as to Abelard's demand that her policies as abbess be guided by himself as male advisor, in practice her autonomy must have been considerable.[8] Her responsibilities as abbess required considerable administrative and doctrinal skill. This was especially true because, as Heloise complained, so little had been done to define the terms of a monastic rule for women. In contrast, Abelard had miserably failed in monastic life.[9]

Even more decisive than her actual position of authority, however, is the substance of Heloise's stated views on love and morality. In her first letter, written after an extended silence on Abelard's part and in response to his autobiographical exposition of their relationship, Heloise's subject is not her frustrated sexual urges. Rather her concern is with Abelard's failure to love and to understand the nature of love. Her argument focuses on the key concept of responsibility. Abelard professed love for her, but he did not and does not love, she argued, because he does not recognize the personal responsibility that is the actual content of love. This responsibility is multifaceted. We are responsible to those on whom we inflict wounds, to what we have established, to those who love us, to those whom we can make happy, to those who have done what we have asked them to do. Relations based on these obligations are the substance of love.[10] What Heloise asks of Abelard is not the now impossible sex act but the concern, care, presence to her, if only in letters, that would fulfill these obligations. On this understanding of love, Abelard's castration is irrelevant; a love based on mutual responsibility and care survives physical disability. It is clear, Heloise concludes, that Abelard never loved, but was driven by a selfish craving for genital satisfaction. He married to ensure his exclusive possession of the object of his craving; when the seat of the craving, his genitals, was removed, so was his lust. Nor is his failure to love a fact over which he has no control; he ought to have loved and he ought to love still.

Abelard's response to this argument is cool. In the impersonal tone he might take to a stranger to whom he owes nothing, peppering his text liberally with erudite biblical and scholarly references, he assures her that he has confidence in her ability to administer her convent. If she needs further instruction in spiritual matters, he is at her disposal; otherwise he would like her to leave him alone. In a second letter, goaded to a "rational" defense of his position by Heloise's refusal to obey and be silent, he makes explicit what is implicit in his first response. Of course, he says, sexual love is lust. Nowhere in any of his ethical writings is there any indication that he thought there was any other kind of sexual love between men and women. Sexual "libido," or lust, he continues, is ugly and degrading. He could not keep himself from "dirtying himself as in a pigsty"; he was bound to her "with the flames of concupiscence"; he craved "miserable, obscene pleasures." The "place from which lust rules" and the "sole cause of these desires" is the organ that God has mercifully eliminated in his case (MS XV, 89; 147). In fact, it is not so much Abelard as it is his "member" that God has punished. In his way, God "cut him off from the dirt in which he had been immersed," "cleansed rather than deprived him" in removing what is only "sordid and worthless" (MS XV, 89; 148).

So goes Abelard's "rational" argument. Yes, he said, of course he only used Heloise to satisfy his vile pleasures (MS XV, 92; 153). What man does any differently? How much better, he exhorts her, is the monastic life he has chosen for her than if she had married someone else and again "given herself up to the sordidness of carnal pleasures and painful childbirth" (MS XV, 90; 150). Abelard's alternative to lust is not another earthly love, which he cannot imagine as different, but spiritual love for Christ and, derivatively, of others as brothers and sisters in Christ. Throughout her letters, Heloise persisted in her refusal to share this view of sensual passion as a vile genital craving.[11] Her mutually responsible love is not a sexless love. Even after the physical act of love has become impossible, she treasures memories of erotic pleasure. "The pleasures of love we shared," she says, "were for me so sweet, they cannot displease me, nor can they be erased from memory; not only what we did, but the places and times in which we did it, along with you yourself, are fixed in my spirit, so that I live it all over again with you and cannot, even in sleep, be at peace" (MS XV, 80–81; 133).

If Abelard's body-phobic indictment of sensuous pleasure has been taken as "reason" or "philosophy" in contrast to Heloise's unphilosophical "passion," it can only be because a certain dualistic metaphysics is taken for granted as philosophy's conceptual underpinning. There are two parts to a man, a lower part that is the body and a higher part that is the soul. The body, especially certain parts of the body, is the obvious source of the appetites, including the sexual appetites. This is the metaphysics that is the basis for Abelard's celebrated ethics of intention. In the *Ethics*, he argues that sensual appetites are weaknesses or defects embedded in a man's physical nature or bodily constitution and that these defects are the correlate and necessary condition for virtue, which is seated in the other part of a man, his rational soul. In his soul part, a man may refuse to "consent" to bodily appetite in conformity to God's command. Vice, therefore, is only in intent, in the refusal to withhold consent, and so in the "contempt for God and offending against him" (*Ethics* 4). The essence of vice is "to consent to that which should be refrained from according to God" (*Ethics* 16). The basis of virtue, or good intention, on the other hand, is that "you believe that what you do pleases God and are not in any way mistaken in that belief" (*Ethics* 54). Abelard's innovation as a moral philosopher is to argue that virtue is neither in deeds nor in good will, as Augustine argued, but, regardless of what is done or willed, in the correct rational attitude to what we do or will. If, for Augustine, good will remains linked to the living and acting body, for Abelard the rational consent that constitutes virtue is completely severed from and set in opposition to the body and to any feelings and desires linked to the body. Abelard's "consensus" and "intentio" are not the intelligent and feeling interior spirit that is the spring of action, but an alienated rational obedience to a higher will.[12]

This ethics, which most commentators have claimed Heloise borrowed from Abelard, generates a number of morally questionable consequences, some of which Heloise explicitly denies. The majority of Abelard's examples, perhaps predictably, have to do with sex, the area in which a man's natural bodily defects are supposedly strongest and, therefore, most available to be a pretext for virtuous judgment. For Abelard, the more licentious and lustful a person is, the more chance he or she has to be virtuous by withholding consent.[13] Good thoughts, on the other hand, do not necessarily make an action right. A servant who is attacked by his master and to defend himself has to kill the master does not have an evil will, but a good will toward his own defense; nevertheless, says Abelard, he is guilty of sin because he consents to kill his master. He should have "endured" his own murder (*Ethics* 8, 24).[14] These morally dubious results are a necessary consequence of a dualism in which moral reason is severed from human life. They are also a symptom of the lack of moral development Heloise criticizes in Abelard. In his ethics, there is no impulse to spiritual regeneration; vicious appetites are accepted, or even encouraged, so as to be the occasion for resistance and contrition.

Heloise's conception of love and obligation, on the other hand, is not based on the same dualistic categories. For Heloise a person is not a body joined with a rational soul, but a complete organism. She makes no opposition between the rational soul and the sinful body but instead distinguishes between outer works and inner spirit. If this is a morality of "pure intention," as most commentators have repeated after Gilson and Muckle, it is very different from Abelard's virtuous intention as will to obedience. Heloise's "it is not so much what is done that is to be weighed, as it is the spirit in which it is done" (MS XVI, 251; 175), in Abelard's *Ethics* becomes "the merit or the praiseworthiness of the doer is not in the deed but in the intention" (Ethics, 28).[15] No matter what sinful things we do or will—and of course we will be malicious, greedy, lustful—if we do not intend to disobey God, we have achieved virtue. Far from adopting such an ethics to excuse herself, Heloise specifically refuses it in her own case. Unlike the biblical villainesses she cites, she did not mean to ruin Abelard, although in fact she brought his ruin about. *But* "even if innocence clears my spirit, and no consent makes me a party to this crime, so many sins went before, that I cannot be completely immune from guilt" (MS XV, 80; 131). In other words, no simple lack of consent can excuse wrongdoing, guilt and blame are instead a result of a complex of actions and feelings. For Heloise, what dirties or purifies the soul is not "intention" in the sense of disobedience or righteous judgment, but "what comes from the heart (corde), thoughts of adultery, or murder, etc."; vice is to have one's "spirit corrupted by a depraved will (*prava voluntate*)" (MS XVII, 250–51; 174). Vice is not in the external act of murder or se-duction; it is in the spirit of hatred or lust in which such acts are done. The "feeling of the doing is what is criminal" (MS XV, 72; 115). Heloise's virtuous "animus" is not obedience to law but the "affectus" of an action, the beneficence, as opposed to the malevolence, that prompts it (MS XV, 72; 115).[16] Even what we owe to God, in her view, is not so much obedi-ence as it is heartfelt "devotion," expressed in offerings, prayers, and thanks (MS XVII, 251; 175–76).

Heloise's ethics is consistent with her view of love. The interlocking re-sponsibilities that are the substance of love are owed to a whole person. Responsibilities of care and devotion do not develop in a private battle between physical lust and spiritual obedience but in a complex web of concrete interactions, dependencies, and shared pleasures that constitute loving relationships. Such a conception of love is all but inexpressible in the terms of Abelard's dualist metaphysics. Because the battle between ap-petite and law that such metaphysics mandates cannot be won in any but a temporary way, there can be no redemption in human love. Abelard's newfound virtue can only be the renunciation of love for obedience to divine authority; and the transfer to human beings of "love in Christ." In his own case, Abelard concedes, this redemption had to be won through extreme means—the actual mutilation of the uncontrollable part of his body. Although we might have thought the great logician's rational soul ad-equate to the task of mastering the passions, Abelard confesses he had a particular difficulty with self-control. This might be, he speculates not without a note of pride, because his appetites, like his reason, were ex-traordinarily virile.

Heloise refuses to think in terms of a metaphysical dualism between soul and body and rejects the morality of command and will that accom-panies it. This continues to be evident when she writes of the monastic life. When Abelard forbids any discussion of their personal relationship, Heloise continues her questioning in the only terms that Abelard is willing to accept. If the only permissible topic is to be the spiritual guidance of her order, then this will have to be the bond between them and the means for them to continue their dialogue on the nature of obligation and virtue. What, she challenges him, should be the rule for a convent? The Benedictine rule was written for men. "Certainly, those who wrote the rules for monks were not only completely silent about women, but also laid down regulations that they knew were not at all appropriate for them" (MS XVII, 243; 162). What rule would accommodate the different body of a woman, could take account of the fact that she menstruates and has less muscular strength? Should the Benedictine rule be relaxed to take account of women's physical frailty?[17]

Initially, Heloise's questioning focused on the weakness of women and the necessity of adapting the Benedictine rule to their deficiencies, an approach likely to get Abelard's willing attention.[18] As her argument develops, however, it is no longer the weakness of women that is in question but the adequacy of any moral order based on law, command, and obedience. The goal of monastic life must be the highest form of virtue, she argues, but should virtue be identified with the "outward show" of dietary laws, special clothing, and penances? If the rule for women is relaxed so as to include only the giving up of personal possessions, continence, and adherence to the morality of the Gospels, would that not be enough? It was enough for the apostles, and even for Christ himself. "Would that our religion could rise to this height—to carry out the Gospel, not to go beyond it, lest we attempt to be more than Christians" (MS XVII, 245; 164). No longer is it women's frailty that requires a relaxed rule. Heloise indicts any code of monastic ethics that sets itself above the simple morality preached by Christ.

First, she argues, an attention to outward actions rather than the "state of the heart" encourages hypocrisy. In her denial of repentance for her sexual desires, Heloise already had made clear how little she valued any "outward show of penance," whether to oneself or to others. She would not pretend to be contrite when in her heart she still desired and treasured memories of sexual pleasure. Inevitably her very body, she said, would betray her in movements in her sleep and involuntary cries of pleasure. She expresses her impatience with those who "rashly profess monastic observance" and vow to follow rules that cannot be kept and under which "nearly all men give way, or rather fail" (MS XVII, 246; 167). It is not only women who are unsuited to asceticism. To propose rules against which the body will inevitably rebel is to invite dishonesty whatever the sex. Heloise, as handy with Scripture as Abelard, quotes Paul: "Law intervenes to multiply law-breaking" (Romans 5: 20; MS XVII, 245; 165).

Second, Heloise suggests that a monastic rule that goes beyond Gospel morality is an affront to Christian faith. Who is to say that the teachings of Christ are not good enough or that the virtue of the apostles is inferior? Jesus did not forbid wine or meat to his apostles or insist that they wear special kinds of clothing. They were to live as men among men. He instructed them only to avoid giving offense to other people by what they ate or drank according to the usages of those around them. A morality of obedience to law or rules, Heloise argues, is completely alien to Jesus' moral teaching. Far from instituting dietary rules and ritual observances, Jesus criticized the observance of the Law in Jewish practice. Virtue is not obedience to the Law, he taught, but consideration for others and purity of heart. Paul, writing to Timothy, goes so far as to identify dietary rules with "subversive doctrines." The essence of the Christian message is the difference between "virtue and the show of virtue," between a "natural habit of virtue" and obedience to laws that are inevitably the laws of men (MS XVII, 249–50; 173).

Heloise's virtue does not require the heroic act of will of Abelard's dualist metaphysics. In Abelard's ethics, the inner evil of appetite is irradicable, desirable even, so that the rational mastery of the soul over vice can be exercised. Virtue can never be a "natural habit," because such a thing is impossible. Heloise's virtue requires not willpower but a change of heart, a change of heart, for example, in which a man might learn to love, seeing a woman not as an object on which to gratify his lust but as a person with whom he has a relation involving mutual responsibilities. In such a reformation, he would win the "freedom of the Gospel" and not the "yoke" of the Law (MS XVII, 251; 176).

Abelard is unmoved by Heloise's argument. In the lengthy directions he gives for her order, he constantly emphasizes discipline and obedience. What does following Christ mean? he asks. It means one puts aside possessions, affection for those related to him, and his own wishes and "commits himself to be ruled by another's rule, not his own" (MS XVIII, 244; 186). The house of God is an "armed fortress" with a commander and a clear delegation of authority (MS XVIII, 250; 196). The abbess is in charge, taking her orders from her spiritual husband Christ as well as from his subordinates in the nearby monastery responsible for directing the external affairs of her convent. Their ultimate superior is God who gives commandments to men, commandments to be followed in obedience to the pope, the bishop, the abbot, and, finally, the individual's will in mastery over his sinful body. For this reason, there must be a strict law for a woman's order and no loose, unsupervised arrangements.[19]

In the convent the abbess rules, but she must rule according to regulations. Abelard, apparently belatedly realizing the mistake of liberally encouraging women to be independent scholars, admonishes Heloise on the proper conduct of an abbess. She should be over sixty—a requirement that Heloise will not be able to meet for some years. If she is "not lettered"—there is no insistence here that all nuns be educated—she should "accustom herself not to philosophic studies as dialectical disputations but to the teaching of life and the performance of works." If she thinks she must refer to the Scriptures in order to understand better, she should not hesitate to "inquire and learn from the educated" (MS XVIII, 253; 201).[20] Abelard is particularly emphatic about the necessity for male direction:

> And so truly we believe that convents observe more firmly the religion of their calling if they are governed by the foresight of spiritual men (*spiritalium virorum*), and the same pastor is set over the ewes and the rams: that is, the same one presides over women and men, and always

according to the apostle: The man is the head of the woman, just as
Christ is the head of man, and God the head of Christ. (MS XVIII, 258;
210)[21]

In the chain of military command that is Abelard's God's world there is a
clear hierarchy that allows the ethic of obedience to operate effectively.
As Abelard lays out the correct forms of convent life, the split between
body and soul is institutionalized as the authority of the ruling masculine
soul over the various evils of the female body, and the authority of male
clerics over convent life.

The restrictive framework of this dualistic metaphysics is particularly
evident in one of Abelard's most striking "rational arguments," as he attempts to persuade Heloise to forget him and rejoice instead in her religious vows. There should be a great pleasure for her, Abelard tells her, in
the bed of Christ, the new husband to whom he has relinquished her.
Apparently not remembering or understanding Heloise's indictment of op-
portunistic marriages, he urges on her "a happy trade (*commercium*) of
your married state, for where you were before the wife of a miserable man,
now you are in the sublime bed of the King of Kings" (MS XV, 83; 138).
Remember, he tells her, the Ethiopian woman, black flesh on the outside
and therefore ugly and poor, but white in bones and soul on the inside and
so lovely she is loved by the king. The king, Abelard extends his metaphor,
must visit his black lover secretly because of her blackness, just as Heloise
will have intercourse with Christ in the privacy of the convent.

In this dubious but common reduction of the sensuality of the Song of
Songs to heavenly love, which Abelard spins out with great rhetorical flour-
ish, is evident the conceptual infrastructure of Abelard's rationality. The
argument is not only strictly constructed according to the familiar dualism
of body and soul but uses metaphorical extensions of that opposition to
draw complementary contrasts between inferior woman/superior man,
black flesh/white soul, evil body/chaste soul. These dichotomies are the
founding conceptual frame for much of mainstream Western philosophy
since Aristotle.[22] Their implications in racism, sexism, and sexual repression have been well documented. What characterizes Abelard's thought,
however, is not only the specific body-phobic, racist, sexist oppositions
that structure it but also the very discipline of thought and language that
originally constitutes universal concepts and that holds speech to a particular form. If Heloise's thought is seen as irrational, it is not only because
she refused to accept the inferior status of women, or black skin, or the
body, but also because her thought has no rigid institutional scaffolding.
Instead of structural relations between mind/body, white/black, man/
woman, Heloise's thought has the flowing quality that Abelard found so
dangerous in the female tongue. Unrestrained by any canonical conceptual

order, such a thought and speech can, in truth, as Abelard feared, deviate from orthodoxy and "run all over the world," as it flows directly from desires, from the body, from the tongue itself as the organ of speech.[23]

Abelard's most renowned contribution to philosophy, his theory of universals, is the theory of the conceptual discipline that is to redeem such loose talk. In a subtle negotiation between nominalism and Platonic realism, much admired by contemporary linguists, Abelard argued that a universal is not a thing or material essence, but a use of words. That use of words, he argued against the nominalists, is caused by a resemblance between things. But the resemblance in which universals can be grounded is not intuited in sensual experience. The ability we have to institute universal concepts such as "man" or "soul" is the essence of rationality. Sensation and imagination give us only confused ideas of a thing, but with a universal, we grasp what something really *is*—for example, that it is a substance, or a body, or white. A universal is neither a *res* (thing) or a *vox* (sound) but a *sermon* (term) whose meaning depends on a "human institution" based on a rationally intuited resemblance between things. It is with these universals that we are able to put our thoughts in order. The soul can be opposed to the body, white to black, man to woman by way of oppositional qualities and a logic constructed that eliminates contradictions from discourse.[24]

Heloise not only refuses to adopt the particular conceptual order urged on her by Abelard—soul over body, man over woman, white over black—she does not think in fixed oppositionally defined concepts at all. An example is her correction of Abelard's incomplete and therefore distorted account of her arguments against marriage. She begins by asserting not a hierarchical opposition but an apparent contradiction: to be the whore (meretrix) of Abelard would be more honorable than to be the wife of an emperor (imperatrix) (MS XV, 71; 114). Whore is not oppositionally defined as a woman who is not a wife, nor is wife defined as a woman who is not a whore. Instead the semantic dissonance of the combination of wife/dishonorable and whore/honorable is explored by noting contradictions in the actual institution of medieval marriage as experienced by women. When a woman marries for status and money, says Heloise, as twelfth-century women were often forced to do, it is the same as prostitution. Such marriages will always be unstable, and the partners prone to infidelity. As the woman wonders whether she made the best bargain, she becomes a whore, willing to "trade in" her old marriage for a more advantageous one.[25]

This critical insight suggests in turn a new concept of the marriage relation, based on the commitment to hold each other in the highest esteem, believing that "there is no better man or worthier woman on earth" (MS XV, 71; 114). Attributing these words to the Greek philosopher Aspasia, Heloise calls them "truly saintly, more than philosophical opinion (*senten-*

tia), they should be called wisdom (*sophiae*) rather than philosophy" (MS XV, 71; 114).[26] Fidelity in marriage can only be assured when each believes the other to be the best. The possibility of such a love based on mutual esteem cannot be thought within the conceptual framework of Abelard's universals. The opposition between mind and body reflects instead an internal battle between lust awakened by a woman and obedience to God. For Abelard marriage can only be motivated by jealousy, by the need to secure the object of lust. As he admits to Heloise, he insisted on the secret marriage that has ruined both their lives because "had you not been joined to me before in marriage, at my withdrawal from the world, either at the suggestion of your parents or for the delights of carnal pleasure, you might easily have clung to the world" (MS XV, 90; 149). He is incapable of appreciating Heloise's fidelity assured by mutual esteem for the other, which would require a moving beyond and out of the solipsistic drama of reason pitched against appetite. Abelard's judgment can only be that Heloise is irrational. She has not thought in universals; she has not separated things into their correct metaphysical categories; she has not structured her argument according to what things *are* in their essence.

Instead Heloise thinks through conflictual ideas and conflictual reality to move toward new conceptions of love and marriage. The idea of prostitution helps her to understand the actual reality of its supposed opposite, marriage. Observations of marriage as practiced suggest the idea of a new and different kind of marriage. Instead of Abelard's thought held rigidly in place by fixed categories of being, Heloise's thought is, just as Abelard charged, flexible and moving. Marriage and prostitution change in meaning as concepts come into contact with the experienced reality of medieval marriage.

In Heloise's thought there is a more complex relation between words and things than in Abelard's "institution" of universals that reflect supposed permanent resemblances between things. As she works through reciprocal interactions between concepts and reality, Heloise is able to advance understanding of their situation where Abelard is not. His only escape from the dichotomy of soul and body is to elevate that dichotomy to a higher level, to an imaginary spiritual relation between the ruling soul of God and the subservient reason of man. Similarly, the only solution he can suggest for Heloise is that she accept the surrogate embraces of his superior in lieu of his own. This, needless to say, is an inadequate solution in Heloise's view. She refuses to accept Abelard's insistence that the failure of earthly love can be made good by a transfer of lustful affection to God.

In Heloise's thought, there is a different kind of relationship between passions and concepts than in Abelard's logic. It is not surprising that Abelard has recently been discovered by semioticians.[27] The "signifying chain" of his rationality, although often troubled by irruptions of bodily drives which he sees as both sinful and irrational, constantly reestablishes itself as symbolic structure. From the standpoint of Heloise, and, I think, most readers who are not philosophers or linguists committed to contemporary constructed or deconstructed versions of Abelard's dialectic, this can only constitute a kind of pathology. Abelard is not able to understand what Heloise writes to him or to respond in any meaningful way. Throughout his "rational" arguments is evasion and irrelevance that infuriates Heloise and also the reader. The cause of this communicative disability is the very separation of passion and reason in which he takes such pride as a philosopher. On the one hand, there is logic, conceptually structured by dichotomous universals; opposed are the evil appetites to be repressed and mastered. The result is that Abelard's rational thought, detached from the issues at hand, becomes an exercise in conceptual dexterity. At the same time, his repressed emotions stagnate, breaking out in irritable and sometimes manic expressions of impatience and disgust.

For Heloise, there is no such separation between passion and thought. Her love and anger are constantly present in her language. Her passions are as thoughtful as her language is passionate. Her desire is not thoughtless physical reflex, fixed in genital sensation that, when blocked, results only in disruptive irritability; it is embedded in a matrix of approaches and responses, exchanges and dependencies, understanding and conflict between persons. Her language is not fixed in categories divorced from experience that support only defensive assault on rival positions, but flows from her past and present experience. Her speech is not the involuntary expression of bodily impulses, nor is it a pure emotionless logic of the soul, but rather moving and changing conceptualizations directed to and shaped for the responses of others.

The mutual understanding that Heloise tries to establish is not the same as the logical necessity forced on her by Abelard. The instrumental value of logical necessity was well described by Abelard:

> I will take your accusations one at a time to answer, not so much to excuse myself as for an instruction and encouragement to you, so that you will assent more willingly to my requests when you understand the facts of reason, so that you will listen to me more carefully in regard to your claims as you find me less wrong in mine, and so that you will be that much more afraid to condemn as you see me less worthy of blame. (MS XV, 83; 137)

Heloise's concern, on the other hand, is not to get Abelard to do what she wants but to achieve an interpersonal understanding of the catastrophic events that have shaped their lives. Disturbed by the distortion in Abelard's autobiography, Heloise writes to reestablish a mutual understanding of what has happened, to grasp interpersonally the real dynamics of events and their consequences, of actions and their motivations. In this project, I think it is fair to say, Abelard shows no interest at all. For Abelard, speech is an exercise of will, a way to force acquiescence to his wishes and opinions.

This is hardly the first or the last time a man and a woman have misunderstood each other because of different conceptions of language and its purpose. But their failure to communicate also raises a larger question. If Heloise refused to accept the discipline of Abelard's dialectic, if she refused the style of logical debate that has shaped the philosophy curriculum and the institutional structures of the modern university, is this prophetic of the future? Will women continue to be judged unsuccessful as students and philosophers? Will they continue to disappoint their male mentors? Even though we now recognize as sexual harassment Abelard's ruse to seduce an innocent young girl, the answer is still in doubt. If rationality, logic, and correct methodology are structured according to universal categories that are sexist, racist, and body phobic, women may not be logical or rational. If logical thought requires that categories stay rigidly fixed, not coming into contact with lived experience and changing as a result, then women may again fail to succeed. If philosophy persists in being a professional discipline divorced from passionate experience and aspiration, women may not be interested.

Heloise's thought not only has the negative quality of being unlike Abelard's, it also offers a positive example. What would a philosophical community be like in which Heloise's thought would be at home. It would have to accommodate passionate speech that comes from the problematic experience of women and of men. It would be motivated by a concern for mutual understanding that can stabilize and repair relations between persons. Its discussions would be critical and, at the same time, constructive of new forms of understanding. Positions would be articulated not in battles of rival wills maneuvering within an accepted framework of concepts that may have lost any reference to experienced reality, but in the kind of free and open discussion that Abelard refused. If philosophy as we know it has often perpetuated and articulated that refusal, might a new philosophical community be informed by Heloise's and Aspasia's wisdom, their subtle, sensitive, mobile, flexible women's tongues? Might philosophers finally admit what Saint Paul and Abelard denied, that a woman can be the teacher of a man?

NOTES

1. References throughout the text are to the Latin texts of *Historia calamitatum* (Abelard 1933) and of Heloise's and Abelard's letters (Heloise and

Abelard 1950–56); the translations are my own. References are also appended to Betty Radice's recent translation of the letters (Heloise and Abelard 1974). References to Abelard's *Ethics* are to the Latin text edited by D. E. Luscombe (Abelard 1971; my translations).

2. *Animus* is more general then *corde*, or "heart," which is the usual translation. One's *animus* can be one's reasoning, mind, conscience, will, as well as feeling and emotion.

3. Abelard confesses that he did see the need for physical discipline throughout the tumultuous course of their pedagogical and erotic relationship. Later, when Heloise grew more resistant to his sexual demands, the tone is harsher: "Even when, unwilling, reluctant, and trying to dissuade me, you resisted as much as you could, because yours was the weaker nature I often forced your consent with threats and beatings" (MS XV, 89; 147). For this method of instruction, Abelard claimed good authority. God also punishes, he tells Heloise to exonerate God's harshness to them, but "this is a father's rod, not a persecutor's sword; the father strikes to correct, and to strike down an enemy who kills" (MS XV, 92; 153).

4. See Muckle's extensive review of the arguments and evidence for authenticity in his introduction to the Letters (MS XV, 47–68). Muckle concludes that the evidence is inconclusive, but there is nothing in the manuscripts that casts positive doubt on authenticity. His main worry is the unlikeliness that such a revered nun could have such a "sensual mind," as well as that Heloise could have done the final editing. She, he is sure, hardly would have wanted to "leave such a character sketch of herself as her 'monumentum perennis' (MS XV, 67). See also Dronke's more recent review of the evidence and his argument that it was the "profane" passages in Heloise's first two letters, and not textual evidence, that originated the claim that the letters are inauthentic (Dronke 1984, 108). Especially interesting is Dronke's linguistic analysis of Heloise's style as distinct from Abelard's, which would seem to put to rest the view that the whole series was written by Abelard.

5. Muckle's introduction to the *Letters* (MS XV, 52, 59).

6. For example, Robertson (1972). Robertson finds Heloise's arguments so "absurd" (124) and "ludicrous" (126) that he insists that the letters are not genuine but a fiction manufactured by Abelard for the edification of the nuns of Heloise's convent. Abelard's intention, he says, is "to show how desperately Heloise needed instruction" and to expose the "self-righteous unwillingness on her part to assume any responsibility for her condition" (128). Grane (1970) gives a more balanced interpretation that gives some credit to Heloise's accounts of love and marriage. Grane admits that a "very reasoned attack could be mounted against [Abelard's] monkish piety and grim asceticism" (69), but he concludes that Abelard has been able to regain his "intellectual integrity on a completely different plane" with love of God (67), while Heloise remains regressively committed to the "synthesis of the heart's urge and the mind's clarity that had always motivated her" (70).

7. For example, Waithe (1989): "In a long discussion Gilson identifies the philosophical foundations of Heloise's views on love and friendship. . . . it is clear that Heloise based her view of love on Cicero's philosophy . . . she is devastated to

realize that the very arguments and principles of morality she learned from Abelard and to which she subscribed, did not move him or guide his actions towards her" (73).

8. Although Abelard complains in his autobiography about how often he was required to visit and advise the nuns, Heloise insisted that he had neglected his duty to the convent. I am inclined to take her account over his, especially as during the time of his supposed visits he is known to have been busy elsewhere defending himself against charges of heresy and poor administration.

9. After his maiming, Abelard retired to the monastery at St. Denis; there, his high-handed criticisms caused general hatred among the brothers and he was banished to a separate school on the grounds. Accused and convicted of heresy, he was imprisoned for life in St. Medard, only to be released by the papal legate. When he returned to St. Denis, he infuriated everyone further with a charge that the monastery records were incorrect. The monks complained to the king and Abelard had to flee again. Understandably, after all these difficulties, he was granted permission to live alone as a monk, but after a few years he was named abbot of St. Gilda's in Brittany. There his relations with his charges were so troubled that the monks tried to kill him and he only escaped under armed guard. Further charges of heresy occupied him until the end of his life. By any standard, Abelard, who set himself up as Heloise's mentor, had no distinguished record of monastic leadership. In contrast, Heloise's administration was universally commended. In their first year at the Paraclete, the king exempted the nuns from taxes; the convent was supported financially both by the church and by lay endowments. Even the uncompromising Bernard of Clairvaux, about to become Abelard's mortal enemy, had nothing but praise after his visit in 1131.

10. Heloise's philosophy of love is not, as most commentators have repeated after Gilson (Gilson 1960, 56), Cicero's view of the ideal masculine friendship as expressed in *De amicitia*. First, Cicero is describing relations between men and not sexual relations between men and women. Second, the problematic of the Cicero piece is conflicts that arise between loyalty to friends and public duty. Finally, Cicero's answer is that one must choose friends carefully so that they are as like one as possible and not for mutual advantage, so as to minimize the chance of such a conflict. Heloise may have read Cicero, and even used Cicero, but her view is not his.

11. Many commentators have wanted to see a conversion on Heloise's part, as in her later letters she turns to less personal topics. See Dronke (1984, 137) for a review of the sources. It is true that she acquiesces before Abelard's insistence that only convent matters be discussed, but her tone, as I read it, does not indicate agreement but rather acceptance of the only terms on which Abelard is willing to communicate with her.

12. Although both Augustine and Abelard reject a purely exterior ethics that defines sin as the commission of some one or more of a list of proscribed actions, there are significant differences in their ethics. Augustine distinguishes between the doing of willful evil and the involuntary doing of evil, but the will is still essentially linked to action as the choice of which of our inclinations should be gratified.

Abelard rejects the will as the seat of sin, making a distinction between will, on the one hand, which is wanting or desiring to do evil, and consent, on the other, which is obedience to God's command (*Ethics* 32). Over the will is a rational judging that an action is forbidden by God that is completely autonomous of the body.

13. Abelard argues in the *Ethics* that evil will is a necessary condition for virtue because it gives us something to struggle against. If we simply did what we want or will, we would not be commendable in God's eyes. Only a restrained evil will can win the "crown of glory"; there is no reward in doing good "willingly" (*Ethics* 12). Virtue is in submitting our will, good or bad, to God's (*Ethics* 12). In his second letter to Heloise he applies this ethics to her case. She is fortunate, he says, because she is young and not mutilated, and so still has the "thorn of desire" that can be the occasion for a virtuous refusal of consent in accordance with God's will (MS XV, 93; 154).

14. This is not a radical pacifism on Abelard's part. There are occasions when consent to killing is innocent—for example, when a convict is hung out of "zeal for justice" (*Ethics* 28).

15. Many have commented on the similarities in wording between Heloise's and Abelard's formulas: "it is not what is done, but the spirit in which it is done." The similarities, Muckle concludes, can only be explained by common origin or imitation. Disastrous, however, to the popular thesis that Heloise imitated Abelard is the fact that Abelard's *Ethics* was written well after the letters. Not ruling out the possibility that "the common source is Abelard's mind," Muckle admits the possibility that the wording in Abelard's *Ethics* and other later writings may have been borrowed from Heloise. Added evidence is that Abelard's early wording in *Sic et Non* is very different (MS XV, 55–56).

16. In this, Heloise's ethics might seem to be closer to Augustine's than Abelard's. One can only speculate what some of the differences might be if more of Heloise's writings were available. Augustine's *lex aeterna* might have been much less prominent. Also, Augustine's struggle with concupiscence might have been resolved not by a choice of abstinence but in an inner transformation of lust into more developed forms of friendship, commitment, exchanges of pleasure.

17. Heloise cites a number of specific problems for a woman's order. The rule that all clothing should be wool is impractical, considering menstruation. A diet without meat may not be appropriate, considering women's special needs for nutrition. Because women are less prone to drunkenness, a strict prohibition of wine may not be necessary. Is the abbess to rule in the same way as the abbot? What should be her practice when male guests come to the convent, or worldly women? What should be the requirement, if any, for manual labor?

18. Heloise had no developed feminist position that women and men are or should be equal or the same. The emphasis in her discussion of a monastic rule for women is not on women's equality but on their differences from men. Some of those differences, she notes, are actually beneficial in monastic life; for example, women are constitutionally less likely to fall prey to gluttony or drunkenness (MS XVII, 245–46; 165–66).

19. Abelard warns Heloise in no uncertain terms of the dangers of a life independent of male authority: "There are those who will not stand any restriction at all from monks, and who disperse themselves throughout villages, cities, and towns, and even live alone without the observing of any rule, and are so much the worse than worldly men as they fall away more from their vocation. They name their dwelling places obedientaries, where no rule is followed, abusing them as if they were family or private homes, and there is nothing to be obeyed but stomach and body there where they live as they wish with friends or family, the more free in their own manner the less they have to fear from their own consciences. Indeed, in such shameless apostates, there is no doubt there are criminal excesses that might be venial sins in others. You should forbid yourself not only to consider but even to hear about such a life" (MS XVII, 250; 195–96).

20. Some commentators have cited Abelard's insistence that nuns understand the meaning of the words in hymns and prayers as support for scholarship in convents. Abelard's concern, however, is with women's "ecstatic language" and the possibility that nuns may delight in the melody of their singing, rather than doctrine. The antidote he suggests is not thought or philosophy but listening and reading Scripture with attention to received meaning as opposed to mystical ecstasy (MS XVIII, 286–87; 258–59).

21. See the end of *Historia calamitatum* (MS XII, 208–9; 101) for a similar argument, but compare MS XVIII, 259; 213–14, where Abelard cautions that in order to ensure harmony and peace, men's rule should not go against the will of the abbess. Abelard's ambivalence reflects the many conflicts in the patriarchal church's thinking about monastic life for women. The dangerous heritage from paganism of women's sacerdotal power still evident in many local religious practices and unpleasant memories of disturbances caused by powerful noble abbesses in the early days of monasticism provoked the church to insist that nuns be closely controlled by male monastics. This created new problems as monks and church officials came into contact with women and were tempted by lust. On the other hand, if the convents were shut down, there would be no place where loose women, women unattached to men or "virgin," could be cloistered. Also troublesome were the hermitesses of the early eleventh century, who represented a resurgence in female mysticism and a spiritual power uncontrolled by the male church; convents were necessary so that those who withdrew to the wilderness (*anachoreta*) could be enclosed (*inclusa* or *reclusa*), confined under the auspices of some recognized church institution. Throughout shifting policy, a precarious balance was sought between the segregation of women monastics from men and the control of women by men. Similar conflicts might have motivated Suger to expel Heloise's nuns from Argenteuil and make it necessary for them to settle on Abelard's land near Troye.

22. Aristotle's *Politics* (book I, chapter 5) is the foundational text. Aristotle sets up a mutually confirming set of symmetrical oppositions between mind/body, reason/emotion, human/animal, master/slave, man/woman to justify the natural dominance of men over women, masters over slaves, and Greeks over barbarians.

23. See Dronke's study of the stylistic characteristics of Heloise's writing—rhythms, cadences, dynamic tensions—that constitute its expressivity (Dronke 1984, 107–39).

24. Abelard discusses universals throughout his *Logica ingredientibus* (Abelard 1933). See my extended discussion of his logic in Nye (1990).

25. See also Dronke's discussion of Heloise's *Problemata, Patrilogia latina*, 178, 677–730 (Dronke 1984, 134–39). These were a series of unresolved problems in the interpretation of doctrine and Scripture encountered by the nuns of her order in their studies that Heloise submitted to Abelard for consultation. Unlike Abelard's own *Sic et Non*, which set out contradictions among various authorities to be resolved by textual editing and logic, Heloise's problems were more closely related to contradictions in the lived experience of a moral or spiritual life and, in many instances, were a continuation of themes in her personal letters: Can you obey a law partially? Why should a converted sinner be welcomed with more joy? How is any sin forgivable? Can you sin in doing something your husband and master commands? Abelard's answers to these, one might say, loaded questions were cool and mechanical, based, for the most part, on abundant quotation rather than on thought or reference to religious experience.

26. In a footnote, Radice (Heloise and Abelard 1974, 114) follows tradition by insisting that Heloise derived her knowledge of Aspasia from Cicero: although Heloise refers to Aeschines Socraticus, who wrote a dialogue about Aspasia, "this is no proof that Heloise knew Greek as the passage was well known in the Middle Ages from Cicero's translation of it in *De inventione*." Heloise's reference to Aspasia, however, goes considerably beyond Cicero's brief reference in *De inventione*. In order to illustrate what induction is, Cicero used as an example a scrap of conversation from Aeschines' dialogue in which, according to Cicero, Aspasia uses the following argumentative strategy: she gets Xenophon and his wife to agree that if they believe that their neighbor has a better spouse they would want a better spouse too; then she makes them draw the inference that if they are to be happy together they will have to make it so they are each the best. Cicero makes no comment on the philosophy that underlies this move, but produces it only as an example of inductive argument.

27. See, for example, Kristeva (1984). Kristeva has developed a dualistic theory of language in which necessarily alienated and oppressive symbolic structures are opposed to the primitive "semiotic" expression of drives and body sensation. My reading of Heloise differs radically from deconstructive readings inspired by such a linguistics—for example, Peggy Kamuf's, in which Heloise is understood as transgressing or disrupting Abelard's symbolic structures (Kamuf 1982). In my reading, the woman speaking is not condemned to transgressive play on the margins of rational language; rather she attempts to restore communicative relations that are mutual and productive of interpersonal understanding.

REFERENCES

Abelard, Peter. 1933. *Philosophische Schriften*, ed. Bernhard Geyer. In *Beiträge zur Geschichte der Philosophie des Mittelalters* XXXI, 1–4. Münster.

————. 1971. *Peter Abelard's Ethics*, ed. David Edward Luscombe. Oxford: Clarendon Press.

Dronke, Peter. 1984. *Women writers of the Middle Ages*. Cambridge: Cambridge University Press.

Gilson, Etienne. 1960. *Heloise and Abelard*. Ann Arbor: University of Michigan Press.

Grane, Lief. 1970. *Peter Abelard*. Trans. Frederick Crowley and Christine Crowley. New York: Harcourt Brace and World.

Heloise and Abelard. 1950–56. *Letters*, ed. Joseph Thomas Muckle and Terence Patrick McLaughlin. *Medieval Studies* XII, XV, XVII, XVIII.

————. 1974. *The letters of Abelard and Heloise*, ed. and trans. Betty Radice. Harmondsworth: Penguin.

Kamuf, Peggy. 1982. *Fictions of feminine desire*. Lincoln: University of Nebraska Press.

Kristeva, Julia. 1984. *The revolution in poetic language*, trans. Margaret Walker. New York: Columbia University Press.

Nye, Andrea. 1990. *Words of power: A feminist reading of the history of logic*. New York: Routledge, Chapman, Hall.

Robertson, Durant Waite. 1972. *Abelard and Heloise*. New York: Dial Press.

Waithe, Mary Ellen. 1989. *A history of women philosophers II*. Dordrecht: Kluwer.

CHRISTINE DE PISAN AND THOMAS HOBBES

KAREN GREEN

Recent feminist political theory has been highly critical of the social contract tradition (see Pateman 1988, 1989). Liberalism, in particular, has been deemed an inadequate foundation for feminism, and some have argued that feminist political theory should be grounded in a non-contractual understanding of society (Jaggar 1983, 50; also Held 1987). It has been suggested that in a feminist, non-contractual, political theory, relations between citizens would be modelled on those between mothers and children. In this paper I hope to illuminate the points of difference between contractual and non-contractual conceptions of society by comparing the political writings of the mediaeval feminist Christine de Pisan with those of Thomas Hobbes.[1] Christine de Pisan, I argue, can be interpreted as endorsing a more 'maternalist' conception of political authority than other monarchist thinkers. Her writing thus offers us one version of a non-contractual understanding of political relations. However, the consequences that she draws from her understanding of political rights and duties, modelled as they are on maternal and filial obligations, are not compatible with the modern feminist commitment to egalitarianism. In order to illuminate the strengths and weaknesses of social contract theory I first discuss one of Carole Pateman's criticisms of Hobbes and show that it is flawed. I then offer my own criticism of Hobbes' reasoning, arguing that the situation of women serves to demonstrate a dramatic failure in his logic. However, the nature of this failure is not sufficient to undermine all forms of social contract theory. What it shows is not that social contract theory is completely defective, but that it is incomplete. The nature of this incompleteness is further illuminated through a discussion of the political writings of Christine de Pisan.

Like Hobbes, de Pisan wrote a number of political treatises, including *Le Livre du Corps de Policie*, at a time of impending civil war, and in the

This article originally appeared in *The Philosophical Quarterly* 44: 177 October 1994.

hope of promoting peace. Like him, she was interested in upholding the authority of the sovereign (cf. Hobbes *EW* vol. 2, pp. 78–80). Unlike him, she also wrote explicitly and at length on the place of women in society, and her views cast a new light on Hobbes' advocacy of political subjection. There are further similarities in their thought, which will be discussed below. And there is also an important difference, which resides in their assumptions concerning moral psychology and moral education. Hobbes believes that reason by itself must be able to give us a reason for being ethical, for 'the Lawes of Nature (as *Justice, Equity, Modesty, Mercy* and (in summe) *doing to others, as wee would be done to*) . . . are contrary to our naturall Passions' (*L* ch. XVII, pp. 87–9). De Pisan, by contrast, writes within the framework of a Christian Platonism which treats the love of the good as a natural tendency, distinct from reason. For her, moral motivation is *sui generis*, and is not identical with prudence. I shall argue that feminist objections to Hobbes are most cogent if they are understood as objections to his moral psychology, but this moral psychology is not an essential part of social contract theory. This indicates the possibility of developing a version of political theory which is both contractual and ma-ternalist, in a sense to be developed later.

The Feminist Critique of Hobbes

Hobbes introduces his discussion on commonwealths with the observation that humans are by nature equal. They are all equally possessed of reason, the desire to preserve their own life above all things and, importantly for his argument, the capacity to preserve it (*L* ch. XIII, p. 63). According to a standard interpretation, he then argues that humans are self-interested and that the state of nature is a state of war. Since a state of war is in no one's long-term interest, people are led by reason to enter into a social contract and to give up their freedom in exchange for the protection which the state provides. Thus the existence of the state and its laws is justified in the light of the rational egoism of all humans. Reason leads to the recognition that the best way to preserve one's own life, liberty and material possessions is to submit to the power of a state that will protect them (*L* ch. XVII, pp. 87–90).

The existence of women and children poses an immediate difficulty for Hobbes' political views, for women in civil society are not men's equals, and it is extremely odd to think of our ethical relations with children as based on contract (see Brennan and Pateman). Yet, unlike so many male theorists, Hobbes resists the temptation of explaining this social inequality by postulating women's natural inferiority, and he does not interpret marriage as naturally involving women's subordination. With ad-mirable consistency, he insists that in the state of nature men and women are equals and that any authority that husbands have over wives is the result of civil society. He points to the possibility of a society like the Amazons, who according to tradition governed themselves, contracting with neighbouring tribes of men for intercourse and giving them any boy children who might be born, while retaining exclusive control over their daughters (*L* ch. XX, p. 105; and *EW* vol. 2, p. 116). In the state of nature, Hobbes argues, authority over children rests with mothers exclusively, for, without the social structures that ensure paternity, paternity cannot be proved, and 'since every man by law of nature, hath right or propriety to his own body, the child ought rather to be the propriety of the mother, of whose body it is part until the time of separation' (*EW* vol. 4, p. 154). Nevertheless it is not generation but preservation which entitles the mother to dominion over her child, and should she expose it and it be brought up by some other, the right of dominion would pass to that other. Having made these observations, Hobbes says nothing explicit regarding the justice of the usual relationship of husbands to wives in the society in which he lived. He observes merely that for the most part civil law gives dominion over children to the father because commonwealths have been erected by the fathers and not by the mothers of families (*L* ch. xx, p. 105).

Something is clearly missing from Hobbes' story. If his premises were true, and if society were founded on a social contract between equals, we would expect women to be among the contractors as well as men. Individual women are not, as Hobbes admits, necessarily weaker than individual men, and in any case, weak men as well as strong ones are party to the contract that founds society. So how did the subjection of women arise?

Feminist critics of liberalism have suggested a number of places where the Hobbesian story falls down. Many have objected to his premises concerning human nature, and in particular to the claim that humans are rational egoists (e.g., Jaggar p. 45). Some (e.g., Flax) have modified this claim by suggesting that only men are rational egoists, and that consequently the view of human nature that Hobbes offers is distorted and purely masculine. In support of the first of these criticisms it can be pointed out that Hobbes' story is not borne out by anthropology, and in order for infants to survive, mothers must be, at least partly, altruistic. So, it can be argued, Hobbes' assumption of universal rational egoism is not borne out by the facts.

While the difference between those social contract theories which are compatible with feminism and those which are not depends, I shall argue, on whether Hobbes' moral psychology is adopted, by themselves these observations do not take us very far as criticisms of Hobbes' logic. Humans may not be total egoists, but it is not reasonable to assume that they are total altruists either. Although most people act altruistically towards some individuals, many cannot be relied upon to extend this behaviour to a very wide group. If they could, there would be no need for laws and institutions to protect our rights. As Hobbes observed, in response to contemporary objections to his jaded assessment of human nature, we shut our doors when we go to sleep and defend our coasts, thus manifesting our belief that others will not necessarily treat us altruistically (*EW* vol. 2, p. 6). And in fact all that Hobbes needs to assume for the sake of his argument is that even if we are by nature reasonably altruistic to those who are close to us, by blood relationship, proximity or in virtue of some other trait that excites our sympathy, we place our own self-preservation very high among our interests and that in fact, in general, it is an over-riding consideration (see Coady 1990).

Another common criticism of Hobbes is that there never was a state of nature in which people lived as isolated individuals. But as it stands this falls short as a compelling criticism. One *can* read Hobbes as suggesting the implausible hypothesis that there once was a state of nature populated by isolated individuals, but there are places where he clearly thinks of the state of nature as populated by family groups, in conflict with each other, who are brought together into a commonwealth by the social contract. This suggests the following development of the feminist critique. Either Hobbes accepts the unrealistic hypothesis that there was a state of nature in which humans lived as isolated atoms, or he must admit that the family constitutes the first society, and that since the family is held together by natural altruistic sentiments, morality cannot simply be grounded in reason.

Yet Hobbes can be read as having pre-empted this criticism, and as having rejected it on the grounds that natural ties of affection are not sufficient to hold families together. He speaks of the families of 'the savage people in many places of America' as being held together only by 'natural lust', and he also says that there exists in the state of nature 'the natural inclination of the sexes, one to another, and to their children' (*L* ch. XIII, p. 65 and ch. XX, p. 105). But, he says, such ties are weak and easily broken. The family must therefore be held together by a compact that reflects in miniature the compact that founds civil society (see Chapman). Members of a family consent to the absolute authority of the family head in exchange for the protection provided by membership of the family. Since children owe their lives to the protection and nurture of the one who has brought them up, who need not be a natural parent, that person has dominion over them derived from the child's consent, 'either express or by other sufficient arguments declared' (*L* ch. XX, p. 105). So Hobbes understands the development of civil society as a two-stage process. Individuals contract to come together in family groups, which are, as a matter of fact, usually patriarchal; and then patriarchal family heads contract together to form a commonwealth. The state of nature that exists in an abstract and theoretical sense between individuals, exists historically as a state of war between families and exists even now between nations.

The resulting Hobbesian explanation of the inequality of women in civil society is that commonwealths are set up by fathers, and civil society accords dominion to fathers, because mothers are already subjugated within patriarchal families. And there is contemporary evidence that this is how the state was formed (Lerner 1986, 89, 121–2). But this only pushes the apparent inconsistency back a step. For how is it that fathers have obtained dominion over mothers and hence over their children? One answer might be that Hobbes is simply wrong about the natural equality of all individuals and that men and women are not equal in natural liberty. Indeed Hobbes himself equivocates over this, and at one place admits that the equality he has in mind is possessed by 'all men of riper years' (*EW* vol. 2, p. 115). This admission would be strengthened if one took into account the fact that, although an individual man may not be stronger or more able than an individual woman, women as a group are less strong than men. It is also plausible given the particular disadvantages women suffer because of pregnancy. Women wishing to preserve their infants' lives are likely to surrender in the face of a threat to their children, even if they could sacrifice the infant and then possibly vanquish their aggressors. And, because of the possibility of pregnancy, women are subject to a kind of attack, rape, that may have consequences for them different from any that a man will ever suffer. Pregnancy also has another consequence. So long as children are seen as an asset, women will be a valuable resource and so will be treated as booty, rather than enemies, in war. There is historical evidence that the first slaves were women captured in battle and spared the death that automatically awaited the men of their vanquished tribes (Lerner pp. 78–89). Since men have little motivation to kill women, women have little to gain by attempting to vanquish men. Hobbes himself makes no explicit mention of the natural disadvantages that women face due to childbearing, but they remain in the background of his account.

In her book *The Sexual Contract* Carole Pateman considers a Hobbesian story of this sort, and argues that it is not consistent with Hobbes' general assumption that people are rational egoists. If choosing to care for infants puts women at a disadvantage, and all individuals are rational egoists, then women would not care for infants, and so the first generation would be the last (p. 49). But this is too quick a rebuttal of the Hobbesian story. Hobbes' individuals are interested, first and foremost, in the preservation of their lives. In the face of conflict with a potential enemy there are always three options: to flee; or, if it is too late for that, to submit to the other party and contract into their service; or to fight to the point where either the other is vanquished (killed or submits) or one loses one's own life. If it comes to battle, some women may take the former, some the latter course. Since the children of those women who take the option of fighting to the death are less likely to be born, if the woman is childless, and more likely to die, if she has children, over time there will be more children who are brought up by those women who have accepted submission. So the assumption that the first aim of all is self-preservation leads to the conclusion that, in the state of nature, if there is a life-and-death conflict, the women whose children survive will tend to be those who are prepared to accept submission in order to increase their children's chances of survival and who are, in this sense, reasonably altruistic, at least towards their own children.

More recently, Pateman (1991 p. 70) seems to have given up her criticism of the cogency of Hobbes' story and to have recognized in his work

> an early version of the argument, presented in the later nineteenth and earlier twentieth centuries in elaborate detail and with much ethnographic data, that civilization and political society resulted from the overthrow of mother-right and the triumph of patriarchy.

This is surely right. Hobbes, with his mention of the Amazons, shows some awareness of the very myths of the historic 'defeat of women' which fuelled later speculation about the existence of an original matriarchy. But interpreting Hobbes in this way throws into question the success of the Hobbesian project, just so long as we interpret that project as involving a demonstration of the rational justification of obedience to the moral law.

This emerges because we can establish that, while the Hobbesian framework does provide an explanation of the origin of women's subordination within the patriarchal family, it cannot provide a justification of that subordination. Pateman's intention, in her early rejection of the consistency of Hobbes' argument, would seem to have been to preempt any rationalization of the subjection of women which took it to be, like the subjection of servants to masters, and citizens to the state, grounded in consent, even consent obtained in circumstances of duress. Instead, she interprets woman's historical situation as one of slavery imposed upon women by the fraternity of men in order to guarantee men's right of sexual access. But her total rejection of social contract theory leaves nothing in place for the reconstruction of a feminist theory of justice. Although social contract theory may be flawed, properly interpreted it can provide a plausible account of justice, understood as fairness. It would be hasty to reject it in its entirety until such time as a better alternative becomes available. It therefore seems worth while to take a longer route in order to see what is at fault with such Hobbesian rationalizations of women's historical subjection.

There is in the literature on Hobbes some controversy over the interpretation of his intentions (see Greenleaf). On one traditional view, he gives a description of political society, based on what he takes to be scientific premises, which leads him into ethical relativism and the claim that might is right. He says that there is no justice outside civil society and that what is just depends on the civil law. This would apply, in particular, to matrimony. The civil law is whatever is promulgated by the sovereign, and the sovereign gains its legitimacy from its power to protect the citizens subject to it. Subjection to the sovereign is rational, because it is only through the consent of each individual to be ruled that peace can be preserved, and peace is the precondition for the preservation of life. The subjection of women to their husbands will be rational, by the same reasoning, if civil society has patriarchal laws. It will be rational in the state of nature also, in so far as it is a means of preserving peace. If might is right, then, if one is not one of the mighty, obedience and service to the powers that be is the most reasonable and prudent course of action, the best way of maintaining the protection of the mighty and the benefits of their good favour. So, if Hobbes is correct, women's traditional acceptance of submission is grounded in their desire for self-preservation and their consequent desire for peace. Although this reading of Hobbes might appear to rationalize women's historical subjection, it also has emancipatory implications. If men hold sway over women merely on the grounds of consent obtained through the use of force, and women are able to reverse the situation, perhaps because changing technology has altered the importance of muscle in the distribution of power and diminished the disadvantages of pregnancy, then women have a natural right to do so. All spoils will go to the victor in the battle of the sexes, and woman must be expected to retrieve her natural dominion over her children and the fruits of her labour whenever she has the power to do so. But at the same time this reading undercuts the possibility of articulating a satisfactory theory of justice between the sexes that could be acceptable to both men and women, because it denies that there is any justice beyond the laws which are upheld by those in power.

On another reading, Hobbes is arguing that there is a God-given natural law, the study of which is the science of natural justice, and this law is perceptible by the light of reason (L ch. XXXI, p. 197). Such a law is ineffectual except when upheld by a civil authority, but at the same time a civil authority will ultimately be ineffectual unless it understands and obeys the natural law. Rational individuals subject themselves to the state, in order to ensure that the natural law is upheld, and any state that is to preserve itself must have a civil law in keeping with the law of nature (*EW* vol. 4, pp. 213–20). Because people enter civil society in order to preserve as many of their natural rights as is compatible with a recognition of the rights of others, a stable civil government will extend liberty to its citizens. Hobbes elucidates (*ibid.* p. 215):

> By liberty, I mean, that there be no prohibition without necessity of any thing to any man, which was lawful to him in the state of nature; that is to say, that there be no restraint of natural liberty, but what is necessary for the good of the commonwealth.

This reading of Hobbes has even more obvious emancipatory implications for women. If, as he allows, women in the state of nature have dominion over their children and the right to their service, how can one justify their giving up these rights in civil society? If one gives the Hobbesian answer, that women submitted to men at a stage of the development of society earlier than the institution of great states, since women's liberties were not preserved, this now goes against the principle of natural law as spelt out by Hobbes, and so begins to look like a grave injustice.

The picture that would fit best with this edict of natural law would be one in which a woman gave up some liberty, notably the liberty to have sexual relations with any man other than her husband, in exchange for the protection of herself and her children, while the husband gave up some comparable liberty, presumably the liberty to dispose of his surplus production at will, in exchange for the secure knowledge of paternity. If the institution is to conform to the natural law, as characterized by Hobbes in this passage, it should involve the loss of no further liberties. So natural law would suggest that, since this contract is between equals, it should guarantee the parents joint dominion over their children. At least one earlier English commentator seems to have seen the family in this way (see Hinton pp. 292–3). Hobbes, however, does not consider this possibility, for he assumes that either the husband or wife must rule, insisting that 'No man can serve two masters' (*L* ch. XX, p. 105).

If we emphasize the normative elements in Hobbes' work, which stress the rational law of nature and each individual's equal right to those natural liberties that are compatible with a like liberty for others, the subjection of women to their husbands stands out as a manifest injustice. In fact, it indicates a fatal flaw in Hobbes' reasoning, which undermines his whole attempt to show how ethical behaviour and obedience to the state can be justified. What is interesting about Hobbes' argument is that it seems to provide reasons for behaving ethically which are compelling *even for an egoist*. As I pointed out above, one does not need to attribute to Hobbes a belief in an implausible psychological egoism: he only needs to assume that a usually over-riding motive in human psychology is self-preservation. This does not detract from the claim that the argument, if good, will convince an egoist. For the achievement of all aims, whether they are egoistic or altruistic, almost always depends on one's own survival. However, whether one starts with the assumption that humans are by nature rational egoists, or with the weaker assumption that self-preservation is a primary motive, Hobbes' attempt to place obedience to the natural law on a rational foundation fails. It is worth going into the reasons for this in some detail, for it shows where the limitations of the attempt to ground morality in reason lie. As already mentioned, feminist writers have insisted that the attitude of the rational egoist comes more naturally to men than to women. But this observation by itself does not show that Hobbes' argument collapses. Indeed, the Hobbesian explanation of women's subordination suggests that women will be more likely to have to seek their self-preservation through submission than men are, and that this will be particularly the case if their aims include the preservation of their offspring; but it offers no criticism of this situation, which is perpetuated at the expense of women. If we are to show the flaw in Hobbes' reasoning we need to show how a situation which does not accord with the natural law, as Hobbes outlines it, nevertheless can perpetuate itself with the consent, under duress, of those who are deprived of their natural liberties.

We can see this once we admit that women have an equal natural right to liberty. Since men do not have to take into account, to any very great degree, the threat that women pose to men's survival, they do not need to recognize the natural rights of women. For women, as a group, are disadvantaged in relation to men, as a group. Women clearly could murder their fathers and husbands, as they do in one of Herodotus' stories (Herodotus 1945, 114). But they are unlikely, given their average inferiority in physical strength, to be able to maintain men in a state of submission grounded in the threat of superior force. By contrast, men, since they have little fear that women will succeed in any rebellion, are able, as a group, to maintain women in a state of submission without fully recognizing their equal natural right to liberty. Hobbes attempted to show that adherence to the natural moral law is rational, for both subject and sovereign, given that the desire for self-preservation and liberty is primary. The situation of women suggests that when the sovereign is a member of a group which is stronger than another group in the society, the sovereign can avoid such adherence in relation to members of the weaker group. This appears to be the historical situation of women, and of other subordinate groups or classes, whose rights have not been recognized by the rulers of the societies in which they live.

At the root of this failure in Hobbes' reasoning is an ambiguity in the concept of the equality of individuals. The argument that founds moral and political obligation on the desire for self-preservation depends crucially on a claimed equality of power, which is plausible so long as we think of people as isolated individuals, but which breaks down because real power is not merely an individual attribute, but belongs to individuals partly in virtue of the group to which they belong. At the same time, Hobbes recognizes an equality of natural right which exists independently of our power to enforce it. It is our grasp of this moral notion that enables us to recognize that there are situations in which individuals may be forced to consent to unjust pacts, and that consent does not of itself entail justice. It is the obviousness of this natural equal right to liberty which has been taken up by later feminists, and, it is important to note, the notion can be defended independently of implausible assumptions concerning our actual independence and equality in the state of nature, or our intrinsic egoism. Modern versions of social contract theory, epitomized by Rawls, abstract away from claims about actual equality of power in order to maintain that the principles of justice are those principles that we would consent to be governed by were we all rational and equal in power (see Rawls p. 11).

Christine de Pisan's Problematic Feminism

Interest in the writings of Christine de Pisan has been fuelled by her claimed status as the first known feminist. Yet her right to be deemed a feminist has been hotly contested. Recently Sheila Delany has asserted (p. 181) 'that she was not even by the standards of her own day a reformer or protofeminist'. And Delany is only one of a number of feminist writers, going back at least as far as Mathilde Laigle (pp. 120–3), to question de Pisan's feminism. De Pisan ends *The Book of the City of Ladies*, her major defence of women against the slanders of men, with the advice (p. 225) that women who are married should not disdain being subject to their husbands. This pronouncement is quite inconsistent with modern feminist doctrine. Maureen Quilligan, who is interested in defending de Pisan against her critics, and who finds in her writing an elegant defence of female authority, is tempted (p. 244) to dismiss this ending as 'the first effect of the failure of will of a weary author'. But this response is quite superficial. It fails to take into account that de Pisan's advice to married women is part and parcel of her general political theory. If this theory is, as I shall argue it is, plausibly deemed maternalist, then this consequence shows that maternalist political thought can carry with it some of the same dangers as paternalist thinking. Nevertheless I hope to show that there are some strengths in de Pisan's political philosophy which can be re-appropriated by a 'maternalist' contract theory.

De Pisan's advice to married women is completely consistent with her general understanding of political subjection and social duty. In her earliest discussion of the function of the sovereign, she gives (*FBM* p. 5) an account of the origin of political authority rather like that given by Hobbes:

> when the human race began to populate and fill the countries of the earth, then, since perversity is natural to the human race, when it is not moderated by reason, the people, having no law, took to extortion and committed infinite evil against each other, pillage, killing and many outrages without regard to justice and without any constraint; then the people, taught by the gift of nature, long experience and by reason, decided that it would be good, in order to avoid these ills, that one of them, the most dignified and appropriate in virtue and knowledge, should be established superior and prince and thus by common consent they gave authority and sovereignty to this person.

She is thus quite clear, from the outset, that the role of the sovereign is to preserve the peace, and that dutiful subjects will do what they can to reinforce the sovereign's legitimate power. In her biography of Charles V she excuses the rather rosy picture that she paints of the character of the French royal family by suggesting that for her to criticize the ruling house in public would be inappropriate. Since people are much more likely to notice other people's faults than their own, such acts are more likely to be dangerous than useful. Princes, she believes, should be criticized in private, by those who are close to them (*FBM* p. 33). Insubordination of all kinds is anathema to her way of thinking. The body politic which she describes is governed by a prince or princes who correspond to the understanding, from which derive all the movements of the body. The knights and nobles are the arms and hands which carry out the sovereign's decisions, and the ordinary people are the stomach, feet and legs (*CP* pp. 2–3). Each individual has an appropriate role to play, according to this hierarchical and organic model. Different individuals have different duties, derived from their social positions, and each position provides equal scope for the honour people deserve in proportion to their virtue (*CP* pp. 3–4). The justice which the prince will uphold is, says de Pisan, quoting Aristotle, a measure which will render to each his right, and, like Aristotle, she believes that different kinds of people have different rights and obligations (*CP* p. 61). In particular, men are more adequately equipped with 'strong and hardy bodies' which enable them to uphold the laws by physical constraint and force of arms, so men more naturally administer laws and rule than do women (*TCL* p. 31). Women, then, even when they are married to princes, are in the position of subjects, and like other subjects they should serve well, for their own sakes and for the sake of the general good. But de Pisan's endorsement of political subjection should not be read as an approbation of servile or thoughtless obedience. It is partly prudent, for in the society that she describes most people are both subject and sovereign. It is also exemplary, and, she believes, has the power to move the powerful to recognize their own duty of subjection to the moral law.

The sketch so far provided of de Pisan's political thought does little to distinguish it from standard patriarchal thinking. There are, however, two related features of her treatises on political relations which warrant attributing to her a 'maternalist' conception of the sovereign. The first has to do with the function of love in her political thought. The second involves her depiction of women as paradigmatic sovereigns and subjects.

Because the function of the sovereign is to protect the country from its external enemies and to uphold justice within, the health of the body politic depends on the sovereign's virtue and love of justice. So de Pisan in *Le Livre du Corps de Policie* turns early to the education of princes (pp. 5–14). And in her manual of advice to women *The Treasure of the City of Ladies* she also discusses the education of children and the best way to instil virtue (pp. 66–8, 85–9). She suggests that children will more easily learn from someone that they love and respect. The teacher who wants to teach virtue must be a mirror or model of virtue for the child, but at the same time should not be too solemn, but make sure the child has time to play. The teacher should win the child's affection with small presents and story-telling. The mother, tutor or governess teaches largely by example. And, like the mother, the good prince is responsible for the moral welfare of his subjects, so he too has a duty to act as a moral exemplar. In contrast to Machiavelli, who (p. 96) answers the question 'Is it better for a prince to be loved or feared by his people?' in favor of fear, de Pisan (*TCL* pp. 71–4) advises the princess that it is the love of her subjects which is her surest protection and which she should work to deserve. De Pisan's enlightened views on education are plausibly seen as deriving from practical traditions of child-rearing, and are extended in the sphere of government to the status of a general principle, that subjects will be more strongly motivated to please and obey rulers they love and respect, than those they fear and despise. Within a good family, the position of child is not more onerous than the position of parent. Though the child owes its parents obedience, it is free of the responsibilities that go with parental power. The greater the power that individuals have, the greater their responsibility for the moral and material welfare of those within their charge, and it is in the light of these views that de Pisan can both be considered a feminist and consistently judge that women should not scorn their lack of independence.

Virginia Held is just one of a number of writers who have been influenced by Carol Gilligan's claim that there are different masculine and feminine ethical voices and by Sara Ruddick's related suggestion that women have a sense of self related to their position as potential mothers. Reading de Pisan confirms this hypothesis. She uses a vocabulary which places far more emphasis on love, virtue and ethical devotion than that of most male writers. Like modern proponents of the maternalist ethic, she also sees women as having an important role to play in the preservation of peace (Ruddick 1987 and de Pisan 1985, 50–2, and 1984). Yet this maternalist ethic, when it is pursued by those who lack power, can easily transmute into a quietist acceptance of virtuous subordination. This emerges from the way in which, for de Pisan, women's subordination is exemplary. Like Hobbes, she sees marriage as a political relationship. And she is well aware of the Greek and Roman myths which, as suggested above, plausibly lay behind Hobbes' belief that there had been a historical defeat of women. The way she treats these myths is interestingly different from their usual treatment, for she emphasizes women's active participation in the constitution of the state in which individuals accept their subordination to the law. She repeats the history of the Amazons in a number of places (e.g., *BCL* pp. 40–51). But, while the Athenians stressed the defeat of the Amazons, de Pisan uses them as proof that women are capable of great strength and courage, and she leaves obscure the decline of their empire, which she says had lasted eight hundred years. She does not mention the role that the defeat of the Amazons was alleged to have played in the foundation of Athens (duBois 1982, 67–70; Tyrell 1984, 113–28). She is, however, interested in the Sabine women and the part they played in the foundation of Rome. She introduces their story in the second part of *The Book of the City of Ladies*, where she is dealing with the benefits brought by women to the world, and she uses it as one of a number of stories which illustrate the spiritual good women have done (pp. 142–50). Like the Virgin Mary, Judith and Esther, the Sabine women bring a spiritual benefit and save their people from destruction. The rape of the Sabines is a story which fits in well with the Hobbesian explanation of the subjection of women. The Sabine women are captured by the trickery and force of the Roman men. Their status as wives is the same as their status as captives. But de Pisan emphasizes those aspects of Plutarch's story which attribute the institution of the law and peace to the intervention of the women (see Bryson 1986). The Sabine men attempt to avenge themselves on the Romans and to win back their women, but the women, carrying their children, throw themselves between the battle lines in order to bring about peace. They want neither the victory of their fathers and brothers, for whom their children would be enemies, nor the victory of their husbands, who will kill their fathers and brothers. Instead, they sue for peace and the recognition of the rule of law. Whereas Hobbes makes the subjection of women an act of self-interest in the face of superior force, for de Pisan it is rather a conscious ethical choice made for the greater good. In subjecting themselves the women act in a way which has both material and spiritual value.

There are many passages in de Pisan's writing which warn against the danger in doing evil, but she does not attempt to show, as Hobbes does, that unrestrained self-interest is irrational in virtue of its bad effects in this world. She relies on two different arguments to persuade the powerful to be ethical, one which stresses that true happiness depends on honour, and a second which evokes the possibility of punishment in the world hereafter. Her reliance on this second argument may seem to be a weakness in her work, as compared with Hobbes'. But, in fact, this apparent weakness could be taken to indicate an awareness on de Pisan's behalf that the claim that political immorality is against one's rational self-interest is simply implausible, if one considers only the consequences in this life. As the situation of women attests, and so long as what is meant by reason is merely self-interested reason, the very powerful may well never have reason to worry about the rights of the powerless. Unless one accepts that virtue and honour are intrinsic goods, morality and rational self-interest cannot be guaranteed to coincide.

For our purposes, it is in the first argument that the more interesting aspects of de Pisan's thought reside. She recognizes that society, in the end, depends on the promotion, in its powerful members, of ethical motivation, or love of honour, and she attempts to show the powerful how such love of honour is integral for securing happiness. Her arguments, grounded in her own experience, start out from a profound sense of our dependence for happiness on the good-will of others. Virtue, in her scheme of things, makes that dependence more secure, and, in the last instance, it can be an inalienable source of solace, in the face of the kinds of change of fortune that it is beyond our power to prevent (Pisan 1974, 8–11, and Hindman 1986, 123–28). Virtue makes one's situation more secure, partly through giving others no reason to hate oneself, and partly because we are creatures who learn by imitation. By practicing virtue we teach it to others, particularly to our children and subordinates, on whose virtue we ultimately depend. By contrast, Hobbes begins with a state of nature in which it appears that we are all independent agents. Morality is introduced as a restriction on our natural liberty, which we accept only because we are forced to by a recognition of the strength of others. For de Pisan, we have natural inclinations in childhood which, if properly fostered, will lead us to virtue, and by discovering that virtue is an end in itself, we achieve not just the good of others but our own true good.

Behind Christine de Pisan's philosophy it is plausible to find a thought of the following kind. It is in the interests of those who are relatively powerless to foster in others a sense of their duty towards the powerless, for, being unable to force others to recognize their rights, they are constrained to rely on reason and persuasion, on stimulating the sympathy or gratitude of others, or on teaching by example, in order to achieve their aims. Since we are all really quite powerless, no matter how our good fortune might mask this fact at any time, we should all adopt this path. The good prince should recognize that he is 'as frail as another man and no different from others except for good fortune' (*CP* p. 16). The political philosophy which results from this thought has a great weakness and a great strength. Its weakness is that the methods it suggests can be pursued for a long time without making those who are powerful and immoral change their ways. Its strength is that there is no conflict between the means advocated to achieve the ultimate end of a good society, and the end aspired to. The end is a society in which those with power recognize and fulfil their duty to exercise their power in defense of the well-being and liberty of all (with the exception of those who threaten the liberties of others); the means is simply to live, as far as possible, according to the principles that would be adopted were all to aspire to this end.

De Pisan's writing emphasizes love, dependence and the duties of those in positions of power to care for the less powerful. The kind of ethical impulse which is motivated by love of the good cannot be reduced to rational self-interest, although it is in general in accord with prudence. But it would be a mistake to think that, having showed that Hobbes' attempt to reduce morality to rational self-interest fails, we should simply jettison social contract theory and replace it with the imperative to fulfil one's personal duties to care for others. For there are significant limitations to de Pisan's philosophy which should give pause to recent feminist advocacy of a simple turn from justice to care. Socialists and feminists have pointed out the illusoriness of the image of man, the independent, autonomous individual which is evident in Hobbes' works (e.g., Jaggar 1983, 39–46). At the same time, much feminist thought, in particular that of Wollstonecraft and de Beauvoir, owes much of its inspiration to this conception of humanity, and for this reason it has recently come under critical scrutiny. Many feminists now assert that women value connectedness, care and dependence. Yet Christine de Pisan reasons from our dependence on others to the wisdom of the acceptance of subjection in marriage, and this cannot be embraced by any who consider themselves genuine feminists. Not all relations between citizens should be modelled on the natural inequality of power and responsibility that exists between mothers and children. In the remainder of this paper I suggest that the resolution of this conflict is to combine the principles of justice that can be derived from hypothetical versions of social contract theory with a moral psychology of the kind implicit in de Pisan.

A Maternalist Contractualism

The moral psychology articulated by de Pisan involves an originally Platonic way of thinking of the moral individual, in which it is assumed that the soul is divided into three parts. She follows a Christianized version of this tradition in her assumption that love of the good, and the pursuit of virtue, are the true ends of man, and the means to a happiness which is not subject to changes of fortune. Love is here associated with the force that motivates us to do good. It can be love of the good, and the desire to do others good, as well as love of the beloved for what is good in them. The picture assumes that humans tend to have a natural desire to do good, which nevertheless needs to be stimulated and fostered, and which makes us by nature moral beings. Within Hobbes' psychology, the suggestion that there is a natural moral motivation is vigorously rejected. It is claimed that our primary motivation is towards self-preservation, liberty and power. Morality is thought of as a system of rules, which reason dictates it is in our interests to adopt. But morality is not an end in itself. It thus becomes extremely difficult to demonstrate why those who have freedom and power should bother about morality, in the many situations in which their immorality cannot rationally be seen to threaten their self-interest. It is ultimately to this feature of Hobbes' moral psychology that feminists are objecting when they reject his rational egoism. But the alternative view, held by Christine de Pisan, that virtue is an end in itself, can be seen to be deeply problematic when it is pursued by individuals who themselves exist in a situation of oppression.

Modern liberal thought has been deeply influenced by Rousseau's consignment of the reproduction of the citizen to the private realm of the family, governed by a feminine love and sentiment quite different from the rational justice of the public realm. Neither Hobbes nor de Pisan operated with a clear distinction between the private and the public realm. Much of de Pisan's advice to women is directed towards princesses, and she assumes that sexual morality is just as important to matters of state as are the virtues of justice, and the art of making peace. Her emphasis on the good that women have wrought casts a new light on Hobbes' explanation of women's submission. If Hobbes is right, and citizenship involves acquiescence to the rule of the sovereign, and the first sovereigns are heads of families, then a woman's acquiescence to her husband can be taken to be a paradigm of citizenship. De Pisan remained unperturbed by women's subjection to their husbands just because she saw it in this light. Her defence of women can be read as a moral defence which highlights the moral excellence of women, in their devotion to duty and subjection to the moral law. Her orientation gives her political philosophy a moralistic cast, noted by a number of commentators. In a sense, this makes her development of the parentalist metaphor in political life more consistent than Hobbes'. One of the weakest aspects of Hobbes' thought is his attempt to transform child-parent relations into relations of consent. De Pisan, by contrast, takes for granted that the relation of parent to child is the paradigm of an ethical relation, and the situation in which the duties of the powerful to the powerless and the consequent rewards of virtue are clearest. She sees quite clearly that children learn by example and that the best means to encouraging a child to develop a good character is for it to love someone of good character. She extends this idea to the political realm. Thus at the centre of her political philosophy are ethics, moral education and the development of the love of God in those in positions of power. She sees these as bound up with relationships between members of the society which foster ethical behaviour, trust, truthfulness and love. Her advice seems to have been naturally adopted by many generations of women, who have seen devotion to the duties of wife and mother, and care for the physical and moral well-being of others, as more immediately important than the overthrow of structural injustice.

What de Pisan's political philosophy lacks, however, is a criterion of justice which can be used to clarify the difference between those situations in which such devotion to personal duty counts as consent under duress to servitude, and those in which it counts as the voluntary pursuit of virtue. Hypothetical versions of social contract theory, such as Rawls', can fill this gap. Because the focus of political philosophy has shifted since the time of de Pisan and Hobbes, from reasons for political subjection to the defence of individual sovereignty, the question which was uppermost in de Pisan's mind, 'How to instil in the individual political and moral virtue?', has dropped from sight. With Locke's introduction of the distinction between political and parental power, and Rousseau's alignment of the private ethical realm with women and of the public realm of justice with men, this question has been relegated to the sphere of the personal and sentimental. What the situation of women shows is that Hobbes was wrong: morality cannot be identified with rational self-interest, because history and nature have left a legacy of great actual differences in power. In the wake of the failure of attempts to overcome the limitations of liberalism, by abolishing all actual inequalities, it is worth turning back to the question which was central in de Pisan's political philosophy. How does one promote in citizens, no matter how great a portion of power fate has dealt them, virtue, love of honour and subjection to the moral law?

As we have seen, one cannot turn back to this question without holding on to demands for justice. But retaining liberal methods for determining which situations are unjust does not imply an acceptance of Hobbes' moral psychology. Actual liberal societies have largely relied on the subjection of women within the family for the reproduction of morally motivated citizens. But as women overthrow that subjection, the question of the subjection of the individual to the moral law becomes more urgent. Without an understanding of the production of the individual who loves honour and justice, social contract theory is incomplete. But without social contract theory, we have little understanding of how we might settle questions of justice. A feminist contractualism should, therefore, place the reproduction of the moral individual at centre stage and could thus plausibly be deemed maternalist.

NOTE

1. Dates are 1364–1431 for de Pisan and 1588–1679 for Hobbes.

REFERENCES

du Bois, Paige. 1982. *Centaurs and amazons*. Ann Arbor: University of Michigan Press.

Brennan, Teresa, and Carole Pateman. 1979. "Mere auxiliaries to the commonwealth": Women and the origins of Liberalism. *Political Studies* 27: 183–200.

Bryson, Norman. 1986. Two narratives of rape in the visual arts. In *Rape*, ed. S. Tomasselli and R. Porter. Oxford: Blackwell.

Chapman, Richard Allen. 1975. *Leviathan* writ small: Thomas Hobbes on the family. *American Political Science Review* 69: 76–90.

Coady, C.A.J. 1990. Hobbes and "The Beautiful Axiom." *Philosophy* 65: 5–17.

Delany, Sheila. 1987. "Mothers to think back through": Who are they? The ambiguous example of Christine de Pisan. In *Medieval texts and modern readers*, ed. L. Finke and M. Schichtman. Ithaca: Cornell University Press.

Flax, Jane. 1983. Political philosophy and the patriarchal unconscious: A psychoanalytic perspective on epistemology and metaphysics. In *Discovering Reality*, ed. Sandra Harding and Merrill Hintikka. Dordrecht: Reidel.

Gilligan, Carol. 1980. In a different voice: Women's conception of self and morality. In *The future of difference*, ed. Hester Eisenstein and Alice Jardine. Boston: G.K. Hall.

———. 1983. *In a different voice: Psychological theory and women's develop-ment*. Cambridge: Harvard University Press.

Greenleaf, W.H. 1972. Hobbes: The problem of interpretation. In *Hobbes and Rousseau*, ed. M. Cranston and R.S. Peters. New York: Anchor Books.

Held, Virginia. 1987. Non-contractual society: A feminist view. *Canadian Journal of Philosophy*, Supplementary volume 13: 111–37.

Hindman, Sandra L. 1986. *Christine de Pisan's "Epistre Othea"*. Toronto: Pontifical Institute of Medieaval Studies.

Hinton, R.W.K. 1967. Husbands, fathers and conquerors. *Political Studies* 15:291–300.

Hobbes, Thomas. [1651] 1966. *The English works of Thomas Hobbes*, ed. Sir William Molesworth. Aalen: Scientia Verlag.

———. [1641] 1979. *Leviathan*. London: J.M. Dent.

Jaggar, Alison M. 1983. *Feminist politics and human nature*. Totowa, NJ: Rowman & Allanheld.

Laigle, Mathilde. 1912. *Le libre de trois virtus de Christine de Pisan et son milieu historique et littéraire*. Paris: Librairie Spécial pour l'Histoire de France.

Lerner, Gerda. 1986. *The Creation of Patriarchy*. Oxford: Oxford University Press.

Machiavelli, Niccolo. [1514] 1975. *The Prince*. Trans. G. Bull. Harmondsworth: Penguin.

Pateman, Carole. 1988. *The sexual contract*. Standford, CA: Stanford University Press.

———. 1989. *The disorder of women*. Stanford, CA: Stanford University Press.

———. 1991. "God hath ordained to man a helper": Hobbes, patriarchy and con-jugal right. In *Feminist interpretations of political theory*, ed. Mary Shanley and Carole Pateman. University Park, PA: Pennsylvania State University Press.

de Pisan, Christine. [1404] 1836. *Le livre du fais et bonnes meurs du sage Roy Charles*. In *Nouvelle collection des mémoires pour servir à l'histoire de France*, vols. 1–2, ed. Michaud and Poujoulat. Paris: Edouard Proux.

———. [1407] 1967. *Le livre du corps de policie*, ed. R. Lucas. Geneva: Librarie Droz.

———. [1402] 1974. *Le livre du chemin de long estude*. Geneva: Slatkine Reprints.

———. [1407] 1977. *The Middle English translation of Christine de Pisan's libre de corps de policie*, ed. D. Bernstein. Probably trans. Stephen Scrope. Heidelberg: Carl Winter.

———. [1405] 1983. *The book of the city of ladies*. Trans. E.J. Richards. London: Picador.

———. [1405] 1984. An epistle to the Queen of France. In *The epistle of the prison of human life*. Trans. J. Wisman. London and New York: Garland Library of Medieval Literature.

———. [1405] 1985. *The treasure of the city of ladies*. Trans. S. Lawson. Harmondsworth: Penguin.

Quilligan, Maureen. 1991. *The allegory of female authority: Christine de Pizan's Cité des dames*. Ithaca: Cornell University Press.

Rawls, John. 1971. *A theory of justice*. Cambridge: Harvard University Press.

Ruddick, Sara. 1980. Maternal thinking. *Feminist Studies* 6(2): 342–67.

———. 1984. Preservative love and military destruction. In *Mothering: Essays in feminist theory*. Totowa, NJ: Rowman & Allanheld.

Tyrell, W. B. 1984. *Amazons: A study of Athenian myth-making*. Baltimore: Johns Hopkins University Press.

POLITY AND PRUDENCE
THE ETHICS OF ELISABETH, PRINCESS PALATINE

ANDREA NYE

In accounts of Descartes's philosophy, Elisabeth[1] appears, if at all, as muse, admirer, student, intelligent but respectful critic of aspects of the great philosopher's work, but not as an original thinker. In her letters, however, Elisabeth made it clear that she thought quite differently from Descartes on a number of topics. The question she is known for—how can an immaterial soul move a material body?—was only the beginning of a long reflective collaborative commentary on the passions, the good life, the nature of philosophical inquiry, methods of reading philosophy, and the connections between epistemology and ethics.

How possible or desirable is emotionless objective science? What is the connection between science and practical life? What is the role of emotion in the making of good judgments? Can the best thing to do be determined by science? How is it possible for soul to have the substance that makes thought effective or body the intelligence that allows actions to be guided by thought? These questions raised by Elisabeth, as they addressed metaphysical dualism at its most vulnerable point, mingled questions of body and mind in a way which was neither rationalist nor materialist. Yes, in certain circumstances, one can become a thinker detached from one's body; yes, one can view one's own and other's bodies as mechanical appendages; yes, one can excise from science meaningless moral essences and refuse to allow fact to be sullied with emotion, but what is the result for ethics and one's private and communal sense of how to live the good life? For Elisabeth, not sheltered in laboratory or University but involved in a chaotic social life of household, family, community, and country, the latter question took priority. Descartes's ethics of prudence, the logical complement to rationalist epistemology, was inadequate to answer it. Furthermore, urged Elisabeth, this is an inadequacy which signals fatal flaws in the epistemology and metaphysics of the *Meditations*. As Elisabeth put it in one of her early letters:

> [Your] letter made me see clearly the three primary ideas we have, their objects and how we must use them. I see also that the senses show me that the soul moves the body, but not really (any more than the Understanding or the Imagination does) the way in which it does. For that, I think, there are properties of the soul, unknown to us, which could, perhaps, overturn what your *Meditations* persuaded me of with such good arguments: the nonextension of the soul. This doubt can be founded on the rule which you yourself laid down there in speaking of the true and the false: all errors come from forming judgements on things which we do not see clearly enough. (L: 7/1 1643)

In her letters, Elisabeth often complained of affairs of state and court which distracted her from pursuing philosophy as rigorously as its difficulty demanded. On several occasions, she alluded to her sex: to the restrictions on the movements of women of her class, their lack of opportunity for exercise and rejuvenating manual work such as gardening, their constricting dress, all of which caused physical maladies which interfered with intellectual work. Descartes, himself, tried to distract Elisabeth from "metaphysical" questions, perhaps influenced by the prevailing view that philosophy was too taxing for frail women. He hesitated at one point to send her a math problem, afraid that it might be too difficult for her.[2] But the differences between them cannot be understood simply as opposition between dominant masculinity and oppressed femininity; these are philosophical differences.

Descartes answers Elisabeth's first written inquiries in an admiring, respectful tone very different from the dismissive irritation with which he answered many of his academic critics. Acknowledging that we cannot understand how the immaterial soul can move the corporeal body either by intellect or by imagination, he gave her an analogy that he hoped would put her questioning to rest:

> . . . when we think of a body moving another body, we tend falsely to imagine qualities of body, like heaviness, as separate substances which do the moving. And we understand such fictitious qualities with both soul ideas and body ideas. The soul then can be understood to move the body in the same way a fictitious "heaviness" might move a body. (L: 5/21, 1643)

Elisabeth, after her usual disarming compliments, quickly disposed of this suggestion:

[You] will excuse my stupidity, I hope, to not have been able to understand the idea by which we must understand how the soul (not extended
and immaterial) can move the body, by an idea we have in another
regard of heaviness, nor why a power—which we have falsely attributed
to things under the name of quality—of carrying a body toward the
center of the earth must persuade us that a body could be pushed by
something immaterial, especially when the demonstration of a contrary
truth (which you promised in your Physics) confirms us in thinking it
impossible. This idea [of a separate quality of heaviness]—given, that is,
that we are not able to pretend to the perfection and objective reality of
God—could be invented out of ignorance of that which truly propels
bodies towards the center of the earth: because no material cause represents itself to the senses, one attributes heaviness to matter's contrary,
the immaterial, which, nevertheless, I would never be able to conceive
but as a negation of matter and which could have no communication
with matter. (L: 6/20, 1643)

Descartes answered with somewhat less confidence and with a frankness
he did not often allow himself with his other critics. Here was the difficulty:
he did not want to ask her to put ordinary common sense understanding of
the union of soul and body away, so he used an analogy. And he didn't
worry that the analogy was false because he thought she had already accepted his proofs for the separation of mind and body. This was only a way
for her to be able to think about their union and not a proof. Anyway, if you
attribute materiality to the soul, this only leads to another contradiction
because matter is at a certain place and excludes other bodies and soul
does not. In any case, the best method is to establish truths of metaphysics
like the separation of mind and body and then leave them alone. Assume
that they are true and get on with science based on understanding as opposed to opinions based on imagination and sense (L: 6/6, 1643).

But Elisabeth did not see metaphysics or philosophy in the same light.
For Descartes, metaphysics is foundational, the establishment of truths
supporting scientific inquiry and establishing science's consistency with
religious belief. Foundations once laid, a philosopher's job is defense: refutation of counter arguments and the handling of inconsistencies. Foundations laid and commitments made, fictitious examples can be used to
smooth over difficulties. For Elisabeth, philosophy is neither foundational
nor defensive. The problem of the influence of mind on body, and of body
on mind, is related to the nature of morality and the role of the emotions
in judgement. For her, philosophy is not a matter of justification of preex-
isting practices, but an existential inquiry bearing on the terms of practical human life.

Interaction between thought and bodily existence is the personal and
political problem which occupies Elisabeth throughout her correspondence with Descartes.

I confess that it is easier for me to concede the matter and the extension of the soul than concede that a being that is immaterial has the capacity to move a body and to be moved by it. For if the former is done by giving information, it is necessary that the spirits which make the movement be intelligent, which you do not accord to anything corporal. And although in your *Meditations*, you show the possibility of the soul being moved by the body, it is nevertheless very difficult to comprehend how a soul, as you have described it, after having had the faculty and habit of good reasoning, would lose all that by some sort of vapors, or that being able to subsist without the body and having nothing in common with it, it would allow itself to be so ruled by the body. (L: 10/20, 1643)

A fact of most human lives, and certainly a fact of Elisabeth's life as she lived through recurrent family tragedies and the tortured politics of the Thirty Year War and its aftermath, is an intermingling and mutual influence of mind and body made contradictory by Descartes's philosophy. If, in Elisabeth's political and familial experience, felt emotions, vital interests, incapacitating griefs constantly trouble the most rational of judgements, at the same time the intelligence of animal spirits sometimes helps toward right judgement. The union of mind and body, which Descartes delegated to a philosophically irrelevant and "vulgar" common sense, is for Elisabeth a primary factor in active knowledge and judgement. The motivation of her questioning, therefore, is not the need to establish unassailable and religiously acceptable foundations for rationalist science, but a prior need to know how to live in the world, an understanding which might determine the terms of rationalist science but which cannot be supplied by it. On this view, philosophical epistemology, important as it is, is not impenetrable bedrock, but answers to a deeper strata of thought involved with medical hygiene, political judgement, and personal ethics.

Doctor Philosopher

Elisabeth's health was never robust. She suffered from recurrent fevers, digestive upsets, skin problems, and, at times, incapacitating depression at her family's follies and bad fortune.[3] From the beginning there was disagreement between her and her friend Descartes as to the cause. Although she was willing to attribute a role to psychological factors, she was also insistent that physical ills and physical circumstance can disrupt mental functioning. Descartes, on the other hand, pressed on her a rational philosophical therapy for illness that asserted the mind's dominance over the body. A "noble soul," Descartes tells her, speaking out of the mainstream of philosophy since Plato, is not ruled by passion but by reason. In order to restore health and happiness, she should detach herself from both her body and her emotions, she should view painful events as if they take place in a play in a theater, she should take pleasure in her power to control even the most painful of emotions, and she should compare herself to those less fortunate than herself. If all else fails she should rest and divert her mind.

Firmly, Elisabeth responds that she is accepting a medical cure, giving as reason her conviction that a large part of her troubles have physical causes.

> Know then that I have a body imbued with a great part of the weakness of my sex, know that it registers very easily afflictions of the soul and does not have the strength to be quit of them, being of a temperament subject to obstructions and remaining in a climate which contributes to illness. For persons who cannot do much exercise like myself, a long oppression of the heart from sadness is not needed to disrupt the spleen and infect the rest of the body with vapors. I think that the slow fever and dry cough which is still there even with the heat of the season and the walks which I take to rally my forces, comes from that. (L: 5/24, 1645)

Here as elsewhere, Elisabeth is quite gentle with what she obviously takes as the philosopher's failure to understand a woman's life, or any life of civic and familial responsibility. Her problem, she explains patiently, is not that she pays too much attention to worldly fortune and misfortune, it is the physical circumstances of her life, and more important, the fact that when those to whom she is attached suffer, she can in no way see their suffering as other than evil or keep from being moved by it (L: 5/24, 1645).

Descartes persists: she should experience events only with her mind and not with imagination or senses, when events are over she should immediately forget them and think of something else, she should always look at things with a "bias" that makes them seem as favorable to herself as possible, she should try not to want anything not in her power to accomplish. Elisabeth's responses to these philosophical prescriptions, however sweetened with protestations of gratitude for Descartes's friendship, were firm. He makes her feel better even when he cannot instruct her, she reassures him, but she cannot follow his advice without failing in her duty. A bias against herself rather than in her favor is necessary in court with its constant flattery and hypocrisy. It is not possible to practice detachment given that events in time are always surprising. There is no way to rationally ready oneself or detach oneself completely from the sadness that events cause. If she was either all sense or all reason, as he suggests, yes, but in fact, she is human, which means that she is part rational and part sensate which is what makes her situation so difficult.

At this point of impasse, Descartes suggests the remedial reading of Seneca on "The Happy Life." But even as Elisabeth obediently takes up her assignment, the divergence between them continues. Descartes immediately regrets his choice. Seneca is not analytic enough, he complains, he does not follow the proper method, he does not define and deduct. He himself, Descartes laments, could have done so much better in defining the highest good and the best life. It is so simple: rationally you figure out what is best, you resolutely do it; you don't desire what is not in your power. If you follow these steps you never have reason for repentance or regret. Even when results are bad it is not your fault and so you do not suffer. You are not unfeeling, but you restrict yourself to good desires, those subject to reason. This much clear, he proceeded with a lengthy analysis of the weaknesses of not only Seneca but of all of classical ethics.

Although she agreed with many of Descartes's critical points, Elisabeth read Seneca differently. First, unlike Descartes she took pleasure in the reading of Seneca's "bon mots," his seductive language. Her giving of herself to his prose prompted a different interpretation of classical ethics. What Descartes may have missed, she points out with her usual tact, is Seneca's aim, which is not logical consistency but the winning of adherents. For this purpose, making one's views attractive to others is more effective than logical deduction. What Descartes did not appreciate was the specific rhetorical force, the purpose and interest, the expression in classical ethics of radically different ways of seeing things. As she puts it:

> I attributed the obscurity, which is found in [Seneca] as in most of the ancients, to the way he explains himself which is very different from our own. The same things which are problematic with us can pass for hypotheses with them, and the lack of logical connection and order Seneca observes is with the aim of acquiring admirers by surprising the imagination, rather than of acquiring disciples by informing the judgement. (L: 8/16, 1645)

Elisabeth's reading allows for critique that is not mere surface logical critique.

> When Epicurus tells a lie at his death bed, assuring his friends he is well instead of crying out like an ordinary man, he is living the life of a philosopher not of a Prince, Captain or courtier. He knows that nothing outside prevents him from following his rules and acting like a philosopher.
>
> But with the Prince or Captain, repentance is inevitable, and one is not able to defend oneself with the knowledge that failure is as natural for a man as being physically ill. For one does not know that one can be exempted from each particular fault. (L: 8/16, 1645)

Epicurean ethics, like Descartes's ethics, is addressed to a small special-ized group detached from active life. In contrast to a life of leisured reflec-tion, an active life results in repentance regardless of platitudes about human fallibility; there, what matters is not abstract acknowledgement of error in general but after-the-fact realization of faults which could have been remedied. Regret, Elisabeth suggests, even if scholars are exempt, is inevitable in a life of responsibility to others.

A year later, after a new round of painful events results in her banish-ment from her Mother's court in The Hague, Elisabeth makes a suggestion for remedial reading: Machiavelli's *The Prince*. Descartes, devoted to his royal friend and concerned for her, agrees, but again is critical. Also again, Elisabeth questions his understanding. Against Descartes's rather naive protests that Machiavelli's Prince is tyrannical and unjust, once more Elisabeth proposes attention to motives. It is not that Machiavelli is prais-ing usurpers, she tells Descartes, it is that he chooses the hardest case to show most clearly how power can be kept.

> It also seems to me that to teach the governing of the state, he takes the state most difficult to govern—where the prince is a usurper, at least in the opinion of his people. In this case, any opinion he might have himself as to the justice of his cause may serve to put to rest his own conscience but not his affairs, when the laws restrict his authority, or the powerful undermine it, or the people speak against it. And when the state is so dis-posed, great violence is less evil than little violence since the latter of-fends as much and gives pretext for a long war. The former takes away from the powerful courage and any means which they can undertake. Similarly, when violent acts come quickly and all at once, they cause anger less than surprise, and are more bearable for the people than the long train of misery that civil wars bring. (L:10/10, 1646)

Elisabeth's intelligent empathy leads to a different kind of critique. Machi-avelli presents a paradox—to be good, the Prince must be bad. Isn't he only doing what so many philosophers have done? "I think it is from plea-sure that [philosophers] take to saying paradoxes that they can later ex-plain to their students" (10/10, 1646).

The Nature of Passion

Neither the reading of Seneca nor Machiavelli solved the philosophical problems that Elisabeth posed. It is she who put her finger on the real key to the difficulty. Descartes says that passions can be controlled by the mind and that rational thought can be detached from emotion; Elisabeth doubts whether this is possible or desirable. But, how can the question be decided without knowing what passion is? And how can the philosophical question of the relation between mind and body be solved if emotions are not understood. The omission of a treatment of emotion, Elisabeth suggests, constitutes a defect in Cartesian epistemology and one that Descartes needs to remedy.

> I would like to see you define the passions, in order to know them better, because those who call them disturbances of the soul would persuade me that their force only consists in shattering and subjecting the reason if my reason didn't also show me that there are some that lead to rational actions. But I am assured that you will shed more light on this, when you explain how the force of passion renders it any more useful when it is subject to reason. (L: 9/13, 1645)

Again Descartes replied confidently. This is easy, he says. She has already read his Treatise on animals and so understands how impressions registered on the brain cause agitations or physiological effects in the "spirits" of the body. Passions—sadness, joy, desire—are thoughts which come from a particular agitation of the animal spirits and which are felt in the soul itself (October 6, 1645). But again, confidence was short-lived. After a preliminary distinguishing of passions from sense impressions, dreams, moods, and bodily sensations, Descartes broke off.[4] It is eight days before he takes up his pen again. He was going to enumerate the passions, he confesses, but had trouble. Then he was distracted by another letter from her asking new questions and by new charges against his philosophy in the schools and so he has had to put the passions aside to answer new queries.

They were, however, a subject that Elisabeth was not going to let drop. The means to morality and the good life, as Descartes presents it, is rational distance from and control of the emotions. One is to observe events detached from any imagination of what might happen and any painful feelings. One calculates and deducts the best course of action; one acts. One's responsibility is over. One forgets and gets on with other things. In thinking of events, one represents them always with a positive bias, seeing them in the light most favorable. Descartes admitted that the mind could not directly control passions caused by bodily agitations; it could not will itself to feel love or not to feel fear, but it could neutralize and manipulate passion so as to keep passion from troubling rational thought. A person can refuse to act on emotion, she can divert her mind with pleasant images, she can cultivate interior emotions of self-satisfaction that override bodily passion.

The basis for this ethic of prudence, which Descartes went on with Elisabeth's urging to develop in detail in *The Passions of the Soul*, is metaphysical dualism: the view that bodily processes are mechanisms independent of the mind. In *The Passions*, he describes a living body as a dead body with mechanisms working: "We may judge that the body of a living man differs from that of a dead man just as does a watch or other automaton (i.e., a machine that moves of itself), when it is wound up" (P: Art. VI). Although the mind can move parts of the body and can receive neural messages from the body, it does so from a distance. Most bodily processes go on independently of the mind. The long first part of the treatise is taken up with a detailed description of the animal "spirits" or bodily mechanisms that cause passion: blood pumping, caloric heatups, tightening of muscles, vibration of nerves.

If it were not for the fact of human action and passion—of the direct influence of the mind on muscles and nerves and the direct influence of bodily sensation on the mind—the strange device of the pineal gland circuit between mind and body Descartes is forced to introduce in his treatise on the passions might not have been necessary.[5] The mind as receptacle of ideas might clearly and distinctly represent to itself bodily motions, understand that God has arranged all for the best, and leave it at that. The body might have gone on operating according to physical principles, monitored and corrected by rational will. However, as Elisabeth constantly pointed out, the soul is so "intimately" connected to the body that agitations of "animal spirits" from the body and rational desire and will, no matter how "noble," are constantly intermingling, making it impossible to detach emotion from judgement or reason from passion. The passions of the soul which animal spirits cause—variable, contradictory, and often painful—push the rational will here and there and can lead to a very unhappy state of mind. Reason, thinking itself independent, may only ratify natural dispositions and attitudes. This is why, if Descartes is right, and the key to the good life is rational control and training of the passions but not total unfeeling anaesthesia, it is necessary to understand passions and temperaments, to separate out good and bad in them, and to prescribe ways in which they should be handled.

In response to this questioning, Descartes developed in his treatise a "theory" of the passions. At all passion's root, he argued, is wonder or surprise, which becomes esteem or disdain depending on whether wonder is at a thing's bigness or smallness, or love or hate depending on a thing's harmfulness or pleasurableness. Six primitive passions branch off: wonder, love, hate, desire, joy, and sadness, which in turn have various permutations depending on the obtainability of, or current possessor of, harmful or pleasurable objects. If Descartes distinguished the branches of knowledge by the various judgements and ideas that come from them, he distinguishes passions physiologically, as bodily mechanisms which branch off from a primal reaction to a new event: digestion, heats and chills which accompany love, fear, joy.[6] Such complexes of movements, he says, registered on the soul via the pineal gland, are functional: they get the soul to consent to what is good for the body, they warn the soul that the body is in danger; they predispose the soul to will defensive or positive actions. Like other bodily mechanisms they require adjustment. Bodily passion is often exaggerated and painful to no useful purpose at all. In these cases, if one cannot directly control one's bodily reactions, one can divert one's mind, or in extreme cases practice therapeutic self-deception. "Even a false joy is often of more value than a sadness whose cause is true."

Preferable for the purpose of self-preservation, when possible, is rational judgement on "what is best" and action based on that judgement. Such rational judgement and action can result not in the perhaps uncontrollable bodily agitations, but a new kind of "sentiment" initiated in the soul itself congruent with what is rationally possible and obtainable. Here was an alternative to Stoic a-pathy. The way to achieve a good life is to ignore passionate bodily feeling and desire, to achieve distance from the passion, but to foster "interior emotions" that originate in the soul, the most important of which is "generosity;" Descartes's generosity, however, is not a giving to others; it is a generosity to oneself, an esteeming of oneself as highly as one can given the acknowledgement of undeniable faults. He illustrated the difference with an example. A husband's wife has died; outwardly the man grieves with all the physiological and mental effects of grief, but inside his soul he is generous. Judging that he is not responsible for his wife's death and that *rationally* he would be sorry to see her again, even as he outwardly grieves, "yet he feels a secret joy in the inmost parts of his heart, the emotion of which possesses so much power that the sadness and the tears which accompany it can do nothing to diminish its force" (P: CXLVII).

No matter what happens externally or to others, Descartes over and over claims this inner self-satisfaction and self-sufficiency, as "a species of joy which I consider to be the sweetest of all joys" and the most reliable source of happiness and goodness. In order to achieve an unshakable and pleasant notion of his own worth, all that a man need do is "live in such a way that his conscience cannot reproach him for ever having failed to perform those things which he has judged to be the best." Then he will have a "satisfaction which is so powerful in rendering him happy that the violent effects of the passions never have sufficient power to disturb the tranquility of his soul" (P: CXLVIII). He will know how to honor and respect people according to their rank (P: CLXII). He will have no remorse, and almost no cowardice or fear (P: CLXXV-CLXXVII). He will have none of the ordinary kind of pity which "feeble" people have, probably, Descartes speculates, because they represent the evil that happens to others as possibly happening to themselves. He will feel only a mild pleasurable pity from a distance, able to take satisfaction in the fact that he is virtuously acknowledging the suffering of others (P: CLXXXV-CLXXXVI).

Much as she paid her old friend the compliment of avowing his work to be her guide, Elisabeth never accepted this account of the passions. So repugnant is it to her that politeness and respect for Descartes did not prevent occasional irritation and even shock at his recommendations. Commenting on the final manuscript of *The Passions of the Soul*, after initial compliments on the completeness of his treatment and congratulations that he has "gone well beyond" what other philosophers have written on the subject, Elisabeth notes the inadequacy of a mechanistic account of passion. How is it possible to distinguish one passion from another—love from lust, repentance from anger—physiologically?

> I do not see how one can know the diverse movements of the blood, which cause the five primitive passions, since they are never alone. For example, love is always accompanied by desire and joy, or desire and sadness, and to the measure that it is strong, others think also . . . [defect in the manuscript here] . . . contraire. How is it then possible to tell the different beating of the pulse, the digestion of meats, and other changes of the body, which serve to reveal the nature of these movements? Also, as you note, none of these passions is the same in all temperaments: mine is such that sadness takes away the appetite, as long as it is not mixed with any hate and is such as comes only from the death of a friend.
>
> When you speak of the exterior signs of passion, you say that admiration, joined to joy, makes the lungs fill up with many jolts to cause laughing. To which I ask you to add in what way admiration (which, according to your description, seems to only operate on the brain) could open up so promptly the orifices of the heart to create this effect.
>
> The passion that you note as the cause of sighs does not seem to be what you say since dress and the fullness of the stomach can also cause sighs. (L: 4/25, 1646)

Different emotions—love, hate, fear—are not distinguishable in Descartes's mechanical man; his physiology may be in various states but these are not identifiably human feelings. Nor can the registering of bodily agitations on the brain account for different passions felt in the soul. All the soul would recognize is anonymous agitation in animal spirits. It could not on the basis of physiology distinguish generosity from vanity, or disapproval from mean-spiritedness, and if neither passion nor emotion is distinguishable, there is no way to tell the good emotions, the licit passions, from the bad passions. One is back with either unfeeling Stoic rationalism, fortified by a sense of self-sufficiency and superiority, or acceptance of all passion no matter how destructive.

The problem, of course, is that emotion and passion, unlike pain and other bodily sensations, seem to involve a judgement on events, a judgement which not only the mind but also the body seems to make. The body loves or fears; the body judges that an object is desirable or dangerous. Such an intelligent body cannot be accounted for physiologically. Alternately, passion, if seen as a mental phenomenon, has a substance and thickness, an intractability not consistent with mental operations as Descartes understands them, i.e., as assent and dissent to ideas and their disinterested manipulation. Emotion drags the body into thought, implicates feeling in the very process of judgement, weighs down ideas with bodily experience that blurs their clarity and distinctness. If bodily mechanisms might be simply ignored by independent thought, such a thinking feeling or feeling thinking cannot be.

Descartes's rational therapy might be effective for pain management, but for emotional upset it was ineffective. Here Descartes's financial stability and lack of emotional involvement with others, whether by choice or temperament, was a deficit. Elisabeth, alive to the social world around her, must constantly deal with reactions to actual changing events and adjust herself to new circumstances:

> But I find still less difficulty in understanding all that you say about the passions, than I do in practicing the remedies that you prescribe for their excess. For how can one foresee all the accidents that can take place in life, when they are impossible to count. And how can we prevent desiring with ardor things that tend necessarily to the conservation of man (like health, and the means to live) and that nevertheless do not really depend on free will. For knowledge of the truth, the desire is so just that it is naturally in all men; but an infinite knowledge would be needed to know the just value of goods and evils that customarily move us, since there are many more than a single person could imagine, and it would be necessary to know perfectly all the things that are in the world. (L: 4/25, 1646)

In her reflections on ethics, Elisabeth repeated many of the objections which prompted her original questioning of Descartes's immaterial soul. Temporal life, unlike the mental world of eternal innate ideas, involves surprise. It is often, if not usually, impossible to decide ahead of time what is the best course of action. Perfect prejudgment on the infinitely variable facts of material life is impossible, she argued. Judgements made in the press of human affairs are never final. Descartes's emotional hygiene might describe a certain kind of temperament, but is unpracticable for anyone in public life. Many of the good things of life, like health and the means to material subsistence, must, by the very terms of bodily material life, be desired, whether they are in one's power to achieve or not. Given the flow of temporal events, regret and sadness are inevitable unless one is exceptionally well-favored by fortune. We must act with and for others and, in that regard, our private rational judgement of what is best may not count for much, may actually be detrimental to an accurate estimate of what needs to be done.

What is needed, she tells Descartes, is not a morality for a sequestered life, but morality for real involved life in the world.

> Since you have already told me the principles of a life on one's own, I still would like to know your maxims in regard to a civil life, in which we are dependent on persons who are little rational. In such a life, up to now, I have always found that experience serves me more than reason in the things which concern it. (L: 4/25, 1646)

Elisabeth, as an involved family member and active politician, required a practical ethics, not an artificial rationality that does not engage with the complexity of human affairs. She needed a morality such as Machiavelli attempted to deliver in *The Prince*. There, she notes, the concern was not so much the state of one's own conscience or pious hopes for an after life, but actual states of human affairs which cause painful emotions of grief, guilt, fear, or repentance (L:10/10, 1646).[7] In such a worldly life, there is no possibility of perfect forethought; success depends on an attention to changing reality, which can rule one like a "governess." As Elisabeth put it, "Birth and misfortune force me to use my judgement promptly in order to lead a life itself sufficiently difficult and free of prosperity to prevent me from thinking of myself, just as if I were forced to trust in the rule of a governess" (L: 10/13, 1645).

Elisabeth chides Descartes for thinking that her unhappiness is due to an unhealthy dwelling on material misfortune and her own inadequacies. The difference between them is philosophical: the good life for Elisabeth is not an atemporal beatitude apart from human affairs, but a successful dealing with life in time where surprise and catastrophe constantly challenge judgement and arouse emotions of regret and anger.

> I am persuaded that the accidents that surprise people governing the public, who are without the time to find the most expedient means, carry them (no matter what virtue they have) into actions that afterwards cause the repentance you say is one of the principal obstacles to happiness. It is true that a habit of valuing goods according to how they contribute to contentment, and measuring that contentment according to the perfections that make pleasure remain, and judging without passion those perfections and pleasures, protects from many

faults. But to evaluate goods, it is necessary to be completely acquainted with them. To be acquainted with all those among which we must choose in an active life would require an infinite science. You say that one must be content when one's conscience witnesses that one has used all possible precautions. But this never happens, because one does not simply find one's story; one always revises things which remain to consider. (L: 10/13, 1645)

Events as lived and experienced cannot be understood in an eternal present of clear and distinct ideas in which what is best is marked out ready to be discovered. Instead, what has happened, its meaning and significance, its goodness and evil, is constantly reconstituted in reflection and memories of bodily experiences in the world.

Again and again Elisabeth comes back to this problem of surprise in moral life. A practical ethics never deals with the same situation twice; life in all its variety is seldom predictable. The perfect forethought and resolution that Descartes recommends as antidote to emotional upset is not at all possible when one has temporal responsibilities. There is no infinite knowledge of goods; events must be experienced and digested for the good and bad in them to be recognizable. Descartes urged Elisabeth to cultivate the contentment that comes from inner satisfaction that to the best of her knowledge she had done the best thing. For Elisabeth, what happened and what is best is not a fixed fact that one "finds." Instead it is a "story" constantly revised as one considers actions in retrospect. For Descartes, vulnerability to surprising events and regretful reflection is moral weakness. For Elisabeth it is at the center of moral life.

An Ethics of Polity

The problem that Elisabeth's inquiry into the passions was meant to address had been elided in Descartes's account of the passions. He had produced a theory of the passions, but he had not convinced Elisabeth that the theory was any more than a description of a particular emotional economy, one not desirable or possible in practical life. Most important, no guidance had been given as to how to solve the primary problem of morality as Elisabeth understood it: what is the right balance between one's own self-interests and the interests of others. As she put it in one of her earlier letters:

To measure contentment according to the perfection that causes it, it is necessary to see clearly the value of each thing, to see if those that only serve themselves or those that make us more useful to others are preferable. The latter appear to be valued more in an excess of spirit which torments itself for others, the former in an excess of spirit which only lives for itself. And nevertheless, each inclination can be supported with reasons strong enough to make them continue all our lives. It is the same with other perfections of the body and the spirit—an unspoken sentiment makes reason approve, which you ought not to call passion but rather approval by something innate. Tell me then, if you please, to what point we should follow such a sentiment (being a gift of nature), and how to correct it. (L: 10/13, 1645)

Again Elisabeth had undermined the stability of Descartes's rational soul. In the place of a sentimental bedrock of self-satisfaction that one has judged the best and acted on it as well as one can, she puts "temperament," an inner but perhaps correctable tendency to feel either for oneself or for others, a tendency for which reason could always find justifying arguments. How much should one follow such a tendency? How should or might one correct it?

But even as he worked on the passions, Descartes had a way to finesse this issue. Do what rationally appears to you as best and there is no need to regret, he said; for the rest we can trust in God that events are arranged for the best and at the very least, we can look forward to the afterlife.[8] Specifically on the problem of self and other, God's plan conveniently allows for adjustment of self interest and the interests of others, Descartes argued; he has arranged the social world so that we are not materially independent but must live in a family, community, state. We need others to survive, meaning that there is a prearranged coordination between self-interest and altruism in practice. Of course, one would not sacrifice oneself for some small gain for others, and if a man is worth more than his whole town, it might not do to destroy him to save it. Certainly, to survive successfully, a person must have discretion, knowledge of the world; he must understand which things will cost a possible benefactor little so as to know which favors to ask. But providentially, things are arranged so that what is of small cost to one person is worth much more to another, with the result that favors when asked by a man of prudence are easily granted (L: 9/15, 1645).

Behind Descartes's ethics is a man of the world, but in a different sense: here is someone who, with his emotions under control or perhaps no longer accessible, plays the system, knows the ropes, curries favor in the right places. Again Elisabeth expressed some frustration. God's plan for the world, she answered, might be reassuring in natural disasters, but it cannot reconcile one to evil which is the fault of the free will of others. If hopes for an after life were sure, one would commit suicide immediately. No, the real problem, she says, is to be able to make the proper kind of judgement between one's own interests and the good of others. How is it that you can objectively evaluate your own worth against others' worth? How can you weigh the value of civility, the price to be paid of boredom and irritation for going through the motions of politeness, for indulging the needs of others that seem less important than one's own? In a life involved with family and politics, Elisabeth was often distracted, not only with nursing sick brothers and sisters, counseling relatives on treaties, handling family quarrels, arranging marriages, but also with social occasions and frivolous demands on her time and energy.

> The consideration that we are a part of a whole, whose advantage we ought to seek, is really the force behind all generous actions, but I find much difficulty in the conditions that you prescribe. How measure the trouble which one gives oneself for the public against the good that would come of it, without it appearing more grand, in as much as its idea is more distinct. And what rule would we have for the comparison of things which are not really equally known to us, such as our own merit against that of those with whom we live? A natural arrogance would make us always tip the balance our own way; a natural modesty would esteem our own merit at less than its value. To profit from the particular truths of which you speak, it is necessary to know exactly all the passions and all the predispositions, the majority of which are insensible. Also, in observing the mores of the countries where we live, we sometimes find in them much that is irrational but nevertheless necessary to observe to avoid even greater inconvenience (L: 9/30, 1645).

Descartes, genuinely concerned but at a loss, continued doggedly to press what he took as the source of his own tranquility: the inner sense of satisfaction that is philosophical virtue as he sees it. Maybe she should stop studying, maybe her spirit is too fragile for philosophy. Even when events turn out badly she should not blame herself. She should think about what has happened positively, always with a bias in her own favor, perhaps even cultivate a "false" joy in fictional merits. After all, trouble and evil do not really exist. Rather surprisingly, he cited the teaching of his old enemies, the theologians. Evil is, unlike good, only privation, so no matter how bleak the situation, it is always possible to find some good that can give satisfaction.

Elisabeth's reaction to these suggestions betrays for once a sense of shock.

> After having given so many good reasons why it is better to know the truth to our disadvantage rather than to fool oneself agreeably, and showing that, nevertheless, given that all things admit different considerations equally true, you should stop at the one which gives you most contentment, I am astonished that you want me to compare myself to

those of my age in respect to what is unknown to me rather than what I cannot ignore even though that might be more to my advantage. There is nothing that could tell me if I would have profited more in cultivating my reason than others have with the things that they care about. (10/28, 1645)

The crux of the matter, as she saw it, was continually passed over in Descartes's moral advice. How are we to judge between self and other? The point is not to achieve at all costs the pleasant sense that one is superior, that one has done nothing wrong, or to bring about an economy of emotion that causes no pain. It is rather to do the right thing in complex circumstances. For that the biggest danger is not false modesty, but the down-playing of one's faults.

> In fleeing repentance for faults we have committed as an enemy to felicity, one runs the risk of losing the concern to correct them, especially when some passion has produced them, since we naturally like to be emotionally moved and to follow that movement. There is only inconvenience that comes from this flight which teaches us that recognition of faults could be harmful. (10/28, 1645)

In the place of Descartes's theory of the emotions, Elisabeth suggests another hygiene, not rational suppression of painful emotion which is impossible anyway, but rather a channeling of emotion in which pity and shame elicit the "concern" that prods remedial action. For Elisabeth, regret and repentance are not evils to be avoided but play a primary moral role in adjusting behavior and attitude. It is not mind that rules passion, a rule which can be self-deceptive as passion easily finds reasons to justify itself. Rather it is thought fused with passion that leads to emotional and moral growth. Elisabeth's "prudence" is not a balancing of self-interest and prudent concern for others dictated by an assumed order of the world; it is a human achievement. As she put it:

> in possessing (such a judgement), one would not fail to do justice to others as to oneself. If it is a fault that a brave spirit loses sometimes the means to serve his country in abandoning himself too easily to his own interest, it is also a fault if a timid spirit loses himself in his country, to the fault of risking his own good and fortune for its preservation. (10/28, 1645)

In this moral balancing, emotion plays a primary role, not only in weighing the advantage of self against other, but also in determining what is good for others. This, for Elisabeth, is not a question of balancing costs or keeping a foot in all camps or fostering a positive inner sense of self-worth, but a difficult and ongoing maintenance and balancing of interests to which emotion, in constant touch with bodily physical circumstances, contributes.

Rational satisfaction at the core of the soul can be no substitute, especially when it disturbingly mutates to a divine sign. Writing to her in Germany, relieved at the apparent easing of her unhappiness, Descartes, with some embarrassment, confesses that he sometimes feels there is a supernatural force to his interior emotion of joy. When he has it and gambles in the casinos he finds he almost always wins. Something like Socrates' genie seems to guide him to the right play (November, 1646). To this new surprising suggestion that self-satisfaction might miraculously bring about fortuitous events, Elisabeth responds dryly, no doubt chastened by this equation of the real tragedy of her situation to a gambling game. She herself hopes, she said, for no such divine voice or miraculous good fortune. Unfortunately, Socrates' genie would be no help in the misfortunes she and her family had suffered. Nor did it do much good for Socrates, she wryly observes. Descartes's good fortune when he feels good about himself is no doubt due to the fact that he plays on those occasions with more abandon. A better guide, she tells him, given that much of unhappiness depends on bodily existence—physical health, pleasant and wholesome environments—is "ordinary" emotion of grief, pity, anger.

> I also have observed that times when I follow my own inclinations, I have succeeded better than those in which I let myself be led by the advice of those wiser than me. But this I do not attribute so much to the felicity of any genie, as to the fact that having more affection for what touches me than anyone else does, I am better able to examine the ways which might harm or be advantageous than are those on whose judgement I might rely. (L: 11/29, 1646)

To illustrate the difference between their ethics, Descartes's several responses to the tragedies in Elisabeth's life are illustrative. The first caused a rift between them that went on for a number of months. Elisabeth's exiled family had inherited from Elisabeth's father, Frederick, leadership of the alliance of Protestant Princes who opposed the autocracy of Catholic rule in the Holy Roman Empire. When, in 1645, Elisabeth's brother was cajoled or seduced into the Catholic camp and persuaded to marry a Catholic Princess, Elisabeth was devastated. Not only did the marriage call down ridicule on her family, it also cheapened and degraded the Protestant conviction and struggle for reform. Descartes, feeling a slight to his Catholic religious affiliation, delayed for months in responding to the letter in which she expressed to him her grief and frustration. When he did respond, it was only after an anxious inquiry on her part and he did so coldly. He would have thought she would have understood, he said, the virtue of making friends in all camps. In response to her anguish that her brother had changed religions the way he might change a hat, Descartes told her that it is possible to be brought to the true faith by chance events. In any case, she should forget the incident and get on to other things. If the deeply religious and committed Elisabeth made any response to these assurances, it is lost.

The next major tragedy in Elisabeth's life was so explosive that there could be little mention of it in their letters. Unlike the scholarly Princess Elisabeth, her mother, Queen Elizabeth of Bohemia, and her sister, Princess Louise, had a reputation for frivolity, intrigue, and flirtation. At one point, their indiscretions threatened to erupt into open scandal when both had liaisons with a loose-mouthed courtier who boasted of their favors. Furious at the scandal and forced to defend his mother's and sister's reputation, Elisabeth's brother Phillip became involved in a street brawl in which he stabbed the lover to death and then fled from the police. Elisabeth, critical and disapproving of her mother's and sister's behavior, was, nonetheless, suspected of collusion and banished permanently from her mother's court to live with relatives in Germany. What Descartes said to her when he visited her twice at The Hague, as she was preparing for the journey that would keep them apart for the remaining years of his life, we cannot know. But his letters to her in Germany after this incident, urging prudence and forgetfulness, evoke a new sharpness in the tone of Elisabeth's replies. She is impatient with Descartes's insistence that she rest, do nothing but smell the flowers, forget painful events, and live for simple pleasure. There is no way to erase past events even when one is in pleasant circumstances, nor does being in Germany mean that she could or would detach herself from political responsibilities.

Descartes's reaction to the incident that permanently dashed the fortunes of Elisabeth's family was perhaps the most interesting. In 1649, Elisabeth's uncle, King Charles I, was beheaded in England. Hearing that Elisabeth had become gravely ill, Descartes again wrote to urge prudence on her. If he did not know that she was a philosopher like Socrates, he wrote, he would fear that she was upset by her Uncle's beheading. As it is, she is accustomed to changes in fortune, so she will not have been surprised or even troubled to learn of the death of one of her relatives. Even if such a death might seem more horrible than dying in one's bed, really it is more glorious, more out of the ordinary. With such a death one is mourned, praised, and regretted by everyone; one's good points are publicized. No doubt, in his last moments, her Uncle had more satisfaction from his good conscience than pain from indignation. As for pain, it wouldn't have been involved because beheading goes so fast (L: 2/22, 1649). Again, no answer is recorded from Elisabeth.

In these responses, it is possible to see what can be the practical import of a morality of prudence: therapeutic insensitivity to the suffering of others, blindness to the political consequences of intellectual or spiritual belief, forgetfulness of painful events which might have given cause for regret or repentance. These were consolations of philosophy that Elisabeth would never accept. Even in their last exchange of letters, the differences between them were apparent. Descartes, flattered by overtures from a new royal patron, Queen Christina of Sweden, went to the Swedish court, prudently continuing to tell Elisabeth of her precedence in his regard. It was best to have friends in all camps, and, even though the camp of a reigning Queen must have seemed more secure than that of an exiled Princess, Descartes continually assures Elisabeth that she has his favor and that he is her Ambassador to the Queen. Elisabeth, hopeful at first of an ally, and then resigned to the Queen's lack of serious interest in her or in philosophy, writes to Descartes in Sweden a few months before his death, one last time trying to correct his misapprehension. Referring to Descartes's constant apologies, Elisabeth wrote:

> Do not ever think that a description [of the Queen] so advantageous gives me reason for jealousy; rather it makes me value myself a little more than I did before, to have the idea of a person so accomplished, an idea which can only clear our sex of the imputation of imbecility and weakness pressed on it by Messieurs the pedants.

No doubt, Elisabeth had painful emotions as Descartes embarked on the trip to Sweden, the trip which would bring about his premature death: pain for herself that she might be losing one of the few friends who was her intellectual equal, pain for Descartes that he was deceiving himself as to Christina's seriousness and regard. She, however, seems to have achieved a moral equilibrium different from Descartes's prudence: a passionate welding together of personal interest and the well- being of others.

The Role of Philosophy

Neither Descartes nor Elisabeth was guilty of the superficiality that Elisabeth noted in some philosophical thought. Neither of them invented puzzles so they could impress students by solving them. Neither of them had as primary aim a circle of admiring followers. Both were serious and impassioned thinkers. Elisabeth expressed her admiration and respect for Descartes in each of her letters no matter how critical. Descartes answered her concerns without the impatience and contempt he often had for academic criticism. Still, inherent in and enlivening their correspondence were very different conceptions of philosophy. Descartes understood philosophy as it is often defined in the "mainstream" of Western thought. Philosophy is foundational; its purpose is to establish theoretical bedrock on which knowledge is founded. If it is not true to say that metaphysics comes after the fact for Descartes, certainly it comes in the midst of ongoing commitment to science which it grounds and justifies. Once the foundations for that science are laid they should not be disturbed. As he tells Elisabeth, one establishes metaphysics, in this case the independence of the soul and the existence of God, and then one gets on with research.

In contrast, for Elisabeth, philosophy is generated and regenerated in practical life, in conflicts and uncertainties in time and in relation to other people. Her changing philosophical questions reflect these existential origins. How can one balance the needs and desires of self and others? How can one act when changing circumstances make hindsight different from foresight and there is no perfect scientific knowledge of the infinite variety and complexity of human affairs? Which of the emotions should be censored or controlled?

But these differences make no exclusive opposition. If Elisabeth comes to metaphysics out of practical concerns, Descartes comes back to practical concerns from metaphysics. Metaphysics may be the roots and physics the trunk of knowledge for Descartes, but the "branches" of knowledge are mechanics, morals, and medicine. Without them science and the philosophy which establishes it is a dead letter. If, for Elisabeth, philosophy is the reflection that makes life in the world coherent and effective, for Descartes philosophy is the roots that allow the flowering of morals and medicine without which science is useless. It is at that intersection of different lines of thought that Elisabeth, devoted family member and stateswoman, and Descartes, isolated and often embittered scholar, meet, with affection, mutual concern, and intellectual respect.

The common ground on which they collaborated was the medicine and morals which for Descartes must be the flowering of philosophy and which for Elisabeth is the matrix of philosophy. With Elisabeth, Descartes is no removed cerebral rationalist disdainful of practical refutations of pure mathematical science. He expected and demanded of his philosophy and the science it supports that it provide cures for disease and means to health and growth. Unlike so many of the complaints from Descartes's academic critics, Elisabeth's initial and continuing objections to Descartes's philosophy were not an adversarial finding of superficial inconsistencies but were generated out of immediate painful experiences as she dealt with constant conflicts between self-interest and duty to others, with the pain of inevitable regret and repentance and seemingly natural inclinations to certain kinds of behavior. As such, Descartes always treated them with respect. Coming from different but converging concerns—Descartes that philosophy and science be useful, Elisabeth that chaotic and painful experience be intelligible—they engage in a thinking-together that would have been impossible for either of them alone. If they had never met, Descartes might never have worked on the passions, never have moved past an inadequate account of the mechanics of animal physiology to describe emotions specific to humans and their cognitive functioning. He might never have acknowledged the role the body plays in thought. Similarly Elisabeth never stopped expressing her indebtedness to the Cartesian philosophy which had allowed her an intellectual grasp of her situation and helped her to put order into her experiences and to understand the complex interactions between bodily life and mental life.

Separated by her exile to Germany and Descartes's death, their collaboration was interrupted and short-lived. Descartes moved past the careless "provisional morality" of the *Discourse* to the realization that emotions play a role in thought and in the good life that can not be willed away. He had not yet rethought the adequacy of the prescription to wait for the perfect knowledge of science and in the meantime imagine happy things, foster a bias in favor of self, and restrict one's action. He had not given up what Elisabeth saw as an untenable and dangerous faith that God had arranged all things for the best or a superstitious faith that a natural inclination could be taken as a divine sign. He had not given up the claim that thought could be detached from passion. Although after Descartes's death Elisabeth continued to prove an invaluable advisor to her brother, Charles Louis, the Palatine elector, and, later, became an able administrator as Abbess of the great Imperial Abbey at Herford (Westphalia), she did not produce a body of philosophical writing or an alternate theory of the emotions and their relation to science and ethics.

Somewhere, however, in the short collaboration between Descartes and Elisabeth might be the roots of a philosophy of the future. Not a positivist or materialist or functionalist philosophy, ratifying the rational control of minds over bodies and devising thoughtlessly direct controls on emotion that Descartes lacked: antidepressant drugs, shock treatment, cognitive therapies, and brain surgery. Not a professionalized mathematical logic artificially removed from the political and emotional concerns of everyday life. But a philosophy that is a collaboration between theorists and activists, one that works out an epistemology that might, as Descartes demanded, flower in morals and medicine, one that takes account of Elisabeth's concerns for emotional equilibrium, for balancing the needs of self and others, for redress of poverty and restrictive sex roles, and above all, for the power of human beings to change not only their "bias" but also themselves and the natural and social circumstances in which they live.

NOTES

1. Frequently referred to as Princess Elisabeth of Bohemia (1618–1680).

2. See his letter to Pollot, 10/21, 1643. When to his surprise he hears that Elisabeth has solved the problem, he is delighted. She has both the aptitude and the concentration necessary for mathematics. ". . . I was only afraid that patience, which is necessary to surmount, at first, difficulties in figuring, might be lacking. For it is a quality which is extremely rare in person of high birth and noble condition" (10/21, 1643).

3. In 1619, when Elisabeth was a small child, her father, Frederick, the Elector of Palatine, lost the family's Palatine territory by accepting and then losing the throne of neighboring Bohemia, resulting in the family's exile to Holland. When Elisabeth was 10, her eldest brother was drowned in a boating incident in which her father was involved. Her father died three years later of melancholy and despair. In The Hague, Elisabeth, the most level-headed and intelligent member of a large family, struggled to keep the family's reputation and fortunes afloat, by keeping her brothers out of trouble, arranging advantageous marriages for her sisters, all the while weathering the enmity of her frivolous and designing mother.

4. In a general sense, Descartes argued that any thought in the soul that is not caused by the soul's own will is a "passion." However, he distinguished the passions proper from 1) sense impressions, 2) interior body sensations like pain, thirst, hunger, 3) dreams and involuntary day dreams. All these are suffered by the soul but are not strictly speaking thought of as passions or emotions. He also distinguishes mood or temperament, where as a general course, bodily spirits are sad or gay and so result in generally sad or happy thoughts.

5. In Art. XXXI of the *Passions*, to bridge the gap between the immaterial mind and the material body, Descartes posits an interior node in the deepest part of the brain on which bodily impulses converge to be transferred to the soul—"the most inward of all [the brain's] parts, to wit, a certain very small gland which is situated in the middle of its substance."

6. For example: love is characterized by a strong pulse, heat in the chest, quick digestion; hate by uneven pulse, hot and cold in the chest, nausea; joy by strong pulse, heat throughout body, sluggish digestion; sadness by slow pulse, constriction in chest, chills, good digestion; desire by acute senses, heart agitated. Also Descartes distinguished external effects of these internal processes: skin color, eye movement, languor, tremors, tears, groans, sighs.

7. See letter of 10/10, 1646, quoted above. Elisabeth does not so much approve the morality of Machiavelli as she rejects Descartes's failure to understand the context of Machiavelli's reflections. Machiavelli is not laying down natural law, he is recommending an ethics for a particular difficult situation, the situation in which one has newly taken over a government, perhaps by force, and in which there is a real present danger of civil war and real necessity to reestablish order and peace. In such a situation, one may have to choose the lesser of evils. She, however, makes it clear that she would hate to be in that situation.

8. Calvinist fatalism is somewhat surprising in Descartes, but on this, the major question of the day—How is it possible to reconcile freedom of the will and moral responsibility with the omnipotence of God?—there were many permutations of both Catholic and Protestant opinion that not only divided Catholics from Protestants but also created divisions among Catholics and Protestants. Calvinist deviants like Arminius argued, against a strict view of predestination, that God could be moved by moral prayer and good works, while Catholic Jansenists argued the unredeemable evil of human will. Descartes, himself, tries some fancy logical footwork to get around the problem, arguing that a distinction can be made between the freedom we feel we have and the logical necessity that all things depend on the will of God (11/3, 1645). In another letter, he suggests an analogy strangely reminiscent of a tragic event in Elisabeth's life, her brother's killing of a man who was his mother's and sister's lover: a King has forbidden duels, but, knowing that two men are incensed with each other and will fight if they meet, nevertheless brings it about that they are in the same place at the same time. The men, says Descartes, still choose and can be punished for their crime (1/?, 1646).

REFERENCES

L: The letters of Descartes and Princess Elisabeth. *Oeuvres de Descartes*, Volumes III-IV, ed. C. Adams and P. Tannery. Paris: Librairie Philosophique, J. Vrin, 1972. (My translations.)

P: René Descartes. *The Passions of the Soul. The Philosophical Works*, Volume I, trans. E. S. Haldane and G. R. T. Ross. New York: Dover Publications, 1955.

Adam, Charles. *Descartes, ses Amities Féminines*. Paris: Boivin, 1937.

Foucher de Careil, A. *Descartes et la Princesse Palatine*. Paris: Auguste Durand, 1862.

Godfrey, Elizabeth. *A Sister of Prince Rupert: Elizabeth Princess Palatine and Abbess of Herford*. London: J. Lane, 1909.

Néel, Marguerite. *Descartes et la Princess Elisabeth*. Paris: Editions Elzévir, 1943.

ANNE VISCOUNTESS CONWAY
A SEVENTEENTH-CENTURY RATIONALIST

JANE DURAN

Anne Viscountess Conway (1631–1679) was a seventeenth-century phi-losopher and author in the tradition of Descartes, Spinoza, and Leibniz. Until recently, her work was almost lost to us because of the difficulty of translation and semi-anonymous manuscript attribution. Her longest piece, *Principles of the Most Ancient and Modern Philosophy*, was erro-neously attributed to her friend and collaborator F. M. van Helmont. Within the past decade, however, there has been a surge of interest in Lady Anne Conway's work. It has been recognized by many that some of the more salient and original strands of thought in the *Principles* antici-pated Leibniz, and that indeed his usage of the term "monad" was prob-ably due to his originally having seen it in her *Principles*, shown to him by the peripatetic person of letters, van Helmont (Merchant, 1979, 265–266).[1] Several recent commentators have remarked not only on the originality and profundity of the Viscountess Conway's philosophy—she tackles many difficult and perplexing questions having to do with *de re* modality, the nature of time, essence vs. accidents, and so forth—but on her having served as a source for other thinkers (among them, again, pre-eminently Leibniz) in a particularly helpful and fructifying way (Mer-chant, 1979, *passim*).

Since a spate of recent journal articles and books have either touched upon Conway's life or gone into it in some depth (and since there remains, in any case, the superb *Conway Letters*, by Marjorie Hope Nicolson, pub-lished during the '30's), I will devote most of this piece to a discussion of some of the major points in the Conway rationalism, and the respects in which her *Principles* differs from the work of other rationalists.

Hypatia vol. 4, no. 1 (Spring 1989) © by Jane Duran

Anne Conway's work is most easily compared to that of Spinoza and Leibniz, since she is from the start a monist, and far from being a Cartesian dualist. She was, we are informed by all sources, extremely well-read in both Latin and Greek—she had read Plato and Plotinus in Latin and possibly Plato in Greek as well. She had also read Descartes and Spinoza, and it was the former, apparently, who became in some sense the indirect catalyst for her own philosophical work, since she found so much of the Cartesian system erroneous (Conway 1982, 15). She was also in pronounced disagreement with Thomas Hobbes. In any case, our purpose here will be to achieve a commentary on specific portions of the *Principles* where intersection between Conway and Descartes, or to some extent between Conway and Leibniz is most pronounced. Up to this point the work on Conway has been more biographical than philosophical, and save for the meticulous comments by editor Peter Loptson on her *Principles*, more along the lines of intellectual history than rigorous philosophy itself. But if it is the case that, as Loptson and Carolyn Merchant both argue, Conway's philosophical views are sufficiently sophisticated that they merit study in their own right, surely a natural point of departure for such a task is the *Principles*, specific portions of which may easily be contrasted with the work of the other rationalists.

I

A large part of the opening section of the *Principles* has to do with the nature of God. Standing within the framework of the Christian tradition, and a close friend and intellectual confidante of the Cambridge Platonist theologian and philosopher Henry More,[2] Conway wrote in such a way that some of her work seems more theological than philosophical. It is an intriguing aspect of her treatise that, as the commentators have noted, she had taken into account works of Judaica only recently available at the time, especially certain portions of the *Kabbala*. Such work emphasized views of the nature of God, both from the standpoint of substance and from the standpoint of God's relation to a divine offspring, not in accordance with Christian belief and hence somewhat heretical. We will not be concerned with those views here, but Conway's description of God as substance is noteworthy because it leads directly into her monadic view of substance in general.

Briefly, Conway holds that God is a being of infinite spirit, the attributes or particulars of which are infinite in number and necessarily part of God's essence. Specifically, Conway writes:

> God is a Spirit, Light, and Life, infinitely Wise, Good, Just, Mighty, Omniscient, Omnipresent, Omnipotent, Creator and Maker of all things

visible and invisible. . . . In God there is neither Time nor Change, nor
Composition, nor Division of Parts: He is wholly and universally one in
himself, and of himself, without any manner of variety or Mixture. . . .
(Conway 1982, 149)

In Conway's ontology, God is one sort of substance (as God will become
one sort of Monad for Leibniz). All of the rest of creation is another sort of
substance, save for Christ, who is a third sort of substance standing mid-
way, ontologically, between God and the rest of created things. This somewhat pared and terse account may help us bear in mind the Conway
ontological hierarchy, as it has important ramifications for the rest of her
philosophy. Her notion of Christ, peculiar (in English, at any rate) to her
philosophy, is derived partially from the *Kabbala* and its traditional
notion of a being metaphysically halfway between God and the created
world, Adam Kadmon, in Kabbalistic terminology. As Conway writes,
"And for the same reason he is called of Paul . . . the First Begotten of all
Creatures; wherein is signified the relation he hath to Creation. . . . That
the Ancient Cabbalists acknowledged such a First Begotten Son of God,
whom they called the Heavenly Adam" (Conway 1982, 149). More importantly, however, these two ontologically superior entities have an interesting and complicated relationship to the rest of creation, which is itself
metaphysically complex and ontologically intriguing. Both of the ontologically prior entities are in a sense eternally co-present with the rest of creation, since God is by nature a creator *de re*. (This is a sophisticated
point, on which Loptson has extensive commentary.)[3] But more interesting for our purposes is the relationship of the rest of creation—animal,
vegetable, humankind and so forth—to itself. Conway is, as Merchant is at
pains to point out, a vitalist. Hence she is a monist; she sees matter and
spirit as intermingled and inseparable (Merchant 1979, 258).[4] All of creation can be broken down into infinitely many small parts, called monads,
which have the capacity to penetrate and intermingle—hence the interaction one sees among the creatures. She writes of this substance, of
which all except God and Adam Kadmon consist:

> . . . Infinite Divisibility . . . how all creatures from the highest to the
> lowest are inseparably united with one another, by means of Subtiler
> Parts interceding or coming in between, which are the Emanations of
> one creature into another, by which also they act one upon another at
> the greatest distance; and this is the Foundation of all Sympathy and
> Antipathy which happens in creatures. (Conway 1982, 164)

This original and striking metaphysics attempts to account for the
internally felt "action" of one being upon another, what Descartes would
have labeled a "passion" (Descartes 1969, 353–368), by the "Emanation

of one creature into another", achieved by "Subtiler Parts interceding or coming in between." Whatever the lack of clarity here, (Conway holds that this substance has the capacity to be "less gross" and "less corporeal" in some entities, "more gross" and "more corporeal" in others), it is worth contrasting this point specifically with Leibniz's celebrated account of the purely spiritual monads in *The Monadologie* (Leibniz 1951, 533–551). One of the chief difficulties of the Leibnizian account of the monads is, of course, the nature of their effect upon one another, since, as he held, they mirror each other without directly interacting with one another (1951, 534–536). Leibniz writes of the monads, to the puzzlement and chagrin of future commentators:

> 7. . . . The monads have no windows through which anything can enter or depart. The accidents cannot detach themselves nor go about outside of substances, as did formerly the sensible species of the Schoolmen. Thus neither substance nor accident can enter a monad from the outside. . . .
>
> 13. . . . For since every natural change takes place by degrees, . . .
>
> 14. . . . the passing state . . . is nothing else than what is called *perception* . . .
>
> 17. It must be confessed, moreover, that perception and that which depends upon it *are inexplicable by mechanical causes.* (1951, 534–536)

The commentary on Conway and Leibniz (Merchant 1979, *passim*) is at this point fairly well developed, so we will simply note that a difficulty in Leibnizian metaphysics—not to say the Cartesian system, with its conundrum of interaction between the two substances, a source of dismay from Arnauld on down—is handled by Conway in her own system in such a manner that any questions which are raised about the nature of the interaction are at a different level of gravity and at a metaphysically less crucial point.

Conway also held *de re* notions of God's essence which enable her to forestall to some extent the sorts of problems inherent in Leibniz's account of God's creation of Judas.[5] Leibniz notoriously had held that everything exists for a reason, and the reason for the existence of any one given particular or entity is that the overall plan is such as to yield the most perfect set of compossibles (Couturat 1972, 28). Here is Leibniz on the creation of Judas (a problematic area, of course, for Christian theorizing and for the notions of good and evil):

> For God foresees from all time that there will be a certain Judas, and in the concept or idea of him which God has, is contained this future

free act. The only question therefore, which remains is why this certain Judas, the betrayer who is possible only because of the idea of God, actually exists. To this question, however, we can expect no answer here on earth excepting that it is because God has found it good that he should exist notwithstanding the sin he foresaw. This will be more than overbalanced. God will derive a greater good from it, and it will finally turn out that this series of events in which is included the existence of this sinner, is the most perfect among all the possible series of events. (1951, 333)

Leibniz's view of the deity includes the difficulty that the deity is supposed to have engaged in ratiocination with regard to the set of all compossibles, yet other accounts of the nature of God by rationalists have held that it is inconsistent with the nature of God and the divine attributes to suppose that God engages in ratiocination at all. Conway's view has the virtue of being more appealing in the sense that she has a temporal view tied into her overall description of God which saves her from having to give us the notion of a God who weighs and calculates, however ultimately beneficial such weighings and calculations. Loptson aids us in coming to grips with this portion or Conway's view on God's *de re* essentiality and its relationship both to temporality and to the notion of God's being a creator:

> That which does not change is outside time. Change is evidently to be understood internally, and not relatively: when God creates a new substance, which from its first appearance undergoes change, this involves change only in the creature, not in its creator. God in short is immutable and changeless, and therefore outside time. . . . Conway's conclusion—that time is infinite and has always contained created substances—will follow in any case from her view of the essence of God. For her God is essentially, not merely creator, but creative, and ubiquitously so. . . . Hence there have never not been—according to Conway—created substances. (Conway, Loptson (commentary), 1982, 30–32)

As I have asserted at an earlier point, Conway is remarkable in her treatise (which is comparatively short in length—approximately 100 printed pages) for the number of philosophical positions to which she makes reference and in some cases actually attempts to refute. To reiterate, Conway cites (among major thinkers), Descartes, Hobbes, and Spinoza and makes some effort (greater in the case of Hobbes, who, of course, wrote in English) to refute all three. We have already adumbrated some of the respects in which the Conway metaphysics anticipates that of Leibniz, and we have emphasized Conway's use of the term "monad" and the fact that

Merchant, among others, believes that Leibniz probably derived this term from material by Conway which was presented to him by van Helmont (Merchant 1979, 264–265). In the remainder of the paper I will attempt to show in what ways Conway differs from—and intersects interestingly with—Descartes. It is worth mentioning in passing, however, that Loptson, among others, cites as particularly noteworthy Conway's allusion to Spinoza, since his work was not well known in England at the time and since much of it (the *Ethics*, for example) was actually published after Conway's death. Loptson hypothesizes that Conway was familiar with Spinoza's *Tractatus Theologico-Politicus* from her discussions with Henry More. Much of More's own work was either dedicated to Anne Conway, or, according to some, such a direct outgrowth of his discussions with her that she might be thought to be the author of major components of it (Mackinnon 1969, xiv).

II

Along with Hobbes, the other chief object of Conway's interest in the *Principles* is Descartes. Crudely speaking, the large part of her rebuttal against Descartes is apparent from the start of her treatise: she is a monist, and Descartes is a dualist. Her idea of matter, as we have already seen, is a form of vitalism which encompasses both spirit and raw matter *simpliciter* in the same ontological compound. Descartes, of course, was known for having "clearly and distinctly" perceived that mind and matter were separate, and for having come to the conclusion that his essence was thinking (Descartes 1969, 165–179). As Merchant and Loptson both assert, it is a virtue of Conway's metaphysics that she has achieved a view which allows for a continuity between humankind and other living creatures (even, to be sure, between living creatures and non-living creatures). There is no clear line of demarcation for Conway between the human and nonhuman or the living and non-living; rather, ". . . all Kinds of Creatures may be changed into another . . . " (Conway 1982, 222–224). Thus, although she has a *de re* view of individual essence (Paul, for example, to employ a person she utilizes for such purposes, cannot be changed into another individual.), she—unlike some contemporary thinkers—does not have a *de re* view of natural kinds or species essence. She holds that, by gradations, a human might be transformed into a mayfly. Cursorily, she holds that such transformations would be related to the amount of gross corporeality in the individual person—in other words, some might more readily be transformed into mayflies than others.

Insofar as the Cartesian view is concerned, however, there are other noteworthy points of contrast which might be developed above and beyond the obvious juxtaposition of the two views on the nature of substance. It might prove worthwhile to attempt to construct an epistemology for Conway, a feat which is somewhat difficult to perform adequately because epistemology must be pulled out of her writings—she is not particularly explicit on any epistemic point. But her metaphysics would seem to indicate—as it does for most of the rationalists—that there is a natural and patent linkage between her ontology and epistemology, and it does not seem to be straining unnecessarily to try to articulate such a linkage. In addition, and perhaps more intrinsically interesting because it is not addressed as fully in much of the secondary literature, there seems to be an account of the passions embedded in the *Principles*, and here the comparison between Conway and Descartes might be somewhat easier to construct, since Descartes' views on the passions is spelled out in full, and Conway's view is at least more developed than her espistemology.

To proceed with matters epistemological, Descartes held a view on knowledge and the knowledge that tied his epistemology and metaphysics together somewhat more neatly then did Spinoza's, for example. The procession of ideas for Descartes, from "confused" to "adventitious" to "factitious" to "clear and distinct", moves carefully along a line from ideas of purely sensory origin to ideas acquired at least partly through the senses but which generalize over data and hence are somewhat scientific, to ideas which have no sensory admixture and hence are "clear and distinct" (Descartes 1969, *passim.*)[6]

In the *Meditations*, Descartes' systematic doubt is the method by which he paves the way for a new intellectual perspective which is ultimately to yield epistemic criteria. His two principal criteria for knowledge will come to *clarity* and *distinctness*. But it becomes evident by the Third *Meditation*, if not sooner, that the Cartesian notions of clear and distinct are related in an interesting manner to the Cartesian metaphysics. In a brief passage in the middle of his attempt to prove the existence of God, Descartes writes:

> This idea [the idea of God] is also very clear and distinct; since all that I conceive clearly and distinctly of the real and true, and of what conveys some perfection, is in its entirety contained in this idea. . . . [and] I should judge that all things which I clearly perceive and in which I know that there is some perfection, and possibly likewise an infinitude of properties of which I am ignorant, are in God formally or eminently; so that the idea which I have of him may become the most true, most clear and most distinct of all the ideas that are in my mind.
>
> (Descartes 1969, 188–189)

Now because of God's infiniteness and the emphasis that Descartes places at other points on the notion of a "simple" as related to clarity and distinctness, the preceding passage and passages like it have posed some difficulty for Descartes scholars. But we are concerned here with their relationship to Conway's metaphysics, and here it is plain that the passages are helpful and even instructive. For Conway's ontological hierarchy is such that, as we have seen, God is the only substance in her hierarchy which is purely spiritual, the Adam Kadmon substance having an interesting mixture of spiritual and nonspiritual qualities, and the rest of created being containing a much greater admixture of the corporeal.[7] As the admixture of the corporeal becomes greater, and as the beings descend down the ontological hierarchy, it becomes more difficult to construe their constituents and to articulate what proportion of which being is corporeal, what spiritual, etc. It is in this sense, I believe, that Conway has given us a beginning epistemology, and nascent epistemic principles. For it is clear, although Conway does not explicitly say so, that for her, too, the idea of God is the most clearly held and most articulable idea we possess. The ontological descriptions of God at the opening of the *Principles* are straightforward and unproblematic; descriptions of other creatures at a later point are much less so. To quote again, here is the opening of the *Principles* with its description of God:

> 1. God is a Spirit, Light, and Life, infinitely Wise, Good, Just, Mighty, Omniscient, Omnipresent, Omnipotent, Creator and Maker of all things visible and invisible. (1982, 149)

For purposes of contrast, here are some passages from a much later point in the *Principles* which attempt to contrast animals and humankind:

> And First, let us take an Horse, which is a Creature indued with divers degrees of perfection by his Creator, as not only strength of body, but . . . a certain kind of knowledge, how he ought to serve his Master, and moreover also Love, Fear, Courage, Memory and divers other Qualities which are in Man: which also we may observe in a Dog, and many other animals. . . . Now I demand, unto what higher perfection and degree of Goodness, the Being or Essence of an Horse doth or may attain after he hath done good service for his Master, and so performed his Duty, and what is proper for such a Creature? Is a Horse a mere Fabrick or dead Matter? or hath he a Spirit in him, having Knowledge, Sence and Love, and divers other Faculties and Properties of a Spirit? (1982, 180–181)

The obvious difficulty Conway has here is in articulating precisely what the proportions of the vitalist mixture which the horse comprises actually are. Not, of course, that this could be done, even in theory, but this passage and others similar to it support our notion that Conway's implicit epistemology is hierarchical, somewhat like Descartes', but without depending on his dualism. For Conway, obviously, any ideas we possess of God are among our clearest ideas.

Additionally, as we have noted at an earlier point, Conway's philosophy is remarkable in its account of the effects of motion or action from one individual substance—a dog, horse, or person—on another. We had cited this material with regard to the distinction between Leibniz's monadology and Conway's, since it is clear that a problem for Leibniz is his account of how the monads "mirror" one another, given that he does not posit direct interaction. Conway, as we have seen, holds that

> . . . all creatures from the highest to the lowest are inseparably united with one another, by means of Subtiler Parts interceding or coming in between, which are the Emanations of one creature into another, by which also they act upon one another at the greatest distance; and this is the Foundation of all Sympathy and Antipathy which happens in creatures. (1982, 164)

Now Descartes has, of course, an entire work, *The Passions of the Soul*, which attempts to account for passionate interactions between individuals. Briefly, Descartes accounts for the fear we feel when we see a Bengal tiger ahead of us in the grass in Northern India as a movement of animal spirits conveyed throughout different parts of the body by the image or figure of the animal which is imprinted on a portion of the eye. The difficulty with the *Passions* is not really a difficulty with Descartes' physiology, for we can certainly make allowances for the very little that was known about the functioning of the human body at that time. Rather, the difficulty that we face in the place is never fully resolved (nor, of course, is it ever resolved elsewhere in Descartes' work, at least according to many of the commentators, beginning as early as *Objections and Replies*). Here is Descartes on what takes place when we see a ferocious animal:

> Thus, for example, if we see some animal approach us, the light from its body reflects two images of it, one in each of our eyes, and these two images form two others, by means of the optic nerves, in the interior surface of the brain which faces its cavities; then from there, by means of the animal spirits with which its cavities are filled, these images so radiate. . . . And, besides that, if this figure is very strange and frightful—that is, if it has a close relationship with the things which have been formerly hurtful to the body, that excites the passion of apprehension in the soul and then that of courage. . . . (1969, 363–364)

It is not that Descartes' account, again, is not in some sense more fully developed than Conway's. It is rather that it leaves more difficult sorts of questions open. To try to argue for at least the partial superiority of Conway's account is to offer the following construal of the material: On Descartes' account, everything hinges on the body/mind interaction, which is the least developed and most infamously difficult portion of his metaphysics. One moves from the optic nerves, for example, to some form of thinking—to utilization of the mind to recognize the tiger—and also to the "passion of apprehension . . . and then that of courage." It is not clear how this interaction proceeds, and, as I have indicated earlier, this was one of the chief sticking points in *Objections* of both Gassendi and Arnauld. On Conway's account there is direct action between me and the tiger (". . . Subtiler parts interceding or coming in between . . . "), and it is not necessary to wonder how my mind could interact with my animal spirits (themselves affected by the image of the tiger, *ex hypothesi*), as it is on the Cartesian view.

To return once more to the notion of God, both in Descartes and in Conway, there is still another comparison which can usefully be made. To recapitulate briefly, according to Conway we know God innately (1982, 149–150). According to her doctrine, the idea of God is the clearest idea we possess. More importantly, perhaps, since we already have a conception of God which includes his essence and subessences, as Loptson terms them, we can deduce most of the rest of what we know about being/creation from them. We know of Adam Kadmon (as Conway, following the *Kabbala*, terms Christ) because his existence and characteristics follow necessarily both from the existence of God and the existence of visible creation. We know of the substance of visible creation—it being, as we have said, both "Corporeal" and "Spiritual," and "inseparably united with one another"—from our knowledge of Adam Kadmon (Conway 1982, 164).

But it is interesting and valuable to compare Descartes and Conway both on the notion of the idea of God and on what can be derived from it. In order to perform such a comparison, we must go into Descartes at greater length, delineating the problematic areas, and then utilize Conway's work for purposes of comparison.

We alluded at an earlier point to the difficulties caused for commentators by Descartes' statement that ". . . so that the idea that I have of him may become the most true, most clear and most distinct of all the ideas that are in my mind" (Descartes 1969, 188–189). From the Cartesian point of view, one wonders whether or not it is the case that, if Descartes' idea of God is such that "nothing in the world could be more clear or intelligible" (Descartes 1967, 107), it could in some way be said to be the simplest and least complex idea. Preliminarily, one wants to answer with a solid sort of "no." Descartes describes God in the *Meditations* as the Being in which there is an infinitude of properties of which we are ignorant. Certainly, insofar as sheer numbers are concerned, the infinitude of God's properties outweighs any degree of complexity which might adhere to a lesser being. It is here that the crux of the problematic area arises: Is God (insofar as he can be known or comprehended at all by the human mind) most easily described as a concatenation of properties, each of which may be perceived or apprehended clearly and distinctly? And can these properties themselves be described as simples? If all of this is the case, it does lend some credence to the notion that the idea of God as a whole is the most clear and distinct of Descartes' ideas, particularly since it must be remembered that it is at least in part the concept of the greatest degree of perfection's necessarily existing that makes any idea of God so distinct.

But to develop the difficulties with the Cartesian material along the lines of merely one commentator whose work is well-known (Kenny), just because I have a clear and distinct idea of x, a clear and distinct idea of y, and a clear and distinct idea of z, it does not follow that I have a clear and distinct idea of $x + y + z$. It is entirely possible that my idea of the concatenation of these three may be less clear and distinct than my idea of any one of them alone (Kenny 1968, 137). Worse still, the idea under consideration here (that of God) is the idea of a being with an infinite number of properties. If there is any clarity at all in the concept of infinity, it can only be because the concept of infinity is a mathematical concept. The idea is clear insofar as the fact that even the mathematically unsophisticated can grasp that infinity proceeds arithmetically is concerned; it is clear that, for every whole number of which I can think, there is always that number + 1. But surely, one is tempted to say, this is not what Descartes originally meant. Somehow one senses that the antecedent spirit of "clarity and distinctness" has been violated or not adhered to. To repeat Conway's definition of God one more time, she writes:

> God is a Spirit, Light, and Life, infinitely Wise, Good, Just, Mighty, Omniscient, Omnipotent, Creator and Maker of all things visible and invisible. . . . In God there is neither Time nor Change, nor Composition, nor Division of Parts: He is wholly and universally one in himself, and of himself, without any manner of variety or Mixture. . . . (1982, 149)

Now whereas Descartes seems to be at pains to emphasize God's properties—and it is this emphasis which creates some of the difficulties with the notion of "clarity" and "distinctness" of the idea of God—Conway prefers to emphasize God's unity. It may perhaps be the case that, were she philosophically pressed, Conway's account of God would become somewhat more similar to Descartes'. But, again, we have only the *Principles* to go on, and we can only analyze what she has written there and perform some small extrapolation. To be fair, Descartes no doubt delineates God's properties carefully so as to be in a better position to bolster other arguments which he makes on the nature of humankind, for example. (In the Sixth *Meditation*, for instance, one needs to be assured of God's goodness so that one can have more confidence in the information imparted to the senses.) But this merely underscores our overall point. Because Conway does not emphasize God's properties in an enumerative sense (although, as I have indicated, it might be possible for her to do this, since goodness and wisdom, among others, are listed), difficulties with the innateness of a complex idea, or with the clarity of such an idea, do not occur. In its metaphysical simplicity, Conway's conception of God more closely resembles Plato's Form of the Good than it does the Cartesian conception of God, particularly since she specifies that He is ". . . wholly and universally one in himself, and of himself, without any manner or variety or Mixture. . . ." Thus, although the epistemological question of what, precisely, constitutes the knowledge of God is certainly clearer and less fraught with difficulty in Conway's account of God, it is again along the lines of the sorts of difficulty we have with Plato's notion of the Good—we would like to know more about it.

The second major point of comparison between Descartes' alembicated account of God and Conway's is with regard to what one can derive from it. On this score Conway's metaphysics seems at once clearer and more consistent, although it is not, of course, nearly as thoroughly developed as Descartes'. One must, of course, be just and repeat the caveat implicit at an earlier point: the body of Descartes' work (or, for that matter, Leibniz' or Spinoza's) is so much greater that it seems, on the one hand, unfair to make the comparison. But comparison can and should be made, since to slight Conway with the excuse that the *Principles* is not fully developed enough to be compared to, for example, the *Meditations*, is to simply repeat the injury historically done to women philosophers. We must utilize the available material and try to infer what else, consistent with the available material, springs from it.

From Descartes' account of God alone, little can be derived. The metaphysical problems inherent in trying to square his account of God with the rest of creation are more analogous to those we cited with regard to Leibniz at an earlier point. Although he does not go into the problem in any depth, Descartes implicitly seems to be saying (à la Leibniz) that God possesses the capacity for decision-making, ratiocination, and so forth, and that He decided to create the world as it is, so to speak, because it affords the greatest amount of good (Fifth *Meditation*). Nor can we derive any notion of what, necessarily, God creates from Descartes' account, since there is a complete ontological break between the substance that is God and any other substance. Stating the matter crudely, Descartes seems to be given to complete breaks, as it were, since the break or split between matter and spirit is itself another instance of this same sort of theorizing.

Conway solves the problem of the ontological relation between God and the rest of creation by gradations, as we have seen at an earlier point with the brief contrast to the work of Leibniz. All the rest of creation proceeds by gradations, which mimic the gradation between God, Adam Kadmon, and the rest of created things. If this still leaves the nature of the relationship problematic—as it does—it leaves us with what we might be inclined to dub a more holistic account, since there is at least a hierarchical relationship implicit in what she postulates. In Descartes' ontology one senses no such line of interaction or gradation between postulated entities. More importantly, one can derive in Conway, deductively, the rest of creation from the existence of God, since (as Loptson so admirably summarizes)

> God in short is immutable and changeless, and therefore outside time.... Conway's conclusion—that time is infinite and has always contained created substances—will follow in any case from her view of the essence of God. For her God is essentially, not merely creator, but creative, and ubiquitously so.... Hence there have never not been—according to Conway— created substances. (Conway, commentary, 1982, 30–32)

To argue briefly for Conway, this might be thought, in a preliminary fashion, to have bettered Descartes' account in the following sense: since God is *de re* creator, creation flows from Him with no necessity for ratiocination. Thus one metaphysical problem is disposed of. And since there is the obvious hierarchy from God to Adam Kadmon and the rest of created things, the separateness and splitting that plague the Cartesian system are, at least on first view, eliminated.

In sum, then, points of contrast between Conway and Descartes, for example, are not nearly as precisely stated from her perspective as one would like, and hence the contemporary commentator must extrapolate. But there are many fruitful points of comparison, both between Conway and Descartes and Conway and other rationalists, if one is willing to grant that certain sorts of views seem to follow naturally from the explicitly stated Conway ontology. That Conway anticipated Leibniz is now acknowledged in the literature and has received fairly extensive comment. What should be acknowledged, I argue, are the various sorts of ways in which Conway can usefully be contrasted with the other major seventeenth-century rationalists.

III

Throughout this paper I have endeavored to develop a view of the philosophy of Anne Conway which would enable us to see her as a philosopher working within a certain tradition of her own time, a tradition which we acknowledge to have two strands, broadly speaking. The first is its Christian heritage, which nevertheless is much less orthodox in Conway than in some other thinkers, at least partially, one hypothesizes, because of her extensive use of the *Kabbala* as a source (Merchant, 1979, *passim*; Coudert, 1975, *passim*). The second is, of course, the tradition of rationalism, of which Conway is a very worthy proponent. I have chosen to contrast Conway largely with Descartes since there is already an extensive commentary on his work and since Conway has specifically cited him as a thinker whom she attempts to refute in the *Principles*. Somewhat heretically, I have tried to go beyond the obvious sort of contrast between Conway and Descartes on the notion of substance (which is well developed, in any case, by Loptson) to a broader set of contrasts, including elements of epistemology and an account of what was then referred to as the "passions." Necessarily, one goes somewhat beyond the text here, but Conway's text implicitly asks us to do that.

In any case, it is clear that Conway was an original and incisive philosopher of her time, whose work, as has already been acknowledged, influenced Henry More, anticipated Leibniz, and was in stated disagreement with that other English-language philosopher, Hobbes.[8] Merchant describes Conway as a woman whose ". . . ideas, praised and respected in her own day, have been almost forgotten in ours" (1979, 255). In our endeavor to celebrate and remember women philosophers, we can do no better than to take special note of Anne Conway, whose erudition and knowledge were so great that they were even acknowledged by seventeenth-century men.

NOTES

I would like to acknowledge the generosity of the University of California, Santa Barbara Graduate School of Education, where work on the rationalists, particularly Leibniz, was done. Additional thanks are due to Noel Fleming, members of his Spring 1985 seminar on Leibniz, and to offshoots of Eastern SWIP, where fruitful discussion of the doctrines of Spinoza and Descartes, in particular, was had for a period of many years. We all owe a debt of gratitude to Antonia Fraser and Carolyn Merchant for bringing Anne Conway to the fore again.

1. In addition to Merchant, see Fraser and Coudert. Fraser is superb at placing Conway in intellectual context, and Coudert provides an illuminating commentary on the Judaic sources utilized by Conway.

2. All of the commentators and literature cited attest to this fact, and to the rare nature of their friendship. See Powicke (1926), Lichtenstein (1962) and Mackinnon (1969).

3. See Conway (1982, 30–31). Loptson, the editor, is especially careful with the technically difficult points of modality in Conway, many of which bear comparison with today's work on modal topics.

4. Cf. Fraser (1985, 352–353), points out Conway's goal of unifying Christian beliefs and the new science. Cf. also Conway (1982, 164 and 43–46 of commentary).

5. This particular passage from the "Discourse on Metaphysics" is frequently cited as a paradigm elucidation of the problem of the existence of evil. These aspects of Leibniz's work are the very aspects which gave rise to the Voltairean satire. (Leibniz (1951, 333)

6. Descartes' epistemology can be developed using the *Meditations* and *Discourse* alone, although there are also hints of it in the *Rules*.

7. See Conway (1982, *passim*). Loptson feels that she would insist that angels, etc., are purely spiritual, but she does not discuss such beings in any detail.

8. More is said to have remarked that he ". . . turned to her, as naturally as the needle turnes North." (Lichtenstein 1962, 15)

REFERENCES

Conway, Anne. 1982. *Principles of the most ancient and modern philosophy*, Peter Loptson, ed. The Hague: Martinus Nijhoff.

Coudert, Allison. 1975. A cambridge platonist's kabbalist nightmare. *Journal of the history of ideas* 36 (4): 634–652.

Couturat, Louis. 1972. On Leibniz's metaphysics. In *Leibniz: a collection of critical essays*, Harry G. Frankfurt, ed. Garden City, NY: Anchor.

Descartes, Rene. 1967. *The philosophical works of Descartes*, Elizabeth S. Haldane and G.R.T. Ross, eds. Cambridge: Cambridge University Press.

Descartes, Rene. 1969. *The essential Descartes*, Margaret D. Wilson, ed. New York: New American Library.

Fraser, Antonia. 1985. *The weaker vessel*. New York: Vintage Books.

Kenny, Anthony. 1968. *Descartes: a study of his philosophy*. New York: Random House.

Leibniz, Wilhelm Gottfried. 1951. *Leibniz: selections*, Philip P. Wiener, ed. New York: Charles Scribner's Sons.

Lichtenstein, Aharon. 1962. *Henry More: the rational theology of a Cambridge Platonist*. Cambridge, MA: Harvard University Press.

Mackinnon, Flora Isabel, ed. 1969. *Philosophical writings of Henry More*. New York: AMS Press.

Merchant, Carolyn. 1979. The vitalism of Anne Conway: Its impact on Leibniz's concept of the monad. In *Journal of the history of philosophy* 27 (3): 255–270.

Nicolson, Marjorie Hope. 1930. *The Conway letters: The correspondence of Anne Viscountess Conway, Henry More and their friends, 1642–1684.* Cambridge: Cambridge University Press.

Parkinson, G. H. R. 1954. *Spinoza's theory of knowledge.* Oxford: Oxford University Press.

Powicke, F. J. 1926. *The Cambridge Platonists.* London: F.M. Dent & Son.

de Spinoza, Benedict. 1955. *On the improvement of the understanding.* R. H. M. Elwes, ed. New York: Dover.

SOR JUANA'S FEMINISM
FROM ARISTOTLE TO IRIGARAY

DONALD BEGGS

The Mexican nun Sor Juana Inés de la Cruz (1648?–1695), although best known as a poet, had encyclopedic interests that launched her into thinking we can understand better through the history of philosophy. She explains in her *Response* (1690)[1] how she created a room of her own out of her convent cell (which may have been the most important salon at the time in the New World) in order to pursue her research, writing, and reflection. What provoked Sor Juana to produce the *Response*, her last prose text, was an admonition by her bishop that her life-long writing, study, and teaching were improper, and should cease.

The *Response* answers this by developing a complex, many-layered defense of her life choices interwoven with autobiographical narrative. Sor Juana appeals to essential concepts of Aristotelian and Thomist natural law to argue that there are inconsistencies and inadequacies in the Church's threatened interdiction against her teaching and writing, a prohibition that would extend to the scholarly activities and public learning of all women. Central among the concepts Sor Juana uses to defend herself is her elaboration of her "inclination toward letters." On this basis she develops an argument against institutionalized gender bias which is, in effect, an innovative "Aristotelian standpoint"[2] against the patriarchal Church. For reasons like these, she has been called the first feminist in the New World, and the *Response* "the Magna Carta of intellectual liberty for women in America" (Sor Juana 1951–1957, xliii). Unfortunately, this Aristotelian line of argument—however sound—seems to end in an impasse. For an apparently unresolvable conflict arises between the Church's authority to guide its members and the force of Sor Juana's (Aristotelian) arguments about inclinations as natural kinds and rational norms. I will argue that Sor Juana subverts this dilemma with aspects of neoplatonism that make her position, paradoxically, both ontologically gendered and foundationless.

In sum, this philosophically unrecognized text is a powerful autobiographical document as well as an important moment in early modern philosophy. It is, on one level, a narrative of Sor Juana's inclination toward letters; but, because it includes arguments about the meaning and legitimacy of letters and learning for women, and because these arguments incorporate epistemological, ontological, and ethical reflections that appeal to Aristotelian, Thomist, neoplatonist, and hermetic modes of thought and categories, Sor Juana's overall argument is both strikingly original and oddly contemporary. Its strategy, quite simply, anticipates the shifting juxtapositions that typify "postmodernism." Sor Juana's position is not, however, fundamentally consistent with postmodern thought. In this, she is more like Luce Irigaray who, according to Margaret Whitford, insists on "multiplicity," like postmodernists, but also "on the strategic necessity of mimesis and the assertion of (an apparently essentialist) feminine, in order to make a space which resists colonization. If multiplicity is to be celebrated, it has to be *after* sexual difference and not, as at present, by simply bypassing it (Whitford 1991, 84, italics in original). Surely Josefina Ludmer is right to conclude this about Sor Juana:

> To the question of why [in the history of philosophy until recently] there have been no women philosophers [acknowledged], one can answer that women have not engaged in philosophy from the space delimited by classical philosophy but rather from other zones; and if one reads or listens to their discourse as a philosophical discourse, one can effect that transformation of thought. (Ludmer 1991, 93)

The history of philosophy lacks women not only because of the effect of practices which explicitly excluded them from learning and doing well, but also, as Ludmer says, because of a failure to read some thinkers in the right way, a failure of recognition, a hermeneutic blindness. The *Response* can and should be read as philosophy; its full argument can be reconstructed, and this is what I begin to sketch here. As I shall suggest at the end, like Irigaray, Sor Juana intervened "in philosophical debates in order to change the nature of philosophy itself" (Whitford 1991, 186).

In the following, in order first to contextualize a relatively unfamiliar figure, I will sketch Sor Juana's life. Then substantive inquiry will begin by addressing the theme of silence, secrets, and hiddenness, which Ludmer brings forcefully to our attention. Finally, the two phases of Sor Juana's distinctive and ironic argument can be articulated: her Aristotelian, standpoint feminism, and its neoplatonic subversion by what she calls "the philosophies of the kitchen."

Background

In his widely praised study of Sor Juana, Octavio Paz has emphasized how the baroque style of juxtaposing opposites was typical in New Spain's literature and culture.

> It has often been said—both in praise and deprecation—that the Mexican baroque was an exaggeration of its Spanish models. Indeed, like all imitative art, the poetry of New Spain attempted to surpass its models: it was the extreme of baroqueness, the apogee of strangeness. This excess is proof of its authenticity. . . . The unique aesthetic of the Mexican baroque corresponded to the historical and existential uniqueness of the criollo [mixed blood]. Their relationship was not one of cause and effect, but of affinity and coincidence. The criollo breathed naturally in a world of strangeness because he was, and knew himself to be, a strange being. (Paz 1988, 59)

Paz shows how chromatic cultural contrasts became resplendent in the rich tapestry of the criollo Juana Inés's life and work. He contextualizes her life by developing such examples as the complex unity of religiously sanctioned monogamy alongside the widely accepted presence of many illegitimate children (e.g., Juana Inés and all her siblings), the asceticism of Sor Juana's scholarly activities contrasted with the eroticism of her poetry, and the confines of the religious dogma and practices she lived within and the aesthetic sensuality of her "cell." This characteristic of baroque style can help us to understand Sor Juana's apparent contradictions.

According to Paz, Sor Juana "represented the ideal of her era: the monstrous, the unique, the singular example" (274). Although much more than a prodigy, the conditions of her unpromising birth gave her no significant opportunity to develop her talents. Fortunately, her mother took a new lover who enabled Juana Inés to go away to the Court in Mexico City to show off her autodidacticism. And so she arrived, by all accounts a beautiful, poor, "unprotected" virgin, fabulously alert at age fifteen. She impressed the newly arrived Viceroy and Vicereine, who "protected" her. This secular period of early awakening is not described in *La Respuesta*. In any event, we know that Juana Inés must have learned the restraint and elaborate satisfactions of courtly eroticism: writing and reading poetry, staging plays, witty conversations about erudite matters, and endless flirtation.

But such a life had to be a dead-end for her since virtually all the courtiers were already married, and she could not remain at court indefinitely. More importantly, as we learn from *La Respuesta*, Juana Inés had a "total negación" (31) toward marriage. So, after much study, and exposure to new ideas and ways of being, her knowledge and insight grew beyond what her contemporaries could have expected into realms they could only guess. We may suppose that she had begun to understand her "real" place in society and the cosmos. As for her day-to-day existence, her best option was to join a religious order. Many young women took that course not because of a single-minded religious vocation but because there were no other places where society could grant illegitimate, unmarried women security and respect.[3] At age twenty Juana became a Carmelite novice— for three months. Since that asceticism did not allow personal possession even of books, she soon took the vows of the more open convent of San Jerómino (1669), for which the Vicereine provided the dowry. (As a nun, Sor Juana became a bride of Christ.) Then Sor Juana began her studies and writing in earnest. We must not overlook, of course, that she also began a full and busy life as a nun. For twenty-seven years she worked as the convent *contadora* (treasurer and bookkeeper) and archivist, and she became the confidante for many of her sisters.

During this period there were at least sixteen convents in Mexico City. San Jerómino had about fifty nuns, each with approximately five "maids," who might be girls sent to the convent by their families for education, or Indian slaves. The building itself was imposing: two stories, roughly 120 yards on each side, with a central garden and courtyard. Thus, each "cell" had two floors, and many were very nicely equipped. Sor Juana had frequent visitors from the Court and elsewhere, for her reputation was widespread.[4] And these guests brought gifts: scientific devices, musical scores and instruments, works of art, jewels, and books—it is estimated that Sor Juana's library (the one she was at last forced to surrender) had between two and three thousand volumes. In addition to her many visitors, Sor Juana had a constant, special relation to the Vicereine, María de Gonzaga, Countess de Paredes; she dedicated many poems and plays to her that blend erotic and religious imagery.

And this nun engaged in scholarly and literary activities to an unprecedented extent. In effect, she transgressed several social, "natural," and moral expectations. Paz emphasizes the transgressive character of New Spain's culture in general and of Sor Juana's creativity in particular: for her "the act of knowing [was] a transgression" (384). Indeed, her "cell" had almost become a laboratory and workshop; it was certainly a fabulous study and library and an important salon in the intellectual and cultural life of New Spain. Moreover, her relation to the Vicereine challenged conventions because the women openly acknowledged each other as equals, otherwise an impossibility for royalty and a common criollo nun.

The transgression that brought about the bishop's demand that she quit her studies was her refutation of a forty-year-old sermon by a prominent Jesuit favored by the archbishop. Her analysis was circulated without her consent or knowledge by the bishop. (Who took the name Sor Filotea for the occasion.) It scandalized and astonished many. Sor Juana's intrusion into an ecclesiastical and theological debate with the Bishop of Puebla and the Archbishop of Mexico, Aguiar, her "natural" and spiritual superiors, could not be ignored. The bishop may have been partially sympathetic, but could not openly or fully support her. In the end, none in the patriarchy could countenance her intellectual superiority; envy, fear, and misogyny prevailed. And just then, in the course of a regular replacement cycle, the Viceroy and Vicereine had to return to Spain. Sor Juana gave in to the demand to stop writing and studying, and to surrender her library and most of her possessions (1693). She lived two more years.

Silence, the Problem of the *Response*

Sor Juana begins the *Response* by contrasting her silence about her intellectual debts to Sor Filotea (the bishop) with St. Thomas's silence about his debts to his teacher. "Must not I too be silent? Not, like the Saint, out of humility, but because in reality I know nothing I can say that is worthy of you" (16). The irony here cannot be overemphasized. Then, self-consciously referring to one of the techniques of baroque style, she says that digression is a form of silence about one's proper subject matter (18). But what is the proper subject of a text that begins in irony and digresses immediately, that continues these tactics to its conclusion, and that is addressed to a man who has taken a woman's name? Speaking of the *Response*, Ludmer says,

> Sor Juana's text is a vast machine of transformations running on a very few elements: the matrix of the letter contains only three—two verbs and the negative: *saber* (to know), *decir* (to speak or say), *no*. Modulating and interchanging them in an unlimited *ars combinatoria*, conjugating the verbs and shifting the negative, Juana composes a text that works through the relationships, posited as contradictory, between two spaces (places) and two actions (methods): one of each must be ruled by the negative if the other is present. To know and to say or speak, Juana demonstrates, constitute opposing fields for a woman: whenever the two coexist, they occasion resistance and punishment. (87)

Saying and knowing, silence and ignorance, resistance and punishment are used to articulate the boundaries of a new discursive terrain. Let's identify a few more of these features.

As she begins narrating the episodes from her early life, we learn that Juana Inés had been forbidden to read the *Song of Songs*—in part a description of the sexual delights of newlyweds—and this prohibition was a kind of intellectual silencing (and not only of her, for even younger, learned men were forbidden to read this sacred text) (22). In secretly reading it (24), she began a pattern of transgression: expressing her early sexual interest defied gender conventions; we are surprised by her reading independently so early; and customs are violated that would have girls obey their mothers. Indeed, she had at first kept secret from her mother that she had begun to learn to read; then she enlisted her help in disguising herself as a boy so she could further her early education (28). Finally, one of the primary lessons she learns concerns the peaceful silence of books (32): she will have "no other master than mute books, an insentient inkwell [will be her] only colleague" (40).

She says that if she knew all she should know, she would not write, for that would be to know the mysteries that are below the foundation of knowledge. This is why at the start of her narrative she describes for us the modes of silence that Ludmer alludes to: having nothing to say being connected to not knowing, and having too much to say connected to knowing (18f). Like the Sibyls, Sor Juana will "speak" mysteries (66). But, in contrast, again like St. Peter, she speaks without really knowing (56); mere lovers (not possessors) of wisdom will be persecuted (58). She tells us that she was able to "open [the] doors of her heart" to the bishop as a kind of truth telling that revealed her most deeply hidden secrets (28). But, just as Moses asked God to show His hidden face, she wants the bishop to show his (20). She wants Sor Filotea to show himself as the superior who will not let her speak but who has evoked from her this text that demonstrates their true relative abilities. From the blossom of acclaim came vipers to silence her speech (44), but even more injurious than vipers are those of good intent (Sor Filotea?) who tell her not to engage in letters, who command her to become both self-executioner and martyr. And so she casts her letter onto the waters of silence like the baby Moses onto the Nile (90). The narrative closes with the ironic assertion that she has an inclination to silence (92).

How are we to explain this loquacious irony? Clearly, it is not enough to say that because God is absent, then silence is more divine (as Tavard, see note 8 below). In all this, as Ludmer says, it was

> her trick: not to say but to know, or saying that one doesn't know but knowing, or saying the opposite of what one knows. This trick of the weak, which here separates the field of saying (the law of the other) from the field of knowing (my law), combines, as in all tactics of resistance, submission to and acceptance of the place assigned to one by the other, with antagonism and confrontation, retreat from collaboration. (Ludmer 1991, 91)[5]

Thus, blending the secular and the sacred through allusion and irony, she affirms the continuity of a silence that continues to speak after three centuries.

Aristotle and Ironic Obedience

Sor Juana lived and worked when assertions of intellectual and religious independence had begun to shake the European world out of its medieval habits. The impact of Descartes and Luther was possible because the power of the idea of freedom in secular and sacred domains was already at work. Modern philosophy is emphatically announced with the Cartesian "cogito," which epistemologically established the ego even before God's existence could be proven; and modern society separates church and state, enabling the latter to develop unabated, an arrangement consistent with Luther's argument for the absolute freedom of Christians.

Descartes and Luther were both metaphysical dualists, a perspective that modernity has consistently associated with the mind's or soul's freedom. Though we find in Sor Juana an obedience that seems to be wrapped in the medieval worldview, a closer reading discovers that her final acquiescence to religious authority was deeply ironic. In other words, the freedom that characterizes modern philosophy, religion, politics, and culture, also undergirds Sor Juana's *Response*, but in a veiled way. But her freedom, as I will show, in no way relies on ontological or value dualisms. For the *Response* is above all a complex narrative of her inclination toward letters (64). To understand Sor Juana's modernity, the possibility of her unique feminism, then, the scope and meaning of "letters" and "inclination" must first be understood.

Earlier I described Sor Juana's convent cell as a salon. This is our first indication of what "letters" signifies. When we make allowances for the socioeconomic functions of, and constraints on, communication in New Spain, we see that the multifarious activities within her cell, as opposed to either church or court, must have had primary importance to her. She *taught* the women and men who came regularly, among other reasons, to enjoy her erudition and wit; there were poetic, dramatic, and musical *performances* by Sor Juana and others; and, *discussions* ranged freely from philosophical, religious, scientific, and aesthetic topics to court and ecclesiastical gossip. During her time alone she *wrote*, mostly sacred and secular poetry and plays (and she must have had correspondence with other intellectuals), and devoted a great deal of time to the *study* of literature, nature, theology, philosophy, and much else. In this regard, however, she tells us (and the authorities suspicious of her scholarship) that books were the least source of her learning, that nature itself was a continuous source, and that culture, the social-historical world, provided her the greatest opportunity for developing "letters."

The *Response* narrates her "inclination" to all these domains of learning and activity. Juana Inés recognized her inclination very early on, so we are not surprised to learn that it was "inflamed" (28) when she saw her older sister going off to school. In a passage that combines a reference to the Cartesian "light of reason" with a reference to the medieval notion of natural "inclination," Sor Juana introduces us to the central theme of her narrative, and we glimpse her distinctive blending of modern and premodern motifs.

> I have never written of my own choice, but at the urging of others, to whom with reason I might say, *You have compelled me*. But one truth I shall not deny . . . which is that from the moment I was first illuminated by the light of reason, my inclination toward letters has been so vehement, so overpowering, that not even the admonitions of others—and I have suffered many—nor my own meditations—and they have not been few—have been sufficient to cause me to forswear this natural impulse that God placed in me. . . . I have prayed that He dim the light of my reason, leaving only that which is needed to keep His Law, for there are those who would say that all else is unwanted in a woman, and there are even those who would hold that such knowledge does injury. And my Holy Father knows too that as I have been unable to achieve this (my prayer has not been answered), I have sought to veil the light of my reason—along with my name. (Sor Juana 1987, 26)

The "inclination to letters" is a natural, God-implanted impulse, *part of her nature*, and this is why she cannot overcome it and why prayer is not answered. In the course of her narrative, she mentions four groups of reasons that show that letters was her specific inclination, in the natural law sense, and not merely a perverse pleasure. This inclination was: evident from a very early age, consistent throughout her life, firm against all obstacles, and highly developed in spite of everything.

What are we to make of those, past and present, who claim that, in her case, "knowledge does injury"? Given what we know of her attitude toward letters, we can see that Sor Juana does not agree that *knowledge* injures women. It is clear that those who think so are not those who have urged her to study and write, to develop the natural talents that she discovered as soon as she could think. The damages of knowledge arise because some begin by asserting that it is wrong for women to acquire it; the injuries result from insisting that a long-standing social convention (based on a false belief) be superimposed upon a natural condition, in this case, a woman's creative talents, "inclinations." Thus, Sor Juana sought to disguise and mask her reason, her "name," her true nature. In effect, she is telling (some of) her readers to look behind and below the surface of the text. Ironically, because her meaning is veiled by irony, this natural inclination is more deeply revealed.

What is the scope and meaning of "inclination"? Since a survey of Sor Juana's references to this important concept, though obviously essential, is not sufficient, we will need to briefly review the theory of natural law. In the theory of natural law, inclination is the specific expression of God's will upon nature (whether natural objects, cosmic forces, species, or persons). The ground of inclination is "natural law."[6] St. Thomas Aquinas, incorporating Aristotelian physics and ethics into Christian doctrine, defined law (*Summa Theologica*, Question 91) as a rule or measure of acts. And there are three kinds of law: eternal, natural, human. Eternal law is God's conception of natural *kinds* at the moment of creation; each thing is (or is imprinted with) its proper acts and ends. For example, the proposition of Newtonian physics that bodies attract one another according to the product of their masses and inversely according to the square of the distance between them is God's conception of what gravity shall be, eternal law written into the nature of physical mass. Natural law, on the other hand, is what enables rational creatures to be subject to divine providence "more excellently"; they partake of a share of Divine providence in being provident for self and others. Natural law is a "share" of eternal reason "whereby it [the creature] has a natural inclination to its proper act and end; and this participation of the eternal law in the rational creature is called natural law"; "an imprint on us of the divine light." Sor Juana's understanding of her "inclination" consists of these Aristotelian and Thomistic elements.[7]

So it would be a mistake to take literally Sor Juana's reference to her inclination to letters as her worst enemy, as merely a means of self-development rather than something done for the glory of God (Sor Juana 1987, 32).[8] For if she believes her inclination to be God-given, and if it is the source of her life's meaning because its development is equivalent to glorifying God, and if the damages of knowledge result from institutionalized male bias and ignorance, then there is deep irony in her characterizations of her inclination as her worst enemy. Hagiographic readings must miss important dimensions of her thought.

Similarly ironic is her reference to this "dark inclination" (negra inclinación) conquering all else (Sor Juana 1987, 42). After all, her inclination was the ungovernable force (44) that turned her toward letters. Her reflective reason is beyond her will to control (60), even in dreams (64). Since she was made rational, she argues, she should become learned. The role of institutionalized religion in her actual vocation was to provide for her support, and to protect an unmarried woman from the vicissitudes of life, and, as poet and scholar, to shield her from and permit her to manage the distractions of society. In other words, her becoming a nun was what made letters at all possible for her. What was not possible for her was to obey the prohibition to not study (58), to be intellectually silent.

In the end, her obedience in giving up her books and silencing her pen is thoroughly ironic. The scope and meaning of "inclination" ranges over

Sor Juana's entire existence: it extends back into her childhood, shaping it, carries her from court to convent, and causes her to confound, as long as she can, the orders of her religious superiors. The obedience then is paradoxically both modern and medieval. In modern *defiance* of the dominant institution Sor Juana continues to foster her inclination toward letters in obedience to her Aristotelian or medieval *nature*.[9] She finally does conform to the powerful conventions embodied in Church authority, but she ironically uses her insistent inclination to speak and subvert important aspects of those domains in the act of obedience itself.

Neoplatonic "Philosophies of the Kitchen" and Irigaray

Sor Juana's distinctive feminism calls into question a simple Aristotelian-Thomistic basis for her argument against New Spain's patriarchy. From the philosophical meaning of inclination she infers an equality beyond natural differences; nevertheless, she qualifies such equality by appealing to aspects of neoplatonism that reconceptualize fundamental differences as equal. In effect, Sor Juana uses the Aristotelian-Thomist perspective to establish equality (attack patriarchy), but goes on to argue that sex differences have basic relevance for equal social arrangements and opportunities. Thus, she implicitly asserts two kinds of equality.

We have seen that there should be equal access to some spheres of activity. Since the different sexes as such can have equal inclinations and capacities in some spheres, then they should be equally educated and have equal opportunities to develop themselves in those spheres; women should not be proscribed from certain secular spheres, in particular scientific and literary (including pagan) areas, nor any of the sacred domains of letters. So one equality refers to persons irrespective of inclinations that derive from sex. But the sexes do not naturally engage in all the same spheres of activity; some inclinations are sex-derived. Thus, we must recognize a second sort of equality such that all spheres are equal. Therefore, women's domains should have equal status, for they have as great a potential to teach us about spirit, society, and nature, and to contribute to our well-being, as do men's.[10]

What narrative details support two kinds of equality, one independent of reference to sex characteristics and one consistent with natural (or basic) differences? With respect to the first sort, we have seen that Sor Juana cites examples from sacred literature of women having pursued and excelled in letters. The Church fathers permitted letters for women; Paul and others mentioned in Scripture allowed letters to all. As I mentioned above, Sor Juana's own inclination toward secular letters is well demonstrated by the details of the narrative itself: her Aristotelian "substance" as a natural and specific self inclined toward letters is evident from the earliest age, was consistent throughout her life, was firm against all obstacles, and became highly developed in spite of everything. Moreover, her developed gifts greatly benefitted others. In using the philosophical resources of patriarchy against itself, Sor Juana exemplifies the first sort of equality: women should have equal access to domains where differences are not natural but only conventional or socially constituted.

Sor Juana's proto-feminist standpoint on inclination goes far beyond what the Church of New Spain was able to accommodate. And yet she is not satisfied with that standpoint strategically because it comes to an impasse, and not satisfied theoretically because its categories are limited to Aristotle and Aquinas. When honoring the first sort of equality, if men teach women (an allusion to Abelard and Heloise), history shows that domination and other perils are typical. These would result in an injury to "nuestra república" (75, see also 72–76). Today, we should refer to this as an injury to the body politic arising from the institutionalized arrogance of sexism. But conversely, when women teach men we find murder (Hypatia of Alexandria, murdered by monks in 415 (66)) and other dramatic persecutions (Sor Juana herself). And note the nature of one of the prominent obstacles Sor Juana mentions: some men believe they are wise merely because they are "hombres" (69). Sor Juana suggests that one reason women should teach women is so they may become cultured for themselves and in their own ways. Of course, there are also dangers in intimacy with men. History and culture, then, issue in conflicts with nature's inclinations. So, equality based on the Aristotelian-Thomistic standpoint, while good in itself, results in a strategic impasse.

And these limitations echo the problems that Sandra Harding has found with "standpoint" feminisms. In "The Instability of the Analytical Categories of Feminist Theory" and elsewhere,[11] Harding has analyzed problematic, conflicting developments in feminist theory. She finds internal correspondences between the modes of patriarchal power institutionalized in society, on the one hand, and the legitimate forms of knowledge discovery and justification within those societies, on the other. The essentialism of both traditional empiricisms and rationalisms, their postulation of some sense experiences or rational insights as Archimedian, constitute them as "master" theories. But attempts to reform such empiricisms or rationalisms, to produce "successor" standpoints which critique and reform the masculine-constituted standpoints, incorporate mastering or "policing" aspects of those views. In short, Handing argues that standpoint theories and their offshoots in successor sciences are inadequate (though necessary) models for feminist theory since they fail to overcome, since they conceal within themselves, forms of illegitimate social power.[12] The way out of such theoretical impasses, Harding thinks, is to "embrace the instability" of feminist theories' analytical categories, to see that they have no foundation, even as one uses them to critique standpoints that claim foundations or essential truths. This introduction of perspectivism (or postmodernism) is claimed to be more productive than standpoints because critical leverage can then be immanent but partial (not totalizing), and dynamic but stable (because continuous with previous categories).

> How can feminism afford to give up a successor science project if it is to empower all women in a world where socially legitimated knowledge and the political power associated with it are firmly lodged in white, Western, bourgeois, compulsorily heterosexual, men's hands? Yet how can we give up our distrust of the historic links between this legitimated knowledge and political power?
> One way to see these two tendencies in feminist theory is as converging approaches to a postmodernist world—a world that will not exist until both (conflicting) tendencies achieve their goals. (Harding 1987, 295)

How does Sor Juana get beyond her strategic and theoretical impasse? How does the second sort of equality get articulated in the *Response*? To see this double move we must first set forth the neoplatonic aspects of the *Response*, for they function as her foundationless "perspectivism"; they destabilize, without abandoning, the Aristotelian standpoint. And in this way the second sort of equality is grounded.

The neoplatonic tradition[13] was embodied in a trope that became constitutive for European thought, society, and culture. The "great chain of being" (Lovejoy 1960) was a value-ranked scale of creatures and entities, an ontological series of continuous links and gradations. The core concepts for all this come from Plato: the Idea of the Good in the *Republic* was the logical foundation for Plotinus's inward, ethical movement (reditus); the Demiurge of the *Timaeus* created a sensible world modelled on the intelligible world, what Plotinus calls the outward, ontological movement (exitus). Thus, the cosmic tree of life is continuous and full, a plenitude in the continuum of *logos* or reason, a great chain of being.

The neoplatonic aspects of Sor Juana's writing, especially her poetry, are widely recognized.[14] So, as with the cluster of Thomist and Aristotelian notions centered on the concept of inclination, it is not surprising to find neoplatonic elements in the *Response*. The great chain of being is what guides and grounds her reference to the hierarchical scale of reason. "For no other cause except that the angel is superior in reason is the angel above man; for no other cause does man stand above the beast but by his reason" (Sor Juana 1987, 52). And it informs her use of the image of the face of Moses being changed merely by being in conversation with (the face of) God (48). Her repeated use of the idea of "hidden links" reinforces the medieval great chain and connects it to the complex modern theme of silence (see Sor Juana 1987, 20, 38, 48, 58, 62). And the scale of being is taken to an audacious height when, in an extended passage, Sor Juana uses it to compare herself to Christ (46–58).

At the conclusion of her chain of neoplatonic interventions, Sor Juana announces that if Aristotle, the philosophical father of inclination, had "prepared victuals, he would have written more" (62). With this, Sor Juana moves away from the personal, historical, and intellectual impasse of an Aristotelian inclination that faces institutionalized patriarchy. But the ground of inclination is not simply replaced by the neoplatonic chain. For by invidiously placing Aristotle in the kitchen she also breaks with the traditional great chain of being to move toward a *gendered* neoplatonism[15] (and see note 10), naming this crucial move her "philosophies of the kitchen" (62). This does indeed subvert inclination as fundamental, but it simultaneously preserves differences in the continuity of the chain of being. Sor Juana's discovery of "natural secrets," the many hidden links of the chain, points back to a paradoxically *bottomless* foundation. For beyond the hidden links between phenomena and the scales of reason and being we saw that Solomon's Temple, whose Author was God, was foundationless in the sense that there is "no foundation without mystery" (34). No point is Archimedian. And yet, gender remains basic to her perspective in that women must teach women, some women simply cannot marry, and communication among sybils cannot be substituted for.

Gendered neoplatonism is consistent with Sor Juana's Aristotelian feminism. The Aristotelian standpoint acknowledges inclinations specific to the natural kinds of sex; this is the ontological, outward movement in the neoplatonic scheme. At the same time, she can claim that there are different spheres of activity based on these inclinations that are equal to each other; this corresponds to the neoplatonic ethical, inward movement. However, in her philosophies of the kitchen Sor Juana recognizes possible exchanges between nature and culture that cannot be discerned using positivist categories of Aristotelian natural law (or what we might now call Kuhnian normal science or Harding's successor science), and neither can they be reduced to (what we would now call) the nominalism of socially constituted practices, the postmodernist trumping move Harding recommends we somehow enact.

Different from yet similar to both the feminism of the Aristotelian standpoint on inclination and the postmodernism of foundationlessness analogous to some contemporary perspectivists, Sor Juana's two forms of equality constitute a distinctive version of the neoplatonic inward movement. And we also find a distinctive outward movement that overcomes contemporary feminism's liberal Charybdis and postmodern Scylla, its ontological essentialism versus relativism (social constructionism), on the one hand, and its epistemological realism versus nominalism, on the other.

These global features of Sor Juana's *Response* bring her very close to what Luce Irigaray calls an "ethics of sexual difference." For virtually her whole life Sor Juana refused what Irigaray calls the "ethical mistake" of woman's "destiny," and thus was able to develop "access to mind," "to find and speak her meaning" (Irigaray 1993, 126). Nevertheless, she was "faithful to a process of the divine which passe[d] through her . . . without . . . falling prisoner to . . . the question of 'God'" (118). I will conclude this essay by indicating some of these Irigarayan parallels.[16]

Like Irigaray, Sor Juana rejects androgyny because "the world is not undifferentiated" (126); "each sex has its own interests, needs, and desires, and therefore represents limits to the interests, needs, and desires of the other sex. . . . Women's needs for autonomy, freedom of movement, sexual self-determination . . . clash with male desire for their containment, enclosure, or control" (Whitford 1991, 165f). Indeed, Sor Juana's "total negación" of marriage seems based on a belief, like Irigaray's, that "women and men are ontologically *incommensurable*" (Irigaray 1993, 209n6, italics in original). Correlated with these ontological differences for Irigaray, as for Sor Juana, are ethical and political norms. Sex "difference needs to be *represented* so that women exist as such in systems of representation, and *a fortiori* so that women have a distinct legal, civil, and ethical status" (Irigaray 1993, 173, italics in original). And yet, neither ontological nor ethical differences should be interpreted as essential. Sor Juana is not essentialist insofar as she subverts Aristotelian ontology with a foundationless neoplatonism. Similarly, Whitford explains that Irigaray uses the language of fixed identity in order to get beyond it.

> Irigaray's insistence on nature, then, is not at all crude biologism. It is intended to expose the complicity of philosophy in maintaining a completely traditional symbolic division between the sexes. Her so-called essentialism is primarily a strategy for bringing to light the concealed essentialism of philosophy. . . . It is ironic that someone who is arguing for the *re*structuring and *re*symbolizing of male and female 'nature' should be seen as essentializing, i.e., as assigning a fixed nature to each sex. (Whitford 1991, 94, italics in original; see also 84, 103, and 135f)

By simultaneously incorporating being and meaning, the ontological and the ethical, into her perspective, Sor Juana goes beyond Aristotle, just as Irigaray goes beyond traditional "philosophy" by strategically mimicking and using it. But in this Irigaray is not really postmodern, according to Whitford, since she argues that, whatever the avatars of the history of 'truth,' whether in its deeply influential Platonic version, or whether in the anti-Platonic critiques and the 'postmodernist' pluralism that they have ushered in, the scene of representation allows only the 'same' and the 'other of the same' to take the stage. Plato and his critics have that much in common. For that reason, women [should] not simply oppose a female truth to a male truth. (Whitford 1991, 105; see also 143, 154)[17]

This seems to be a feature common to our general and Sor Juana's particular situations: one's "historical location, in which the current necessity for affirmative political action appears to be undercut by the necessity for theoretical negativity" (124). These characteristics are seen in Sor Juana's resistance to authority through ironic subversion. Like Antigone, according to Irigaray, we have to "take the negative upon ourselves" (Irigaray 1993, 120).

As a last correspondence[18] I would like to refer to the striking fact that each of these thinkers has issued a call for a dual conception of rights. I argued above that Sor Juana claims that two sorts of equality should be taken into account, given historical and social conditions as they were, an equality within shared spheres and an equality of different spheres. Whitford's interpretation of Irigaray refers to the former, traditional rights as short term and to the latter, as yet undeveloped ones, as longterm; the former are preconditions of the latter. Irigaray argues for equal rights as "the first condition for the question of specific women's rights to be raised at all. . . . So it is necessary to distinguish between rights in the short term and rights in the long term. . . . [T]he price paid for equal rights [alone] in an otherwise untransformed society can be too high" (Whitford 1991, 184f).

Sor Juana's life became a blend of beliefs in the hidden powers of the natural world, the ontologically outward movement, together with the faith that with effort one could ascend to truth, the ethically inward movement. Paz says that her cosmos, unlike Dante's, was infinite, and that her God, contrary to Aquinas's, was a primal power, not a personal presence. As a philosopher, Sor Juana located and then developed a space from which to speak, necessarily ironically in her case, a *logos* of silences and mysteries but with which sacred and secular learning, and social and historical observation and evaluation, were bound up. From this space she put forward a complex argument for a complex equality whose terms we have not yet clearly discerned how to articulate. Her feminism takes off from the literal but socially constructed kitchen and any other traditionally constituted categories and domains of theory and practice. For Thomism, inclinations establish natural kinds and are determining for all, and some inclinations establish inequalities over time; for neoplatonism, gender as a social convention subverts the great chain or cosmic order because there is no foundation. Together these contrasting perspectives did not quite create an instability, but allowed Sor Juana to develop a space of profoundly fecund silences into which, at the end of her life, she withdrew in ironic obedience.

NOTES

1. I use Margaret Sayers Peden's translation (on facing pages), *A Woman of Genius: The Intellectual Autobiography of Sor Juana Inés de la Cruz. A Sor Juana Anthology*, Alan S. Trueblood, trans., contains not only the *Response (La Respuesta)*, "First Dream," and several other poems, but also a useful "Introduction."

2. Sandra Harding has critically elaborated the notion of "standpoint epistemology," explained below. In brief, it includes reference to the privileged epistemological and moral insights available to those who have had to bear systematic oppressions and who, as a result, have come to better understand the systems of oppression they must survive under.

3. See Arenal 1983, 178. Arenal argues that convents were a form of semiautonomous culture that allowed women to develop their talents.

4. "Until Sor Juana's final years, her life as a bride of Christ was anything but that of a typical nun. Having spent nearly five years as a lady-in-waiting at the Viceregal court in Mexico City, she continued her ties with the secular world, often receiving the Viceroys and other prominent figures of the day as visitors in the cloister and writing commissioned secular verses and drama (the majority of her literary production)"(Myers 1990, 455).

5. Ludmer goes on to argue that Sor Juana thus finds "a space beyond sexual difference" (92) by "changing, from within [her] assigned and accepted place, not only its meaning but the very meaning of what is established within its confines. As does a mother or homemaker who says, 'I accept my place, but as a mother or homemaker I will engage in politics or science'" (93). In my view, Sor Juana does not accept the place authority assigns her to, even as she submits; rather, she changes its meaning by challenging some and shifting other of its fundamental assumptions. It would be interesting and instructive to make explicit and further elaborate Ludmer's semiotic reading of the *Response*. For while such an approach is what prevents her from seeing that Sor Juana does not accept her place, since the structural possibilities dictate otherwise, it nevertheless could be used to reveal and explore unsuspected meanings in the text.

6. This notion, in turn, derives from the Greek understanding that there is a *kosmos*, a natural order and beauty. Heraclitus described the natural order ontologically as an everliving fire, with measures kindling and measures going out;

Antigone, in Sophocles' *Antigone*, refers to permanent values, inherent in the nature of things, that are neither conventional nor written, that are not subject to change in history, however our recognition of them may vary. In *Romans* 2:14–15 nature is said to have engraved a law in the heart of pagans which they can know. Later, the Stoics claimed that reason interprets the order of the world in the form of natural norms. In modern philosophy the idea of natural law has been refashioned through Protestant jurisprudence, especially Grotius's work in the seventeenth century. It became the model for positive (human) law, and a kind of limit concept for law givers. With such a grounding notion, it is thought, we are enabled to improve and to critique human law. For example, it was with this sense of natural law that Martin Luther King, Jr. was able to justify civil disobedience. Other functions of natural law include enabling us: (1) to *see* the applications of positive law where precedent is inadequate; (2) to *regulate* the conflicts between laws (e.g., person vs. property); (3) to *create* new laws.

7. The Aristotelian and Thomistic aspects of her poetry have been very carefully detailed. For example, Gerard Flynn says that her most important single poem, which many say is her most important single work, *El sueño* (The Dream, commonly known as "First Dream"), "is an Aristotelian-Thomistic explanation of the nature of human knowledge" (Flynn 1971, 27). Constance M. Montross has analyzed the two main texts of Sor Juana's corpus, the *Response* and "First Dream," for their Thomistic (and thereby Aristotelian) elements (Montross 1981).

8. This is the hagiographic type of interpretation Montross consistently presents. Thus, she takes literally Sor Juana's claim that writing about theological matters was particularly difficult for her (6). More plausibly, however, we should see the rhetoric of courtly and ecclesiastical conventions at work in such self-effacement. Montross also takes literally Sor Juana's repeated characterization of her inclination to letters as an "excess," in spite of the repeated claim that it was God-given and the evidence that it was beneficial to her and to others. In other words, *for Sor Juana*, the inclination is an opportunity for virtue, but for Montross and others its development is excessive, not normal, and so a vice. This, of course, simply takes the point of view of the Church patriarchy that some women may have talents that would be unnatural, hence immoral, for them to develop. Similarly, George Tavard's interpretation of Sor Juana's motive empties her of spirit. "It is well known that Sor Juana has written out of obedience (to the demands of her patrons)" (Tavard 1991, 168). Tavard also claims that for her "basic understanding of the self, she squarely chooses Platonism" (185). This in spite of her Aristotelianism and neoplatonism (which I show below).

9. In his "Introduction" Trueblood oddly denies that Sor Juana would affirm her own intellectual independence (Sor Juana 1988, 9). More consistently, he later acknowledges that her stand against the authorities was taken "with what her sympathizers must have seen as reckless defiance" (10). And later, speaking of her "lack of a formal education," he notes her "vast intellectual ambition and the self-reliance needed to pursue it" (21).

10. Merrim follows Ludmer and Myers in arguing that Sor Juana, probably like most contemporary feminists, does not defend sexual difference.

> Sor Juana militantly defends a woman's right to education and, by implication, participation in the male order. All of this together, added to the example of her own literary life, but substantiates the obvious: that—as is entirely natural in view of the context in which she wrote—rather than asserting or projecting women's "difference," both ideologically and literally Sor Juana sought to *negate* their difference, to introject or appropriate the masculine realm for the feminine and to place them on the same continuum. (23, original emphasis)

This interpretation neglects the two-edged argument for equality that Sor Juana puts forward using both Aristotelian and neoplatonic categories. The former, based on inclination, does indeed set difference aside, but the latter, I argue below, uses neoplatonic ontology to establish gendered perspectives. Hence, the "philosophies of the kitchen."

11. Harding 1987, 1989.

12. Of course, not all social power in knowledge production is illegitimate. See Longino, 1990.

13. This last of the great pagan philosophies found its systematizer in Plotinus. Programmatically, we may note five characteristics of neoplatonism: (1) it rejects all dualisms, particularly in metaphysics and ethics; (2) the One is the center and all else is *emanation* or creation from it; (3) emanation occurs by and through *logos*, and this in a double movement; (4) metaphysically *from* the One and ethically *to* the One; so that in the end (5) all things are unified in a normative hierarchy of being. Although neoplatonism has mystical tendencies, Flynn argues persuasively that Sor Juana should not be considered a mystic in any of the usual senses because of her emphatically intellectualistic inclinations.

14. Jose Pascual-Buxó argues (and Paz agrees) that "First Dream" not only reconciles Aristotelian psychology and neoplatonic teleology, but that it also bridges the Aristotelian psychological and hermetic doctrines that Sor Juana adapted from the Jesuit Kircher and the *Corpus Hermeticum* (11, 7). Ptolemaic cosmology, Aristotelian and Galenian physics and physiology—in other words, the whole tradition of Alexandrian neoplatonism—according to Pascual-Buxó, permit her simultaneously and productively to use apparently irreconcilable systems (3, 13). Paz simply calls this her syncretism. Given her feminism, I think we have to see her syncretism as her having opted neither for a quasi-modern Aristotelian standpoint nor a quasi-postmodern neoplatonic perspectivism. Rather her foundationlessness is ironic. Referring to Kircher in the *Response*, she says that "the Reverend Father Athanasius Kircher [demonstrated] in his curious book, *De Magnate* [that a]ll things issue from God, Who is at once the center and the circumference from which and in which all lines begin and end" (40).

15. So Myers, like Merrim, is misleading to argue that Sor Juana's feminism is best based on a neoplatonic androgyny of soul. Soul, as opposed to intellect alone, cannot be simply an androgynous blend for Sor Juana, since inclinations specific to her as a woman are such strong features of it. Besides, it does not make sense to say that Sor Juana is androgynous but "accomplishes this task [of negating sex differences] through her appropriation of masculine discourse for her own ends" (464) when we know that some of those ends are sex-specific, e.g., establishes women's discourse and education. I think some readers have confused Sor Juana's use of an Aristotelian standpoint, which recognizes sex specific characteristics, with androgyny. On the other hand, it is true that Sor Juana incorporates other features of inclination into her discussion, and that her neoplatonism of the intellect uses androgyny. But her feminism is not reducible to either of these perspectives.

16. Elaine Showalter has described a similar configuration in the "first wave" of feminist male literary criticism.

> Where Derrida insists that hierarchical oppositions (such as man/woman) must be deconstructed through reversal rather than denial, feminist critics must put this principle into action, must choose whether to ally themselves with the reformist position of sexual equality, which denies difference, or with the radical position which asserts the difference, the power, and the superiority of the feminine. Their position on the specificity of women's writing, their critical style and voice, will be determined by this choice. [Jonathan] Culler [*On Deconstruction*] recognizes that both positions are valid, although as a Derridean he prefers the rhetorical reversal. Most feminist critics, in fact, play both ends against the middle—advocating social, academic, institutional equality, but textual difference. These positions are not oppositional, but responsive to women's different roles as citizens or as writers. (Showalter 1983, 140)

Showalter goes on to critique male feminists who do not acknowledge the limitations of their interventions into feminist discourse. "Reading as a feminist . . . is not unproblematic; but it has the important aspect of offering male readers a way to produce feminist criticism that avoids female impersonation. The way into feminist criticism, for the male theorist, must involve a confrontation with what might be implied by reading as a man, and with a questioning or surrender of paternal privileges" (143).

17. For other indications of Sor Juana's anticipations of postmodernism, see Merrim n41, n44.

18. There are other important features I do not have the space to develop, but I will mention one other important one. Irigaray's notion of a "sensible transcendental" (*An Ethics*, 129; see also Whitford's discussion) functions as does Sor Juana's neoplatonism, as the subversive moment for both theoretical and practical problems that neither destroys the defining elements nor depends upon them, but uses them to get bearings on a "horizon." But it is not so perspectivalizing as Harding's embracing the instability as to make her a postmodernist.

REFERENCES

Arenal, Electa. 1983. The convent as catalyst for autonomy: Two Hispanic nuns of the seventeenth century. In *Women in Hispanic literature: Icons and fallen idols*, ed. Beth Miller. Berkeley: University of California Press.

Flynn, Gerald. 1971. *Sor Juana Inés de la Cruz*. New York: Twayne.

Harding, Sandra. 1987. The instability of the analytical categories of feminist theory. In *Sex and scientific inquiry*, ed. Sandra Harding and Jean F. O'Barr. Chicago: University of Chicago Press.

———. 1989. Feminist justificatory strategies. In *Women, knowledge, and reality: Explorations in feminist philosophy*, ed. Ann Garry and Marilyn Pearsall. Boston: Unwin Hyman.

Irigaray, Luce. 1993. *An ethics of sexual difference*. Trans. Carolyn Burke and Gillian C. Gill. Ithaca: Cornell University Press.

Juana Inés de la Cruz, Sister. 1951–57. *Obras completas de Sor Juana, IV*, ed. Alberto Salceda. Mexico: Fondo de Cultura Economica.

———. 1987. *A woman of genius: The intellectual autobiography of Sor Juana Inés de la Cruz*. 2nd ed. Trans. Margaret Sayers Peden. Salisbury, CT: Lime Rock Press.

———. 1988. *A Sor Juana Anthology*. Trans. Alan S. Trueblood, Cambridge: Harvard University Press.

Longino, Helen. 1990. *Science as social knowledge*. Princeton: Princeton University Press.

Lovejoy, Arthur O. 1960. *The great chain of being: A study of the history of an idea*. New York: Harper and Row.

Ludmer, Josefina. 1991. Tricks of the weak. Trans. Stephanie Merrim. In *Feminist persepectives on Sor Juana Inés de la Cruz*, ed. Stephanie Merrim. Detroit: Wayne State University Press.

Montross, Constance M. 1981. Virtue or vice? Sor Juana's use of Thomistic thought. Washington, D.C.: University Press of America.

Myers, Kathleen A. 1990. Phaeton as emblem: Recent works on Sor Juana Inés de la Cruz. *Michigan Quarterly Review* 29 (3).

Pascual-Buxó, José. 1989. Sor Juana egipciana (Aspectos neoplatónicos de *El Sueño*). *Mester* xviii (2).

Paz, Octavio. 1988. *Sor Juana: or, The traps of faith*. Cambridge: Harvard University Press.

Showalter, Elaine. 1983. Critical cross-dressing: Male feminists and the woman of the year. *Raritan* 3 (2).

Tavard, George. 1991. *Juana Inés de la Cruz and the theology of beauty: The first Mexican theology*. South Bend, IN: Notre Dame Press.

Whitford, Margaret. 1991. *Luce Irigaray: A philosophy in the feminine*. London: Routledge.

DAMARIS CUDWORTH MASHAM
A SEVENTEENTH–CENTURY FEMINIST PHILOSOPHER

LOIS FRANKEL

Damaris Cudworth lived from January 18, 1659 to April 20, 1708. She was the daughter of Ralph Cudworth, a prominent member of the Cambridge Platonist school, who authored a lengthy but unfinished treatise, *The True Intellectual System of the Universe*, a criticism of atheistic determinism. He had intended, but never accomplished, the addition of a criticism of Calvinism. This opposition to Calvinism, combined with opposition to Hobbes, were central features of Cambridge Platonist philosophy. In addition, the Cambridge Platonists held that God is essentially rational and that true Christians ought to emulate that rationality. They held also (as did Leibniz) that God should be adjudged good based on its works, rather than God's works being considered good just because God performed them. Many of these views, as we shall see, play important roles in Damaris Cudworth Masham's work.

Though denied access to higher education, as were all women of her time, Damaris Cudworth grew up accustomed to philosophical discourse. She shared many philosophical views with her father and many with Locke (indeed, often the two men's views were compatible) and frequently wrote in defense of both their views (Passmore, 91).[1] Her relationship with Locke was close, and was personal as well as philosophical. They had enjoyed a romantic attachment prior to her marriage to Sir Francis Masham in 1685, and continued a close friendship thereafter. It was at the Masham home, Oates, that Locke ended his days in 1704, having been a resident beginning 1691. Locke wrote admiringly of Masham:

> The lady herself is so well versed in theological and philosophical studies, and of such an original mind, that you will not find many men to

Hypatia vol. 4, no. 1 (Spring 1989) © by Lois Frankel

whom she is not superior in wealth of knowledge and ability to profit by it. Her judgment is excellent, and I know few who can bring such clearness of thought to bear upon the most abstruse subjects, or such capacity for searching through and solving the difficulties of questions beyond the range, I do not say of most women, but even of most learned men. From reading, to which she once devoted herself with much assiduity, she is now to a great extent debarred by the weakness of her eyes, but this defect is abundantly supplied by the keenness of her intellect (Bourne II, 213).[2]

During Locke's residency, the household was visited by Isaac Newton (Bourne II, 219), with whom Masham and Locke discussed the Bible, and Francis Mercury Van Helmont (Cranston, 374), the latter a close friend of Anne Conway, author of *The Principles of the Most Ancient and Modern Philosophy*, and a strong influence on Leibniz.[3] Although there is no direct evidence that Conway's work was discussed in Van Helmont's visit, it is not unlikely that it was. Masham had at least a passing acquaintance with Conway's work through Leibniz, who mentions Conway in passing to Masham in a letter of December 14/25 1703 (Gerhardt III, 337). Additionally, Ralph Cudworth's fellow Cambridge Platonist Henry More was a close friend of Conway's.[4]

Faith and Reason

Masham's works include *A Discourse Concerning the Love of God* (1696, a reply to John Norris' *Practical Discourses*), *Occasional Thoughts in reference to a Virtuous or Christian Life* (1705), and correspondence with Locke and Leibniz. Masham wrote to Locke on April 7, 1688 in praise of an abridgement of Locke's *Essay*, which he had recently published in order to elicit criticism and interest in the full work. Masham apologized for her limited knowledge of philosophy, mentioning her poor eyesight and that she had been discouraged from reading philosophical books. It is unclear whether this discouragement was solely on the grounds of her failing sight, or because those who discouraged her considered such reading unsuitable for her. Nevertheless, in agreement with her father's position on the issue, she challenged Locke's denial of innate ideas, suggesting that his difference with those who believed in such ideas was not 'really so great as it seems,' because the proponents of innate ideas had not claimed that specific ideas were innate, but only that there was 'an active sagacity in the soul' (Cranston, 300).[5]

Masham's correspondence with Leibniz primarily addressed metaphysical subjects, including Leibniz's Pre-Established Harmony, the relationship between mind and body, free will, and Cudworth's account of "plastic natures." She also mentioned frequently her friendship with Locke, whose "direction" she credited for the successful upbringing of her son (Gerhardt III, 365).[6] She had sent Leibniz a copy of her father's *The True Intellectual System of the Universe*, writing that "The esteem you express for that work pleases me very much . . . and . . . it is a new confirmation to me of the worth of that performance" (Gerhardt III, 337).[7]

While Masham had some interest in metaphysics, as we have noted above,[8] her writings emphasized Christian theology, epistemology, and moral philosophy. On this score, her interests included the relationship between faith and reason and the question of the morality of worldly pursuits. In particular, Masham wished in *Occasional Thoughts* to support Locke against Stillingfleet[9] on the relative merits of reason and revelation. Stillingfleet had claimed that Locke upheld reason at the expense of revelation:

> Your answer is, That your Method of Certainty by Ideas, shakes not at all, nor in the least concerns the Assurance of Faith. Against this I have pleaded. 1. That your Method of Certainty shakes the Belief of Revelation in general. 2. That it shakes the Belief of Particular Propositions or Articles of Faith, which depend upon the Sense of Words contained in Scripture.[10]

In his chapter "Of Enthusiasm" (Essay IV.xix, added in the fourth edition), Locke decries "enthusiasm," the rejection of reason in favor of revelation, as an attitude which

> takes away both reason and revelation, and substitutes in the room of them the ungrounded fancies of a man's own brain, and assumes them for a foundation both of opinion and conduct. (Essay VI. xix. 3)

Locke adds that reason and revelation are not so opposed as the enthusiasts believe, but are instead closely related, reason being "natural revelation" and revelation "natural reason enlarged by a new set of discoveries communicated by God immediately" (Essay IV. xix. 4). While genuine revelation is absolutely true and certain, he continues, we must first be certain of having received a revelation, and such certainty must be more than "ungrounded persuasion" of our own minds (Essay IV. xix. 11). It must at least "be conformable to the principles of reason" or be attended with some outward sign of revelation, such as a miracle (Essay IV. xix. 14).

Writing in support of Locke, Masham reiterates his claims that revelation may provide rational grounds for belief (1705, 34), but that reason must be employed in order to determine whether a revelation has indeed occurred. Absurdities must be denied the status of revelation, for no revelation could be contrary to reason (1705, 35). In this position, she is in accord with the Cambridge Platonist view that God is essentially rational and that good Christians ought to emulate that rationality.

Masham argues further that a preference for revelation alone over revelation scrutinized by reason would lead people to consider Christianity to be unreasonable, resulting either in the rejection of reason in favor of faith ("enthusiasm") or in the rejection of faith in favor of reason: skepticism. Nevertheless, she argues in *Occasional Thoughts* that religion provides the only sufficient support for virtue, based on anticipation of divine reward and fear of divine punishment (1705, 14–5). Although many of the Christian rules of morality are, she thinks, derivable from reason and the "light of nature," our passions will tend to overwhelm us without the steadying influence of religion and a "rational fear of God," "experience showing us that natural light, unassisted by revelation, is insufficient to the ends of natural religion" (1705, 55–6).

> Religion has, I think, been rightly defined to be *the knowledge how to please God,* and thus taken, does necessarily include virtue, that is to say *Moral Rectitude* (1705, 84). . . . . a farther impediment to men's obeying the law of nature, by virtue of the mere light of nature; which is, that they cannot, in all circumstances, without revelation, make always a just estimate in reference to their happiness. (1705, 103)

However, in order to believe that a deity can guide our actions and influence their consequences, we must have solid evidence for religious beliefs (1705, 16). Therefore, Masham objects (perhaps following her father's opposition to dogmatism)[11] to mere rote teaching of catechism (1705, 18ff). If studied only by rote, she argues, the pronouncements of religion often seem contrary to common sense (1705, 20). But Christianity should not seem to be teaching doctrines contrary to reason, for the discovery of its (seeming) absurdity leads people to doubt the reasonability of religion. Masham adds that women are especially susceptible to this doubt, not having the advantage of education to overcome the "ignorance or errors of their childhood" (1705, 21).

Women, Education, and Reason

When examining the works of long-ignored women philosophers, particularly those women who lived during times when philosophy was considered an inappropriate occupation for women, one is moved to look for evidence of feminist attitudes. One first looks for such fairly obvious indications as protests about women's lot in life. These abound in Masham's work, as we shall see in this section. In addition, we might seek more subtle manifestations of feminism, depending on what we count as feminism: Is it meaningful, for example, to speak of epistemology, ethics, theology, or metaphysics as capable of being informed by feminism? Much contemporary work in feminist philosophy suggests that it is indeed meaningful to speak in such terms. Without addressing that issue directly, we will consider in the next section how such a broader interpretation of feminism might shed light on Masham's work.

Explicitly feminist claims are found in several of Masham's arguments: First, she objects to the inferior education accorded women, but primarily on the grounds that such inferior education (a) makes them unfit to educate their children properly and (b) conduces to impiety in women and their children. Impiety occurs because those not properly educated will believe in Christianity out of habit, or rote, rather than out of understanding and therefore will be unable to defend their faith against any doubts with which they may be confronted.

> For if Christianity be a religion from God, and women have souls to be saved as well as men; to know what this religion consists in, and to understand the grounds on which it is to be received, can be no more than necessary knowledge to a woman, as well as to a man: Which necessary knowledge is sufficient to enable any one so far to answer to the opposers or corrupters of Christianity. . . . (1705, 166)

Although by late 20th-century standards Masham's brand of feminism is weak indeed, we must consider the extreme antifeminist times in which she lived. Masham laments the fact that women of her time were discouraged from intellectual endeavors. Being barred from formal higher education was a major impediment which she herself must have felt deeply. Young women of the upper classes were kept busy with social diversions, so that they had no time to spend on the improvement of their understanding (1705, 151). About women of other classes, Masham unfortunately has nothing to say. However they were obviously barred from intellectual activity also. Even though Masham herself was encouraged in her studies by Locke, Leibniz, and her father, it appears to have been the sort of indulgent, paternalistic encouragement given by learned men to exceptional women of leisure. In general, however, she notes that women are dependent on the good opinions of men, and blames the attitudes of men who, for the most part, were not over fond of learning themselves, and thus threatened by educated women, for this sorry state of affairs:

> The improvements of reason, however requisite to ladies for their accomplishment, as rational creatures; and however needful to them for the well educating of their children, and to their being useful in their families, yet are rarely any recommendation of them to men; who fool-

ishly thinking, that money will answer to all things, do, for the most part, regard nothing else in the woman they would marry: and not often finding what they do not look for, it would be no wonder if their offspring should inherit no more sense than themselves. . . . girls, betwixt silly fathers and ignorant mothers, are generally so brought up, that traditionary opinions are to them, all their lives long, instead of reason. (1705, 162)

Thus wretchedly destitute of all that knowledge which they ought to have, are (generally speaking) our English gentlemen: And being so, what wonder it can be, if they like not that women should have knowledge; for this is a quality that will give some sort of superiority even to those who care not to have it? (1705, 174)

As for other science, it is believed so improper for, and is indeed so little allowed them, that it is not to be expected from them: but the cause of this is only the ignorance of men. (1705, 169)

In addition, Masham objects to the double standard of morality imposed on women and men, and especially to the claim that women's 'virtue' consists primarily in chastity (1705, 21). Masham objects to this as insufficient, seeing chastity as a low-level necessary condition, without which a woman would be "contemptible" (1705, 22), and opposes its being considered "the chief merit [women] are capable of having" (1705, 22). To regard chastity in this way, she argues, lowers women's self-esteem or (justifiably) makes them think men unjust. She also points out that being over-proud of one's chastity, while ignoring other virtues, leads to conceit. Chastity should not be considered solely a woman's virtue, but a sacred duty for both sexes:

Chastity (for example) is, according to the Gospel, a duty to both sexes, yet a transgression herein, even with the aggravation of wronging another man, and possibly a whole family thereby, is ordinarily talked as lightly of, as if it was but a peccadillo in a young man, although a far less criminal offense against duty in a maid shall in the opinion of the same persons brand her with perpetual infamy: The nearest relations often times are hardly brought to look upon her after such a dishonor done by her to their family; whilst the fault of her more guilty brother finds but a very moderate reproof from them; and in a little while, it may be, becomes the subject of their mirth and raillery. And why still is this wrong placed distinction made, but because there are measures of living established by men themselves according to a conformity, or disconformity with which, and not with the precepts of Jesus Christ, their actions are measured, and judged of? (1705, 155)

Here Masham has reminded the reader that conventional moral and religious teaching is not always in accord with rational Christianity. True virtue is action in accord with "right reason" and the Gospel, which are "one and the same, differently promulged" (1705, 97–8), not the exact observance of custom or civil institutions (1705, 96). Virtue is not just following the rules, as religion is not just reciting the catechism. Both require the proper employment of the understanding.

Epistemology, Feminism, and Moral Philosophy

It has been argued recently by Nancy Chodorow (1978) and Carol Gilligan (1982) that the 'male experience' resulting from child-rearing practices in our society encourages males to define their masculinity in terms of separation and detachment, while the same practices result in a 'female experience' which encourages females to define themselves in terms of relation and connection. These self-definitions, Gilligan argues, shape our moral life, females tending to make decisions in terms of relationships, males in terms of rules and abstractions.[12] Nancy Holland (1986) has extended these theories to epistemology, pointing out the atomistic structure of Locke's epistemology, where simple ideas are combined to form all other ideas, including ideas of substance and of relations, and abstract general ideas. Holland sees this as exemplifying the "repression of relation and connection that Chodorow describes as characteristic of male experience" (1986, 4). While I am not entirely convinced of the Chodorow/Gilligan thesis (the claim of a universal 'female experience' and 'male experience' is supported primarily by anecdotal evidence and psychoanalytic theory), it nevertheless suggests criteria for identifying 'feminine,' if not necessarily feminist approaches to philosophy. Accordingly, we can now look for examples of appeal to relation and rejection of atomism; and we do indeed find some in Masham's work.

The *Discourse on the Love of God*, Masham's other published book, is a response to John Norris' *Practical Discourses*, the latter based on the *Principles* of Malebranche. Masham particularly objects to Norris' claim that we ought not to love creatures at all, because doing so is incompatible with loving God. She argues that love of creatures is a necessary prerequisite to the love of God, that Norris' and Malebranche's arguments are insufficient and even injurious to piety, and that one can love creatures and God without any incompatibility. In this passage, Masham responds to Norris' claims (indicated by Masham's italics):

> But another reason, besides the narrowness of our capacities, Why *we cannot divide our love* between God and the creature, is, *because we cannot love either of them, but upon such a principle as must utterly exclude the love of the other;* which is thus offered to be made out: We

*must not love any thing but what is our true Good: There can be but
one thing that is so: And that must be either God, or the creature,*

What is our *True Good*, he tells us is that which can both *deserve and
reward our love*. But certainly whatever is a good to us, is a *true good*;
once whatever pleases us, pleases us: And our love, which he says is to be
deserved and rewarded, is nothing else but that disposition of mind,
which we find in our selves towards any thing with which we are pleased.
So that to tell us, that we must not love any thing but what is our *True
[Good]*; Is as much as to say, that we must not be pleased with anything
but what pleases us; which it is likely we are not in danger of. (1696,
89–90)

Here we see Masham poking fun at Norris and objecting to his dualistic
and atomistic thinking with regard to the sharing of love between God and
creatures. The love of God and of creatures is not so separable as Norris
had claimed; indeed, she argues, the love of God is *based* on the love of
creatures. Masham's position could, by the criteria discussed above, be
considered feminist because it rejects separation in favor of connection.

Male philosophers have traditionally associated women with nature,
the earth, the body, and everyday or 'worldly' things in general, while associating men with God, the spirit, and 'otherworldly' things. One form of
feminist response (and my own preference) is to reject such dualistic
stereotypes; another, which Masham embraces to a limited extent, without identifying it as a feminist move, is to rehabilitate the so-called female
side of the dichotomy, rejecting some of the more austere values embedded in patriarchal systems. Masham objects to any strong proscriptions
against loving 'the world,' arguing that only 'inordinate' love of the
world conflicts with our duty to God. Here she is in accord with her
father's emphasis on the virtues of "the good of the system" and "public-
spiritedness"—the social life, as opposed to the contemplative life advocated by Norris (Passmore 1951, 79).

[S]uch declamations as are sometimes made against pleasure absolutely
(not the irregular pursuit of it) as if pleasure was in its own nature, a
false, and deceitful, not a real and solid good, have produced this ill
effect, that many from the absurdity hereof are confirmed in an evil in-
dulgence of their appetites, as if to gratify these was indeed the truest
wisdom of a rational creature. . . . (Masham 1705, 79)

That happiness consisting in pleasure, we are so much the happier as
we enjoy more pleasure must unquestionably be found true; but that
the gratification of men's desires and appetites cannot therefore be that
which should always, as they are rational agents, determine, or regulate
their actions in pursuit of happiness, is no less evident; in that we per-

ceive our selves, and the things to which we have relation, to be so
framed, and constituted in respect one of another, that the gratification
of our present desires and appetites, does sometimes for a short, or
small pleasure, procure to us a greater and more durable pain. (1705,
75)

> . . . the love of pleasure implanted in us (if we faithfully pursue it in
> preferring always that which will, on the whole, procure to us the most
> pleasure) can never mislead us from the observance of the law of
> reason: and that this law enjoins only a right regulation of our natural
> desire of pleasure, to the end of our obtaining the greatest happiness
> that we are capable of: so that there is an inseparable connection, or re-
> lation of moral good and evil, with our natural good, and evil. (1705,
> 77–8)

Finally, rejecting the patriarchal preference for pure power (activity is
preferred to passivity, existence to nonexistence, strength to weakness, ri-
gidity to flexibility), Masham argues that God is not to be loved simply because it is our creator, and more powerful than we, but because God is
good and the source of our happiness. Mere existence is not necessarily a
good thing, for the damned and many unhappy people in this world do not
consider it so. It is more reasonable, therefore, to worship the author of
our happiness than the author of our mere existence (1696, 62–3). Thus,
things in this world must be worthy of love in order that their creator,
which must be more perfect than its creations,[13] may be worthy of our
greatest love (1696, 64). In other words, worship and love are due to a
creator only if it uses its power for our benefit, not simply on the grounds
that it has power over us:

> For God as powerful (which is all we should know of him, considered
> barely as a creator) is no more an object of love than of hate, or fear;
> and is truly an object only of admiration. It seems therefore plain, that
> if any could be without the love of the creatures, they would be without
> the love of God also: For as by the existence of the creatures, we come
> to know there is a creator; so by their loveliness it is that we come to
> know that of their author, and to love him. (1696, 64–5)

Any assessment of the claim that the positions discussed in this section
constitute a feminist approach to the issues involved, or represent a particularly 'feminine' perspective, depends on the assessment of something
like the Chodorow/Gilligan thesis, i.e. that Masham's positions represent
'female' value-systems in opposition to those of the male establishment.
That task requires more discussion than is possible here. Nevertheless, it
is clear that Masham's calls for improved education for women and an end

to the double standard regarding chastity represent at least a limited feminist orientation. And perhaps that is the most that we can expect from a woman of the seventeenth century.

NOTES

1. Passmore comments in a footnote that Masham wrote to Bayle to defend her father against the claim that his views led to atheism. Passmore adds that the belief that Masham abandoned her father's theories to take up those of Locke is a result of ignorance of Cudworth's unpublished work.

2. Citing MSS in the Remonstrants' Library: Locke to Limborch, March 13, 1690-1.

3. See Frankel (1991, 41–58).

4. She employed with their son some of Locke's educational methods, apparently with great success. Replying to Molyneux, who wrote in praise of Locke's educational methods on Molyneux's son, Locke writes:

> [Masham's son], but nine years old in June last, has learnt to read and write very well is now reading Quintus Curtius with his mother, understands geography and chronology very well and the Copernican system of our vortex, is able to multiply well and divide a little, and all this without ever having had one blow for his book. (Bourne II 267, citing 'Familiar Letters,' p. 57, Locke to William Molyneux, August 28, 1693)

5. Citing B.L. MSS. Locke, c.17, f. 154.

6. To Leibniz, November 24, 1704.

7. To Leibniz, March 29, 1704.

8. See her correspondence with Leibniz, Gerhardt III, 333–375.

9. See Christophersen, 41–2.

10. Answer to Mr. Locke's second Letter; wherein his Notion of Ideas is prov'd to be Inconsistent with it self, and with the Articles of the Christian Faith. London, printed by J.H. for Henry Mortlock, etc. MDCXCVIII, pp. 178 in 8vo, p. 65; quoted in Christophersen, 41–2.

11. Passmore, 81.

12. Gilligan, 100, cited by Nancy Holland, "Gender and the Generic in Locke", presented at the Pacific Division meeting of the American Philosophical Association, March, 1986.

13. Masham shares this principle with the Platonists.

REFERENCES

de Beer, E. S. 1976. *The correspondence of John Locke*. (vol. 2). Oxford: Clarendon Press.

Bourne, Henry Richard Fox. 1969. *The life of John Locke*. (2 vols.). London: Scientia Verlag Aalen.

Chodorow, Nancy. 1978. *The reproduction of mothering*. Berkeley: University of California Press.

Christophersen, H. O. 1968. *A bibliographical introduction to the study of John Locke*. New York: Burt Franklin.

Cranston, Maurice. 1957. *John Locke: A biography*. New York: MacMillan.

Frankel, Lois. 1991. Anne Finch, Viscountess Conway. In *A history of women philosophers, III*, ed. Mary Ellen Waithe. Dordrecht: Kluwer.

Gerhardt, C. I., ed. 1875–90. *Die philosophischen Schriften von Leibniz*. (7 vols.). Berlin.

Gilligan, Carol. 1982. *In a different voice*. Cambridge: Harvard University Press.

Holland, Nancy. 1986, March. *Gender and the generic in Locke*. Paper presented at the Pacific Division meeting of the American Philosophical Association, Los Angeles, CA.

Locke, John. 1959. *An essay concerning human understanding*. Alexander Campbell Fraser, ed. (2 vols.). New York: Dover.

Lowrey, Charles E. 1894. *The philosophy of Ralph Cudworth: A study of the true intellectual system of the universe*. New York: Phillips and Hunt.

Masham, Damaris. 1696. *A discourse concerning the love of God*. London: A. and J. Churchil at the Black-Swan in Paternoster-Row.

Masham, Damaris. 1705. *Occasional thoughts in reference to a virtuous or christian Life*. London: A. and J. Churchil at the Black-Swan in Paternoster-Row.

Passmore, John A. 1951. *Ralph Cudworth: An interpretation*. Cambridge: Cambridge University Press.

SOME ASPECTS OF THE PHILOSOPHICAL WORK OF CATHARINE TROTTER

MARTHA BRANDT BOLTON

I

Catharine Trotter (whose married name was 'Cockburn') is certainly not unknown to students of early eighteenth-century philosophy and especially the philosophy of John Locke.[1] She wrote a very able short treatise, *A Defence of Mr. Locke's Essay of Human Understanding,* published anonymously in 1702. It was prompted by three anonymous letters critical of the *Essay,* written by Thomas Burnet. Trotter's defense was praised by several astute persons,[2] including Leibniz and Locke himself, who wrote a letter of thanks to the author when he discovered her identity.[3] Accordingly Trotter and her *Defence* are generally mentioned in accounts of the controversies that engulfed Locke's *Essay* within a decade or so of its first publication and her views are occasionally given brief attention in detailed discussions of Locke's account of moral law.

Although known to philosophers nowadays mainly because of this connection with Locke, Trotter produced several other philosophical tracts. Most of them follow a similar pattern. All but one undertakes to defend the views of some prominent philosopher against attacks from authors now considered of marginal importance. Soon after her defense of Locke against Burnet, Trotter published a short work, called *A Guide to Controversies,* that does not exactly conform to the format. It consists of two letters on the then still-sensitive question of the method of resolving disputes over Christian doctrine. These were private letters Trotter wrote while studying the fundamentals of the Roman Catholic Church and the

This article originally appeared in *The Journal of the History of Philosophy* 31:4 October 1993. Reprinted with permission.

Anglican Church, a process that ended with her conversion from the former to the latter.[4] Even here, her second letter follows the rebuttal-pattern, for it is a detailed reply to her Papist correspondent's arguments for an infallible earthly authority.[5] Her third philosophical tract is a second defense of Locke, this time in rebuttal to a sermon on the doctrine of resurrection preached by Dr. Winch Holdsworth.[6] Then for a lengthy period she was occupied with raising a family under financial duress, due in large part to the fact that she married a clergyman who, for reasons of conscience, was unable to take the oath of loyalty to George I. When she returned to writing philosophy, she expanded her response to Holdsworth, who in the meantime had produced a book in reply to her earlier *Letter* to him.[7] She went on to publish two additional treatises: the first, called *Remarks upon some Writers in the Controversy concerning the Foundation of Moral Virtue and Moral Obligation.* There she describes herself as undertaking to defend Samuel Clarke's account of the foundation of moral virtue and obligation. She considers a series of objectors: Edmund Law, Isaac Watts, William Warburton, and two authors of anonymously published essays on morality, Thomas Johnson and George Johnston.[8] Her last philosophical work, *Remarks upon the Principles and Reasonings of Dr. Rutherford's Essay,* has as its subtitle: *In vindication of the contrary principles and reasonings, enforced in the writings of the late Dr. Samuel Clarke.*[9] As this brief survey shows, Trotter did not hesitate to advertise herself as defending the views of Locke and Clarke against specific objections raised by selected contemporary orators and writers. A woman publishing anonymously, she apparently thought this the most effective way to attract the audience she wanted.

In any case, the formula-description of Trotter as a defender of Locke and Clarke caught on. Those who have mentioned her as a philosopher in the last two hundred years have invariably described her in these terms. Although the formula is accurate in a general way, it is a mistake to think it gives the sum and substance of Trotter's philosophical work. For the description suggests her opinions are derivative and may encourage a dismissive attitude of the sort expressed in the article on Catharine Cockburn in the *Dictionary of National Biography.* There we are told that in later work she defended the ethical theory of Clarke "and it is not much to the credit of her philosophical acuteness that she does not perceive it to be inconsistent with the theories of her old teacher Locke."[10] Of course the formula that describes Trotter as a defender of Locke and Clarke need not imply any lack of perceptiveness, but it does not do justice to her philosophical accomplishment. The purpose of this paper is to bring out some other dimensions of Trotter's work. I will focus especially on some aspects that offer special insights in moral theory and, at the same time, help us to understand what engaged this remarkable woman to do philosophy, and why she chose the format of defending views identified with others.

II

My first contention is that although Trotter describes herself as defending the moral theory of Clarke, she did not derive the doctrine in question from that philosopher. She anticipated the main points of Clarke's moral theory in her first defense of Locke. Some information about what prompted this defense is necessary background. Thomas Burnet's *Remarks upon an Essay concerning Humane Understanding* asked Locke to clarify what the principles of his *Essay* imply concerning certain claims in moral theory and natural and revealed religion. Locke's only public response was a defensive and uncomplimentary reply to the first of the letters that comprise the *Remarks*.[11] No doubt this accounts for the fact that the three letters grow increasingly hostile and aggressive. In the third letter, Burnet ends by charging Locke with intending the *Essay* to insinuate Deist views, such as that finite minds are parts of the one mind of God. Putting that aside, Burnet's queries and charges focus mainly on three topics: (a) Locke's account of the grounds of the moral distinction, i.e., "the Distinction of [moral] Good & Evil, Virtue & Vice, *Turpis & Honesti*" (Letter I, p. 4); (b) whether Locke's principles of knowledge suffice to prove the veracity of God and, thereby, establish the truth of *revealed* religion; (c) the charge that Locke hinders belief in the resurrection, because he professes uncertainty about the immateriality of the soul and he doubts that the soul always thinks. These three disputed issues are not entirely separable, but the one of most abiding interest to Trotter is the first.

Burnet suspected that Locke maintained (whether privately or in the *Essay* is not entirely clear) that morality depends entirely on reward and punishment distributed in accord with the arbitrary will of God. In other words, what makes just or charitable actions virtuous is nothing but God's commandment to be just and charitable and the sanctions associated with that command. God could equally well have commanded us to be *unjust* and *selfish*, and then that would have been what we ought to do. The specter of this extreme "voluntarism" had haunted British moral thought since the early seventeenth century.[12] Often the views that right and wrong are determined by convention and that duty reduces to self-interest were attributed to Thomas Hobbes. But a theistic voluntarism closer to what Burnet envisioned had been urged earlier by John Selden.[13] Burnet was well acquainted with the view and produces a list of its undesirable consequences: it implies there is no fixed notion of moral good and duty and that God is entirely free to alter the commandments; it implies that moral behavior is nothing but prudence dictated by God's unavoidable sanctions—thus even conformity to the commandment to *love God* is based on nothing but self-interest; and it implies that the arbitrary (rationally inexplicable) content of the moral law can only be known by revelation, thus that heathens are not subject to moral law. Did the *Essay* commit Locke to these dire results? Burnet gave the following reasons for suspecting, and later on asserting, that it did: (i) Locke failed to recognize that we have an intellectual faculty for noninferential apprehension of the moral distinction (Burnet eventually ties this to Locke's denial of innate moral principles); (ii) although Locke hinted that a demonstrative science of morals might be possible, he said almost nothing about its first principles; (iii) Locke endorses the view that God's will determines duty, especially in the following passage which Burnet quotes: "What duty is cannot be understood, without a Law: nor a Law be known or supposed without a Law-maker, or without Rewards and Punishments."[14] These three points sum up Burnet's main worries about whether Locke subscribed to a voluntarist view of moral good, virtue, and duty.

Trotter took the main challenge to be to show that Locke's principles of knowledge are adequate to ground *certainty* with regard to a nonvoluntarist account of moral good and that Locke's remark concerning the source of duty is *consistent* with such an account. She explains that her main aim is "to vindicate [the *Essay*] from a defect in the foundation of certainty, in those things, which are of greatest concern to us: which I doubt not to do; it being clear to me, that whatever we can know at all, must be discoverable by Mr. *Locke's* principles; for I cannot find any other way to knowledge. . . " (Works I, 53). She proceeds to proffer an account on which the moral distinction is nonvoluntarist and to argue that it can be known with certainty according to the theory of knowledge in the *Essay.* She tries briefly to show that Locke himself endorsed this same moral theory and I do not think she succeeds. But that is not essential to her main project.

Burnet claimed against Locke that moral principles are known independently of experience and noninferentially. Trotter surmised, no doubt correctly, that Burnet assumes we have immediate knowledge of *eternal* moral truths. That is, moral propositions are "eternal" in the strong sense that their truth is independent of the existence of actual things signified by their propositional terms. Access to a realm of such immutable truths was assumed in standard theories of innate knowledge. In rebuttal, Trotter argues that some judgments of moral value are not immediate, for we cannot assess the justice or injustice of a type of action without understanding natural and conventional rights.[15] Locke actually insisted that there are *no* self-evident moral rules (*Essay,* I, iii, 1 and 4).[16] Trotter does not go that far, but she does not need to in order to rebut Burnet's view of moral knowledge in general. Further, she suggests that Burnet is extravagant in assuming that moral truths are "eternal" in the traditional sense. She argues that a moral principle is "sufficiently established, if it is, and always must be true, supposing those things, to which it relates, to exist" (*Works,* 56). In later works, however, Trotter distanced herself from these roughly Lockean views and openly advocated a more Platonist metaphysics, positing moral truths as eternal objects of God's knowledge;[17] in this, she may have been influenced by Clarke. It is important to notice, however, that her acceptance of this metaphysical thesis is not inconsistent with her adherence to main tenets of Locke's analysis of knowledge (including his anti-innatism). In any case, these issues are not at the heart of Burnet's challenge.

That concerns what Locke's philosophy implies concerning the basis of moral good and his remarks on a necessary connection between duty and a maker and enforcer of law. Trotter's reply to this proceeds as follows.

(i) She begins by using Lockean principles to argue that we do not need innate knowledge of the nature of God in order to know what moral good is: ". . . for we cannot know that the nature of God is good, before we have a notion of good. It must be then by reflecting upon our own nature, and the operations of our minds, that we come to know the nature of God; which therefore cannot *be to us* the rule of good and evil; unless we will argue in a circle, that by our notion of good, we know the nature of God, and by the nature of God, we know what is good" (*Works* I, 58). The crucial implication of this is that our knowledge of human nature (available in conformity with Locke's principles) is the ground of our knowledge of moral good: "From whence it will follow, that the nature of man, and the good of society, are *to us* the reason and rule of moral good and evil; and there is no danger of their being less immutable on this foundation than any other, whilst man continues *a rational and sociable creature*" (*Works* I, 58).

(ii) Trotter's second move is to claim that Locke's principles of knowledge suffice to ground natural religion, in particular, knowledge that God requires us *to do* what is morally good. More exactly, God commands that we do those things that we perceive to be suited to our nature and "annexed" to our happiness. Her argument is that Locke's tenets enable us to prove, first, that God is the supremely wise creator of all other things[18] and, next, that we can know what is suitable to our nature and conducive to our happiness (which she says here is necessary for the motivation to act). Then she argues as follows (in this passage, what Trotter calls the "end" of a created thing is what God wills that thing to be or do): ". . . it is inconsistent with that divine wisdom . . . to have formed us after such a manner, that if we employ those faculties, which he has given us, we cannot but judge, that such things are fit to be done, and others to be avoided, and this to no end at all. Much less can we suppose he has designed us to act contrary to the necessary motives of our actions, and judgment of our minds; it being a flat contradiction, that infinite wisdom and power should form any of his works so disproportionate to their end" (*Works* I, 59). In other words, we apprehend that certain ways of acting are suited to our nature and conducive to our happiness, and this gives us a certain motive to act in those ways. We can conclude that this is what our supremely wise creator wants us to do; otherwise God created us with a sort of natural necessity of acting in ways to which God is indifferent or opposed—hardly the course of wisdom. I will return to this argument shortly. For now, Trotter's second move is to contend that Locke's theory of knowledge can account for how we have natural knowledge of what God commands. It follows that the content of the divine command is not *arbitrarily* determined. (Accordingly Burnet professes to be uncertain whether Locke thinks morality capable of demonstration.)

Trotter presents this line of argument as correct by her own lights. In addition, she tries to show that *Locke* endorses it, by quoting the following passage from *Essay,* IV, iii, 18: "The *Idea* of a supreme Being, infinite in Power, Goodness, and Wisdom, whose Workmanship we are, and on whom we depend; and the *Idea* of ourselves, as understanding, rational Beings, being such as are clear in us, would, I suppose, if duly considered, and pursued, afford such Foundations of our Duty and Rules of Action, as might place *Morality amongst the Sciences capable of Demonstration* . . . " (*Works* I, 61). It does not seem to me the passage *does* show that Locke subscribed to Trotter's strategy of deriving the law of nature and divine command from a teleological perspective on the nature of rational and sociable creatures. But that does not count against her main contention, that Locke's theory of knowledge is adequate to ground certainty concerning a nonvoluntarist moral law.

(iii) Trotter's third move deals with Locke's remark that in order to know our duty, we must know there is a lawmaker who rewards those who conform to the law and punishes those who don't. She urges that Locke is speaking of what gives morality the *force of law,* not what determines what is morally good or virtuous. As she argues: ". . . the Remarker cannot deny, whatever he thinks, *the first grounds of good and evil;* or, however clearly we may see the *nature of these things,* we may approve or condemn them; but they can only have the force of a *law* to us, considered as *the will of the Supreme Being,* who can, and certainly will, reward the compliance with, and punish the deviation from that rule, which he has made knowable to us by the light of nature" (*Works* I, 61). The thesis that there is no law without an authority and sanctions was familiar enough, for instance, from Suárez's influential treatise on law. Trotter's contention is that Locke does not mean to say that *morality* cannot exist without a giver and enforcer of laws, but just that this is required for morality to have the status of *law*.[19]

These three moves comprise Trotter's response to Burnet's challenge. What are the key points? In a footnote in his book, *Locke and Burnet*, S. A. Grave says Trotter's defense consists in separating the grounds of the content of moral law and the basis of the obligation to obey it. Whereas the difference between moral good and evil is determined by human nature, moral obligation presupposes law and thus it is created by divine authority.[20] Now the separation of the ground of moral good from God's commandments does exonerate Locke from a certain sort of "voluntarism." But, I want to argue, this is not Trotter's defense. It misrepresents her view on the source of moral *obligation*. My claim that Trotter did not derive her theory of moral obligation from Clarke depends on this point, so I will consider it in some detail.

In fact, there is direct evidence that Trotter did *not* hold in the *Defence* that God's command is the source of obligation. A note to this effect was added to the force-of-law paragraph in the posthumously published *Works*. In her later works, Trotter clearly advocated the view held by Clarke, that human nature is the source of obligation, as well as the ground of the moral distinction. The note denies that this marked a change in her view: "Some who had lately read this defence [of Locke], have thought, that the author's sentiments, on *the ground of moral obligation* were different when this was wrote, from what they now appear to be in some late pieces. But the author thinks there is no real difference: the grounds of moral obligation are not here discussed at all; the notion of founding morality on arbitrary will is carefully rejected; and the nature of God, or the divine understanding, and the nature of man, all along supposed to be the true grounds of it."[21] (On the question who actually wrote this note, see above note 17.) So Trotter's point that moral rules have the force of law in virtue of divine command is *not* to be taken as an account of what obliges us to be moral. Although Grave's interpretation occurred to some of Trotter's contemporaries, we know from the author that it is wrong.

Where *does* Trotter locate the ground of obligation in the *Defence?* As the note explains, the source of moral obligation (the rational motive to be moral) is not explicitly addressed in that work. Nevertheless I want to argue that Trotter tacitly supposes that obligation, like moral good, is grounded in human nature. Thus, both are separated from God's commands, which carry the force of law. My contention is that the theory that moral obligation *derives from human nature* is implied by what she says and presupposed in her argumentation.[22]

The view is implicit in the second move in Trotter's defense, the argument that on Locke's principles we can *know* what God commands us to do. Recall her argument: human nature dictates that it is morally good for us to behave in certain ways;[23] therefore, God wills that we behave in accord with these dictates, for otherwise God would not be supremely wise. He would be indifferent or opposed to the realization of what is required by the nature of what he created. But does this requirement of nature *obligate* us antecedently to God's commands? I contend that Trotter must suppose it does. For surely she thinks there is a moral obligation to do what God commands, whatever its source. So her argument must be that human nature supplies a reason to conclude that God wills us to do those things we are, indeed, obligated to do. But human nature offers no *reason* adequate to ground obligation-carrying divine commands, unless human nature itself gives rise to obligation. In other words, if the value of acting in conformity with our nature plus our recognition of that value do not obligate us, then there is an element of arbitrariness in God's creating an obligation by his command. Thus Grave's suggestion that Trotter takes obligation to be created by divine command injects a degree of arbitrariness into God's will, which is incompatible with her argument for the knowability of the divine command.

There is further evidence that Trotter's argument presupposes that human nature obligates us to certain sorts of behavior. Even in the argument we have been considering, she says that the judgment that certain actions are fit to our nature supplies "necessary motives of our actions." Moreover, she immediately goes on to argue: "It will not be much from the purpose here, to take notice of the folly of those men, who think to weaken the authority of religion, by calling it a politic contrivance, established for the good of government or society; which is as much as to say, it is the less obligatory, because it is necessary. Whereas that very thing shews it to be our indispensable duty, and of divine authority, without any revelation; since the divine workmanship, *human nature,* could not subsist without it" (*Works* I, 59). Here again we have the argument: what our nature and society requires, we are obligated to do, and that in turn shows that God commands us to do it.

We can now look briefly at Samuel Clarke's moral theory. Clarke was invited to give the Boyle Lectures in 1704 and he devoted them to demonstrating, as rigorously as he could, certain propositions about the being and attributes of God. These lectures were so well received that he was invited to give the Lectures the following year. This time he undertook a rigorous demonstration of the main propositions of natural religion and morality. Like many others, he aimed especially to undertook the despised Hobbesian moral theory. Above all, Clarke stressed that God's will is determined, as he put it, by the "eternal *different relations,* that different things bear one to another" and the "consequent *fitness* or *unfitness* of the application of different things or different relations one to another."[24] Clarke's second main contention is that these very same eternal relations "*ought* . . . to determine the wills of all subordinate rational beings. . . ." Or, as he goes on to explain: ". . . these eternal and necessary differences of things make it *fit and reasonable* for creatures so to act; they cause it to be their *duty,* or lay an *obligation* upon them, so to do; even separate from the consideration of these rules being the *positive will* or *command of God;* and also antecedent to any respect or regard, expectation or apprehension, of any *particular private and personal advantage or disadvantage, reward or punishment,* either present or future; annexed either by natural consequence, or by positive appointment, to the practicing or neglecting of those rules" (*Discourse,* 225). Where Trotter speaks of what is "suitable to human nature," Clarke speaks of "eternal differences," "relations," and what is "fit." The note mentioned earlier indicates Trotter considered this to be a mere difference in terminology. It is clear, however, that she welcomed Clarke's pronouncements on the eternality of moral truth, in contrast to Locke's austere doctrine that moral ideas are made by human beings without reference to external archetypes.[25] Nevertheless Clarke's theory of moral good and obligation is essentially the theory Trotter propounds in defense of Locke. Their common aim is to acknowledge the moral relevance of God's will without yielding ground to voluntarism. Their schemes are the same: moral good and moral obligation are determined, *not* by God's commands, but rather by the natural suitability of certain actions; the content of God's commands is determined by these same considerations of fitness; the divine commands and associated sanctions are a reason for moral action, but there is a reason (obligation) to be moral independent of divine sanctions.

Trotter's *Defence* was written in 1701–02 and Clarke's second course of Boyle Lectures was given in 1705. I do not claim that Trotter invented the moral theory she shared with Clarke, but I do claim she didn't *learn* it from him.[26] She advocated that theory, and recognized its importance as an alternative to the voluntarist scheme, before Clarke produced the statement of the view that attracted all the attention.[27]

III

The second point I want to develop has to do with a pattern of exposing a mistaken view of obligation that occurs in various guises among Clarke's opponents. This is only one of the themes that unify Trotter's various works. It is of special interest, because it involves a penetrating criticism of certain accounts of obligation (and rational motivation more generally) and because it is suggestive of concerns that moved Trotter to engage in philosophy.

Clarke's writings on moral theory spawned a good deal of controversy especially among (but not confined to) authors committed to grounding morality in religion.[28] As Trotter followed the debate, she saw that Clarke's opponents repeatedly misconstrued the obligation to be moral, often because they assumed that our only (rational) motive is pursuit of personal happiness. In Trotter's eyes, proliferation of this sort of view grew out of the *mis*interpretation of Locke by Burnet and later by Shaftesbury. She wrote to her niece in the 1740s complaining of Shaftesbury's allegations of voluntarism against Locke.[29] They are inexcusable, she writes, but goes on: "Yet I must own to you, I am not myself satisfied upon a review of what Mr. Locke has said on moral relations. His plan led him to consider them only with reference to the present constitution of things; and though he is very free from the charge of making the nature of morality uncertain, I fear he has given occasion to the interested scheme so much in fashion of late, but carried, I dare say, far beyond what he intended" (*Works* II, 343). The "interested scheme" bases the obligation (motivation) to be moral exclusively on self-interest, the pursuit of divine or natural benefits for oneself.[30] Had Locke given more emphasis to the "eternal and unalterable nature of right and wrong"[31] that grounds God's will, at the same time that he stressed the motivating force of divine sanctions, he would not have encouraged the "interested scheme." Trotter saw that all versions of this scheme resemble theistic voluntarism: by making (some sort of) reward attached to moral action the *only* motive for morality, they make the nature of moral acts irrelevant to the obligation to perform them.

One of her main later works, *Remarks upon Some Writers in the Controversy concerning the Foundation of Moral Virtue and Moral Obligation* (1743) contains several rebuttals to selected authors who advocate, or in some way support, the "interested scheme."[32] Trotter first considers some claims in the notes written by the translator of William King's *Origin of Evil,* Edmund Law.[33] One of Law's notes argues against Clarke's metaphysical thesis that moral truths are strictly eternal. Law objects that eternal relations would be a determining constraint on God's will inconsistent with freedom of will; it must be, instead, that moral truths are due to God's free decision concerning what to create.[34] Here Trotter defends the traditional doctrine of eternal moral truths. Concluding that Law did *not* mean to imply that the ground of morality is "arbitrary," i.e., without rational ground in God's wisdom and benevolence,[35] she replies, in effect, that he has committed a modal fallacy. He has confused two claims: (i) it is necessary that God create things with natures that ground certain moral laws and (ii) it is necessary that if God creates things with certain natures, then certain moral laws will pertain to them. She claims that the former, but not the latter, would be an unacceptable bar to God's freedom. In her words: "To this I answer, the necessary relations of all possible things are *strictly eternal,* as they are eternally perceived by the divine understanding to be unalterably what they are. This depends not on a determination of the will of God, tho' the bringing any possible nature, with its necessary relations, into *actual* existence, proceeds solely from that determination. This distinction the writers on the other side are very apt either *weakly* or *willfully* to overlook, though a very obvious and a very important one in this controversy" (*Works* I, 405; also see 406 and 408–409).

Law quoted with approval the view "that our Interest and our Duty are both of them the same [and] that it is absolutely impossible any thing should be our Duty, which is not our Interest into the Bargain" (*Origin* I, 86). One reason why moral action is in our interest, according to Law, is that we have a consciousness of what ought to be done that is made uneasy when we neglect to do it. Although Trotter has little reason to object to this, she does object strongly to Law's contention that conscience is, as he puts it, "Rule and Obligation."[36] She argues especially that conscience, or moral sense, cannot be regarded as a source of obligation in its own right: "But the obligation seems plainly founded on the *approbation* itself: the uneasiness we feel upon the practice of anything contrary to what moral sense approves, is a *consequence* of obligation, not the *foundation* of it, and only shews, that we are conscious of being obliged to certain actions, which we cannot neglect without standing self-condemned; self-condemnation manifestly presupposing some *obligation,* that we judge ourselves to have transgressed" (*Works* I, 407). Saying that we are obligated to some action if (and because) the prospect of neglecting to do it makes us uneasy, Law gets things the wrong way 'round. In fact, the thought of the not performing the action makes us uneasy, if (and because) the action is obligatory.[37]

Law's error is like that of a theistic voluntarist, who holds that God's command and sanctions create obligation. The truth is the reverse: the fact that we are obligated to certain actions accounts for God's command and its sanctions. And Trotter mounts this very objection to Law's claim that divine sanctions create obligation where there would otherwise be none: "This determination [i.e., God's determination to reward virtue in a future state], it is plain introduces no *new moral obligation,* in the usual sense of that word; . . . on the contrary, the very notion of reward and punishment implies an *antecedent* duty or obligation, the conforming or not conforming to which, is the only ground of reward and punishment. These cannot, therefore, be the foundation of the obligation; tho' the translator supposes all obligation to arise solely from a prospect of them" (*Works* I, 414; also 415). Trotter's position is that moral sense, understood as "a consciousness consequent upon the perceptions of the rational mind," is *one* source of obligation and divine sanction another, but these are secondary. Law goes wrong because he eliminates the primary value of moral actions as ground for the (natural and divinely promised) pleasures that result from them.[38]

Law stated: "That, and that only, can be said to oblige us, which is *necessary to our Happiness,* and every thing does so far oblige as it is necessary" (*Origin* I, 87). He understood this in conjunction with the view that we always act to further our own happiness. Trotter objected to his claim that there are no disinterested benevolent actions: "A benevolent agent has no other prospect but the interest or happiness of another. The delight he finds in having obtained that end, is either the *consequence* of his benevolence, or of the approbation of his own mind, for having done what was right and fit; but in no case the motive of his action" (*Works* I, 412). The familiar point against psychological egoism has special significance, because Trotter subsumes it under the general pattern we have been noting: other-regarding actions are not valued (motivating) because they please us, but rather doing them pleases us because we value (are motivated to) them.[39]

Trotter turns next to an *Essay on Moral Obligation* published anonymously, but written by Thomas Johnson.[40] Johnson was more explicit than Law in urging that morality must be grounded in self-interest which can only be satisfied by rewards and punishments after life. As he put it: "Before it can be determined what can bring such a necessity upon an agent, as is consistent with perfect liberty, which *moral obligation* is supposed to do, it must first be known, what it is he would chuse or refuse as an intelligent free agent: and as it is self-evident, that to every *sensible* being happiness is preferable to misery, and consequently that happiness must be his choice, and misery his aversion, it is plain, that *moral obligation* can be founded upon this principle *only*" (quoted in *Works* I, 419). Trotter does not fail to object (again) to the claim that an intelligent agent always acts with the aim of attaining personal happiness. Nevertheless she does not deny that (as Law said) morality cannot require us to act in ways that oppose or destroy our happiness. And both Johnson and Law argued that morality *does* sometimes require us to do what is inconsistent with personal happiness in this life; their conclusion was that only assurance of rewards in the afterlife can provide the motive necessary to obligate morality.[41]

The crux of Trotter's response is that her opponents have too narrow a view of what constitutes human happiness:

> [Man] is a *rational* and *social* as well as a *sensible* being, and may, nay must be under some obligations as such. . . . A rational being ought to act suitably to the reason and nature of things: a social being ought to pro-

mote the good of others: an approbation of these ends is unavoidable, a regard to them implied in the very nature of such beings, which must therefore bring on them the strongest *moral obligation*. To ask, why a rational being should chuse to act according to reason, or why a social being should desire the good of others, is full as absurd, as to ask why a sensible being should chuse pleasure rather than pain. If such a question is to be answered, the answer will be the same in either case, these ends are to be chosen, because suitable to the nature of beings with such and such capacities. (*Works* I, 420)

The error is failing to see that action in accord with our nature is constitutive of our happiness. Of course we value happiness, but acting in pursuit of *other* things we value is essential to personal happiness. (Law and Johnson make the nature of what makes us happy irrelevant to our being happy.) Trotter concludes that we always have a motive to act in accord with our nature. It is not, as Law said, that divine sanctions fill in where natural obligation lapses, but rather that they make up for "the defects of our strength and resolution to comply with it" (*Works* I, 415).

As for Johnson's radical contention that there is *no* fitness in actions or obligation antecedent to God's command, it cannot be squared with the rectitude of that command: "Nor can a wise and good being make a thing, that is *really unfit* in itself, the subject of his command. Virtue therefore does not acquire its fitness from *Command*: But God commanded it, because he saw, that it was absolutely right and fit, the indispensable duty of a rational and social being" (*Works* I, 423). Neglect of the primary value of certain human actions is shown, once again, to lead to mistakes in the theory of obligation.

Trotter reports that Johnson, as well as others, objected to the notion of "fitness." They argued that fitness must always be specified relative to some end, and that this undermines the claim that morality is based on fitness *per se* (a thing can be fit for bad uses).[42] In defense of the notion, Trotter argues that considered as a general concept, what is fit for a thing is determined by its nature, not by its relations to other things; but specific actions that are fit, e.g., gratitude to a benefactor, obviously entail that the action has a certain end. "The absolute fitness of virtue in general consists in its tendency to promote the order, harmony, and happiness of the world: and every particular virtue, (such at least as respects our fellow-creatures) tends to some good or other, towards the object of it . . ." (*Works* I, 433). All of this is able enough. But Trotter does not, as far as I know, attempt to defend the teleological assumption that actual things have natures that determine ends, or what is fit for those things to do.

She turns next to a pamphlet written under the name 'Phil-orthos', a pseudonym used by George Johnston.[43] The author shared Trotter's view that morality is founded on immutable natures, but argued that these natures are eternal beings that subsist independently of any mind, including God's.[44] Presumably Trotter thought this worth rebutting, because it could be turned to the purpose of those who argued that God's freedom would be compromised if his will were determined by eternal fitnesses. The issue is peripheral to our main concerns. I will just note that (*inter alia*) Trotter makes the nice point that eternal natures could not exist as archetypes of *possible* creatures independently of a being with the power of creation.[45]

Finally, Trotter discusses some claims in the second edition of William Warburton's *Divine Legation of Moses*.[46] That work was meant to refute Pierre Bayle's antireligionist moral theory. Bayle had contended that the essential difference of moral good and evil and moral sense suffices to motivate virtue, and that religion is irrelevant to morality. Trotter warmly approves Warburton's purpose, but contends that he goes too far in making morality depend on religion. For Warburton held that God's command is the primary source of obligation, without which neither moral sense nor the nature of moral acts would have obligating power.

Although Warburton rejected the "interested scheme," he gave a distinctive anti-Clarkean twist to his theory of obligation. What obliges us is, not the selfish desire for reward, but rather the laudatory motive of wanting to comply with God's will. Obligation is grounded in the relation of creator to creature, which makes it fit that the latter should obey the former.[47] Trotter's first response is that if this one fitness of actions to our nature creates obligation, so should all the others.[48] Further, Warburton agrees with her that it is only by recognizing the fitness of certain actions that we have natural knowledge of the content of God's commands. But if nothing but the fitness of certain actions to our nature informs us that God wills us to do them, then the fitness of those actions must be a reason to do them apart from consideration of divine will.[49] Warburton does not escape the sort of difficulties entailed by theistic voluntarism.

In this review of arguments found in *Remarks on Some Writers,* I have only traced one theme. In fact, as the work carefully rebuts the specific arguments of Clarke's opponents, it develops various other themes as well. My aim is just to bring out one recurring insight that unifies a work that might seem diffuse on cursory inspection.

Trotter's last book, *Remarks upon the Principles and Reasonings of Dr. Rutherford's Essay on the Nature and Obligations of Virtue,* is a further effort to undermine the swelling sentiment for the "interested scheme."[50] In the preface, she denounces "the unaimiable and degrading picture of both [mankind and our duties], given us by some late moralists, who profess to do honour to religion by establishing it on the *lowest* motives, upon pretence, that they are the *strongest;* . . . and that no man does, or ought to do, the least beneficent action, or has any sense of gratitude for those done to him, without a prospect of farther advantage to himself" (*Works* II, 8). Rutherford's proposal was this. He stated as a definition that "virtue is that quality in our actions, by which they are fitted to do good to others, or to prevent their harm."[51] (As Trotter points out, the definition precludes self-regarding virtues.) He further maintained that human beings have no natural motive or inclination to beneficent actions, i.e., virtuous actions. So we do not practice virtue "unless some motives of happiness are thrown into the opposite scale."[52] The passage continues: ". . . [virtue] will always remain distinct from vice whatever becomes of its votaries, and that behavior, which does good to mankind, will not only be different from that, which does harm, but will always be the best for those who feel its influence, though the virtuous in the meantime are miserable. But if our happiness is the most natural and most rational end of our actions, then virtue, before we can be obliged to practice it, must be the best for its votaries too and must make them happy." Rutherford concludes that duty and the obligation to be virtuous depend entirely on revealed religion and God's promise to reward virtue.[53] Thus virtue consists in other-regarding action, but the constant motive for being virtuous is the self-regarding prospect of reward. Trotter's discussion sometimes expresses amazement, sometimes scorn, and is always carefully argued. Without going into details, it should be clear that Rutherford's position offered ample scope for the sorts of critical points we have traced in Trotter's earlier *Remarks upon Some Writers*.

In sum, a main theme of Trotter's two last words is to fend off an increasingly influential line of thought on obligation being put forward by religionist authors. I think we can see from this one theme at least part of her purpose. She shared with her opponents the common goal of grounding morality in religion. She repeatedly pointed out that their various views, for one reason or another, could not be entirely dissociated from voluntarism, an association that discredited their common religious purpose. Looking at Trotter's work after two hundred years, one is struck by the fact that she restricts her critique to figures now regarded as obscure. Although versions of the interested scheme were advocated by nonreligionist moral theorists, e.g., Shaftesbury and Hutcheson, Trotter does not discuss them in her published work. She was familiar with their views, as her letters show; certainly she was in a position to deploy her defense of moral realism and objections to the interested scheme against their positions, too. Had she written against their tracts, which we still read nowadays, she might well have had more influence on the development of moral philosophy. Why did she confine her published work to defending the moral theory she shared with Clarke against exclusively religionist opponents?

IV

In this last section, I want to suggest that Trotter's religionist orientation is connected with the fact that she attached a specific political significance to her philosophical work. There is, of course, no question that she was deeply convinced of the *truth* of a theistic moral theory free of voluntarist elements. Her "defenses" very ably use reasoning and close argument in the effort to convince others of what she took to be the true basis of morality. But she also intended her philosophizing to influence the practices of her contemporaries specifically within her own Christian community.

One example is that Trotter thought it crucial to win acceptance of the link between morality and God's will to prevent recurrence of the sorts of outrage committed in the not so distant past. Writing to her niece (1732), she lamented the views of Deists and many other Christians who, as she put it,

> treat moral virtue, not only as distinct from, but opposite to, religion; which I look upon as the most pernicious error in the world, and what has given rise to the grossest superstitions and the wildest fanaticism, that the head of man is capable of. It was from this notion, that *the will of God might be contrary to morality,* that the enthusiasts in *Cromwell's* time committed the most extravagant outrages, and the blackest villainies, under the pretence of serving the cause of God; and it is not to be doubted, that many of them really believed they were doing his will. But they are not the only sort of men, whom this principle has corrupted. Massacres, and judging men to death for religion, have sprung from the same source. . . ." (*Works* II, *268–69)*

Here is a very practical reason for promulgating the union of morality and divine will.

Other instances of the practical significance Trotter attached to her work cluster around her various attacks on clerical dogmatism. This is present to some extent in her first *Defence* of Locke. She saw clearly enough that Burnet's queries assume a dogmatic stance in order to cast doubt on the principles of Locke's philosophy. In his second letter, Burnet protested that his motives were irreproachable: ". . . I can blame none that desire such Principles of *Humane Understanding* as may give them Proofs and Security against such a System as this, Cogitant Matter, Mortal Soul, A Manichean God (or a God without Moral Attributes), and an Arbitrary Law of Good and Evil."[54] Here Burnet is presuming to *know* certain doctrines, some in fact *controversial,* and proceeding to judge Locke's theory of knowledge by this standard. Burnet's reasoning involves a logical fallacy, which Trotter does not fail to expose.

But she also brings out the practical point that dogmatism is pernicious, whereas the antidogmatic programme of the *Essay* is beneficial. As she explained in her prefatory letter to Locke, she was moved to write the *Defence* because Locke had "[broken] in upon [the] sanctuary of vanity and ignorance; and by setting men on considering first *the bounds of human understanding*, [helped] them to a close pursuit of true and useful knowledge. And is it possible for a lover of truth to be unmoved, or silently suffer any injurious insinuations of so excellent a design?" (*Works* I, 46). In contrast to Burnet's dogmatic presumption that evidence for the doctrines of orthodoxy cannot be questioned, Trotter thinks it a mistake to advocate doctrines that cannot withstand questioning. The practical point is this: ". . . no doubt those writers who establish [the science of morality] on the most solid grounds, do the best service to religion, which has received no little prejudice, by the attempts of some well-meaning men to support it upon metaphysical notions, upon false or abstruse reasonings . . ." (*Works* I, 48). Dogmatizing simply plays into the hands of atheists and skeptics.

A similar practical aim of undermining whose who try to repress all examination of orthodox doctrine motivated Trotter's second vindication of Locke. A large portion of this second defense replies to Holdsworth's two specific charges: that Locke denied we will be resurrected with the same bodies we have on earth and that resurrection of the same body is an essential tenet of the faith. Trotter explained why it was important to rebut Holdsworth on these points: "But my reason for [disputing] . . . is not the importance of the question, whether the body raised shall be the very same or not . . . , but the vast importance of not submitting to have a *word* imposed, as a doctrine of faith, [whose meaning] . . . even the most zealous maintainers of the doctrine confess is not determined in Scripture. Thus many sincere *Christians* will be condemned with Mr. Locke, for heretics and infidels . . . who never suspected themselves liable to such a charge . . ." (*Works* I, 377).

The *Vindication* was also intended to exonerate Locke's character from the charges of heresy which, Trotter reports, had damaged his reputation. But her concerns go beyond Locke's particular case. In her initial letter to Holdsworth, she pointed out the folly of attacking the motives or orthodoxy of a respected person (e.g., Locke or Clarke). In effect, it surrenders someone of great influence to the opponents of religion and morality (*Works* I, 118).

Why did Trotter devote her considerable philosophical talent to works defending prominent moral theorists against a series of opponents who have since become obscure? My suggestion is that she thought Clarke had perfectly well expressed the position she advocated. She took on the task that needed to be done. That was to defend the view against rising opposition which although well-meant was in fact damaging religion and morality by tainting both with voluntarist elements. Her special concerns for practice and policy within her own Christian community explain why she wrote against figures we now regard as peripheral. They were the sources of opposition within the circle of religious thinkers of immediate relevance for Trotter's practical aims. Writing philosophy was difficult for her. It is not that she didn't love to write and talk philosophy—her letters are full of it. But she was plagued by fatigue, headaches, poor eyesight and burdened by other demands with first claim on her best time. It may well be that what encouraged her efforts to publish philosophical work despite these difficulties was her expectation that certain immediate practical aims of great importance to her could be accomplished by it.[55]

NOTES

1. Trotter published her philosophical works anonymously. Thomas Birch, editor of the posthumously printed collection of her philosophical writings, gave it the title, *The Works of Mrs. Catharine Cockburn*. Before her marriage, Trotter wrote several plays, both comedies and tragedies, which were produced with some success in London and published under her own name. On Trotter as dramatist, see Fidelis Morgan, *The Female Wits* (London: Virago Press, 1981).

2. See Leibniz, *Nouveaux Essais* (*Leibniz Philosophische Schriften* [Berlin: Akademie-Verlag, 1962]), bk. VI, p. 70; John Toland (see letter from Trotter to G. Burnet, 8 Aug. 1704, in *The Works of Mrs. Catharine Cockburn, Theological, Moral, Dramatic, and Poetical,* ed. Thomas Birch [London: J. and P. Knapton, 1751], II: 175); and James Tyrrell, in a letter to Locke (see John Yolton, *John Locke and the Way of Ideas* [Oxford: Clarendon Press, 1956], 19 n.5). Also see Birch's "The Life of Mrs. Cockburn," *Works* I, xvi.

3. Locke to Catharine Trotter, 30 December 1702, *The Correspondence of John Locke,* ed. E. S. De Beer, 8 vols. (Oxford: Clarendon Press, 1982), 7: 730–31.

4. Although her family was Anglican, Trotter had in her youth embraced the Roman Catholic faith due to the influence of some distinguished friends (see *Works* I, v).

5. The letter is lost and the name of its author is now unknown.

6. Holdsworth (1679–1761) was fellow of St. John's College, Oxford, vicar of Chalfont St. Peter's, Bucks (1733–61) and author of *A Defense of the Doctrine of the Resurrection of the same Body* (1727).

7. Trotter's detailed reply, *Vindication of Mr. Locke's Christian Principles,* was first published in the posthumous *Works of Catharine Cockburn.*

8. *Essay on Moral Obligation* (1731) was written by Thomas Johnson (d. 1737), fellow of Magdelene College, Cambridge. Johnson was one of four edi-

tors of Stephens's *Thesaurus Linguae Latinae,* editor of several editions of Pufendorf's *De officio hominis et civis juxta legem naturalem,* author of *Quaestiones Philosophicae* (1734) and other works. The second pamphlet, *The eternal obligation of Natural Religion,* was signed "Phil-orthos," pseudonym of George Johnston, Reverend of London. Johnston was also author of *Christianity older than the creation, or the Gospel the same with Natural Religion* (1733) and *Religion plain, not mysterious; or reason the judge of all doctrines* (1733).

9. Thomas Rutherforth (1712–1771), as he is called in the *Dictionary of National Biography* (1900 ed.), was Regius Professor of Divinity at Cambridge and also author of *A System of Natural Philosophy, being a Course of Lectures in Mechanics, Optics, Hydrostatics, and Astronomy*(1748), *The Credibility of Miracles Defended against the author of Philosophical Essays* [David Hume] (1751), *Institutes of Natural Law: being the substance of a Course of Lectures on Grotius' de Jure Belli et Pacis* (1754–56), and other works.

10. Article by Leslie Stephen, *Dictionary of National Biography,* ed. Leslie Stephen (Smith, Edler & Co: London, 1887), XI: 183.

11. Burnet's three letters, Locke's reply to the first letter, and an account of notes Locke made in the margins of the second two letters are published together in *Remarks upon an Essay Concerning Humane Understanding* (New York: Garland, 1984). This edition is cited in all references to Burnet's *Remarks* in this paper. Thomas Burnet was a student of Cudworth, master of Charterhouse, author of *The Sacred Theory of the Earth* (1689–90) and a controversial interpretation of Genesis, *Archaeologiae philosophicae* (1694).

12. Stephen Darwall suggests that two different types of "theistic voluntarism" emerged from the efforts of seventeenth-century moralists to explain the rational motivation (obligation) to obey the law of nature. One is a moderate voluntarism (ascribed, e.g., to Pufendorf), in which the duty to obey the law of nature is derived from the will of God and backed by divine sanctions; but the binding force of divine command is itself grounded in a further moral fact to the effect that God has a right to command his creatures. In contrast, an extreme theistic voluntarism (ascribed to John Selden) holds that natural law is binding because God wills obedience and has inescapable power to enforce his commands. (See Darwall, "Motive and Obligation in the British Moralists," *Social Philosophy & Policy* 7 [1989–90]; 137–41.) Trotter understood the issues posed by theistic voluntarism in much the same way, but argued that "moderate voluntarism" could not be defended unless understood as the sort of fitness-based theory of morality she advocated. She wrote in a letter (1743): "But I would ask if the will of God is supposed to be the *only* foundation of moral obligation, upon what grounds we are obliged to obey his will? I can conceive no other, but either his absolute power to *punish and reward;* or the *fitness* of obedience from a creature to his creator. The first of these would bring us down, I fear, to those low principles [her correspondent] disapproves [i.e., self-interest]; and if that is rejected, the other returns us to that reason, nature, and essential differences of things, into which, I apprehend, all obligation must at last be resolved" (*Works* II, 359).

13. See Richard Tuck, *Natural Rights Theories* (Cambridge: Cambridge University Press, 1979) and Darwall, "Motive and Obligation," 133–44.

14. Essay, I, iii, 12, quoted in *Remarks,* Third Letter, p. 13. Also see *Essay,* II, xxvii, 8. All references to the *Essay* are taken from *An Essay concerning Human Understanding,* ed. Peter H. Nidditch (Oxford: Clarendon Press, 1975).

15. *Works* I, 54; also 60. Trotter also pursues an *ad hominem* strategy against Burnet, pointing out several inconsistencies in his theory of innate "natural conscience" as the faculty by which we apprehend moral truths (see *Works,* I, 94–97).

16. This is one of Locke's arguments against innate moral principles, which he assumes would have to be self-evident. The *Essay* does say that morality can be demonstrated. Before concluding that he is committed to proving moral principles from nonmoral premises, however, one needs to investigate what Locke regards as a demonstration, e.g., whether it requires self-evident premises. One needs also to investigate whether Locke supposed that there are propositions with morally evaluative content that are not strictly moral rules.

17. In the posthumous *Works,* the following footnote is added at this point in *Defence*: "This whole paragraph is a partial and temporary consideration of moral truths (as the opposers of Dr. *Clarke* do not consider them) with relation only to the present constitution of things, not to their original ground, as they exist eternally in the divine mind. An error, the author is now sensible of, and that there was no need of this for the defence of Mr. *Locke's* principles. If his plan led him only to speak of the immediate origin of our ideas, or how we come by our ideas of moral relations, his principles are sufficient by the reflections we make on the operations of our own minds, to lead us to the supreme mind, where all truth, and the abstract nature of all possible things, must eternally and immutably exist" (*Works* I, 56).
   This is one of two notes added to the *Defence* in the posthumous edition comparing Trotter's views in that early work with her views in later works in defense of Clarke. Both report the author's opinion in the third person. They were presumably written by Trotter herself although it is possible they were written by Birch. His introduction indicates that Trotter began the editing work for publication of the collected works, but due to her death the preparations were completed by him. The fact that Birch included the notes certainly gives us his assurance that they express Trotter's own views.

18. Burnet charged that Locke's principles are inadequate to prove that God has the moral attributes of veracity, benevolence, and so on. Trotter replied that Locke's account of the origin of ideas can accommodate a notion of perfection that includes moral, as well as metaphysical perfections, and that Locke proves that a perfect being exists (citing *Essay* II, x, 6). Burnet had gone so far as to say that Locke's inability to prove the veracity of God leaves him without support for the claim that human faculties are reliable means of apprehending truth. Trotter neatly points out the circularity in Burnet's position that we need a proof of the veracity of God to warrant reliance on our faculties of proof (*Works* I, 67).

19. It is not clear that this is what Locke intended, although it offers a way of making his remarks consistent, e.g., with the passage Trotter quotes from *Essay* IV, iii, 8. Arthur Wainwright, in his introduction to Locke's *Paraphrase and Notes*

on the Epistles of St. Paul, maintains that Locke changed his mind on whether the content of moral law could be known without knowledge of reward and punishment in a future life. Wainwright maintains that Locke took the negative view in earlier works, but took the positive one in his final *Paraphrase*, which says: "There is no certain determined punishment affixed to sin without a positive law declaring it." This implies that we can know the content of morality (sin) without knowledge of the sanctions attached to moral law. Wainwright suggests Locke may have been influenced on this point by Burnet's criticisms (49). But Locke might equally well have been moved by Trotter's analysis of how we know (by natural means) what God commands. Locke was working on the portion of the *Paraphrase* that contains this statement in 1702, when he wrote thanking Trotter for her defense.

20. S. A. Grave, *Locke and Burnet* (East Fremantle, Australia: Wescolour Press, 1981), 18, n. 30.

21. The note continues (to the end): "New terms have been since introduced into these subjects; we talk now of essential differences, nature, relation, truth, and fitness of things: but the meaning is the very same; for all these are to be sought for in the nature of God, or of man. But Mr. *Locke* is here defended in establishing morality on *the will of God, and rewards and punishments considered, as it it [sic] has the force of law;* there I suppose lies the *apparent* difference, tho' there is none in reality. The author still agrees to that proposition; for strictly and properly speaking a law implies authority and sanctions; and though we say the *law of reason,* and *the law of nature,* this is in a less proper sense, importing, that they are as effectual grounds of obligation, as if they were real laws, but they oblige us, not as *dependent,* but as *reasonable* beings; in the same manner as the Supreme Being, who is subject to no laws and accountable to none, obliges himself to do always what he perceives to be right and fit to be done. In this light the author has all along considered the grounds of moral obligation; and this I presume is not inconsistent with allowing, that the will of God, rewards and punishments, can only give morality the force of a law" (*Works* I, 61–62).

22. It is also implied by a passing remark in the opening Letter to Locke concering his efforts to produce a demonstration of the grounds of morality: ". . . never any age abounded like this with open advocates of irreligion, upon pretended rational grounds. To silence these unhappy reasoners, by a demonstration of *the obligations their nature lays upon them,* is a work worthy of the excellent Mr. *Locke* . . ." (*Works* I, 47, first emphasis added).

23. The connection between what is suited to our nature and moral good or virtue is explicit in the "reason and rule to *us*" passage quoted above, p. 571. Also, in the following: "And if the relation, which moral good and evil has to natural good and evil, were sufficiently observed, there would be as little dispute about the nature and reality of *virtue* and *vice* [as about that of pleasure and pain]. Those, who think they are only notions in the mind, would be convinced they are as real as natural good and evil; all *moral good* consisting in doing, willing, or chusing, for one's self or others, whatever is a *natural good;* and all *moral evil,* in doing, willing, or chusing whatever is a *natural evil,* to one's self or others. . . . And as this

unalterable relation makes the real and immutable nature of virtue and vice undeniable; so also from thence it is plain, *that the nature of man is the ground or
reason of the law of nature; i.e.* of moral good and evil" (*Works* I, 57).

24. *A Discourse of Natural Religion,* in Samuel Clarke, *The Works,* 4 vols.
(New York: Garland Publishing, 1978; reprint of the 1738 ed.), II: 608.

25. See, e.g., Trotter's letter to her niece, *Works* II, (quoted below, p. 148). For
Locke's views on moral ideas (mixed modes) see, e.g., *Essay* II, xxx, 4 and IV, iv,
5–10; on "eternal truths," see especially IV, xi, 14.

26. There are similarities between Trotter's moral theory and views published
before she wrote her defense in works by Hugo Grotius (to whom she refers at
Works I, 58), Nathanael Culverwel, and Samuel Pufendorf. I am not in a position
to say whether Trotter's moral theory is fully articulated by any of these authors.
(There is, however, some reason to think she did *not* agree with Pufendorf on the
source of obligation; see above note 12.) Ralph Cudworth's treatise on moral
theory takes a position very like Trotter's, but was not published until 1731. Locke
wrote in his youthful *Essays on the Law of Nature* that although obligation has its
source in the will of God, it does not arise from fear of punishment, but rather
from "rational apprehension of what is right" (noted by Darwall, "Motive and
Obligation," 138); this is not an unambiguous statement of Trotter's position and,
in any case, this treatise was not published prior to the *Defence.*

27. Clarke made passing remarks adumbrating the theory he shares with
Trotter in the essay on confirmation in his *Three Practical Essays on Baptism,
Confirmation and Repentance* published in 1699. He briefly suggests that God's
commands are determined by the eternal fitness of things and that conformity to
duty is excellent in its own right. (See Clarke, *The Works,* III: 575, 579, 581.) On
the anticipation of Clarke's later moral theory in this early work, see J. P.
Ferguson, *An Eighteenth-Century Heretic: Dr. Samuel Clarke* (Kineton, Warwick:
Roundwood Press, 1976), 11–13. But in this treatise, Clarke is not advocating a
moral theory, much less combatting the voluntarist threat. I have found no evidence that Trotter knew this early work, but even if she did, she could hardly have
learned the view she propounds in the *Defence* from these sketchy remarks.

28. See, e.g., Ferguson, *An Eighteenth-Century Heretic,* ch. 3.

29. Trotter quoted Shaftesbury's "terrible accusation" to her niece: "It was Mr.
Locke, that struck at all fundamentals, threw all order and virtue out of the world,
made the very ideas of these *unnatural;* that, according to him . . . God, indeed, is
a perfect free agent in his sense; that is, free to any thing, that is however ill: for if
he wills it, it will be made good; virtue, may be vice, and vice virtue in its turn, if
he pleases, and thus neither right nor wrong are any thing in themselves" (*Works*
II, 342). The passage is from Anthony Ashley Cooper, Earl of Shaftesbury, *Characteristics of Men, Morals, Manners, Opinions, Times,* ed. John M. Robertson
(Indianapolis: Bobbs Merrill Co., Inc., 1964).

30. The meaning Trotter attached to this term is indicated in *Remarks upon
Some Writers,* where Trotter says that the author of *Essay on Moral Obligation*
sides with the "general scheme" of those "who are for taking away every motive to

virtue but self-interest" (*Works* I, 412). It is more explicitly indicated in a letter to her niece (1747 or 1748): "All we contend for is, that God has given to man such a disposition to benevolence, as should lead him to virtue; should teach him, that he was designed to seek the good of others, as well as his own; and that self-love, or an artificial association of ideas, are not the sole ground of benevolence, or the proper foundation of virtuous practice, as the gentlemen of the interested scheme maintain" (*Works* II, 340).

31. *Works* II, 342.

32. A portion of this book deals with issues prompted by Clarke's claims concerning the being and attributes of God. These matters are not irrelevant to metaphysical aspects of the doctrine of "eternal fitness," but I am not going to examine them here.

33. *De Origine Mali* was written by William King and published in 1702; the English translation together with notes was first published in 1731. Trotter does not mention the translator by name and the name was not given in the first edition. But the numbers by which Trotter refers to the notes indicate that she used the second edition (1734), which did name the author of the notes.

34. Law expresses this view in a section titled "Remarks, referr'd to in Note 10," Remark i: "What is good for me now in these Circumstances and Respects, will always be so in the same Circumstances and Respects, and can never be alter'd without altering the Nature of things, or the present System: but we cannot imagine these *Relations* therefore to be any real *Entities,* or to have existed from all *Eternity,* or to be antecedent to, or independent of the Will of God himself; as some Writers seem to have done. . . . We cannot, I say, imagine them to be either strictly *eternal* or *independent* of the Will of God, because they must necessarily presuppose a determination of that Will, and are in truth only Consequences of the Existence of things proceeding from that Determination." See *An Essay on the Origin of Evil by Dr. William King, translated from the Latin with notes . . .* by Edmund Law, 2nd ed. (printed by J. Stephens for W. Thurlbourn in Cambridge and sold by J. Knapton, R. Knaplock & W. Innys, London: 1734), 2 vols, 1: 85.

35. Trotter writes: "When the author of the notes finds himself pressed with the danger of this principle, of founding good and evil, and placing the obligation to virtue, on the mere will of God, he owns, that *mere will* would of itself be no ground of obligation at all, and that *the will of God must not be separated from his other attributes;* which is, I think, giving up all that is contended for. The moral attitudes of God, his goodness, justice, truth, and rectitude, are chiefly understood by us with relation to his dealings with his creatures, suitably to the nature he has given them, and to their demeanor in it. To say then, that the will of God *must not be separated* from these attributes, *i.e.* must be considered as determining itself agreeably to, or in conformity with them, is the same thing, in other words, with conforming itself to the reason, nature, and fitness of things" (*Works* I, 410–11). Nevertheless, she goes on to rehearse the unacceptable consequences of a "voluntarist" account of moral law, much as Burnet had done. Law did mean to avoid the result that the content of moral law is arbitrarily deter-

mined by God's will: "This author [i.e., Clarke] seems afraid of our placing the *Obligation* to Virtue on the *mere Will of God;* as if his Will were separated from his other Attributes: which would indeed of itself be no ground of Obligation at all, since upon such a blind Principle we could never be secure of Happiness from any Being how faithfully soever we obey'd him, or how much soever we resembled him in Perfection" (*Origin* II: 313,n. 52).

36. Trotter quotes the phrase (*Works* I, 407). Law's note continues: "As a natural *Instinct,* [conscience] directs us to approve such Actions as tend to produce Happiness in others, and so is a *Rule* whereby we determine all such Actions to be virtuous, as it gives us pain, or makes us uneasy at the Neglect of these Actions, . . . it so far *obliges* us to pursue them, or makes the Practice of them necessary to our *Happiness:* which is the true meaning of the word *Oblige*" (*Origin* I: 86–87).

37. A similar pattern of argument is used against Law's contention that reverence of a creature to its creator is ". . . suitable to the nature of the [creature], as productive of his happiness, and to that of [the creator], as agreeable to his will, who originally designed the happiness of his creatures, and therefore bound this and the like duties on them" (*Origin* II: 21). Trotter responds: "But surely this is reversing the order of things. Should we not rather conclude, that reverence from a creature to his creator is therefore productive of happiness to the one, and agreeable to the will of the other, because suitable to their respective natures? If this were not so . . . then God might *originally* have annexed the happiness of his creatures to their *irreverence* towards him and *bound that as a duty upon them*" (*Works* I, 403–404).

38. "But though Dr. *Clarke* and his followers maintain, that the *fitness of things,* and conscience or the *moral sense* . . . have *in themselves* an obligatory power, yet it must be allowed, and they as vigorously maintain, that the *will of God,* with the sanctions of his laws, can only enforce this obligation, so as to extend to all times and all cases. These therefore, as Mr. *Warburton* judiciously observes, make a threefold cord, that ought never to be untwisted. The consideration of the *will of God* must necessarily be taken into all schemes of morality, as the author of the notes justly says; but an endeavour to establish it upon that alone, exclusive of the other principles, seems to me no less a defect in *some,* than the want of that has been in *many* of our modern systems" (*Works* I, 407; also 412–15).

39. As Trotter says in objection to Johnson: "The very supposition of being happy alone, without regard to any person in the world, or whilst all about him were miserable, most [*sic*] appear a contradiction to a social nature: But this dependence of his happiness on that of others is the *effect* of his benevolent affections, not the *cause or ground* of them" (*Works* I, 427).

40. The full title is: *An Essay on Moral Obligation: with a view towards settling the controversy concerning moral and positive duties* [by Thomas Johnson]. *In answer to two late pamphlets: the one entitled: The True Foundation of Natural and Revealed Religion Asserted: being a reply* [by A. A. Sykes] *to the Supplement to the Treatise on the Christian Sacraments* [by Daniel Waterland]. *The other—Some Reflections upon the Comparative Excellence and Usefulness of Moral and Positive Duties: by Mr. Chubb* (1731).

41. Law wrote in note 52 (vol. II): "I grant *the natural Consequence of Virtue is Happiness* (at least would be so, if universally practiced) and as such it carries a partial Obligation in itself, or is so far its own Reward; but what will become of the Obligation (according to my sense of that Word) when this Consequence does not follow? As the Author [Samuel Clarke] very reasonably grants it *cannot* in the present state. . . . To deduce one from the prospect of Reward in a future state . . . is having recourse to the *Will* of God to supply defects and compleat the Obligation, instead of founding it on these *Relations as such,* as *absolutely fit* and *right,* and to be follow'd for *their own sakes* without regard to any farther End" (*Origin* II: 314; referred to by Trotter, *Works* I, 414–15).

Trotter records the following from Johnson: "If we must talk in the language of these advocates for fitnesses, we should call the fitnesses, which they speak of, partial fitnesses, or rather *unfitnesses,* as wanting the most essential part of the fitness of an action, *viz.* Beneficialness to the agent himself. God's command supplies that part of fitness before wanting, and makes it now wise and fitting to chuse what before could not have been *wisely* chosen; for what is not fit upon the whole, is *really unfit*" (*Works* I, 421, reference to *Moral Obligation,* 58).

42. Trotter expresses the complaint as follows: "The opposers of Dr. *Clarke* in general are, I find, greatly prejudiced against the word *fitness.* . . . Absolute fitness, or *fit in itself,* is an absurdity with them. The term is relative, they say, and must be unintelligible, when used without relation to an *end;* (for it is a mistake, common to all the writers on that side, to suppose, that the words *fit in itself,* are meant to exclude all manner of *end,* or relation to any thing;) . . ." (*Works* I, 432).

43. Phil-orthos, pseud. [i.e., George Johnston], *The Eternal Obligation of Natural Religion; or the foundation of morality to God and Man. Being an answer to Dr. Wright's remarks upon Mr. Mole's Sermon* [on the Foundation of Virtue] (London: For T. Cox, 1732).

44. Trotter quotes Johnston: "[W]hether there were a divinity or not, any creator, creature, or not, such moral entities would always subsist, and be just the same that they are now" (*Works* I, 435).

45. "But if these moral entities, the moral natures and differences of things, refer, as this author says they do, to *possible existences,* he should have considered, that by supposing there were no divinity, no creator, he supposes away the only ground of *possible existence;* if there was no divinity, there could be no possible existences, and consequently no truths concerning them" (*Works* I, 435–36).

46. *The Divine Legation of Moses demonstrated, on the principles of a religious Deist, from the omission of the doctrine of a future state of reward and punishment in the Jewish disposition,* 2nd ed. (London: 1742), 2 vols. Trotter specifies the second edition, but I have been unable to verify that it is the edition she used.

47. Warburton argued: "The true principles of morality should have the worthiest motive to enforce it; and the legitimate motive to virtue on that principle is compliance with the will of God." Further: "It is a mistake that will could not oblige without happiness; will could not indeed oblige to unhappiness, but it would oblige to what should produce neither one nor the other, tho' all considera-

tions of the consequences of obeying or disobeying were away" (quoted by Trotter with reference to p. 38 and p. 49, *Works* I, 447–48).

48. "But I think it may with great solidity be concuded, that if the will of God obliges from a fitness, that arises on account of the relation of a creature to his creator, whatever fitnesses arise from other relations, and the essential difference of things, will likewise oblige in their proportion" (*Works* I, 448).

49. "But if these relations, or our perceptions of the essential difference of things, are, as he farther argues, the rule, that God hath given his creatures to bring them to the knowledge of his will, then it must be a rule to all his creatures, whether they consider it as his will or not; and therefore, as reasonable beings, the fitness of obeying the creator's will must be so far from being *infinitely different* from the fitness of complying with a man's perceptions of the necessary relations and difference of things, that, supposing all consideration of the consequences were away, there must be an equal obligation to either, according to the opportunities of discovering them: Besides that without a regard to the right, and reason, and equity of the case, whatever mens actions may be, there is no virtue or real goodness in the person, that does them: the nature and reason of things therefore should seem to be the genuine principle of true morality" (*Works* I, 448).

50. Thomas Rutherford, *An Essay on the Nature and Obligation of Virtue* (London: Printed by J. Bentham for William Thurlbourn [Cambridge] and sold by W. Innys, C. Bathurst, & J. Brieroft, 1744).

51. *Nature and Obligation,* 6, quoted by Trotter, *Works* II, 9.

52. *Nature and Obligation,* 91, quoted by Trotter, *Works* II, 27. Rutherford also says: "Every man's own happiness is the end which nature teaches him to pursue." Also: ". . . our own happiness is what we must prefer to everything else, and therefore is the only end, which we are likely to pursue with steadfastness and constancy. Virtue if it should interfere with this end would soon be deserted . . ." (153).

53. *Nature and Obligation,* especially Chapter X, whose thesis is "The constant and uniform practice of virtue towards all mankind becomes our duty, when revelation has informed us that God will make us finally happy for it in a life after this" (239–72).

54. *Remarks,* Second Letter, 11; also see 12 and 28 and Third Letter, 3–4 and 16.

55. I am grateful to Robert Shaver for suggestions regarding the development of early modern moral theory, and helpful comments on earlier versions of this paper. I also benefitted from discussion with participants in the British Society for History of Philosophy Conference on Women in the History of Philosophy held in Cambridge, April 1992, especially from a section on Catharine Trotter included in (but omitted from the oral presentation of) a paper delivered there by Stuart Brown. Thanks also to discussants at the Northeast American Society for Eighteenth-Century Studies meeting, Amherst, 1990 and the Eastern Division APA session on women in the history of philosophy, Boston, 1990. Comments from an anonymous referee for the *Journal of the History of Philosophy* were especially helpful.

NOW FOOLISH THEN WISE
BELLE VAN ZUYLEN'S GAME
WITH SEXUAL IDENTITY

JOKE J. HERMSEN

'Everything is fashion,' wrote the Utrecht-born aristocrat Belle van Zuylen (1740–1805) in 1789, who lived most of her life in French-speaking Switzerland and was also known by her married name Madame de Charrière. This statement was made in a pamphlet that she wrote under the pseudonym of Thérèse Levasseur, who was the servant, sexual partner, and life companion of the eighteenth-century French philosopher Jean Jacques Rousseau (1712–1778). Belle van Zuylen was quick in pointing out the fickleness of public opinion:

> People and reputations are the toys of fashion, like clothing and hairstyles. Once it was fashionable to love Rousseau, then to pester him, and in these days it is fashionable to idolize him and to slander me. (Charrière, 1988, p. 107)

The sad figure of Levasseur turned out to be instrumental in influencing public opinion about Rousseau. For instance, women who were famous for their Parisian *salons* and for their literary talents, like Madame Germaine de Staël, sided resolutely with the philosopher and went so far as to accuse Thérèse Levasseur of being the cause of Rousseau's suicide. The story goes that Levasseur, who lived with Rousseau for 30 years, was suspected of committing adultery with an 'ordinary' coachman. This blatant act of infidelity allegedly shocked the great philosopher so much that he did not survive it. The modern reader cannot fail to notice that Rousseau's supporters, first and foremost among them Madame de Staël, who fully

This article originally appeared in *Women's Studies International Forum* 16 (1993), no. 4. Reprinted with permission from Elsevier Science Ltd., Pergamon Imprint, Oxford, England.

believed this story, never even paused to consider for one moment the sorrowful fate of his life-companion, Thérèse herself. The poor woman had to stand by as each one of the five children she had with Rousseau was sent to the local orphanage, simply because the great master and celebrated pedagogue refused to spend any time bringing up his own children.

Unlike Madame de Staël, Belle van Zuylen was never very convinced by Rousseau's theories, especially his ideal of the return to nature and his admiration for the noble savage, which I discuss later. Nor did Belle approve much of the intellectual style of Madame de Staël herself; she consequently took the side of Thérèse Levasseur and wrote a whole pamphlet in her defense, trying to clear her of the charge of having driven the great man to suicide. This was the 1789 text: *Plainte et défense de Thérèse Levasseur* (Charrière, 1988, pp. 107–121), which she sent round to French newspapers and literary journals. Belle's valiant attempt to come to Levasseur's rescue, however, did not quite succeed, because friends and servants of the influential Germaine de Staël bought up as many copies of Belle van Zuylen's pamphlet as they could get their hands on. This was a not unusual and highly effective eighteenth-century form of censorship.

Belle's stated belief that 'everything is fashion' was a comment on the way in which intellectual life was conducted in her day; she knew that people and ideas could fall out of fashion as easily as hairstyles and clothes. The author of *The Social Contract* himself was not immune from such twists of fate and falls from grace. In eighteenth-century France, most educated, that is to say upper-class women, like Madame de Staël herself, thought very highly of the great Jean-Jacques, made public professions of faith in his theories of education and morality, and—contrary to the master himself—raised their children according to the principles set forth in *Emile or of Education*. Rousseau advocated a far-reaching and rather abstract ideal of social equality, in the framework of a new system that he wanted to be free from hierarchy and relations of oppression. Nevertheless, he constantly emphasized a natural, that is to say biologically determined, kind of inequality between men and women, especially in *Emile*.

It is precisely this deterministic aspect of Rousseau's theories that has come under increasing criticism from contemporary feminist philosophers and historians of ideas like Geneviève Lloyd (1985) and Sarah Kofman (1982). Feminists have directly taken on his statement that women are subjected *by nature* to the mercy and the superior judgment of men. In the light of this discriminatory approach to women, feminist philosophers have shown that the social equality principle upheld by Rousseau applies to male citizens only, leaving women in a resolutely inferior condition. The vicissitudes of fame and of historical evolution being what they are, Rousseau is nowadays more or less out of fashion, whereas Belle van Zuylen, after years of relative obscurity, is finally in the spotlight. Both feminist and other scholars have rediscovered her ideas and work, finally doing justice to her freedom of mind and lively style.[1]

Unlike so many of her contemporaries, Belle van Zuylen refused to be taken in by an appeal to nature as the explanation for and justification of the differences between the sexes. According to Belle van Zuylen, the differences between men and women should not be looked upon as 'natural,' that is to say inevitable and therefore unchangeable facts, but rather as the consequences of social inequalities and discrimination, sustained over long periods of time.[2] The differences between the sexes are therefore not due to the specific talents of one sex as opposed to the deficiencies of the other. Belle van Zuylen argues instead that: "there is nothing in the constitution of man or woman which *a priori* determines their abilities." (Charrière, 1982, vol. III, p. 217). Belle did not hesitate to express her skepticism vis-à-vis Rousseau in very critical terms. Thus, she ended up being one of the few critics of her day who exposed the inferior role to which Rousseau had confined Sophie—Emile's mistress in the eponymous pedagogical treatise. In her short story "Mrs. Henley" (1784), Belle van Zuylen writes:

> Rousseau has hardly thought about Sophie's rights and ambitions; she is no more than a slave who is raised for the benefit of her master. (Charrière, 1982, vol. VIII, p. 119)

Belle's insight is that Rousseau's educational system, which was based on tuning into the pupil's 'natural' gifts, actively discriminated against women. By being firmly attached to their 'natural' procreative function, Rousseau's system barred women's access to formal education and thus condemned them to a sentimentalized form of ignorance. Belle opposed to this retrograde view a wide-ranging educational project, based on concrete equality of opportunity between boys and girls and aimed at training women to become independent and to think independently. In a letter to a woman friend, she develops this point of view: "All abilities of man and woman are originally the same, and if the rational ability of men is more perfect, then that is a result of education and education only" (Godet, 1927, p. 301). Belle van Zuylen's central point of disagreement remains that whatever kind of inferiority Rousseau and many of his contemporaries saw as the 'natural' lot of women, this was in fact the result of a social and political system that preferred to keep women locked up in a domestic role, instead of allowing them access to the public tribune.

The idea of the social construction of differences between the sexes in a hierarchical scale that equates difference with inferiority has come a long way in feminist practice since Belle van Zuylen's outspoken rejection of Rousseau's essentialism, as I will argue later on.

For an eighteenth-century writer like Belle van Zuylen, however, thinking about sexual difference without reducing it to a biologically deterministic notion was much riskier and more radical than it is for contemporary feminist theorists. She had to struggle against a cultural heritage in which the radical separation of masculine and feminine 'qualities, virtues or attributes,' that is to say an extreme affirmation of sexual difference resulted in and, to a large extent, justified the intellectual and sexual oppression of women. The 'feminine' dimension was determined as inferior or inadequate by the impact first of Christian morality, later reinforced by the scientific creed of the Enlightenment. Both the classical Christian ethos and the new scientific spirit of the eighteenth century saw the female body as a source of inferiority. In the age of the Enlightenment, women, tormented by an allegedly weak and nervous body, were thought unable to reach the necessary level of 'rational' insight, which was needed for social participation. From Voltaire and Kant to the Scottish moral philosophers, the so-called 'inferior body' of woman was thought to be the basis of her social inferiority. Even a writer like Diderot did not dissent from this misogynist and essentialist view.

In this context of extreme affirmation of sexual difference as a mark of inferiority, Belle van Zuylen opposed her equality-thinking to this eighteenth-century form of biological determinism. However, as I show, the equality perspective which van Zuylen defended did not aim to create a *neutral* subject, from which every bodily or sexualized foundation had been eliminated. On the contrary, she wanted to pave the way for innumerable sexualized subject positions in a constant play with sex identities which could not be fixed once and for all. What I hope to show, through the interpretation of a fragment of her novel *Three Women* (Charrière, 1982. Vol. 9, pp. 21–127), is that she manages to sail around the dangers of 'essentialism,' by not focussing exclusively on *The* difference between man and woman, but rather by situating the phenomenon of sexual difference within the subject him/herself. In other words, Belle van Zuylen sees sexual difference as paving the way for indefinite different relations women and men can create to the sign of their sex.

One of the contemporary feminist concerns is the question of how to play on the countless differences between the sexes, while calling into question the ideal of absolute equality. The debate on equality versus difference has been especially lively in the Netherlands (Hermsen & van Lenning, 1991), and the figure and the works of Belle van Zuylen have played an instrumental role in it. The question I would therefore like to raise, speaking within a Dutch context is: What can Belle van Zuylen's simultaneous emphasis on equality—against the essentialism of her day—and desire to play with the many facets of sex identities teach us today? What lesson can she give us on the interaction between equality and difference? In posing the question in these terms, I am agreeing with Joan Scott (Scott, 1988) when she states that contemporary feminists have nothing to gain by polarizing the relationship between equality and difference. A great deal more would be gained instead if we could learn to approach these two notions as interconnected with and, in many ways, inseparable from each other. With the help of Belle van Zuylen's innovative and highly spirited work, I argue that a perspective dictated by enlightened equality need not conflict with difference, nor does it necessarily have to result in the assimilation of women into 'masculine' attributes or ways of knowing, as some suggest (Irigaray, 1987). What I want to argue instead is that such a nuanced approach can create the bases for the exploration and valorization of *all kinds* of differences.

Twofold

Let me add a few remarks to contextualize the contemporary discussion on sexual difference. It was Nietzsche who, with his expression of the 'primal error of equality,' gave the first impulse to a radical philosophical way of thinking that could do justice to difference. Although his work did not have an immediate impact upon feminism, because of his vehemently antiliberationist style, Nietzsche's thought was to become important in the second half of this century through the re-interpretations offered by the French post-structuralist school of difference, to which I return.

Initially, Nietzsche addressed his criticism of equality to the ways in which the eighteenth-century Enlightenment has put the relationship between language and reality. According to this school, the subject was capable of naming objectively the 'essence' of all things surrounding *him* (this kind of epistemologically valid subjectivity was seen at the time as the exclusive prerequisite of men), fixing it in language and thus providing insight into the world while making it also controllable. To Nietzsche this model of objective expression was an illusion. He even wondered whether language is an adequate expression of reality at all, because concepts are created by putting on the same plane different notions or levels of experience, equalizing unequal things. Thus he argued: "Overlooking the individual and the real provides us with the concept" (Nietzsche, 1980, p. 878). No leaf on a tree is actually the same as any other leaf, but to be able to speak we use the general metaphor 'leaf,' which has to refer to all separate and different leaves:

> We think we know something about the things themselves when we speak of trees and colours, but we own nothing but metaphors of things. (Nietzsche, 1980, p. 880)

In other words, language is for Nietzsche an *army of metaphors*, in which the specificity of the thing is sacrificed to a sort of cross-referencing to others, which he calls "equalization or equation." This is the process which enables us to speak and understand each other. That this way of proceeding makes us lose the 'uniqueness' of the very experiences we want to express is also for Nietzsche a way of pointing out the great limitation of scientific claims to objectivity. The claim to objectivity both neglects and denies that words are always metaphors and that consequently the notion of an 'absolute truth' is an illusion. Through this argument, the idea of equality comes under attack as a sort of inner tendency of scientific language to place on the same—allegedly objective—plane, different objects. He criticized the metaphysically deterministic belief in 'truths' as being typical of Christian Western philosophy and proposed instead to restore the uniqueness of things by looking at each experience from many different perspectives.

As I suggested earlier, contemporary French philosophers of 'difference,' such as Derrida amongst others (Derrida, 1967), were inspired by Nietzsche and consequently worked on the critique of objectivity and the notion of the heterogeneity of experience. This agenda spells the decline of the political belief in the eighteenth-century ideal of equality, a point which did not fail to have an impact on Western feminist thinking practice, notably during the last 20 years in France. Sexual difference-thinkers like Luce Irigaray (Irigaray, 1987) and Hélène Cixous (Cixous, 1975) particularly ask for the recognition of difference of women, a difference that should not be suppressed, but on the contrary should be positively re-interpreted. Both Irigaray and Derrida criticize Western philosophy, which they see as being characterized by thinking in antitheses. In this dualistic mode of thought, one pole of the antithesis is considered to be dominant in relation to the second pole. Thus, the 'feminine' can be seen as subordinated to and derived from the 'masculine.'

However, the difference thinkers themselves are divided by their own differences as well. Derrida for instance aims at removing all binary oppositions and advocates an *absolute difference*, in which not a single permanent sign, not a single fixed identity can be established temporarily in relation to any other (Vasterling, 1989). Irigaray on the other hand tries to develop a *double syntax*, in which a feminine identity can be expressed as well. "Female theoreticians who support an articulation of sexual difference opt for duality," argues Rina Van der Haegen in her dissertation on Irigaray and Derrida, "they particularly wish to allow a 'feminine' and a 'masculine' to speak" (Van der Haegen, 1989, p. 57). Irigaray wants to create an alternative 'feminine' system of representation, which separates itself from the prevailing 'masculine' morphology. Irigaray (1977, p. 111) goes as far as to suggest that even the structures of sexuality, desire, and consequently the unconscious are dissymetrical in the two sexes. She defines this as 'the double syntax,' by which sexual difference marks a radical lack of symmetry in the structures of the feminine and masculine subjects. Irigaray thus accomplishes a reversal of the power relation between feminine and masculine, in favour of the former. More importantly, this move leads her to attack the notion of equality as a neutralization of differences that can result only in assimilating women into masculine ways of thinking. Irigaray points to a paradox in the notion of equality: In the present balance of power, equality with men could well mean that women give up all that had made them 'different' from the other sex, thereby losing sight of their identity. Irigaray is no blind believer in equality, because she sees it as a male-dominated principle, which has been historically prevalent since the eighteenth century. She argues that the abstract ideal of equality is implicitly based on a masculine subject, which tries to pass himself off as the universal. Irigaray attacks both the implicit assumption of masculinity and the fact that the eighteenth century notion of the subject is so abstract, that is to say so disembodied. The emphasis on the body is a way of lending support to a more situated, that is, a more accountable vision of the subject.

It seems to me that Irigaray's radical defense of the feminine results in a glorification of the latter, which becomes the privileged site for the affirmation of heterogeneity, whereas the 'masculine' stands for all that is homogeneous and hegemonic. More importantly for me, Irigaray does not fully detach herself from biological determinism and makes frequent references to both biological and psychic essentialism.[3] In my opinion, Irigaray does not see sexual difference as a play with identity, but rather as the affirmation of a new essentialized feminine subject; in this respect, I find myself less in agreement with Irigaray, than with Belle van Zuylen herself.

Three Women

In her novel *Three Women* published in 1796, Belle van Zuylen lets her protagonist Constance conduct a social experiment which is revolutionary for her time because it is in open contradiction with Rousseau's naturalistic approach to education. This erudite and self-willed woman wants to finish "once and for all with the prejudices about sex-specific characteristics" (Charrière, 1982, vol. IX. p. 114). To achieve this, in her novel, she takes orphan twins, a boy and a girl, to a wet nurse and orders her to dress both children exactly alike, so as not to encourage what we would today call gender-stereotypes in their upbringing. Furthermore she demands that the boy be given a girl's name and the girl a boy's name. And Belle van

Zuylen writes: "We will see whether the real Charlotte shall knit, whether she shall be gentle and nice, coquettish and affectionate, and whether the real Charles shall take up the plane and the pick-axe, whether he shall be frank, brave, rough and truculent. I think they will be able to reach the age of twelve or fourteen without suspecting anything. If by then the boy has the mentality and nature and the character of a girl, and the girl the nature and character of a boy, I will make this public and hope that afterwards less silly nonsense is maintained about the difference in nature and in distinctive characteristics of both sexes." (Charrière, 1982, vol. IX, p. 114)

What exactly did Belle van Zuylen want to prove with this exchange of sex roles between the two babies? First of all, she wanted to make it clear that both children are equally endowed with 'natural' capacities and that specific characteristics and abilities cannot be allotted to them on the basis of their anatomical constitution and differences.

I interpret this as criticism of the idea of essentialized sexual difference prevalent in her time, which pins both sexes down to certain roles and characteristics. With her sexual experiment, Belle van Zuylen wanted to show that the sex bestowed by nature does not determine the identity of the individual. In a late twentieth-century perspective, I would add that identity is rather determined by the way in which an individual can and is allowed to relate to her or his sex. In order to argue for a fundamental equality in the very constitution and mental capacities of the two sexes, over and above their differences which are the effect of socialization and culture, Belle van Zuylen had to assume that identity is more than the ex-pression of anatomy. It seems to me that in order to posit equality in the structures of identity, Belle had to imply the notion of an unabridgeable *distance*, a creative *space* that separates the 'self' from whichever sexual morphology one happens to be born with, which in turn determines the kind of social treatment one gets. What I emphasize is that, while arguing for equality in social and political rights for women, Belle van Zuylen paved a way for thinking about difference in the in-depth structures of identity, as that space of differentiation from one's organic or anatomic structures. She thus no longer understood sexual difference as a notion— that is, a factually determinable difference between man and woman—but also as a process, that is, as a never fixed and ever changing relationship which each one can have to one's identity. In the novel in question, the trick of neutralizing sex differences by disguising the sex identities of the two children, also serves the purpose of showing that the sex of the child is not a fixed and given fact but rather a process, that is to say a symbolic structure which the child can make him/herself familiar with in different ways.

I would like to situate this insight in a more contemporary discussion on sexual differences. I do not consider 'sex' as 'a positive fact,' but, with reference to modern semiology, as a 'sign'; this allows me to elaborate further Belle van Zuylen's idea. Although my sex is the 'sign' that characterizes me, the 'I' that is thus expressed does not coincide completely with the sign of my sex, 'I' am not determined only by my sex. My sex is rather, as Derrida puts it, a *trace* left on me, albeit an important one, but which should not be fixed into an identity or 'essence' of my being. Going even further in this direction, Kristeva (Kristeva, 1974) argues that the subject is always a *subject in process*, because the fixing of sex identities is constantly changing, as it also encompasses unconscious processes. Therefore, 'I' repeatedly have to relate myself in new ways to the sign of my sex; in this sense, sex identity is an open-ended process.[4] If the subject does not coincide completely with her/his sex, if she/he carries always a differentiating force, this necessarily implies that the subject is never a 'closed' identity, but is constantly creating the conditions for her or his being-woman or being-man. Quite clearly, male-domination being still the prevalent force in this world today, sexual stereotypes and the inferiority of women tend to prevail as models of identity. But feminist theories and practices of sexual difference have at least made us understand that *political resistance* is possible at the level of identity, by claiming not to coincide with either one of the sexually polarized positions. In other words, sexual difference can empower a political process that consists in refusing to uphold the dualistic scheme of masculine/feminine opposition (Braidotti, 1989). I would go so far as to suggest that the distance that exists between my identity—my 'I'— and my sex opens a space where I can create my sex identity, refusing the stereotypes that society makes available to me. A sexed identity structured against social expectations and fully claimed as such is therefore a feminist political position, because it refuses the subordination to the dualistic scheme that has kept women in prison of their so-called 'natural' bodies for such a long time.

I think that Belle van Zuylen's by now famous statement to James Boswell: "I have no talent for subordination" (van Zuylen, 1988, p. 93) aims at reclaiming this freedom. When she wrote to her epistolary lover Constant d'Hermenches: "To be free has ever been my most ardent wish, to be free and to shake off the etiquette," she meant that she did not wish to comply with etiquette that is connected to her being-woman (Charrière, 1988, p. 114). The modern reader can fully appreciate how, in the eighteenth century, the idea that an individual ought to coincide with her/his 'natural' anatomical sex served the organization of society very well, and still does in many cultures. In this way, women can *a priori* be linked with tasks like motherhood and housekeeping, which are presented as their 'natural' duty in life. By attributing an identity or 'essence' to man and woman on the basis of their sex, society is divided into two categories. Social order also requires that it be made clear in advance to both sexes which pole of antitheses like public-private or reason-feeling they are supposed to identify themselves with. Belle van Zuylen protested against this 'one to one' identification of people with their sex because this imposed identity prevented her from shaping her life the way she wanted. In *Three Women*, referring to the disguise of the babies, she has Constance say: "Even though I am completely woman, I will not be convinced of something because of the use it might have" (Charrière, 1982, vol. IX, p. 143).

Libertine

If the subject does not coincide with her/his sex, if in short it encompasses a difference, this means that we constantly have to interpret our being-woman or being-man. This makes sex into a figure of speech, into a metonymy of the 'self.' A metonymy that does not fix sexual identity, but shifts it and compresses it in new places. Psychoanalytic theory has understood the structure of the individual as a process of claiming as gendered identity, the sex one is born with. This process may go by more or less successfully, but identification with one's own sex will never be complete. A certain distance to one's own sex will always remain a distance that makes the creation of one's own identity possible. The French philosopher Assoun posed in reference to Rina Van der Haegen's thesis on sexual difference: "Freud does not take the sexual fact for granted. There is no sexualized nature which can be fixed as such, but man and woman construct their psycho-sexual identity" (Assoun, 1989, p. 503). However, as Belle van Zuylen demonstrates, the freedom to construct one's own identity is often denied by the social and political structures of society.

Let us now situate this idea of distance between the 'I' and the self in the context of eroticism and sexual difference. I believe this creative play with one's own sex forms also the basis of seduction and eroticism in both heterosexual and homosexual frameworks. What makes desire possible, in other words, is the blurring of fixed boundaries, which I see as a play with fixed identities and a resistance to fixed identifications. As Cixous suggests in her work on female homosexuality, the play with sex identities is also one of the most effective ways of resisting the heterosexual model (Cixous, 1983). In other words, it is not the sexually 'other,' that is to say the one with the *alternative* sex who seduces me, but rather the one with the *altering* sex. Desire requires a subject who can put her/his sexual identity at stake and play with it. At the same time, this desire is only possible if there is no 'one to one' imposed identification of people with their sex and if there is room left to be able to play such an erotic game.

I am quite aware that it would be anachronistic to put such a modern vision of female desire into Belle van Zuylen's mouth. Nevertheless I think it is not coincidental that, in the Dutch context, it was her work that inspired me to think of the 'play with sex identities' as a feminist political position. Her work is full of references to this undecided structure of the sexed self. Thus she sometimes feels 'estranged from' her own sex and she states that she would be 'a less misplaced being as a man.' Then again she rather calls herself a licentious and frivolous woman, who would like best to have gone through life like the seventeenth-century courtesan Ninon de Lenclos:

> Had I neither father nor mother, then perhaps I would be a Ninon and try with virtues to amend for the affront I have offered to society by shaking off the yoke of a neatly established order. (Charrière, 1988, p. 194)

Her desire to play the game of altering sex identities frequently emerges in the letters to Constant d'Hermenches, whom she seduces with statements like: "My senses are like my heart and soul, craving for pleasures" (van Zuylen, 1987, p. 120) and "my senses become ablaze when I still occupy myself with you after midnight" (van Zuylen, 1987, p. 222). She amuses herself and her friend regularly with giving libertine descriptions of herself. At the same time she slips through his fingers, when she tells him about her sexual desires for 'others': "You would be surprised to see how affectionate I can be with this woman, kissing her hands and arms, pursuing her time and again and telling her a hundred times how charming she is" (van Zuylen, 1987, p. 227). In her work Belle van Zuylen takes up numerous different sexual positions and in this way exceeds the bounds that society has imposed on her. However, this 'game' is not without risks.

Madness

In psychoanalytic theory this transgression of identity is considered as a shifting, temporary or otherwise, of the individual to a pre-subjective state, also referred to as 'psychosis.' In this sense, Belle van Zuylen's frequently returning hysterical nervous disorders, her *vapeurs*, indicate not only her objection to the ban on sexuality for women in her days, but seem to indicate as well that time and again she sought out the ultimate limits of her identity. Despite the dangers involved in this transgression of the prescribed boundaries, she knew that in order to live, to love and to write, this creative but also self-destructive 'game' had to be played. In this context, then, the famous description of herself as 'now foolish then wise' gets an unexpected turn. For it expresses precisely this game with the boundaries of identity, in which the temporary attachment of the individual to his/her sex corresponds to the moment of 'wisdom' and the unsettling of this temporarily formed identity to the moment of 'madness.'

In the contemporary reading of Belle van Zuylen with contemporary difference theorists like Irigaray, which I undertook above, I argued that I felt closer to Belle's play with sexed identities than to Irigaray's glorification of the feminine. It seems to me that the differences between these two thinkers are even more striking if you consider the implications of their respective positions for female creativity. To Irigaray, social emancipation is insufficient as a condition to allow female creativity to express itself, although it is a *necessary* condition. What is needed, according to Irigaray, is a female imaginary, a female creative force, even for a female god to sustain the process of expressing the feminine of woman. Irigaray wonders whether women can be creative, that is to say free in their minds, while they still have to relate to a cultural heritage biased by men. According to Irigaray, many women artists have gone mad and besides have not achieved full artistic self-expression because they did not focus on a specific feminine power of imagination. Irigaray writes:

> How can a woman create like a man, without being split up and scattered? Do women have to go mad before they can be artists? Do we have the opportunity to decide on madness, on wisdom? Can we be foolish or wise? (Irigaray, 1985, p. 39)

Unknowingly quoting Belle van Zuylen on wisdom and foolishness, Irigaray argues for the development of a specific feminine aesthetics. As long as women conform to the existing mode of masculine cultural production, a dispossession of their being-woman will always be involved. This detachment from her sexed identity is for Irigaray a source of female madness that ends in death. Therefore, to escape from madness women must relate to themselves and bring about an imagination of their own irreducible feminine identity. As can be gathered from the above, this would be too essentialistic for Belle van Zuylen's taste; what she would call 'madness' is rather the moment of loosening up all identification with a fixed identity, to make room for the blurring of boundaries and the play with different sexes.

With Belle van Zuylen the sense that 'beautiful' works of art are not created from a state of health and a "well-adjusted" consciousness seems to be dominant. In the process of creation, a state is sought out which rather disperses fixed identities. In this state, notions and experiences are explored, which we would not even suspect in our daily lives. All the letters Belle van Zuylen has written during the long night hours in her cold rooms in Slot Zuylen in Utrecht, left her none the healthier, and often she was confined to her bed for days because of severe *vapeurs*. She went, as the Dutch writer Hella Haasse notes, "as far as she could go in intimacy on paper" and "in her writing she played with fire" (Haasse, 1990, p. 63). But exactly by means of this dangerous game she found a kind of freedom which she sometimes called 'criminal,' because it undermined her fixed role in society and made numerous different roles possible. Or, as she writes to d'Hermenches: "the fire of my imagination and the craving of desire urged me to forget my own principles" (van Zuylen, 1988, p. 222). Out of this constant shifting of her limits and her excursions, so to speak, to the verge of madness, her letters, which belong to the most beautiful ones in the eighteenth-century epistolary literature, were born.

Now Foolish Then Wise

Belle van Zuylen's words 'now foolish then wise' can be read as the motto of a female 'aesthetic existence', as the Dutch philosopher Karen Vintges proposes, in which "being a woman can give rise to the design of new styles of life and cultural images" (Vintges, 1991, p. 227). At the same time, van Zuylen's motto can be regarded, in the footsteps of Luce Irigaray this time, as a first move towards the strategy of mimesis. The one who is 'now foolish then wise' realizes that the sexual position she/he takes up at a certain moment is only temporary in nature. Although not without identity, and therefore not without power either, the now foolish then wise one is elusive, and never the person one thinks she/he is. When Belle van Zuylen characterizes herself with these words, she proves herself to be a strategist of mimesis. A mimesis which in the words of the Dutch feminist scholar Mieke Aerts "restructures the conventional stereotypes by means of a playful imitation or perverting repetition" and can be understood to be a "politics of differentiating publicities" (Aerts, 1989, p. 498).[5] Not only in her letters, but in her stories as well, Belle van Zuylen stages moments of transformed mimesis. A clear example of this is her story "Mrs. Henley," which is an imitative answer to the novel *The Sentimental Husband* by Samuel de Constant. In Constant's novel a sensitive man is driven to death by a tyrannical woman. In Belle van Zuylen's mirror story it is not the woman who emerges as the guilty party, but the man who appears to be the source of the problem. She achieves this effect not by simply reversing the roles—the sensitive woman opposed to the tyrannical man—but by subtle shifts in characters and by putting in a differentiation of emotions. As Hella Haasse notices, there is in Belle van Zuylen's work indeed no such thing as "the traditional black-white of the average eighteenth century fictional characters" (Haasse, 1990, p. 65).

The foolishness and wisdom of Belle van Zuylen, her play with sexual identities, her irony and passion still seduce a modern reader. Her work is as much a call to think through sexual difference as it is an invitation to break fixed patterns. By confronting her 'enlightened' body of ideas with modern ways of thinking, her voluminous oeuvre does not have to be declared a 'beautiful but dead' monument, but can continue to inspire our thinking in vital ways. She herself considered it of very little importance to be buried in the Pantheon. She responded mockingly to the fierce discussion in her day whether or not Voltaire should be buried in this prestigious tomb. To her it was of much greater importance that through her work she could 'correspond with people from all over the world.' It is gratifying to see that 250 years after she was born Belle van Zuylen has been able to defy not only the borders of her country, but the limits of time as well. Her motto 'now foolish then wise' can still inspire the development of a feminist subjectivity:

> Let us try as much as we can to get rid of the veils education has cast over our minds. Let us then, free and at ease, ponder on things and, if we feel like it, write about them. In no way we will have to show slavish deference or shy respect to anyone. (Godet, 1927, p. 459)

NOTES

This article is an adaptation of the author's lecture at the foundation of the Belle van Zuylen Institute of the University of Amsterdam on November 14th, 1990. An earlier version of this article was published in: *Lover* 1991/2, pp. 86–92. The author thanks Rosi Braidotti for her help in editing this piece.

Translated by L. C. van der Wolf.

1. The Swiss/Dutch association for Belle van Zuylen/Isabelle de Charrière publish a news bulletin called: 'Lettre de Zuylen et du Pontet'; address: Drs. M. I. Wolff-Craandijk, Rozendaalselaan 22, 6891 DG Rozendaal/Bibliotheque oublique et Universitaire, Place Numa-Droz 3, 200 Neuchatel. The University of Utrecht was the first to honour her memory by endowing the Belle van Zuylen visiting chair in the early 1980s. In 1990 the University of Amsterdam named its Women's Studies Research Institute after Belle.

2. See for this point also my article "Protoféminisme pendant la révolution. Belle van Zuylen en Mme de Staël à propos de Kant", Hermsen (1989), pp. 295–309.

3. As a way of comparison, other feminist philosophers like Rosi Braidotti confront us with the important question: "How do we reformulate the bodily origin of subjectivity, so that the insight of the body as libidinal surface is incorporated?", without referring to biological determinism (Braidotti, 1989, p. 92).

4. See also on this point my article on Kofman and Derrida: "Baubo or Bacchante?" in Hermsen (1990), pp. 190–208.

5. Just like Diderot, Denis, in his *Le neveu de Rameau*, Aerts distinguishes between an 'order-continuing variant' of mimesis, which she calls 'womanism,' and an 'order-disrupting variant,' which she calls 'feminist.' Diderot, however, calls this first form 'passive and feminine' and the second 'active and masculine.'

REFERENCES

Aerts, Mieke. 1989. De neef van Irigaray: Over mimesis en strategie. *Tijdschrift voor vrouwenstudies, 10*(4), 511–520.

Assoun, Paul Laurent. 1989. Het onbewuste als differentie. *Tijdschrift voor Vrouwendstudies, 10*(4), 502–507.

Braidotti, Rosi. 1989. The politics of ontological difference. In Teresa Brennan (Ed.), *Between psychoanalysis and feminism* (pp. 89–105). London/New York: Routledge.

Charrière, Isabelle, de (Belle van Zuylen). 1982. *Oeuvres complètes (Vols. I-X)*. Amsterdam: Van Oorschot.

Charrière, Isabelle, de (Belle van Zuylen). 1988. *Ik heb geen talent voor ondergeschiktheid*. Correspondences with Constant d'Hermenches & James Boswell. Amsterdam: Van Oorschot.

Cixous, Hélène. 1975. *La jeune née*. Paris: U.G.E.

Cixous, Hélène. 1983. *Le livre de Promethea*. Paris: Gallimard.

Constant, Samuel, de. 1975. *Le mari sentimental, ou le marriage comme il y en a quelques uns*. Milan: Cisalpino-Goliardica.

Derrida, Jacques. 1967. *L'ecriture et la différence*. Paris: Seuil.

Godet, Philippe. 1927. *Mme. de Charriere et ses amis*. Lausanne: Editions Spes.

Haasse, Hella. 1990. Belle van Zuylen. In Joke Hermsen & Riette van der Plas (Eds.), *Nu eens dwaas dan weer wijs, Belle van Zuylen tussen Verlichting and Romantiek* (pp. 55–67). Amsterdam: van Genne.

Hermsen, Joke J. 1989. Protoféminisme pendant la révolution. Belle van Zuylen et Mme de Staël. In *Les femmes et la révolution française,* ed. Marie-France Brive. Toulouse: Presses Universitaires du Marail.

Hermsen, Joke J., & van Lenning, Alkeline (Eds.). 1991. *Sharing the difference: Feminist debates in Holland*. London/New York: Routledge.

Irigaray, Luce. 1977. *Speculum de l'autre femme*. Paris: Editions de Minuit.

Irigaray, Luce. 1985. Une lacune natale. *Le Nouveau Commerce, 62/63*, 39–47.

Irigaray, Luce. 1987. *Sexes et parentés*. Paris: Editions de Minuit.

Kofman, Sarah. 1982. *Le respect des femmes*. Paris: Galilee.

Kristeva, Julia. 1974. *La revolution du language poétique*. Paris: Editions du Seuil.

Lloyd, Geneviève. 1985. *The man of reason*. London: Methuen.

Nietzsche, Friederich. 1980. *Samtliche werke, kritische studien aussgabe, band I, nachgelassene schriften 1870–1873*. Munchen: Deutschen Taschenbuch Verlag.

Scott, Joan. 1988. Deconstructing the equality-versus-difference debate or, the use of post-structural theory for feminism. *Feminist Studies, 14*(1), 33–50.

Van der Haegen, Rina. 1989. *In het spoor van seksuele differentie*. Nijmegen: Sun.

Vasterling, Veronica. 1989. Lacan and Derrida: Psychoanalysis or philosophy? *Krisis, Tijdschrift voor Filosofie, 9*(1), 18–33.

Vintges, Karen. 1991. The vanished woman and styles of feminine subjectivity. In Joke J. Hermsen & Alkeline van Lenning (Eds.), *Sharing the difference: Feminist debates in Holland*. London/New York: Routledge.

REASON AND SENSIBILITY
THE IDEAL OF WOMEN'S SELF-GOVERNANCE IN THE WRITINGS OF MARY WOLLSTONECRAFT

CATRIONA MACKENZIE

> When morality shall be settled on a more solid basis,
> then, without being gifted with a prophetic spirit, I will
> venture to predict that woman will be either the friend or
> slave of man. We shall not, as at present, doubt whether she
> is a moral agent, or the link which unites man with brutes.
>
> —Wollstonecraft 1975, 120

I

In a letter written in 1795 while she was traveling in Scandinavia doing business on behalf of Gilbert Imlay, the man who had recently abandoned both her and her child by him, Mary Wollstonecraft wrote of herself: "For years have I endeavored to calm an impetuous tide—laboring to keep my feelings to an orderly course.—It was striving against the stream.—I must love and admire with warmth, or I sink into sadness" (Wollstonecraft 1977, 160).[1] It is reflections such as these, as well as the tempestuous events of Wollstonecraft's personal life, that have led one of her biographers to suggest that Wollstonecraft was unable to live her own life by the ideal of self-governance that she proposed for women in *A Vindication of the Rights of Woman*.[2] The explanation proffered for this apparent discrepancy is that the *Vindication* was written when Wollstonecraft was childless and inexperienced in sexual relationships with men. Her later

Hypatia vol. 8, no. 4 (Fall 1993) © by Catriona Mackenzie

experiences, however, taught her that passion cannot always, or cannot very easily, be governed by reason. More recent feminist commentators have rejected this rather patronizing view of the relationship between Wollstonecraft's life and her writings.[3] But the idea that Wollstonecraft defined self-governance in opposition to passion has not been challenged and still prevails even in feminist interpretations of her work.[4] Jane Martin, for example, argues that Wollstonecraft adopts a "sovereignty model of personality," which posits reason in opposition to feeling as the "ruling element" of the soul and which allows between reason and feeling "no give and take, no interaction, no sensitivity to context" (Martin 1985, Chap. 4).

In this essay I argue that the overriding preoccupations of Wollstonecraft's work, as well as of her life, were to articulate what it means for women to think and act as autonomous moral agents, and to envisage the kind of social and political organization required for them to do so. Although at times she seemed to identify autonomy with reason, defining it in opposition to passion, in a context in which woman was "always represented as only created to see through a gross medium, and to take things on trust" (Wollstonecraft 1975, 142), Wollstonecraft also struggled to develop an account of women's moral agency that would incorporate a recognition not only of women's capacity to reason but also of their right to experience and give expression to passion, including sexual desire. Of particular concern to her was the need to create the possibility for genuinely reciprocal friendships and love relationships between men and women. She was also vehement that women's bodies should be regarded neither as mere objects of use, pleasure, and exchange among men, nor by women as objects of narcissistic attention. Rather, respect for the body is an integral part of both self-esteem and respect for others. Wollstonecraft's view was that such reciprocity and respect could be realized only in a context in which women are able to exercise control of both the external—financial, educational, and political—circumstances of their lives and the direction of their own affections.

Such an interpretation need not deny that there are tensions within Wollstonecraft's account of women's autonomy, as well as difficulties with it for contemporary feminists. In particular, Wollstonecraft's treatment of the distinction between reason/passion and public/private seems to raise problems from a feminist perspective for her understanding of self-governance. But I will suggest that these problems are not as clear-cut as they are sometimes made to seem. First, it is true that at many points in the *Vindication* Wollstonecraft is explicit that virtue must be founded on reason, not sensibility. She also ties virtue to the notion of the perfectibility of the soul. This lends credence to the view that she regards self-governance as a matter of reason's control over unruly passions associated with the body. From a feminist perspective this is problematic because it allies Wollstonecraft's account of self-governance with hierarchical oppositions between soul/body, reason/passion, and masculine/feminine. The supposedly sex-neutral "self" that controls the body is thus implicitly associated with "masculine" virtues while downgrading "feminine" virtues associated with affectivity.[5] While not denying that Wollstonecraft does appeal to the idea of a "soul which knows no sex," I will try to show that, within the inevitable limits imposed by this idea, Wollstonecraft was also struggling to articulate a more subtle view of self-governance, one that would not pit women's reason in opposition either to their bodies or to affectivity. The outlines of this view are certainly present in the *Vindication*, but they are more fully developed in Wollstonecraft's posthumously published novel *The Wrongs of Woman* (Wollstonecraft 1980b) and in some of her travel writings and personal letters.[6]

Second, in the *Vindication* Wollstonecraft makes much of the claim that although virtue must be regarded as the same in both sexes, men and women have different "duties." Women's "duties," associated with the care of children and the running of the household, are considered by Wollstonecraft to follow "naturally" from women's role in reproduction. But as feminists have pointed out, this division of the sexes according to duties, as well as the idea that certain duties are "natural" to women, derives from and preserves the distinction between public and private that is at the root of women's subordination. Moira Gatens, for example, argues that Wollstonecraft's endorsement of a sexual division of labor is a consequence of her attempt to extend the liberal ideal of equality to women (Gatens 1991a).[7] According to Gatens, Wollstonecraft assumes that the liberal notion of equality, and the reason that grounds it, are sex-neutral. In fact, however, the characteristics of the "equal" liberal citizen are defined in opposition to, but also presuppose, those affective virtues associated with women. As a result, the liberal public sphere is a sphere of male equality that can function only through the subordination of women in the private sphere. Wollstonecraft's argument that women can fulfill dual roles as mothers-daughters-wives and as equal citizens thus overlooks the fact that within liberalism women's duties are necessarily tied to women's subordination. According to Gatens, Wollstonecraft attempts to deal with this difficulty by denying the ethical significance of women's embodiment and of those virtues associated with women, and by adopting supposedly sex-neutral but in fact masculine ideals of virtue in both public and private spheres. But given the practical consequences of women's embodiment (in particular, the nature of women's involvement in reproduction), while the ethical significance of sexual difference is denied, difference reemerges at the level of the division of labor. Because the sexual division of labor lies at the heart of women's social inferiority, the net effect of Wollstonecraft's account of virtue is to leave intact the structures of women's subordination.

While I do not deny that the idea that women have certain "natural" duties must be rejected, I do maintain that Wollstonecraft's views on the relation between public and private spheres are more complex than perhaps Gatens allows. Although Wollstonecraft certainly wants nothing to do with the Rousseauian idea of specific "feminine" virtues, she does not deny the ethical importance of the affections. Nor does she overlook the ethical significance of sexual difference.[8] Her concern is to understand the kind of moral character required in order to achieve justice in the public realm and genuine reciprocity in the private. But what motivates this concern is a recognition that male and female embodiment are different and that this difference has ethical and political significance. It was for this reason that she called for not only a "revolution in female manners" but also a complete transformation of the legal and economic relations of both public and private spheres.

It is certainly true that Wollstonecraft was not entirely successful in her effort to combat the representation of women's bodies as obstacles to women's moral agency, a view that came to dominate philosophical and cultural conceptions of femininity from the Enlightenment onward. At times she seems to take over the view that women's bodies are more "dependent" than men's bodies are and hence that women's bodies may be impediments to virtue. Particularly in *The Wrongs of Woman* and in some of her reflections on her own feelings for her daughter, she also seems to suggest that women are by nature more susceptible to the "attached affections" than are men. And, as I stated above, she seems to endorse the idea that certain duties are natural to women. But even here Wollstonecraft shows an awareness that perhaps her views, as well as her own susceptibilities, arise more from "the imperfect state of society" than from the nature of women's bodies.

II

When reading Wollstonecraft it is important to try to disentangle her somewhat sketchy conception of self-governance from the arguments for equality out of which it arises. In her defense of equality she puts a great deal of stress on women's capacity to reason and on the idea that virtue must be founded on reason. This gives rise to the impression that for Wollstonecraft self-governance is equivalent to the rule of reason. I suggest, however, that Wollstonecraft does not straightforwardly endorse the extreme rationalism of the arguments for equality. Rather, these arguments serve the strategic function of directly answering the charges against women's equality that were raised by Enlightenment thinkers—

but in particular, by Rousseau. Although the arguments for equality provide the necessary theoretical underpinning for her account of self-governance, in this account the role of reason figures more as a necessary part of a virtuous character than as the sole authority in all matters.

Wollstonecraft's argument in defense of women's equality works by extending the Enlightenment critique of sovereign power to relations between the sexes. Her claim is that if sovereign power is deemed illegitimate because it sanctions arbitrary power, then logical consistency requires that any exercise of arbitrary power be deemed illegitimate. What she seeks to show is that women's subordination to men is purely arbitrary, that is, it cannot be justified by reason. Wollstonecraft's main method of exposing the arbitrary nature of patriarchal power is via a critique of Rousseau's arguments against women's claims to equality. Her targets are, first, Rousseau's claim that women are by nature inferior to men with respect to those capacities that ground equality—namely reason, independence, and virtue—and, second, his claim that women's equality would subvert the social order.[9] In the *Vindication* Wollstonecraft presents two main arguments against the first claim, an environmental argument and an argument based on an appeal to the perfectibility of the soul. The environmental argument involves a straightforward appeal to empiricist psychology. Following Locke she argues that our capacities are developed and our characters formed in response to our environment, or what she terms "the effect of an early association of ideas." For Wollstonecraft, one of the most significant features of the environment is education or its lack, but environment also embraces customs, habits, opportunities, parental influences, and so on. Her response to Rousseau concedes that women "in the present state of society" do seem to be less capable of both reason and virtue than men are, but she seeks to show that this is simply a product of women's education and environment rather than a natural incapacity.

The environmental argument has, of course, been rehearsed repeatedly under a number of different guises by feminists since Wollstonecraft. A more interesting argument from the point of view of Wollstonecraft's concern with autonomy is the appeal to the perfectibility of the soul. At one level this argument works simply to challenge the coherence of any claim that certain groups of human beings can be naturally subject to others. Women, says Wollstonecraft, are either human beings or they are not—that is, they are either capable of reason and virtue or they are not, they either have an immortal soul or they do not. To postulate the possibility of a being that is neither one thing nor the other is to suggest that women are "beautiful flaws in nature. Let it also be remembered that they are the only flaw" (Wollstonecraft 1975, 122). If women are *not* human beings, then they must be regarded as subject to their impulses and hence incapable of freedom of the will. If this is the case, then their subjection to the authority of others is perfectly justifiable. However, if women *are* human beings, then their subjection to the will of others is completely unjustifiable. Furthermore, if this is the case, it is morally requisite that women be given the liberty and the scope to perfect their souls through the exercise of their reason. Underlying this challenge is the idea that human beings have a duty to improve their souls, more than this, that the highest aim of human life is self-improvement.[10] Thus Wollstonecraft's argument against Rousseau is that by denying women equality, he undermines the foundation of morality because he denies women the possibility of undertaking what is in fact the sternest duty of beings accountable for themselves to God. Shortly we will see how this doctrine of perfectibility underpins Wollstonecraft's conception of self-governance.

In response to Rousseau's claim that women's equality would subvert the social order, Wollstonecraft seeks to show that precisely the reverse would be true.[11] Her argument to this effect focuses on Rousseau's conception of feminine virtue as founded not in reason but in modesty, which, she claims, is not virtue at all but a sham more likely to corrupt and degrade women and the social order than to improve either. The strategy of Wollstonecraft's argument is to concede to Rousseau certain assumptions but to deny the validity of the inferences he makes on the basis of those assumptions. First, she agrees that public virtue must be founded in private virtue, conceding also the importance of modesty and fidelity in relationships between men and women. However, she argues that Rousseau's recommendations for the education of women and his subjection of women to the authority of men will not bring about the desired result. According to Wollstonecraft, modesty must be founded in self-respect and in respect for the integrity of one's body, while fidelity is only a virtue if it arises out of genuine affection. Understood thus, modesty and fidelity are not sexually specific virtues at all. But Rousseau adopts a sexual double standard and makes modesty and fidelity the paramount virtues for women. Furthermore, he grounds these allegedly "feminine" virtues not in women's self-respect and capacity for affection but in male needs. It is clear that for Rousseau the function of so-called feminine virtue is to make women pleasing to men and to ensure that women's own needs are subordinated to this end. Wollstonecraft cites as evidence of this claim Rousseau's injunctions to Sophie to ensure that she is always alluring for Emile, while at the same time insisting that her chastity is her main asset. But pointing to the behavior of the leisured middle-class and aristocratic women whom Wollstonecraft so despised, she suggests that Rousseau's advice is more likely to produce infidelity, or at least sham fidelity, than genuine fidelity because it focuses women's whole attention on "corporeal embellishments" rather than on attaining genuine virtue.[12] The fact that feminine "virtue" must in the end be assured through force indicates that Rousseau was in fact aware of this.[13] Wollstonecraft's joking suggestion is that he abandoned logic on this issue because he succumbed to his own lasciviousness! Wollstonecraft is also outraged by Rousseau's insistence that it is not sufficient for a woman to be faithful; in addition, everyone must know of her fidelity. By making virtue a function of the opinions of others rather than of a person's own integrity and honesty, Rousseau deliberately undermines women's independence. More than this, he quite openly incites women to duplicity and cunning. But by depriving women of integrity and of every legitimate means of exercising power, Rousseau ensures that women will in fact create social disorder because despotism becomes the only path open to them. By being civil and political slaves women become private tyrants (Wollstonecraft 1975, esp. chaps. 4, 5, and 12).[14] Wollstonecraft's conclusion is that Rousseau's recommendations teach women manners rather than morals—hardly an adequate basis for the virtue required to perfect the soul.

Rousseau's second argument in support of the claim that women's equality would subvert the social order is that women's primary function in life is to raise and educate children. Were women themselves to be educated to participate as equal citizens who would take responsibility for this crucial task? Wollstonecraft's response is simple but devastating. Once again she concedes certain assumptions to Rousseau, namely, that the family is indeed the foundation of social life and that women's primary *social* duty is to raise and educate children. However, she points out that if women are trained to be dependent on men, and required to base their judgements on the authority of men, then they will be incapable of raising and educating children. Wollstonecraft's argument is that the task of education demands independence of judgement. This in turn requires a capacity for reflection and generalization. But the education and social position that Rousseau recommends for women denies them the opportunity of developing these capacities. Furthermore, if women are ignorant of virtue and are themselves subjected to arbitrary authority, how likely is it that they will inculcate virtue in their own children? What is more likely is that they in turn will subject their children to arbitrary authority rather than teach them virtue through the use of reason. But having conceded that women's primary *social* duties are maternal duties, Wollstonecraft also argues that women have a duty to which their social duties must always be secondary. This is their duty to themselves as beings accountable to God.

III

Wollstonecraft's views on the perfectibility of the soul are beautifully captured in one of her travel letters written in Tonsberg, Norway. This letter shows that Wollstonecraft's belief in the immortality of the soul did not prevent her from reflecting on the moral significance of human embodiment. In the letter, Wollstonecraft recounts her horror at discovering in the town's church a recess full of coffins containing embalmed bodies. Her horror arose from a sense that it degrades humanity to attempt to preserve the body when all active life has been extinguished, when "the enchantment of animation" is broken. In contrast to the "noble ruins" that are reminders of the exertions and efforts of earlier generations and that "exalt the mind," these futile attempts at prolonging life bring home the "littleness" and mortality of the individual. Reflecting on her reaction, Wollstonecraft writes,

> Life, what art thou? Where goes this breath? this *I*, so much alive? In what element will it mix, giving or receiving fresh energy . . . I feel a conviction that we have some perfectible principle in our present vestment, which will not be destroyed just as we begin to be sensible of improvement. (Wollstonecraft 1977, Letter VII, 158–59)

Although at times Wollstonecraft's belief in the immortality of the soul led her to adopt an attitude of stoicism and resignation in the face of life's sorrows and injustices, her more considered view was that it is by learning from error and experience and by fighting injustice that the soul is improved.[15] As we will see, Wollstonecraft's views on what constitutes virtue or the perfection of the soul shifted somewhat from the *Vindication* to *The Wrongs of Woman*. But the idea that self-governance is essential to virtue and to the possibility of perfectibility or self-improvement remained a constant theme in her work, as did the idea that sexual inequality is immoral because it deprives women of self-governance.

Central to Wollstonecraft's notion of perfectibility and to her account of self-governance is a contrast—not accidentally echoing the same contrast in Rousseau—between independence and dependence. To be dependent is "to act according to the will of another fallible being, and submit, right or wrong, to power" (Wollstonecraft 1975, 135). However, independence, which Wollstonecraft calls "the grand blessing of life, the basis of every virtue" (Wollstonecraft 1975, 85), is not the mere converse of dependence, namely, being self-willed, but is a more complex virtue. In the *Vindication* Wollstonecraft lays great stress on the importance of reason to independence. She characterizes reason in the following terms:

> Reason is . . . the simple power of improvement; or, more properly speaking, of discerning truth. Every individual is in this respect a world in itself. More or less may be conspicuous in one being than another; but the nature of reason must be the same in all, if it be an emanation of divinity, the tie that connects the creature with the Creator; for, can

that soul be stamped with the heavenly image, that is not perfected by the exercise of its own reason? (Wollstonecraft 1975, 142)

According to Wollstonecraft, a person must exercise her reason in a number of different ways in order to achieve independence. The most important of these ways, and the one to which she remains committed throughout her writings, is that exercise of reason which counters the effects of prejudice and which refuses blind obedience to authority. Our actions can be free and virtuous, she wants to say, only if they are based on reasoned judgments, rather than arising out of conformity to social expectations or from notions of duty that require the individual to submit her own judgment to the arbitrary authority of others. In the *Vindication* this view leads Wollstonecraft to condemn military training and discipline as incompatible with freedom (Wollstonecraft 1975, 97).[16] In *The Wrongs of Women* she has Darnford declare that "minds governed by superior principles . . . were privileged to act above the dictates of laws they had no voice in framing" (Wollstonecraft 1980b, 2: 187).[17] These "superior principles" are principles founded in respect for the rights of rational beings, including self-respect, as opposed to the principles of social utility that justify, among other things, the subordination of women and the exploitation of the poor. Her view was that a knowledge of such principles could only be arrived at by "enlarging the mind" through education, sensibility, and experience. By "cramping the understanding," women's education and social position, as well as Rousseau's recommendations on these matters, put the capacity for making independent judgments out of the reach of most women, condemning them to be slaves to the opinions of others.

In the *Vindication* Wollstonecraft seems to follow Rousseau in linking dependence on the opinions of others to being subject to one's own inclinations and passions.[18] In some places she therefore connects that exercise of reason which leads to independence of judgment and virtue with the control of the passions and with a kind of self-denying fortitude. Her complaint against the indolent women of the middle classes, for example, is that their senses are inflamed by the pursuit of pleasure and by momentary feelings. As a result, their reason is prevented from "attaining that sovereignty which it ought to attain to render a rational creature useful to others and content with its own station" (Wollstonecraft 1975, 152). In contrast, the virtuous widow Wollstonecraft depicts for us is a woman who subdues any passionate inclinations, selflessly devotes herself to educating and providing for her children, and then "calmly waits for the sleep of death" (Wollstonecraft 1975, 138–39). In a similar vein, Wollstonecraft also declares that "a master and mistress of a family ought not to love each other with passion. I mean to say that they ought not to indulge those emotions which disturb the order of society" (Wollstonecraft 1975, 114).

However, even in the *Vindication* Wollstonecraft seems to be ambivalent about this view. In a number of places she contrasts the "romantic, wavering feelings" that "inflame" the passions with those "strong, persevering passions" that "strengthen" the passions and so enlarge the understanding and ennoble the heart. (See, for example, Wollstonecraft 1975, 115, 152, 169.) Similarly she contrasts lust with love, sensuality with sensibility, parental self-love with parental affection, and so on, suggesting that although the first term in the pair undermines virtue the second term is essential to it. She also suggests that "the regulation of the passions is not, always, wisdom" and that the reason why men seem to be more capable of independent judgement than women are is because they have more scope to exercise "the grand passions" (Wollstonecraft 1975, 212). Even more surprising, she claims for women the right to sexual desire: "Women as well as men ought to have the common appetites and passions of their nature, they are only brutal when unchecked by reason: but the obligation to check them is the duty of mankind, not a sexual duty" (Wollstonecraft 1975, 238).

In the novel *The Wrongs of Woman*, the character Maria cautions her daughter in a letter to learn to distinguish genuine love and affection from passing infatuation but also urges her not to flee from pleasure and to open her heart to affection, even though that will also make her vulnerable to pain. In an important passage she deplores contemporary moral standards that require women to remain married to men for whom they have neither affection nor esteem: "woman, weak in reason, impotent in will, is required to moralize, sentimentalize herself to stone, and pine her life away, laboring to reform her embruted mate" (Wollstonecraft 1980b, 2: 154). Maria declares that, to the contrary, lack of passion and coldness of heart undermine virtue, and she argues that desire must be reciprocal and women must have the freedom to express "that fire of the imagination, which produces *active* sensibility, and *positive* virtue" (Wollstonecraft 1980b, 2:153). Later she rails against the tyranny of laws that pit women's reason in opposition to their inclinations.

How should these apparent tensions be read, and what implications do they have for Wollstonecraft's conception of self-governance? In the *Vindication* Wollstonecraft does seem to waver between two different ways of thinking about self-governance. On the one hand, especially in her insistence on women's capacity to reason and in her scathing condemnation of the "manners" of contemporary women, she seems to regard the control of the passions by reason as essential to self-governance. On the other hand, she seems also to be moving toward the view that in a well-balanced, virtuous character, reason and sensibility should mutually strengthen and support each other rather than either dominating the other. This seems clearly to be the view of *The Wrongs of Woman*. Why, then, this ambivalence on Wollstonecraft's part? There may be some truth in the claim that the events of Wollstonecraft's own life helped confirm her in the latter view. However, there may also be other reasons for Wollstonecraft's wavering. A clue to these reasons is found in one of her travel letters. Reflecting on her fears and hopes for her daughter Fanny, Wollstonecraft writes:

> You know that as a female I am particularly attached to her—I feel more than a mother's fondness and anxiety, when I reflect on the despondent and oppressed state of her sex. I dread lest she should be forced to sacrifice her heart to her principles, or principles to her heart. With trembling hand I shall cultivate sensibility, and cherish delicacy of sentiment, lest, while I lend fresh blushes to the rose, I sharpen the thorns that will wound the breast I would fain guard—I dread to unfold her mind, lest it should render her unfit for the world she is to inhabit—Hapless woman! what a fate is thine. (Wollstonecraft 1977, Letter VI, 156)

In many other places in her writings Wollstonecraft qualifies her claims with a statement to the effect that what she describes characterizes the situation of women "in the current imperfect state of society." This indicates that Wollstonecraft's apparent devaluation of passion stems from a number of sources. As I argued above, it must be seen, in the context of Wollstonecraft's defense of equality and of women's capacity to reason, as a counter to the Rousseauian depiction of "feminine" virtue. But Wollstonecraft's anxiety about passion is also a response to a social situation that denied to women the scope for expressing desire and passion and hence gave rise to devastating conflicts between reason and sensibility. This is particularly evident in Wollstonecraft's reflections on Fanny quoted above and in her depiction of Maria's marriage to George Venables, a situation that Maria managed to tolerate for six years only by deadening her sensibility. A further reason for Wollstonecraft's ambivalence was her view that "in the current state of society" there was always the danger that women's sensibility was more likely to undermine than strengthen virtue by encouraging "romantic, wavering feelings" rather than "strong, persevering passions." As Maria reflects while gazing out of her asylum window hoping to catch a glimpse of Darnford, "how difficult it was for women to avoid growing romantic, who have no active duties or pursuits" (Wollstonecraft 1980b, 1: 87).

Wollstonecraft's attempt in the *Vindication* to distinguish between those passions that undermine and those that strengthen virtue echoes Rousseau's attempt to make a similar distinction. Like Rousseau, she feels that the very same faculties and capacities, under different circumstances, may give rise to virtue and generosity of heart or self-centered vice. She also shares Rousseau's views about the power of education to shape these faculties and capacities for good or ill. Where she differs from Rousseau is in her acute awareness that virtue and vice arise as much, if not more, from the character of our social and affective relations with others as from our individual dispositions, characteristics, and capacities. Although she often wants to make exceptions for individuals of "genius" and at times portrays herself as Rousseau's solitary walker, requiring solitude for reflection, Wollstonecraft's individuals are nevertheless much more embedded in their relations with others than are Rousseau's.[19] Despite the fact that she condemns the kind of obedient dependence characteristic of subordination, for Wollstonecraft independence is not defined in opposition to a mutually supportive dependence on others. In fact, the values of affection, reciprocity, and love for humanity are central to her account of self-governance. Wollstonecraft's view is that in the absence of genuine feelings for others, self-governance is most likely to be displaced by a kind of self-interested prudence. This was one of the aspects of Imlay that so wounded her, and which she blamed on his involvement with commerce.[20] In the *Vindication* she claims:

> The world cannot be seen by an unmoved spectator; we must mix in the throng and feel as men feel, before we can judge of their feelings . . . we must attain knowledge of others at the same time that we become acquainted with ourselves. Knowledge acquired any other way only hardens the heart and perplexes the understanding. (Wollstonecraft 1975, 215)[21]

And in *The Wrongs of Woman* Jemima is presented as a woman with a great capacity for virtue, but in her "virtue, never nurtured by affection, assumed the stern aspect of selfish independence" (Wollstonecraft 1980b, 1: 82) until Maria treats her with affection and respect.

Many of the tensions in her writings and the conflicts in her life bear testimony to Wollstonecraft's painful awareness that for women "in the current state of society" this kind of self-governance founded in generosity and affection was very difficult to achieve. On the one hand, she argues, women's subordination to men within the family, the idea that women's function is solely to please men, and the denial to women of the right to express or act in accordance with their affections all conspire to make love and friendship founded on respect just about impossible between men and women. This is because the effect of women's situation on *women* is to give rise either to an excess of affectionate sensibility—as Wollstonecraft felt was true of herself—or else to coquetry, while its effect on *men* is to render them lascivious or tyrannical or both. In these circumstances it is highly unlikely that women will have sufficient self-respect, or command sufficient respect from men, to make reciprocity a genuine possibility. In this context it is interesting to note that Wollstonecraft's sometimes prudish remarks in the *Vindication* about the need for bodily modesty arise from the conviction that self-respect and respect for others is necessarily connected with respect for the integrity of one's own body and for the bodies of others. By the time of *The Wrongs of Woman* the prudish aspects of this conviction have disappeared, and Wollstonecraft's comments about marriage laws—"legal prostitution"—that make women and their children the property of men suggest that she regarded women's right to self-governance with respect to their bodies as integral to the demand for equality.

On the other hand, she continues, women's exclusion from the duties of citizenship tends to promote a kind of self-centeredness and leads to a lack of that sense of justice that is necessary if we are to treat others with respect. Here Wollstonecraft points to the behavior of those leisured women who show more concern for their dogs than for their servants. She also points to the kind of parental affection that is an extension of this kind of self-love: "Justice, truth, everything is sacrificed by these Rebekahs, and for the sake of their *own* children they violate the most sacred duties, forgetting the common relationship that binds the whole family on earth together" (Wollstonecraft 1975, 265). Wollstonecraft is adamant that the only solution is a transformation of women's situation in *both* private and public spheres.

IV

One of the major themes of Wollstonecraft's work is that women will not be able to attain self-governance without a certain degree of material—particularly financial—independence. Wollstonecraft's concern with women's financial independence arises out of two firm convictions. The first is that women's emotional dependence and subjection to the tyranny of men will continue so long as women are financially dependent on men and so long as women's independence is not protected by the law. This conviction is articulated most forcefully in *The Wrongs of Woman*, where it is dramatized in the stories of Maria, Jemima, and the various women in whose houses Maria takes lodgings after leaving George Venables, all of whom are victims of the law's inequality. The second is that financial independence, but more importantly, work, is essential to self-esteem and to virtue. As Wollstonecraft remarks in the *Vindication*, "virtue, says reason, must be acquired by *rough* toils, and useful struggles with worldly *cares*" (Wollstonecraft 1975, 143, note 5). These convictions underlie her suggestion that women could very usefully be trained for a number of professions, including medicine, education, politics, and business.

Wollstonecraft was aware that women's financial independence could not be achieved without large-scale changes in the organization of society. To this end she advocated sweeping changes in marriage and property laws, urged the introduction of a system of public coeducation, and suggested, even if somewhat tentatively, that it was not sufficient for women to be citizens, they must also be represented in government. Her view was that these were matters for public, not private, concern and felt that until such changes were introduced women would be unable to achieve self-governance in either their social or their affective relationships. However, Wollstonecraft had no clear proposals for how the changes she advocated might be compatible with the maternal "duties" that she seemed to think were natural to women. For this reason feminists recently have raised two serious objections to Wollstonecraft's conception of self-governance.

First, it is often claimed that Wollstonecraft's ideal of self-governance is an ideal attainable only by middle-class women. In the *Vindication*, for example, her description of a harmonious and fulfilling domestic scene includes reference to a woman "discharging the duties of her station with perhaps merely a servant-maid to take off her hands the servile part of the household business" (Wollstonecraft 1975, 254–55), and it is evident that without such domestic help Wollstonecraft herself would not have been able to devote much of her time to the business of writing.[22] The character of Jemima in *The Wrongs of Woman* indicates that Wollstonecraft became increasingly aware of this problem. Nevertheless, much of the narrative is occupied with the story of the middle-class Maria, who promises, in exchange for Jemima's support, to better her situation. Is the self-governance of educated middle-class women therefore to be achieved at the expense of working-class women who can relieve them of the "servile" aspects of their duties?[23] This question remains pertinent today.

Second, it is argued that despite the importance of Wollstonecraft's critique of property and marriage laws and of her argument that the rights of citizenship must be extended to women if they are going to be expected to fulfill what are after all social duties (the rearing of children), her critique of civil society works by trying to extend the contractual relations of civil society into the private sphere rather than by challenging the association between the masculine/feminine distinction and the tensions within the liberal public sphere between justice and love, contract and kinship, individuality and community. In other words, Wollstonecraft claims for women the capacities of the self-governing male citizen, arguing that relations within the family between men and women and parents and children must be founded on the same basis as relations between equal citizens within the public sphere. Given this starting point, Wollstonecraft can only acknowledge the ethical and political implications of women's specific embodiment by arguing that women have specific *social* duties—

namely, their maternal duties—to which any activities in which they engage in the public sphere must be seen as secondary. Wollstonecraft's conception of self-governance thus compels her to preserve the distinction between public and private spheres and consequently to accept the oppressive representation implicit in this distinction of women's bodies as passive and bound to nature.[24]

These criticisms can begin to be addressed by first assessing Wollstonecraft's views on maternity. Wollstonecraft's remarks about women's maternal duties need to be read fairly carefully for the following reasons. First, it is clear that these remarks play a very important strategic function in her argument in defense of equality. For as was indicated above, what she seeks to show is that even granting the premises of the Rousseauian argument, the conclusions thought to follow from it do not in fact do so. It should not be assumed, however, that Wollstonecraft simply endorses these premises. Second, that Wollstonecraft does not straightforwardly endorse these premises is evident from a number of conflicting remarks she makes about maternity. It is true that she does claim that "the care of children in their infancy is one of the grand duties annexed to the female character by nature" (Wollstonecraft 1975, 265). However, she also claims that "natural affection, as it is termed, I believe to be a very faint tie, affections must grow out of the habitual exercise of a mutual sympathy" (Wollstonecraft 1975, 266). And in *The Wrongs of Woman* Maria remarks that "*in the present state of women* it is a great misfortune to be prevented from discharging the duties, and cultivating the affections" of a mother (Wollstonecraft 1980b, 2: 154; italics added). These remarks suggest that Wollstonecraft's views on maternity pertain to a very specific context, one in which women had few options as far as contributions to society were concerned, apart from the raising of children; in which, given the lack of genuinely reciprocal relationships between men and women, the only outlet for women's affections was in their relationships with their children; in which women were by default primarily responsible for the raising of children because there was no legal or social obligation for men to do so; and in which many leisured women effectively abrogated their responsibilities toward their children.

Given the complexity of this context, Wollstonecraft's views on maternity need to be read on a number of different levels. At one level they are addressed to men, in particular to middle-class men, in the hope of convincing them that the education of their daughters and wives will in fact better enable them to perform those duties that she concedes are "annexed to the female character by nature." At another level, by distinguishing between affections and duties and by suggesting that maternity is a *social* duty, not a merely "natural affection," Wollstonecraft aims to contest the assumption that maternity and self-governance are incompatible virtues by showing that the kind of affections, responsibilities, and skills that arise in the context of childrearing are essential to self-governance. On this basis she can then argue that "maternal duties" are not incompatible with the duties of a citizen. At yet another level, this distinction also enables Wollstonecraft to suggest that women should be able to fulfill their obligations to society in ways other than, or additional to, maternity. Although Wollstonecraft was very well aware that this would not be possible without vast changes in the structure of society, it seems clear that she thought the difficulty was a question of social organization rather than of women's natures.

If this reading of Wollstonecraft's views on maternity is correct, what are its implications for the claim that her ideal of self-governance is an ideal attainable only by educated middle-class women? It is important to distinguish between the issue of whether class distinction is a necessary feature of Wollstonecraft's conception of self-governance and the issue of what she herself says on the matter. As far as Wollstonecraft herself is concerned, she seems to voice a number of somewhat conflicting views, probably reflecting the limited range of conceivable options that were available to her, indeed to all women. In a number of places she suggests that self-governance has less to do with what she calls a woman's "station" than with a woman's dignity and independence. In the *Vindication*, for example, she claims that virtue seems to be most prevalent among poor, uneducated working-class women (Wollstonecraft 1975, 171), and in *The Wrongs of Woman* Maria writes to her daughter: "I fondly hope to see you . . . possessed of that energy of character which gives dignity to any station; and with that clear, firm spirit that will enable you to choose a situation for yourself, or submit to be classed in the lowest, if it be the only one in which you can be the mistress of your own actions" (Wollstonecraft 1980b, 2: 149). Wollstonecraft was aware, however, that poor women, in addition to suffering the "wrongs of woman," also suffered the burdens of the poor more generally, and she believed that poor women were unlikely to be the mistresses of their own actions until both class and sex inequalities are abolished. Yet elsewhere Wollstonecraft seems to align self-governance with "cultivated sensibilities" and to take the existence of servants for granted, even though she is insistent that servants must be regarded and treated as fellow human beings. It is clear, though not surprising, that Wollstonecraft did not really come to terms with the question of who would care for the children of professional women. It is therefore quite possible that she assumed another woman, probably a servant, would take up some of the responsibility. Despite this, I would deny that Wollstonecraft's conception of self-governance presupposes class distinction. For her ideal of self-governance is not committed to the idea that only professional women can achieve independence, even though she is adamant that a certain degree of education is essential for all women. Rather, at the heart of Wollstonecraft's concern with women's independence are the ideas that women must have the liberty and resources to assume responsibility for their own actions and that self-governance is not inconsistent with maternity, affection, or interdependence.

Where does this leave Wollstonecraft with respect to the public/private distinction and with respect to the alleged masculinity of her conception of self-governance? Again, Wollstonecraft's views need to be read carefully. On the one hand, she was aware that, "in the present imperfect state of society," men's equality and reason were achieved at the expense of women's liberty and autonomy and that reason and sensibility, justice and love, citizenship and kinship, and individuality and community seemed irreconcilable, particularly for women. I have tried to show that because she *was* concerned with the ethical implications of sexual difference, Wollstonecraft tried to articulate a conception of women's self-governance that does not simply identify self-governance with one side of these oppositions (the "masculine" side), but rather tries to reconcile them, as well as to disentangle them from their association with the masculine/feminine distinction.[25] I have also argued that Wollstonecraft was aware that her recommendations for women would require massive reorganization of the public sphere, including the political representation of women's interests. That Wollstonecraft in 1792 could not envisage the full extent of this reorganization should not lead us to conclude that she underestimated its difficulty or immensity.

But what is to be made of Wollstonecraft's agreement with Rousseau that the family is the foundation of civil life? And what is to be made of her concession that women's comparative physical weakness may make them more "dependent," and so perhaps less able to achieve virtue, than men? (Wollstonecraft 1975, 80, 109). To some extent this concession should be read as a response to Rousseau's attempt to link his claims about "feminine" reason and virtue to the supposed "natural" passivity and dependency of the female body. Wollstonecraft seeks once again to show that one may accept Rousseau's premises without accepting his conclusion—that virtue is different for the different sexes. This interpretation is supported by Wollstonecraft's frequent arguments to the effect that the physical incapacities to which many women are subject are the direct result of their subordination—in particular, of ideals of feminine beauty that actively discourage women from developing physical strength and skill. However, in light of the fact that Wollstonecraft's text wavers between the character ideal conception of self-governance that I have highlighted in this article and the idea that self-governance is a matter of reason's sovereignty over the body, this concession also indicates that Wollstonecraft was still struggling in the grip of the dominant cultural representation of women's bodies as passive, heteronomous bodies. This is perhaps why in the *Vindication* she could not see a clear solution to the problem of women's subordination except a transformation of the family. The events of Wollstonecraft's life after the publication of the *Vindication*, as well as her later writings, indicate that she became somewhat less optimistic about this solution. But the fact that feminists today are still coming to terms with the problem she so acutely diagnosed, and with some of her solutions, shows that many of the conflicts Wollstonecraft experienced and expressed in trying to articulate an adequate ideal of self-governance for women are still with us.

NOTES

I would like to thank Genevieve Lloyd and Michaelis Michael for helpful discussions during the writing of this paper.

1. I use the terms "autonomy" and "self-governance" interchangeably in this chapter, although only the latter term was used by Wollstonecraft. My tendency, however, is to stick with Wollstonecraft's own term.

2. This view is expressed by Claire Tomalin (1974). Between the time of the publication of *Vindication of the Rights of Woman* in 1792 and her death following childbirth in 1797, Wollstonecraft had lived in revolutionary circles in Paris during the French Revolution; had had an affair with the American, Imlay who was the father of her first child, Fanny; attempted suicide on two occasions following the break up of her relationship with Imlay; and lived with and then married William Godwin, who was the father of her second child, Mary (Shelley). By the standards of her time, and indeed even by our own, her life was extremely unconventional. It is partly because of this that the nature of her personal life has often provided the main context for the reception and interpretation of her work since the publication of *Vindication*.

3. See especially Miriam Kramnick's introduction to the 1975 edition of *Vindication*, and Moira Gatens (1991a). Although my interpretation of Wollstonecraft differs quite markedly from that of Gatens, her discussion in this article helped provoke a rethinking of my views on Wollstonecraft.

4. An exception to the standard contemporary feminist interpretation of Wollstonecraft's work is that of Jean Grimshaw (1989) which I discovered after writing this article. Grimshaw does not specifically discuss Wollstonecraft's views on autonomy, but she does argue that a careful reading of Wollstonecraft's other writings, apart from the *Vindication*, is essential if we are to understand the tensions and shifts in her views.

5. For a scholarly account of the changing associations within the history of philosophy between the reason/passion and public/private oppositions and ideals of masculinity and femininity, see Lloyd (1984).

6. This unfinished novel, which Wollstonecraft tells the reader is the story "of woman, rather than of an individual," is set in an asylum—Wollstonecraft's metaphor for women's "civil death" in eighteenth-century English society (see note 12 below). Its three central characters are Maria, a woman who has been committed and had her child abducted by an unfaithful and impecunious husband (George Venables) seeking to gain control of her inheritance; Jemima, Maria's warder, a working-class woman whose basically virtuous character has been deadened by poverty, sexual abuse, hard labor, and lack of affection; and the ambivalent Darnford, Maria's lover, who seems to embody both the virtues and the vices that Wollstonecraft discovered in men.

7. See also Moira Gatens (1986) and the discussion of Wollstonecraft in Chapter 1 Gatens (1991b).

8. Gatens' arguments in both her articles on Wollstonecraft (Gatens 1986, 1991a) seem to assume that a recognition of the ethical significance of sexual difference entails the idea of a specific feminine ethic. This assumption does not seem to me to be self-evident.

9. Rousseau's proposals concerning the education of women and his attempts to justify these proposals through an account of woman's "nature," occupy most of book V of *Emile* which is an account of the appropriate education for Sophie, Emile's future wife and helpmeet (Rousseau 1974). In book V it becomes clear that the concern with equality that preoccupies Rousseau in the *Social Contract* and the *Discourse on the Origin of Inequality* is a concern with men's equality only, as women are specifically excluded from the rights and duties of citizenship. In connection with this, feminist commentators have pointed out how Sophie's education is designed not around her own needs but around the idea that her role is to be Emile's complement and subordinate: "Nature herself has decreed that woman, both for herself and her children, should be at the mercy of man's judgment. . . . A woman's education must therefore be planned in relation to man" (Rousseau 1974, 328). For a sample of some of these commentaries see the discussions of Rousseau in Lloyd (1984), Martin (1985), Okin (1979), and Pateman (1988).

10. Wollstonecraft's interest in the doctrine of human perfectibility seems to have been aroused by her association with the dissenting theologian and reformer Dr. Richard Price. For an account of this association at various periods of Wollstonecraft's life, see Tomalin (1974).

11. In contrast to Gatens (1991b, 23), who argues that Wollstonecraft's critique of the inequities of Rousseau's educational proposals for women does not take into account the integral role that these proposals play in Rousseau's overall social and political project, the following argument is intended to show that Wollstonecraft was well aware of this connection. In fact, what Wollstonecraft seeks to show is that Rousseau's proposals for women's education will actually undermine his social and political project.

12. In many places in the *Vindication* Wollstonecraft is quite scathing about the coquettish, pleasure seeking, self-obsessed behavior of these women who could take as long as five hours to get dressed! Her observations as well as her

animosity arose from her experience working as governess to the children of a landed Irish aristocratic couple, the Kingsboroughs. Wollstonecraft felt that there was little hope, short of revolution, for changing the ways of the aristocracy. However, she hoped to influence the middle classes, to whom, she claims, her book is addressed. Wollstonecraft was appalled by the way in which the newly leisured middle-class women were attempting to emulate their aristocratic sisters, but, despite her scorn, the argument of the *Vindication* is that the behavior of these women has only one source—their social position. As Miriam Kramnick makes clear (Wollstonecraft 1975), the social position of both middle- and working-class women and the opportunities open to them were dramatically different at the end of the eighteenth century from what they had been one hundred years previously. The rapid expansion of industrialization and mechanization in production had shifted much productive work out of the domestic economy and out of family-based businesses and into factories removed from the home. As a result, middle-class women, who previously had played a significant role in the economy, had become a leisured class dependent entirely on their husbands for economic support and "protection," while working-class women spent increasingly long hours outside the home, performing badly paid menial work with very little time left to care for their children. While working-class women thus ruined their health in factories, middle-class women ruined their health through idleness and through attempts to achieve ideals of "feminine" beauty. Women's economic disenfranchisement became "civil death" when Blackstone announced in 1757 that "the very being or legal existence of the woman is suspended during the marriage or at least is incorporated and consolidated into that of the husband" (quoted by Kramnick in Wollstonecraft 1975, 34). As I will suggest later in this article, sensitivity to this context makes more comprehensible some of Wollstonecraft's more drastic pronouncements against pleasure.

13. According to Rousseau, feminine virtue must be enforced in two ways: first, by ensuring that women not only remain in the private sphere but also lead retiring, almost reclusive lives: "the genuine mother of a family is no woman of the world, she is almost as much of a recluse as the nun in her convent" (Rousseau 1974, 350), and second, through the iron grip of social opinion. Rousseau asserts in *Emile*: "A man has no one but himself to consider, and so long as he does right he may defy public opinion; but when a woman does right her task is only half finished, and what people think of her matters as much as what she really is" (Rousseau 1974, 328).

14. Compare Wollstonecraft (1980b, 1: 137): "By allowing women but one way of rising in the world, thus fostering the libertinism of men, society makes monsters of them, and then their ignoble vices are brought forward as proof of inferiority of intellect."

15. The attitude of stoic resignation is most evident in Wollstonecraft's early novel *Mary, A Fiction*, originally published in 1788 (Wollstonecraft 1980a). At the end of the novel the heroine's response to sorrow and sexual injustice is resignation mixed with joy at the prospect of death and the thought that "she was hastening to that world *where there is neither marrying*, nor giving in marriage"

(Wollstonecraft 1980a, 68). Even here, however, Wollstonecraft's irony gets the better of her resignation.

16. Compare the following remarks, "Standing armies can never consist of resolute robust men; they may be well-disciplined machines, but they will seldom contain men under the influence of strong passions, or with very vigorous faculties; and as for any depth of understanding I will venture to affirm that it is as rarely to be found in the army as amongst women. . . . The great misfortune is this, that they both acquire manners before morals, and a knowledge of life before they have from reflection any acquaintance with the grand ideal outline of human nature. The consequence is natural. Satisfied with common nature, they become a prey to prejudices, and taking all their opinions on credit, they blindly submit to authority" (Wollstonecraft 1975, 106).

17. Compare Maria's picture of her uncle who "inculcated, with great warmth, self-respect, and a lofty consciousness of acting right, independent of the censure of the world," (Wollstonecraft 1980b, 2: 128).

18. Compare Wollstonecraft (1975, 202) on woman "becoming the slave of her own feelings, she is easily subjugated by those of others."

19. In a footnote in the *Vindication* that anticipates contemporary feminist critiques of liberalism, Wollstonecraft suggests that Rousseau's picture of the solitary individual in the "state of nature" overlooks "the long and helpless state of infancy" and so the necessary sociality of human life (Wollstonecraft 1975, 94). Many contemporary feminists have argued that liberal political theory, particularly in its more libertarian guises, is deeply flawed because it assumes a mistaken conception of human subjectivity, namely, that human beings spring out of the earth fully developed like mushrooms, to paraphrase Hobbes. For a sample of these critiques, see Pateman (1988); Jaggar (1983); and Tapper (1986). Whether this characterization is applicable to contemporary forms of liberalism and social contract theory is, of course, the subject of considerable debate among liberals, communitarians, and feminists.

20. See, for example, her letter to him written in Hamburg en route to England from Scandinavia (Wollstonecraft 1977, Letter LXVII, 251). Wollstonecraft seemed to regard commerce as inherently corrupting. Compare her portraits of George Venables and the young Darnford in *The Wrongs of Woman* (Wollstonecraft 1980b).

21. Compare also Wollstonecraft (1977, Letter III, 150–51): "Mixing with mankind, we are obliged to examine our prejudices, and often imperceptibly lose, as we analyze them."

22. Wollstonecraft employed a French nursemaid named Marguerite to care for Fanny.

23. This objection is raised by Gatens (1991a), Martin (1985), and Eisenstein (1981, chap. 5).

24. As was mentioned earlier, this criticism is raised by Gatens (1986, 1991a, and 1991b). Carole Pateman also makes a similar criticism in Pateman (1988).

25. In this respect, her work anticipates some of the preoccupations of contemporary feminist philosophers interested in moral theory and theories of justice. See, for example, Benhabib (1987), Okin (1989), and Young (1990).

REFERENCES

Benhabib, Seyla. 1987. The generalized and the concrete other. In *Feminism as
    critique*, ed. Seyla Benhabib and Drucilla Cornell. Minneapolis: University
    of Minnesota Press.
Eisenstein, Zillah. 1981. *The radical future of liberal feminism*. New York:
    Longman.
Gatens, Moira. 1986. Rousseau and Wollstonecraft: Nature vs. reason. In *Women
    and philosophy*, ed. Janna Thompson. Supplement to *Australasian
    Journal of Philosophy* 64(June): 1–15.
———. 1991a. The oppressed state of my sex: Wollstonecraft on reason, feeling
    and equality. In *Feminist interpretations and political theory*, ed. Carole
    Pateman and Mary Lyndon Shanley. Cambridge: Polity Press; University
    Park: Pennsylvania State University Press.
———. 1991b. *Feminism and philosophy: Perspectives on equality and differ-
    ence*. Cambridge: Polity Press; Bloomington: Indiana University Press.
Grimshaw, Jean. 1989. Mary Wollstonecraft and the tensions in feminist philoso-
    phy. *Radical Philosophy* 52(Summer): 11–17.
Jaggar, Alison. 1983. *Feminist politics and human nature*. Totowa, NJ: Rowman
    and Allanheld; Brighton: Harvester.
Kittay, Eva, and Diana T. Meyers, eds. 1987. *Women and moral theory*. Totowa,
    NJ: Rowman and Littlefield.
Lloyd, Genevieve. 1984. *The man of reason*. London: Methuen; Minneapolis: Uni-
    versity of Minnesota Press.
Martin, Jane Roland. 1985. *Reclaiming a conversation: The ideal of the educated
    woman*. New Haven: Yale University Press.
Okin, Susan. 1979. *Women in Western political thought*. Princeton, N.J.: Prince-
    ton University Press.
———. 1989. *Justice, gender and the family*. New York: Basic Books.
Pateman, Carole. 1988. *The sexual contract*. Cambridge: Polity.
Rousseau, Jean Jacques. [1755] 1973. Discourse on the origins of inequality. In
    "The Social Contract" and other discourses. London: Dent (Everyman's
    Library).
———. [1762] 1974. *Emile*. London: Dent; New York: Dutton (Everyman's
    Library).
———. [1762] 1983. *On the social contract; Discourse on the origin of ine-
    quality; Discourse on political economy*. Indianapolis, IN: Hackett.
Tapper, Marion. 1986. Can a feminist be a liberal? In *Women and philosophy*, ed.
    Janna Thompson. Supplement to *Australasian Journal of Philosophy*
    64(June): 37–47.
Tomalin, Claire. 1974. *The Life and death of Mary Wollstonecraft*. New York:
    Harcourt, Brace, Jovanovich.

Todd, Janet M., ed. 1977. *A Wollstonecraft anthology*. Bloomington: Indiana University Press.

Wollstonecraft, Mary. [1792] 1975. *Vindication of the rights of woman*, ed. Miriam Kramnick. Harmondsworth: Penguin, 1975.

———. [1796] 1977. *Letters written during a short residence in Sweden, Norway, and Denmark*. In *A Wollstonecraft anthology*, ed. Janet M. Todd. Bloomington: Indiana University Press.

———. [1788] 1980a. *Mary, A Fiction*. In *Mary and "The Wrongs of Woman,"* ed. James Kinsley and Gary Kelly. Oxford: Oxford University Press.

———. [1798] 1980b. *The wrongs of woman; or, Maria: A fragment*. In *Mary and "The wrongs of woman,"* eds. James Kinsley, and Gary Kelly. Oxford: Oxford University Press.

Young, Iris. 1990. *Justice and the politics of difference*. Princeton: Princeton University Press.

ANNA DOYLE WHEELER (1785–1848)
PHILOSOPHER, SOCIALIST, FEMINIST

MARGARET McFADDEN

Michèle Riot-Sarcey and Eleni Varikas have recently developed a very intriguing model of the process by which feminist consciousness comes to exist. Taking as examples France in the period of the 1848 Revolution and late nineteenth century Greece, they argue that, over a period of time, a growing awareness of exclusion develops among women. This is brought on by 1) a disintegration of traditional socio-economic structures and a relative absence of women in power positions in the new society; 2) a post-revolutionary society supposedly based on universal ideals; 3) a decline in the position of women, relative to the evolution of the rights of men; and 4) a growth in education, writing and public speech possibilities for women. The consciousness that develops is that of the pariah. This is exactly what Flora Tristan called herself, whereas Virginia Woolf uses the term "Conscious Outsider."

Riot-Sarcey and Varikas identify three forms of this pariah consciousness: 1) *exceptional woman feminism*—this is a tokenism which leads to assimilation, confirms the rule of inferiority, and denies the systematic character of the exclusion of women as a social category; 2) *subversive feminism*—present social structures and institutions are denied or destroyed, leading to social disorder; Claire Démar, the most radical of the Saint-Simonian women, is the example here, with her advocacy of the abolition of even the "law of blood" to free women from maternity; 3) *feminism as the art of the possible*—this form always develops from a collective movement and stresses women's otherness and difference (Riot-Sarcey and Varikas 1986).

In what follows, I wish to test this hypothesis by considering the case of an important early socialist thinker, Anna Doyle Wheeler (1785–1848). While I generally find the Riot-Sarcey/Varikas model to be enormously

Hypatia vol. 4, no. 1 (Spring 1989) © by Margaret McFadden useful and illuminating, there may be some room for refinement. Wheeler seems to be both a subversive and a convention-bound "exceptional woman," depending on which aspect of her thought and life one chooses. In any case, this typology allows us an intriguing entreé into both Wheeler's philosophical ideas and the issue of her somewhat ambiguous historical location.

Anna Wheeler: A Biographical Sketch

Anna Doyle Wheeler was born to an Anglican family of Clonbeg Parish in County Tipperary, Ireland. She was the beautiful and headstrong youngest daughter of a middle-level Church of Ireland cleric, who died when she was not yet two years old. Even though her godfather was the great Irish nationalist Henry Grattan, she was brought up mostly by her father's people, the Doyle's. This family held important posts in the military and civil service for British colonial government, not only in Ireland but also in the American colonies, on the continent, on the Isle of Guernsey, and in India (Doyle 1911).

In 1800, when only fifteen, she was noticed at the races by nineteen-year-old Frances Massey Wheeler, a young inheritor of his family's estate at Ballywire. Wheeler proposed to her at a ball. Her family opposed the match and tried to divert Anna by an invitation to London from her uncle, Sir John Doyle. Anna would have none of this and married Wheeler the same year. In twelve years she bore six children, the first four being girls (Galgano 1979). Rosina, the second daughter, remembers being told about the wrath of her drunken father on learning that Anna had given birth to another girl. Later she had a son, but only Henrietta and Rosina survived infancy. Anna took refuge from her abusive husband in reading. Rosina recalls her mother reading the French *philosophes* and Wollstonecraft on one couch while her mother's maiden sister, Bessie Doyle, read the sentimental novels of the Minerva Press on the other. Rosina tried to learn to draw and not bother them. Both her aunt and her father, Rosina says, would take her (Rosina's) part against her mother, who favored older sister Henrietta. But, she adds wistfully, "I did long for a little of my mother's love" (Devey 1887).[1]

The marriage finally became completely unbearable. In a daring and desperate move, Anna was able to arrange an escape. In August of 1812, she fled with her children, her sister, and her brother, John, to the Isle of Guernsey where her uncle Sir John Doyle was Governor. Francis made no attempt to persuade her to return and refused her any allowance for the rest of his life; predictably, he left her no maintenance in his will (he died in 1820).[2]

In high society on Guernsey, Anna Wheeler was lionized by the aristocratic and wealthy. The aging Duc de Bouillon courted her for 12 years, according to Rosina. Four years after Anna arrived, however, Sir John was forced to resign his office because of his debts. Anna and her family left for London at the same time, beginning the peripatetic life which she was to lead for the next two decades. London, Dublin, Caen, and Paris—these were her principal stops. At Caen she became part of an early Saint-Simonian group and was known, perhaps whimsically, as the "Goddess of Reason."

She returned to Ireland after her husband's death, but was back in France by 1823; in Paris she met Charles Fourier. She always claimed that Fourier's system was essentially the same as that of Robert Owen and Saint-Simon. In all three, she said, co-operation is central; men and women are entitled to both equal education and employment opportunities; and marriage and divorce law changes eliminate the double standard and give women equal rights. For the rest of her life she attempted to bring these three versions of socialism into union. To that end she arranged for Fourier to meet Robert Owen, introduced Saint-Simonian missionaries to Owenites in England, translated Fourierist and Saint-Simonian articles for the Owenite press, sent young people to France with letters of introduction to Fourier, persuaded Owenites in England that Saint-Simonian doctrines were similar to theirs, etc. (see Gans 1964). Through Jeanne-Désirée Véret (who lived for a time with Anna in England and later married the Owenite Jules Gay), Wheeler was connected to the Saint-Simonian women's journal, *Tribune des Femmes*, and translated articles for *The Crisis* (Wheeler 1833b).[3] She became a well-known lecturer at a time when women were not often allowed to speak to mixed-sex groups.

Anna Wheeler also associated with the Utilitarians. Indeed, through her friendship with Jeremy Bentham (begun in Paris) she met William Thompson, whose socialist economic theory so impressed Robert Owen. Thompson, also Anglo-Irish (a large landowner from Cork), formed a close relationship with Wheeler. Together they wrote *The Appeal of One Half the Human Race, Women, Against the Pretensions of the Other Half, Men, to Restrain Them in Political and Thence in Civil and Domestic Slavery* (1825) as a reply to James Mill's essay on government in the *Encyclopedia Britannica*. Mill, in less than a sentence, had dismissed women's rights as unnecessary, since their interests were represented or "covered" by their husbands or fathers.

All the while she continued her networking for co-operative socialism. She was a major influence on the views of James Smith, the editor of the Owenite journal *The Crisis*. When Flora Tristan visited London in 1839, Wheeler helped to guide her around. The chapter on Bethlem Hospital in Tristan's *London Journal* relates an incident in which a French inmate,

M. Chabrier, attacks Anna Wheeler as an atheist who had killed God (Tristan 1982).

When Thompson died in 1833, he assigned an annual annuity of £100 to Wheeler; most of the rest of his estate he willed to the Owenite co-operative movement for the building of an intentional community. The will, however, was contested in court by his relatives on the grounds that Thompson was insane; the process dragged on for a generation, so that she never received the money. Wheeler was an invalid in her last years, but lived to hear of the beginning of the 1848 Revolution in Paris.

Wheeler's Argumentation

A. *The Appeal.* As mentioned earlier, Wheeler and Thompson produced a long, closely reasoned, and well-organized book, *The Appeal of One Half the Human Race, Women.* . . . While it bears only his name, the introductory letter makes the fact of co-authorship clear. The essay begins with the proposition that a social system cannot provide for the greatest happiness for the greatest number if one-half that number is removed from consideration. Part I examines James Mill's general argument that women's interests are "covered" by husbands, fathers, or brothers. In Part II, the first question asks whether there is indeed an identity of interest between women and men. Various sections then focus on the parts of this question: single women without fathers, adult daughters living in fathers' houses, and wives. As one might expect, the essay especially critiques marriage:

> All women, and particularly women living with men in marriage . . .
> having been reduced . . . to a state of helplessness, slavery . . . and priva-
> tions, . . . are *more in need* of political rights than any other portion of
> human beings. (Thompson [1825] 107)

Following eighty pages of philosophical argumentation, the second question in Part II is taken up. Whether a sufficient cause to deprive either group of civil or political rights can be demonstrated, even if an identity of interests could be shown to exist—this is the issue. The argument proceeds by supposing that "the interests of men and women are so involved in each other, that political power possessed by the one *must* be impartially used for the benefit of both" (126, emphasis added). The question of whether one sex should be given exclusive political rights still remains. In a bold and unprecedented reversal, Thompson and Wheeler set forth reasons in favor of giving exclusive political rights to *women*. One of the reasons is, they maintain, that women, being the "weaker party," would never be able to overlook the interests of men since men would never submit to injustice at the hands of women. The most important qualification for those making public regulations for others—i.e., "sympathy with those to be affected . . . or moral aptitude" (114)—is, they assert, to be found more often in women.

Finally, however, they find that no sufficient cause for excluding either party exists, if human improvement is the object. Authentic progress requires that a negative and a positive step be taken: "the negative consisting in the removal of restraints; the positive in the voluntary establishment of co-operative associations" (151).

The third and final question is, "Is there any way to secure happiness to a group but *by means of* equal civil and political rights?" Argued first is the matter of whether women can enjoy happiness without equal civil and criminal laws. The authors point out the evil and degradation that women suffer under present (1825) unequal laws. The second section takes up the question of whether women have any guarantee of equal *civil* and *criminal* law other than their possession of *political* rights. As it stands now, say Thompson and Wheeler, it could often happen that "one fourth plus one" of the adults of the human race, would control "three fourths less one" (174). In other words, a simple majority of men could dictate to the rest of the men and all the women. (This of course takes no account of the fact that not even all men had the vote at that time.)

The essay as a whole is an unequivocal appeal for votes for women, the first to be cogently argued (Wollstonecraft had only hinted at it). In the long, concluding "Address to Women," Thompson and Wheeler exhort women to awaken to their degraded state and join with a system of Co-operation in intentional community such as that espoused by Robert Owen's followers. Interestingly, in an extended footnote, the similarities and differences between Fourier's system and Owen's are discussed. Even here Wheeler tries to unify the disparate strands of socialism. The main difference, she says, lies in the Fourierist system of distribution, one of *inequality*, whereas Owen's goal is *equality* of distribution. Both systems provide for equal education of all children as well as equal rights in marriage and employment for both women and men (Thompson, 204–5).

B. *The Finsbury Square lecture and other statements.* Anna Wheeler soon became a well-known lecturer on women's rights and the various forms of the co-operative movement. A famous address in 1829 at Finsbury Square lecture chapel was directed particularly to women. Entitling it "Rights of Women," she sets out to demolish the main arguments given by men to justify their claim of superiority over women. After a long apology in which she mentions her "depressed health" and "a deep domestic sorrow" (probably Rosina's impending divorce), she says she will be speaking "in my capacity as slave and woman" (Wheeler 1830, 13). As a good utilitarian, she notes that when men refuse to treat women as anything other than as an object of animal passion, men too are degraded: ". . . in refusing to cultivate women's intellectual faculties, men are caught in their own snares; and the ignorance, that they would exclusively confine to women, soon becomes general" (14). "*Prejudice* becomes *fixed principle*" and, like Pandora's box, spills evils throughout all society.

Our institutions, she continues, ostensibly established for "the perfection of human reason" are only caricatures of reason. If we say that nothing can be good that produces permanently evil effects, then our institutions are evil, since they do not recognize the *general* interest of all mankind—which must include women. The problem is, she avers, that individual, personal interest is often set up instead of *general* interest.

She then critiques the two main arguments for male superiority. The first, that men have superior muscular strength, is refuted by evidence from various ancient and primitive societies. She concludes that women's weakness is "a civilized disease," not part of female biology at all. Wheeler challenges the second argument—the alleged moral incapacity of women—also by looking at studies of primitive groups. Here she finds "civilized" behavior wanting. There is no difference in brain capacity, only differences in education. Her argument is buttressed by considering uneducated men. A final part of the argument cites examples of great and heroic women, both noble and common: women during the Terror in France, Madame Roland in prison, and Lady Russell, beheaded for conspiring against Charles II.

Concluding in classic liberal fashion that education will make women equal, she supports this claim by showing how "the greatest vices of women" are all vices of the slave and, as such, can be pedagogically removed.

> We then fearlessly ask for education; equal right to acquire and possess property; equal morals; women themselves responsible for their conduct as members of society; equal civil and political rights. (35)

Political rights for women are necessary, she asserts; otherwise, other rights cannot be guaranteed. Wheeler then invokes the name of Frances Wright, advocate of general education for both women and men, who understood, says Wheeler, that only through the system of Co-operation, sustained by democratic education, could the wrongs to women be righted.

Finally, she calls on women to press for "a sound and liberal education" for their daughters, not being content to wait for others. Women must, she says, form groups of like-minded people, "the ultimate object of which will be to obtain, by all legal means, the removal of the disabilities of women, and the introduction of a national system of *equal education* for the Infants of both sexes" (36). This call for an *organization* of women, demanding equal education and equal property and political rights, marks Wheeler as one of the earliest and most radical of feminists.

Under the pen name "Vlasta," Wheeler published other pieces, continuing to discuss equal education and equal civil and political rights for women and claiming that these were in *men's* self-interest. Because of her knowledge of various societies, she had an important comparative perspective; her strongest criticisms were usually reserved for English women. In an 1832 letter, for example, she caustically comments on women's inability to see their own oppression:

> Fortunately there was not a word about justice to women in the Reform Bill. Else, these poor creatures would have opposed it with more animosity than they did, and most satisfactory it is for us to know that the principle of 'Cannot I do what I like with my own' will suffer only as it relates to men. (Burke 1976, 22)

This criticism of her own sex was not unusual in Wheeler's writing; in this, she is similar to Wollstonecraft.

From Typology to Continuum:
Wheeler's Ambiguous Status

Returning to the framework of Riot-Sarcey and Varikas (1986), we can now see that Anna Wheeler falls between positions one and two: she generally advocated subversive feminist doctrines but was often cast in the exceptional woman's role; indeed, she often saw herself that way (her belittling remarks about women are explicable in these terms, for example). As the Wheeler example shows, it might be better to imagine "exceptional woman feminism" as possessing an inner continuum which moves from the pole of conventionality to the pole of subversion. Depending on which phase of her career and which aspect(s) of her thought one chooses, Wheeler is both a subversive and a convention-bound "exceptional woman."

In a more recent study on the concept of exceptionality, Riot-Sarcey and Varikas have used a notion similar to my idea of a continuum. They discuss two sorts of exceptionality, *vécue* (lived or authentic) and *assumée* (assumed or taken on) and suggest a kind of dialectic between them. They conclude with a helpful metaphor: "The exceptional woman of the 19th century situates herself at the crossing of the feminist consciousness with the world view of the satisfied parvenu" (Riot-Sarcey and Varikas 1987, 11). Wheeler fits this graphic description perfectly. Satisfied with her position as a unique female intellectual, she still calls for a break-up of patriarchal structures and leans toward an attempt at collective work with other women.

During her lifetime most of the antagonism evidenced toward Wheeler had more to do with her political beliefs than with her personal life. Curiously, there is no evidence of scandal about her personal sexual life such as plagued both Frances Wright and Mary Wollstonecraft. Given her views and her friendship with William Thompson, had there been any cause for gossip, it certainly would have been used against both her and her daughter, Rosina. Anna Wheeler was on the outskirts of respectable society, but she was never ostracized as she would have been were she seen as a sex-radical.

Because she never worked within a collective, her feminism was not of the third type, "the art of the possible." Her pariah consciousness was always that of the lone outsider, often disparaging of other women. Indeed, although she never broke the bonds of feminine respectability to become a so-called *"homme-femme"* like George Sand or Daniel Stern, she was still more at home with men than with women. She called for a separate organization of women, but she did not join other women in forming such a group. A mature international sisterhood would have to wait for a larger number of women with fully-developed feminist consciousnesses, a critical mass large enough to overcome the exceptional woman syndrome.

A Concluding Postscript:
Wheeler and the Le Doeuff Thesis

Michèle Le Doeuff's very suggestive article, "Women and Philosophy," describes the way that most women philosophers in history have had access to philosophy, that is, through their passionate relationship with a particular male philosopher. This has been true, she says, from the time of Hipparchia and Crates the Cynic, through Hèloise and Abelard, Descartes and Elisabeth, up to Sartre and Simone de Beauvoir. Women's access to philosophy has not been through the (phallocentric) institutions of philosophic training (from which women have historically been barred), but through their relationship with a mentor. This "erotic-theoretical transference" (Le Doeuff 1987, 185) has meant that women have had access not to philosophy, per se, but to *a particular philosophy*.

If we look at the work of Anna Doyle Wheeler in this context, she becomes another in that line of women playing disciple to a male master, in this case, William Thompson. The way out of the impasse, suggests Le Doeuff, is to try to create in philosophy a "non-hegemonic rationalism," an acceptance of its "intrinsic incompleteness," an ongoing philosophic discourse (206). At the same time, she says, the enterprise of "doing philosophy" should be transformed into a collective enterprise, so that the philosopher as subject disappears. Only thus can philosophy become truly accessible to women. Here, in work groups and other collectives, one may find "a new rationality, in which a relationship to the unknown and to the unthought is at every moment reintroduced" (209). Anna Doyle Wheeler not only had no access to institutional philosophy, she had no concept of doing philosophy collectively. Thus, although she was at the center of many networking activities and advocated an organization of like-minded women, her project was never truly cooperative or non-hegemonic.

NOTES

An earlier version of this paper was presented at the Third International Interdisciplinary Congress on Women, Trinity College, Dublin, Ireland, July 6–10, 1987. The beginning research was carried out and presented in a National Endowment for the Humanities Summer Seminar, "The Woman Question in Western Thought," Department of History, Stanford University, 1986. I would like to thank the following for their helpful suggestions throughout the writing process: Karen Offen (Seminar Director), Catherine Boyd, Bud Gerber, Gail Savage, and Eleni Varikas.

1. The available biographical sources on Anna Wheeler are all dependent on two early sources, written in the wake of the scandal surrounding the separation between Wheeler's daughter Rosina and the British novelist Bulwer-Lytton in 1836. As might be expected, these sources are not entirely dependable, contain several errors, and contradict each other. Louisa Devey's *Life of Rosina, Lady Lytton* (1887) takes Rosina's side, while Michael Sadleir's *Bulwer and His Wife: A Panorama 1803–1836* (1931) puts all the blame on Rosina. The following quotation (describing the family's departure from Guernsey and their uncle Sir John Doyle) is typical of the tone and attitude of the Lytton side of the controversy toward Rosina and her family:

> [Sir John] chose resignation and quick departure, because by this means at least he would be rid of women who had only sought him out for what they could get. . . . Apprised of his immediate retirement to London, Mrs. Wheeler gave way to one final burst of rage and, late in 1816 or early in 1817, sailed for France. In a few months she had become "Goddess of Reason" to a small group of embittered cranks in Caen. Her unhappy children played acolyte on either side of her altar. (Sadleir 1931, 76)

The most sympathetic view of Rosina was that she was the "product" of a terrible upbringing, her mother having abdicated her maternal responsibilities. Anna, therefore, is seen as money-grubbing and, worse, as a radical intellectual, even in the sources sympathetic to Rosina. This view is part of the reason that Anna has been erased from history. Like Mary Wollstonecraft and Frances Wright before her, her political views and personal life were seen as anathema to respectable women, and therefore her life and works simply were omitted from later accounts of early feminism and socialism.

Two examples should suffice to suggest the inaccuracies of these sources. Ballywire is located in County Tipperary; in Devey's account, Rosina says not only that it is in County Limerick (and it *is* on the border of the two counties), but that it is on the western *coast* of Ireland. She describes in great detail the house at Ballywire, and in most respects she is correct. The house does indeed have a stone turret, marble fireplaces, and carved ceilings. But the memory-imagination of the 8-year-old Rosina also imbued the surroundings with a high cliff over crashing waves and a view of the sea to the west (Devey 1887, 10–11). This is pure fantasy; the view is to the relatively tame Glen of Aherlow in the southwestern part of County Tipperary.

Anna Wheeler's father is said to be an arch*bishop* in several of the sources; he was in fact an arch*deacon* and a prebendary, entirely different offices (Leslie 1958, 1: 326). There was a *Catholic* archbishop Doyle (James Warren Doyle, bishop of Kildare and Leighlin) at this time in Ireland, so one can see how the error has crept in.

2. Again, earlier sources disagree as to Francis Massey Wheeler's death date. Galgano (1979) and Pankhurst (1954) follow Devey and use 1820, but Sadleir says 1823. I have been unable to locate a death certificate or grave marker in any available records in Clonbeg Parish or at the Diocesan Library in Cashel. Records for Clonbeg and Galbally Parishes were among those destroyed in the fire at the Public Records Office in Dublin in 1922.

3. I am indebted to Karen Offen, Center for Research on Women, Stanford University, for her perusal of and notes on this letter, and for calling it to my attention. See Wheeler's translation of "Appel aux femmes" (Wheeler 1833a).

REFERENCES

Bell, Susan Groag, and Karen Offen, eds. 1983. *Women, the family, and freedom: The debate in documents.* (2 vols). Stanford: Stanford Univ. Press.

Burke, Stephen. 1976. Letter from a pioneer feminist—Anna Wheeler. *Studies in Labor History* 1: 19–23.

Devey, Louisa. 1887. *Life of Rosina, Lady Lytton.* London: Swan, Sonnenschein, Lowren.

Doyle, Arthur. 1911. *A hundred years of conflict: Being some records of the services of six generals of the Doyle family,* 1756–1856. London: Longmans, Green.

Galgano, Michael. 1979. Anna Doyle Wheeler. In *Biographical dictionary of modern British radicals.* (vol. 1). Joseph O. Baylen and Norbert J. Gossman, eds. Sussex: Harvester Press, 519–524.

Gans, J. 1964. Les relations entre socialistes de France et d'Angleterre au debut du XIXe siecle. *Le Mouvement Social* 46: 105–118.

Le Doeuff, Michèle. 1987. Women and philosophy. In *French feminist thought*. Toril Moi, ed. London: Basil Blackwell, 181–209.

Leslie, Rev. Canon J.B. 1958. *Biographical index of the clergy of the Church of Ireland*. Typescript. Representative Church Body Library, Dublin.

Pankhurst, Richard K.P. 1954. Anna Wheeler: A pioneer socialist and feminist. *The Political Quarterly* 25: 132–143.

Riot-Sarcey, Michèle and Eleni Varikas. 1986. Feminist consciousness in the nineteenth century. A pariah consciousness? *Praxis International* 5: 443–465.

Riot-Sarcey, Michèle and Eleni Varikas. 1987. Reflexions sur la notion d'exceptionalité. Typescript in preparation for *Les Cahiers du GRIF*. My translation.

Sadleir, Michael. 1931. *Bulwer and his wife: A panorama 1803–1836*. London: Constable.

Thompson, William. [1825] 1983. *Appeal of one half the human race, women, against the pretensions of the other half, men, to restrain them in political and thence in civil and domestic slavery*. Intro. Richard Pankhurst. London: Virago.

Tristan, Flora. 1982. *The London journal of Flora Tristan, 1842*. Jean Hawkes, ed. and trans. London: Virago.

Wheeler, Anna Doyle. 1830. Rights of women. *The British Co-operator* 1: 1, 2, 12–15, 33–36.

Wheeler, Anna Doyle, trans. 1833a. Appel aux femmes, by Jeanne-Victoire [pseud.]. *The Crisis*, 15 June; reprinted in Bell and Offen 1983, I:146–147.

Wheeler, Anna Doyle. 1833b. Letter to Charles Fourier, 28 May 1833. Archives Nationales (Paris), Archives societaires, 10 AS25, doss. 3.

"THE LOT OF GIFTED LADIES IS HARD"
A STUDY OF
HARRIET TAYLOR MILL CRITICISM

JO ELLEN JACOBS

Who can tell a life? How can I reconstruct the inside, not merely the shell, of another? Margaret Atwood quotes the end of Arnold Bennett's biography by Margaret Drabble:

> "Many a time, . . . reading a letter or a piece of his journal, I have wanted to shake his hand, or to thank him, to say well done. I have written this instead." "To shake his hand." I suppose this may be what we really want, when we read biographies and when we write them: some contact, some communication, some way to know and to pay tribute. . . . We play Mr. Hyde, constantly, to our various Dr. Jekylls; we supersede ourselves. We are our own broken puzzles, incomplete, scattered through time. It is up to the biographers, finally, painstakingly, imperfectly, to put us together again. (Atwood 1989, 8)

I want to shake hands with Harriet Taylor Mill.[1] I will put the pieces of her life together in a way that will reveal a new portrait, shockingly different from the usual one presented by historians of philosophy who have cast sidelong glances at this puzzling creature in John Stuart Mill's life. I'd like to introduce you to Harriet,[2] not Mrs. John Mill.

I want to shake hands with Harriet Taylor Mill, but that larger project must begin with a history of the critiques written about her, especially in the history of philosophy. And we need to understand why she has been presented as she has. The goal of this article is to begin to uncover the answers to the question "Why has Harriet Taylor Mill appeared in the history of philosophy as she has?" I believe there are several answers, not one answer. The answers intertwine the personality and politics of

Hypatia vol. 9, no. 3 (Summer 1994) © by Jo Ellen Jacobs

Harriet, the sexism of those who wrote of her (which was a reflection of the overall status of women during the periods the commentators wrote), and misunderstandings of the means and meaning of her collaboration with JSM. Some of these answers were first suggested by Le Doeuf (1987), Rossi (1970), August (1975), Tulloch (1989), and Rose (1984). I extend, systematize, and collect their reasons. For example, Rossi demonstrated the sexism of individual commentators on HTM. I show that the history of the critiques is not merely a collection of individual sexist accounts, but parallels the history of progress and backlash in women's concerns. I extend Le Doeuf's analysis of the "Héloïse complex" to the relationship between Harriet and John.

Is there anything new in this article? Yes, the issues of how collaborative writing works and of how the ignorance or refusal of philosophers to use or acknowledge collaborative writing plays an important role in most philosophers' misunderstanding of Harriet's work. Furthermore, no one has pointed out the negative mythology of women's asking questions. Women's questions threaten men's knowledge. Harriet's philosophical thinking resulted in more questions than answers. Questions are more disturbing than answers because their open-endedness disturbs the drive for conclusions. Eve's sin was to desire to eat of the fruit of the tree of knowledge. So was Harriet's.

Philosophers like to think they write a history of *ideas*—sexless, bodiless ideas. If Aristotle has been treated unfairly by certain commentators or during certain historical periods, that is the result of philosophical assumptions or misunderstandings of the commentator—a problem of ideas. We philosophers might be willing to recognize that some political prejudices, say the paranoia about a possible link between Nazism and Nietzsche, creep into the less trustworthy historical analyses, but really, don't we feel above such petty biases as sexism? If not yesterday, then clearly today, we are above the small-mindedness of judging on the basis of sex.

Disclosing the nasty pettiness of her critics will reveal not only the biases against Harriet Taylor Mill. A more general pattern of attitudes toward women thinkers is ingrained in these critiques. I will show that the history of the philosophy of John Stuart Mill reveals that the critique of Harriet centers on her personality while her ideas are ignored. The predominance of ad feminam attacks and an almost complete refusal to consider HTM's ideas makes me suspicious. First, commentators seem to ignore Harriet's ideas automatically, and then they proceed to judge her life on the basis of openly sexist criteria. The unladylike questions that Harriet was famous for and her refusal to accept the passive role assigned by society—Victorian or Anglo-American twentieth-century—are not merely personality quirks that make it difficult for commentators to be fair. The same qualities in male philosophers are universally admired. Her atheism, her ideas about women working outside the home even if they were married (and her insistence on the importance of this idea), and her views on divorce have continued to grate, but they are not openly challenged or confronted. Her "radically" pro-socialist position irritates both those who agree and those who disagree with socialism, but all agree that HTM's ideas are only important insofar as they "influence" JSM's ideas. Philosophers have asked, "How influential was HTM on JSM?" and "Was that influence positive or negative?" They had not set out to ask, "What are HTM's ideas?" or "Are these ideas important or valuable?"

Ahh, you may say, but these comments about HTM are contained in critiques of JSM's work, so obviously the focus is on his ideas. But why has there been no critical biography of HTM? Why no book-length critique of her ideas?

Before I try to answer the question of HTM's place in history, I want to outline the details of that critique. How has Harriet been drawn in the past? I will quickly sketch the raw details of her life; then I will record the slow, dreary history of Harriet as written in academic publications; and finally, I will analyze why this portrait has been drawn as it has. If you are already acquainted with the scholarship on Harriet Taylor Mill, you may want to skip directly to Part 2, "The Analysis of the HTM Criticism." If you want to refresh your memory, or want to learn the details of the history of HTM criticism, read on.

The History of HTM Criticism

The daughter of an obstetrician, Harriet was born in 1807 and married John Taylor when she was 18. She had two children, Harry and Algernon, in the first four years of her marriage. Harriet met JSM a few months after Algernon was born. Their friendship quickly escalated into love during Harriet's pregnancy with Helen, her third and final child, who was conceived when Algernon was less than nine months old. Harriet also began her publishing career during this pregnancy. She published poems, book reviews, and articles in the *Monthly Repository*.

After a brief separation from her husband, she organized living arrangements that provided both the continuation of her intimate friendship with JSM and her formal marriage with her husband. JSM spent weekends and evenings with HTM and traveled frequently with her during the following 20 years. In the 1840s and early 1850s Harriet cowrote a number of newspaper articles on domestic violence despite her near-invalid condition due to consumption and partial paralysis. She wrote one chapter of JSM's *Principles of Political Economy*, the "Enfranchisement of Women" for the *Westminster Review*, and a pamphlet on a domestic violence bill before the legislature during the same period. John Taylor died in 1849, and Harriet and JSM married in 1851. During the mid-1850s, Harriet worked with John on the manuscript that would become *On Liberty* and on his *Autobiography*. Neither was published until after her death in 1858.

Critiques from 1870 to 1900

Historical attitudes toward Harriet are not sympathetic. John was effusive in his praise of Harriet's intellect and sensibilities in his *Autobiography*, dedications to various works, and his tombstone for her. Historians reacted with disbelief, disgust, and disapproval.

The earliest commentators admitted some contribution by Harriet to John's work and acknowledged her own work. In 1873, Henry Richard Fox Bourne wrote, "During more than twenty years he had been aided by her talents and encouraged by her sympathy in all the work he had undertaken," and "Mrs. Mill's weak state of health seems to have hardly repressed her powers of intellect. By her was written the celebrated essay on 'The Enfranchisement of Women'" (Bourne 1873, 504). Mansfield Marston, also in 1873, concluded that "she must have been gifted with the rarest powers of moral and intellectual symathy [*sic*], for she awoke in Mill an admiration as passionate as it was pure. . . . After the death of her first husband, Mrs. Taylor became the wife of John Mill, and never did a philosopher find a more devoted or absorbing companion" (Marston 1873, 9–10).

But it wasn't long before a pattern that would become familiar emerged. S. E. Henshaw announced, in 1874, "What Mrs. Taylor really was it is difficult to decide, amid the colored lights which Mr. Mill is always burning around her, the incense of adulation in which he envelopes her. . . . Men have been blinded by affection, and bewitched by womankind, . . . [but] John Stuart Mill out-Herods them all" (Henshaw 1874, 521, 523). Harriet bewitched poor innocent John: "Under her touch the torpid spiritual faculties of this [John's] ill-used, defrauded, beautiful nature began to stir at last, and the cramped spirit to rise and stretch its wings" (523). According to Henshaw this bewitching was not a metaphor since Harriet's chief sins were her "infidelity and atheism" (522) which complement her erotic "torpid spiritual faculties."

The charge of bewitching would be repeated throughout the history of Harriet criticism. The earliest commentators, like Henshaw, were probably relying on Carlyle's statements about Harriet. Thomas Carlyle, a notoriously biased (not to mention misogynistic) observer, had initially thought Harriet "a living romance heroine, of the clearest insight, of the royalist volition, very interesting, of questionable destiny" (quoted in Hayek 1951, 80). However, his good opinion lasted only as long as he thought her "a young beautiful reader of mine" (81). When Harriet demonstrated that she was not a disciple of Carlyle, he reported that she was "a dangerous looking woman and engrossed with a dangerous passion." In short, she was John's "charmer" (85). Carlyle had "not seen any riddle of human life which I could so ill form a theory of" (85), but that did not stop him from assigning blame to Harriet for "charming" John. Critics and biographers continued to talk of John as "besotted," "bewitched," and "charmed" (even "Bewitched, Bothered, and Bewildered"?) by Harriet. John is seen as a naive goofus who is so innocent of women he is overwhelmed by the first one to cross his path. (Commentators ignored his intimacy with Eliza Flower, Caroline Fox, and Sarah Austin, among others.) Harriet was the evil seductress who used her magic to capture an exotic prey.

In 1882 Alexander Bain, a friend of JSM, attempts an even-handed approach to Harriet's role in John's life, but no matter how he struggles to understand John's attachment to Harriet, he simply could not overcome his traditional views of women. Overall, he seems to agree with John's younger brother, George's, assessment that Harriet was clever enough, but not as wonderful as John thought (166). Bain tries to understand what he takes to be John's misunderstanding of Harriet's worth: "Hard thinkers are most often *charmed*, not by other thinkers, but by minds of the more concrete and artistic mould" (168).[3] Bain recognizes that John might have agreed that Harriet was more concrete and artistic, but JSM would have believed these elements of her genius. John would not have agreed with his deprecation of Harriet's abilities, but Bain can't help concluding, "Such a *state of subjection* to the will of another, as he candidly avows, and glories in, cannot be received as a right state of things. It *violates our sense of due proportion in the relationship of human beings*. Still, it is but the natural outcome of his *extraordinary hallucination* as to the personal qualities of his wife" (171). He tries to understand this odd relationship without damaging Mill's reputation as a great thinker. Bain denies that Harriet is merely a parrot that echoes John's ideas, as some had suggested, or that John is egoistical enough to delight in this reiteration of his ideas (173), but Bain can find no positive explanation of John's attraction other than the vague "witchery of the other sex" (172). Bain's problem is that faced by all JSM scholars: How does one admire JSM, yet account for his "excessive" devotion to this woman?

Later in the decade, William Courtney tries his hand at explaining the "strange influence to which Mill was subjected" in his *The Life of John Stuart Mill*. This infatuation, "for *infatuation* it can only be called when a

man of Mill's intellectual eminence *allows himself* to describe his friend
in terms of such unbounded adulation," suggests two explanations
(Courtney 1889, 115). First, women have a devious way of dressing up
ideas, of making clear and distinct ideas more "picturesque." Like Comte
and Descartes, JSM was an example of "philosophic weakness." A man
who is engrossed in philosophy is often fascinated by "the concrete and
the practical" mind of a woman. "The latter faculty is so far denied to him
that he tends to *overestimate its importance*. It seems like a revelation
from another world if a *woman of wit* and imagination can clothe with
living and palpable flesh some of those arid skeletons among which his
mind has had to make its home" (116). This tendency to overestimate
imaginatively dressed ideas of women is a fault that all (male) philosophers should be wary of. (Interestingly, even in 1960, a commentator on
JSM was still warning others that previous critics who have been favorable
to Harriet have fallen victim to the same enchantment that JSM did and
that Courtney warned of [Pappe 1960, 28].)

The second danger Courtney warned of consists of women's uncanny
ability to jump ahead of logic with intuitive understanding of issues.
"Clever women," unlike intelligent men, often derive their knowledge by
imaginative leaps, not the "hard thinking" and "mental discipline" that
men employ. "A man habitually underrates the woman's quickness of apprehension, and her delicate and intuitive insight into some of the problems with which he has been wrestling. He admires her, therefore, in
proportion to the seriousness of his own logic, not in reference to her own
native powers." Again, like Bain, Courtney recognizes that such an explanation had been explicitly denied by JSM himself. But JSM's insistence on
the similarity of the minds of women and men "would itself support some
such *delusion* as that which has been traced above. It is, at least, *a fact*,
that the *feminine mind* is *surprisingly quick in assimilating and repro-
ducing thoughts* and ideas which have been sympathetically presented to
it. It can adapt itself, perhaps, with greater readiness than the average
masculine intellect to a new medium" (Courtney 1889, 117–18). Again,
John's example serves as a warning to other philosophers who may fall
under the sway of similar feminine intuitions.

Critique from 1900 to 1930

After the end of the Victorian period, especially from 1910 through the
1920s, commentators offered a more sympathetic portrait of Harriet. In
The Life of W. J. Fox, Richard Garnett declared that "Harriet Mill occupies
a position below her desert in the intellectual history of her time. This is
in a measure unavoidable in the case of those who have left no tangible
evidence of their power. *The lot of gifted ladies is hard:* if they write they

are liable to be anathematised as 'scribbling women,' [*sic*] if they are content to guide and inspire, the reality of the invisible influence is called in question" (Garnett 1910, 97). He looks at the work performed before and after John's friendship with Harriet and decides that John "was not the victim of hallucination" although he may have had "a defective sense of proportion" (97).

Mary Taylor, following in the tradition of her aunt, Helen Taylor, and her grandmother, HTM, lambastes a critic who in the 1910s insisted "that no man of superior gifts should have a highly educated helpmeet, lest she by her 'flabby views of life'—a common result, he says, of high education among women—should exert a vulgarising influence upon him" (1912, 358). This critic had openly suggested a type of relationship between an intellectual man and his companion that seems to underlie, but remains unspoken in, many of the negative criticisms of Harriet, both before and after this time. He suggests Rousseau and his mistress as the appropriate model. However, Mary Taylor argues that the type of relationship Rousseau had is hardly the best suited for a man of genius, much less for a man of conscience: "According to the author of *Emile*, he had five children by Thérèse, each of whom he secretly consigned to the Foundling Hospital as soon as it was born. This wronged and unfortunate woman, who could neither learn to read, remember the names of the months, nor tell the time from the face of a clock, and whose deficiencies were made an occasion for jesting between him and his friends, is represented by the *Edinburgh* reviewer as the right helpmeet for Rousseau" (357). Mary Taylor notes that it is sheer ignorance to believe that geniuses could not be aided by smart women: "The remark that 'no one alive' could have rendered to such great writers as Rousseau, Goethe, and Mill any assistance in the formation and expression of their ideas is a species of intellectual arrogance and conceit of which I venture to say no man of genius would be guilty" (358). Substitute Einstein and you will hear the same argument offered in the twentieth century for dismissing the contributions of women companions of "geniuses." Mary points to one piece of evidence in favor of Harriet's abilities overlooked by previous critics: the length of a relationship that for more than twenty years was not legally binding on either party (363).

M. Ashworth, in "The Marriage of John Stuart Mill," confirms Mary Taylor's opinion, claiming that Harriet had "a certain mental quality and critical insight what was wasted on her surroundings" prior to meeting John (Ashworth 1916, 164). Ashworth acknowledges their collaboration: "As the friendship progressed, the two got into the habit of working together. . . . She threw in extra threads—golden ones—into the web of his thoughts" (169–70).

Guy Linton Diffenbaugh, in the 1920s, examined the history of Harriet criticism and concluded, "It appears that with a few exceptions

Mrs. Taylor was esteemed highly by all those who were permitted the opportunity of associating with her" (1923, 198). Yet he quotes with approval Carlyle's statement: "She was a woman full of *unwise intellect*, always asking questions about all sorts of puzzles—why, how, what for, what makes the exact difference—and Mill was good at answers" (quoted in Diffenbaugh 1923, 204). This may be one of the few astute judgments of Harriet by Carlyle, although I doubt that he understood its significance. Like many of the critics of Harriet and John to follow, Carlyle was chagrined by Harriet's penchant for asking questions. Reacting like God in the Garden to Eve's eating of the tree of the fruit of knowledge, most biographers are threatened, not delighted, by Harriet's provocative questions. Diffenbaugh tries to be impartial: "Yet in all fairness to Mrs. Taylor might it not be said that it took at least a clever person to inquire intelligently of Mill—'why, how, what for, what makes the exact difference'; and that it required a woman of remarkable mental gymnastics, at least, to assimilate Mill's answers with a degree of intelligent promptness sufficient to infatuate him mentally" (204). Diffenbaugh sees Harriet's questions as merely "clever," and it is a cleverness designed to infatuate, but at least her "witchery" is based on some sort of intelligence in this analysis.

In Ray Strachey's *The Cause: A Short History of the Women's Movement in Great Britain*, the innuendos about Harriet are examined. "Perhaps it was the fact that she lived apart from her first husband which put her wrong with the world; perhaps she was always socially on the defensive as well as too exclusively devoted to Mill. Perhaps she cared nothing at all for other people, was unsympathetic or even unkind, impatient of stupidity and of conventions. There may have been a dozen such outward difficulties which hid her from the world, and obscured her image in the records which are to be found in the lives and letters of her day. We cannot now judge what it was that made his friends distrust her" (1928, 68). The most important evidence that these innuendos are wrong is that which had been offered by Mary Taylor a decade earlier: John's long devotion.

Critique from 1930 to 1950

In 1930, Knut Hagberg continues the line of criticism first seen in Henshaw in 1874. Harriet is a powerful but bad influence on John. It is neither her socialism nor her Unitarian tendencies that are the problem, but her atheism. Hagberg concludes that Harriet "came to have a decisive influence over Mill. Unhappily, this seems to have been anything but good." She "made him into a Radical rationalist" (Hagberg 1930, 196). It was this rationalism that led her and seduced John into agnosticism or even atheism. As soon as John was free of Harriet's influence, he turned to a

Romantic mysticism. "Mill became a mystic, but only from the moment when he stood alone and detached from her to whose service he, like a medieval knight, had dedicated his life" (198). Here is an explanation that will account for both John's greatness—he had a medieval knight's dedication to his beloved—and the incorrectness of his views—which were due to Harriet's rationalism, and which were corrected upon her death.

In the 1940s Francis E. Mineka shifted the discussion from Harriet's intellectual gifts to her emotional support of John. Harriet could be praised because she offered spiritual sustenance. Harriet Taylor "was a woman of refinement and taste, interested in literature and questions of ethics and politics, but endowed with a strong emotional nature which kept her out of the bluestocking category. . . . However over-colored by emotion his estimate of her powers may have been, there can be no doubt that she was the saving grace of his inner life. Without her, John Mill might well have been a different person, but one can doubt that he would have been as fine, as understanding, or as great a man" (Mineka 1944, 273–75).

Critique in the 1950s

All biographers before 1951 had based their observations on second-hand information about Harriet. Not until nearly one hundred years after Harriet's death, when F. A. Hayek published *John Stuart Mill and Harriet Taylor: Their Friendship and Subsequent Marriage* (1951), did scholars have access to some of Harriet's letters, unpublished essays, and poems. (Hayek also mentions her work on the newspaper articles listed as coauthored in John's handwritten bibliography, although no scholar to date has studied these works carefully.) Hayek notes that "apart from Mill none of those who expressed views about Harriet Taylor's qualities have really had much grounds on which to base them, except W.J. Fox, whose is also the only other voice that joins in her praise" (Hayek 1951, 15). Hayek's opinion after studying these newly available documents was that "her influence on his thought and outlook, whatever her capacities may have been, [was] quite as great as Mill asserts, but that [it] acted in a way somewhat different from what is commonly believed. Far from it having been the sentimental it was the rationalist element in Mill's thought which was mainly strengthened by her influence" (17). The letters Hayek printed for the first time revealed the depth of Harriet's involvement in the writing published in John's name.

Diana Trilling's analysis of Harriet's writings published in Hayek's book expressed a very different opinion of Harriet. Whereas Hayek's examination of these documents revealed that Harriet's early unpublished essays "curiously anticipate[d] some of the arguments of *On Liberty*" (26), Trilling asserts that these essays and letters blow the whistle on Harriet.

"Mrs. Taylor . . . [was] one of the meanest and dullest ladies in literary history, a monument of nasty self-regard, as lacking in charm as in grandeur" (Trilling 1952, 116). Harriet was "prideful, vain and mean-spirited. . . . This intellectual beacon . . . was nothing more than a vest-pocket flashlight of a mind" (120). These pronouncements became the most often repeated comments on Harriet. What evidence does Trilling point to in the letters or other documents? None. She is simply sure that "this was no woman, no real woman—the letters, full as they are of injured vanity, petty egoism and ambition, show no touch of true femininity, no taint of the decent female concerns which support our confidence in the intelligence of someone like Jane Carlyle" (119–20). Harriet's flaw is that she is not a "real woman" and shows no signs of "true femininity." Perhaps if she had gotten up before dawn the way Jane Carlyle did to quiet the chickens so her man would not be disturbed (Rose 1984, 246–67), Trilling would have admired her more.

Michael Packe's *The Life of John Stuart Mill* was the first biography written using the new material found in the London School of Economics archives which Hayek brought to light. Whereas Trilling condemned Harriet for not being feminine enough, Packe (returning to Mineka's approach) believed that Harriet used all her feminine charms to control John. His portrait of Harriet is almost a cartoon of the 1950s view of women. She was a "handsome sprat" that another man could use "to catch an exceptional mackerel" (Packe 1954, 128). Packe decided that at first Harriet had ambitions of her own to write, for example, when she published the reviews, articles and poems in the *Monthly Repository* during the early 1830s. "Harriet, not yet aware of the august mouthpiece she was soon to gain, had a great ambition to become a writer like Harriet Martineau" (131–32). But after a spat with John during which he hadn't done any significant work, her true feminine side surfaced and she finally behaved herself. Harriet gave up her "manful ambition" in order to be of use to John, to "express herself in a more feminine way through her effect on him. . . . Harriet Taylor's influence on Mill at this time was soft and womanly. She soothed him in anxiety; she worried about his health. She afforded him emotional release. In this respect she was completely adequate" (237).[4]

According to Packe, however, as Harriet's beauty evaporated, so did her soft, womanly support. "She was now 34. Her beauty had begun to fade, and, as a result of her nervous disorder, the early vivacity of her quick emphatic temperament became more and more tempestuous" (289). Now Packe's language about Harriet changes. Harriet "insisted on" John changing the *Principles of Political Economy*. "She demanded a complete reversal of his economic treatise in its most essential feature. And she obtained it . . . he was forced to give way" (313). In short, "Harriet's astounding, almost hypnotic control of Mill's mind was not confined to reversing the direction of his economic theory" (315). Oddly, despite these passages, Packe denies that Harriet's influence should be reduced to her "charm[ing] and bewitch[ing] his mind," (316) as other critics put it. He believes that her influence went even further: "The influence she had gradually extended over him now ended in complete ascendancy, and his further writings were not the work of one mind, but of the fusion of two. . . . Her predominance was even more complete than he himself pronounced" (316). John was not only emotionally seduced by Harriet, he was intellectually coerced as well. "Mill ceased to make distinction between Harriet's mind and his. In little things as well as great, he followed where she led" (370). Packe acknowledged the intellectual contributions of Harriet but only by exaggerating her power over John. Instead of contributing to their mutual work, Harriet is seen as dominating John's work. Instead of partnership, Packe sees a matriarchy.

Ruth Borchard wrote *John Stuart Mill: The Man* in 1957. Borchard's Harriet was a "forceful, domineering personality" who "overpowered" John "by her intensely feminine atmosphere" (Borchard 1957, 38, 46). John necessarily obeyed Harriet (55). Harriet's "morbid inclinations" result in an interest in domestic violence, as witnessed by the newspaper articles. "She induced Mill to publish articles against such offenses. . . . This preoccupation with, and passionate railing against, [domestic violence] denote that some primitive spring in Harriet herself was touched. A trace of masochism is part of a normal woman's psychology; it fits her for the job of childbirth. But Harriet's . . . hungry interest in sadistic treatment of women . . . point[s] to a deep-seated masochism unfitting her for normal physical love" (66–67).[5]

What more can one say? Borchard argued that Harriet "had successfully taken his [JSM's] father's place in his life" (72). The charge that Harriet played a man's role in John's life while he played the woman's role is repeated throughout the history of scholarship on the two. Always the assumptions underlying the analysis are that if John wasn't in charge, wasn't dominant, then Harriet must have been; and that roles must be defined along gender lines. Borchard attributes power to Harriet, but only a domineering kind of power that can then be held responsible for all the ideas in John's philosophy that Borchard disapproves of, for example, his socialism. She claims: "Her influence on Mill can hardly be over-estimated. Whatever influence Mill exerted in his own time and over English history must be equally ascribed to Harriet. And the strong impetus given by his books towards socialism and the present welfare state must certainly be attributed more to Harriet than to Mill himself" (99). Would Joseph McCarthy have thought Harriet such a communist that he would have asked her to testify before the House Un-American Affairs Committee? At least Borchard is cleared—along with John. The villain is Harriet.

A couple of small articles in the 1950s tried to balance this picture of Harriet. L. Robbins, in a review of Packe's book, points out Harriet's good sense in her reaction to John's correspondence with Comte (Robbins 1957, 250–9). Maurice Cranston describes Harriet as "a beautiful, forceful, aspiring woman, living like the heroine of a play by Ibsen, in an atmosphere which thwarted her and curbed her spirit, in which she felt a lack of intellectual culture and of visionary ardour" (Cranston 1959, 385). Cranston describes a partnership between them, or what he calls "a marriage of minds," which is unusual among philosophers. However, neither of these were adequate ammunition against the two 1950s biographies of John.

Critique in the 1960s

Although in the 1950s Harriet was drawn as a sort of intellectual vamp, she did appear as powerful (even if the power was a malicious, unhealthy sort). As unbelievable as it will sound after having read the last couple of pages, the writers in the 1950s were considered supporters of Harriet. In fact, they were criticized for portraying Harriet as too important. In 1960 H. O. Pappe's *John Stuart Mill and the Harriet Taylor Myth*, a 48-page monograph that has always received more attention that it deserves, was published. Pappe chastises previous writers on John and Harriet for presenting Harriet as too powerful. He praises Borchard because "[b]eing a woman, she is not overpowered by Harriet's *anima* (as were, I believe, Hayek and Packe). She has enough feminine earthiness to see through some of Harriet's aspirations and devices" (Pappe 1960, 28). Pappe goes on to claim that Borchard herself "does not go far enough in tracing Harriet's masochism" (29). Pappe believes Harriet is not very smart (22) and did not influence John's ideas in any significant way (19, 46). He suggests that all previous scholars have gotten it wrong; instead of Harriet influencing John it was the other way around.

The following year, Jack Stillinger published *The Early Draft of John Stuart Mill's Autobiography*. The draft of JSM's autobiography that had been buried in various libraries and unavailable to scholars was now unveiled. This early draft displays the suggested changes made by Harriet as well as the acceptance of those changes by John. Here we can see their mutual work on this one manuscript—a manuscript that, as an autobiography, should be more exclusively in one person's voice than any other. Stillinger's assessment? "Her alterations in the early draft show her to have had some sense of style and propriety of tone, but they do not confirm Mill's estimate of her intellectual qualities" (Stillinger 1961, 25). He quoted the infamous Trilling article approvingly and signed on to the psychological theory first presented in Borchard that Harriet replaced John's father (28).

In the 1960s, only Gertrude Himmelfarb would argue in a short article that would later develop into a book that Harriet was influential, but again, as in the 1950s biographies, the influence was negative. Himmelfarb claims that John's move toward socialism—the worst idea John had, according to Himmelfarb—was all Harriet's doing.[6]

Aside from one short, virtually undocumented biography by John Ellery (1964),[7] the other biographers in the next several years would try a new approach to Harriet: ignore her. Joseph Hamburger's *Intellectuals in Politics: John Stuart Mill and The Philosophic Radicals* (1965), has only three passing references to Harriet in a book devoted to the period in which Harriet and John were beginning their intimate acquaintance and in which Harriet played a distinct role in John's life. Alan Ryan doesn't even mention Harriet in the index of his biography (1970).

Two "defenders" of Harriet during the sixties offered only lukewarm support. Mineka reiterated his claim from the forties that Harriet was an emotional, not an intellectual, contributor to John's life and work (1963, 306).[8] John Robson, in "Harriet Taylor and John Stuart Mill: Artist and Scientist," says there are two approaches to Harriet, that of the 1950s, that is, that Harriet dominated John, and that of the 1960s, that is, that Harriet contributed little to John's work. Robson adopts the hypothesis that "the relation between Mill and Harriet, it seems likely, was that common, if not invariable, in marriages between members of the *intelligentsia*: frequent discussion, mutual enlightenment, considerable independence in thought, and—the pattern is now changing—subordination of the wife's ambitions to the husband's" (Robson 1966, 171). In his investigation of this hypothesis, Robson focuses on the question of Harriet's specific contributions to John's work by examining her writing. This is a milestone in HTM scholarship. One hundred and eight years after her death, someone finally considers Harriet's writing (even if it is only two paragraphs long!). Mind you, it is only to discover whether or not she contributed to John, not to consider what she had to say. But, at least Harriet's work is finally studied.

Robson's conclusions are a bit confusing. Although he says Harriet's early essays and her "Enfranchisement of Women" "can be seen as forerunners of Mill's *Subjection of Women* and *On Liberty*" (171), his overall assessment is that she didn't influence him, in fact the opposite occurred (172). How can her essays be forerunners of two important works, if "there is no strong indication of influence"? In Robson's study of John's comments on Harriet's share in the work, the reason for the confusion becomes clearer. Using a passage from the last chapter of the *Logic*, Robson casts Harriet as the Artist, and John as the Scientist. Although John believes the Artist's role is fundamental, Robson believes that "the division of labour is rather unusual" (178). Interestingly, this view of woman as the "dreamer," the emotional one; and man as the logical "scientist" is one of the "backward" views of John's that Harriet fought against. That this statement of John's would one day be used to classify her, especially without John's generous affirmation of the importance of such attributes, would have rankled both of them. Robson is willing to declare that Harriet was the more practical of the two: "The persuasion of others, and the practicability of programmes, both derive from experience and habitual recognition of conflicts and contingencies . . . there is no reason to doubt that Harriet Taylor, whose approach as poet and prophetess was more concrete than abstract, also influenced him in this direction" (181). His final pronouncement on Harriet's role is that Harriet encouraged John's "many-sidedness," but "the theoretical groundwork is Mill's. . . . She was not, in any meaningful sense, the 'joint author' of his works" (186). Underlying this analysis is the echo of William Courtney's warning about women's clever kind of knowledge that "leaps ahead of logic" mixed with Mineka's assessment that Harriet provided emotional but not intellectual support. Although this analysis is more careful than most, the prize of male scholarship, the text, is still John's sole possession. Harriet can only dream, support, and suggest.

Critique in the 1970s

What a breath of fresh air it was when, in 1970, Alice Rossi edited *Essays on Sex Equality* by John Stuart Mill and Harriet Taylor. According to Rossi, the resistance to the acceptance of Harriet's contribution to John's ideas is due to three factors: the fight between Philosophical Radicals and Unitarian Radicals (Rossi 1970, 36), the commentator's attitude toward socialism (38), and plain old sexism (45). I will discuss these and other reasons for the currents in Harriet scholarship in Part 2.

Rossi believes, as I do, that Harriet's works need to be studied in order to make an accurate assessment of her work or her influence on John. "None of the Mill scholars have examined the essays collected in this volume for clues to the kind of relationship John and Harriet tried to maintain in their years together. Nor has due allowance been made, in my judgment, for Mill's own intellectual toughness. Mill was not a man to be easily influenced and won over by an idea or person" (Rossi 1970, 39). As is clear from the quotations I've offered throughout this history, Harriet is seen either as noninfluential or as important only because she seduces John into bad ideas. "Though it is couched in terms of detached scholarship, one senses in Mill scholars an unwitting desire to reject Harriet

Taylor as capable of contributing in any significant way to the vigor of Mill's analysis of political and social issues unless it included some tinge of sentiment or political thought the scholar disapproved of, in which case this disliked element was seen as Harriet's influence" (Rossi 1970, 44–45).

Virginia Held, in a review of Rossi's introduction to *Essays on Sex Equality*, supports this approach to Harriet. Held recognizes an important point about Harriet scholarship: "As for Harriet Taylor's coldness, it is more in the eye of the critic than implicit in the evidence" (Held 1971, 406). Max Lerner's pronouncement that "we know [Harriet] was a frigid woman" (in the introduction to *The Essential Works of John Stuart Mill*, quoted in Held 1971, 405) is rejected in favor of this analysis of Harriet's relationship to John and her husband: "She tried to arrive at a reasonable solution that would cause the least pain to all concerned" (Held 1971, 406). What a difference between these new critics and everyone who has written on Harriet before! A couple of years later, the first academic study of John's *The Subjection of Women* was published (Tatalovich 1973). Although this is one text we know Harriet was not involved in writing (it was written after her death), Tatalovich is able to see her influence. Harriet showed John the mental capabilities of a woman and their partnership served as a basis for his description of "the benefits of a marriage [based] on equality" (Tatalovich 1973, 288).

In the 1970s for the first time, a biography of John was written that began to understand the relationship between John and Harriet. Eugene August's *John Stuart Mill: A Mind at Large* (1975), was an important contribution. Instead of Harriet's domination of John, on the one hand, or her insignificance, on the other hand, their work is presented as a partnership. Not the simple partnership of equals in every way, but the partnership of a woman with a good mind but little training because of the educational and social background she had to endure and a man who had both a great mind and extraordinary training. August lets John explain the problem: "Deficiency of education has cut off women from the great traditions of thought and art. Even when a woman hits upon a lucky insight, it is frequently lost, Mill points out (waxing autobiographical again), for want of a husband or friend to evaluate and publicize it. 'Who can tell,' he wonders, 'how many of the most original thoughts put forth by male writers, belong to a woman by suggestion, to themselves only by verifying and working out? If I may judge by my own case, a very large proportion indeed'" (Mill, quoted in August 1975, 218). August sketches a new picture of the Mills's life together: "John's creative energies underwent an astonishing renewal during the collaboration with Harriet. No longer was it *his* genius; it was *their* genius" (August 1975, 136; original emphases).

Have scholars since the early seventies continued to expand and explore the "new" portrait of Harriet? Unfortunately, the backlash began even by the mid-1970s. Three major studies of John, Gertrude Himmelfarb's *On Liberty and Liberalism: The Case of John Stuart Mill* (1974); Bruce Mazlish's *James and John Stuart Mill: Father and Son in the Nineteenth Century* (1975); and Josephine Kamm's *John Stuart Mill in Love* (1977) all return to the view of Harriet found in the fifties and sixties.

Himmelfarb's book, like her article from a decade earlier, argues that all the bad ideas John had, his leanings toward socialism in *Principles of Political Economy* and all of *On Liberty*, were Harriet's doings. Even though Himmelfarb realizes that "the closer any collaboration, the less evidence of it there is likely to be. And a marital collaboration is, of course, the hardest to document" (Himmelfarb 1974, 239); the simplistic ideas and paranoid attitudes she finds in *On Liberty* must be Harriet's (259). The similarities between Harriet's early unpublished essays on tolerance and the ideas in *On Liberty* are taken as evidence for John's corruption. But, as we have seen in other commentators, Himmelfarb still will not attribute authorship to Harriet of the sacred text. John may have been overwhelmed by Harriet's dumb ideas, but the text—the words on the page that really count—is John's. John was "'thoroughly imbued' with a mode of thought that was 'emphatically hers'," but he still owns the text (267). We're back to "Bewitched, Bothered, and Bewildered."

Bruce Mazlish takes a Freudian tack. John chose Harriet not because she was intelligent or provocative but because her name was Harriet. Harriet? you say? Yes, because John's mother and a sister were named Harriet. Mazlish proposes that because Harriet had the same name as John's mother, but had the personality of his father, by loving her John could "possess not only his mother, but his father as well" (Mazlish 1975, 284). And he's not joking. It is John's "bisexuality" that allowed him to be attracted to such a manly woman as Harriet (329). Given the Freudian flavor of this study, it will be no surprise to discover that Harriet is not particularly well thought of. John didn't need Harriet to do the work he did, even though Harriet was not an idiot. (She was an above-average 23-year-old "girl" [307].) Harriet may have a sensitive heart, but she still had "hypnotic power" over John. Mazlish repeats a story about a chair hanging over a cliff that John and his friends visited in Ireland. The folklore declared that whoever had the courage to sit in the chair would rule the house. Neither John nor his friends sat, thus symbolizing an important characteristic of John: he wasn't a "real man," or, as Mazlish puts it, "Conjugal male preeminence was not a prominent trait in his relation to Harriet. Rather, the reverse was true, and willed as such by Mill himself" (309). "The Mill-Taylor relation was almost a parody of the patriarchal family, but with Harriet commanding and Mill obeying" (308). Just as we've seen in Packe and others, the assumption is always that someone must control, must dominate a relationship.

Since it is clear John didn't, Harriet must have. Real sharing of power is not even conceived as an option.

Josephine Kamm's contribution, *John Stuart Mill in Love*, is merely a rehashing of the fifties approach. She virtually repeats Borchard when she says that Harriet's concern with domestic violence is an expression of Harriet's masochism (Kamm 1977, 42). Back is Harriet's rule over John (83). Kamm grudgingly respects Harriet only because she must have been strong in order to force John to acquiesce to her ideas. "What was remarkable was that his largely self-educated woman could, and did, speak and correspond with him on equal terms and, when she felt strongly enough, force him to accept her ideas" (39).

Critique from 1980 to Present

In 1989, Gail Tulloch published the first book-length study of John's views on sexual equality. Although Harriet's name does not appear in the title, Tulloch does include, for the first time in history, a preliminary study of Harriet's essays on equality, including her "Enfranchisement of Women." Tulloch's "judgement is that Harriet Taylor's influence was clearly considerable" (1989, 72). This careful study of John's work and Harriet's in relation to John's is a very important contribution. Tulloch concludes the section on Harriet with the following: "Harriet's position is thus both more consistent in itself and a better guide to practice. It is also consistent with Mill's emphasis on social equality, and is what he too should have said" (99). I only wish she had written the book on Harriet's work primarily instead of secondarily.

Phyllis Rose's *Parallel Lives: Five Victorian Marriages* (1984) is a delightful, provocative study of power relations in the marriages of the Dickenses, Ruskins, Carlyles, and Mills and the common-law marriage of George Lewes and George Eliot (Marianne Evans). Although I admire this book enormously, Rose's attitude toward Harriet and John vacillates. On the one hand, John is a man "with strongly egalitarian politics," yet he is "still subject to domination by [a shrew]" (Rose 1984, 15). Rose says that "Harriet made the decisions. Harriet ran the show. A female autocrat merely replaced the usual male" (137). On the other hand, just the page before, she says, "The Mills were embarked upon a great experiment, something new in the history of relations between men and women—a true marriage of equals. But so unusual was this situation that for Harriet to be anywhere near equal she had to be 'more than equal.' Think of it as a domestic case of affirmative action. To achieve equality, more power had to go to Harriet, in compensation for the inequality of their conditions" (136). "They were a perfect intellectual team" because Harriet "was the executive. She made decisions. . . . She cut crudely, perhaps, but emphatically and practically to important matters." John's mind needed direction, and Harriet was willing and capable of providing direction. John's mind "initiated nothing. He was like an automaton which functioned perfectly when set on course, but could not set its own course or turn itself on. So Harriet, spontaneous, imperious, intellectually passionate, without self-doubt, put the logic machine into motion. She was his starter button. . . . She served as the part of himself that cared" (132, 131). Was this a "perfect intellectual team" or the domination of a good man by a shrew?

Alan Ryan, in "Sense and Sensibility in Mill's Political Thought" (1991) may clarify the attitude toward intellectual history that allows us to sympathize with Rose's ambiguity. He says, "Generosity and flexibility can be aimed at and with luck achieved; a God-like perspective in which all times and places are equally transparent cannot" (Ryan 1991, 122). Harriet and John's relationship was neither simple nor straightforward. It was a mixture of dependency and independence which can only be grasped through a generous shaking of the hand that is offered in letters, essays, manuscripts, and other scraps of information left as a trail through the woods of their lives. Without the trail everyone will get lost in his or her own historical, sociological, and philosophical prejudices. What is needed is to present all of Harriet Taylor Mill's words for the first time, to allow her to speak. When that happens, each of us can listen and try to put together at least one plausible map through the woods.

Analysis of HTM Criticism

Why have critics been so hard on Harriet? There are a number of reasons. First are the three outlined by Alice Rossi: the fight between Philosophical Radicals and Unitarian Radicals; the commentator's attitude toward socialism; and sexism. Philosophical Radicals, such as Bentham, James Mill, George Grote, and others, believed in the reform of the legal system. They believed that the greatest division in society was that between the aristocracy and "the people." The Unitarian Radicals, including William Fox and Harriet Martineau were more concerned with personal and social reforms and were more skeptical of legislative reform. They were more socially unconventional. They acknowledged a deep division between the working classes and middle classes as well as that between the middle classes and the aristocracy. Although the groups overlapped, a certain tension remained between them. Harriet was a Unitarian when she met John and contributed to the Unitarian publication *The Monthly Repository*. John had been moving away from the Philosophical Radicals since his mental crisis in which he questioned all possibility of real advancement of society. Those who liked JSM and were ardent Philosophical Radicals blamed HTM for John's move away from his roots. Those who sympathized with the Unitarian Radicals were kinder in recounting Harriet's influence on John. Not only did this difference of opinion occur among actual participants in these groups but also among the scholars of these groups. As Rossi demonstrates so clearly, Garnett and Mineka, who studied the Unitarians, were the most sympathetic critics of HTM. Laski, Rinehard, Stillinger, Lerner, and Trilling, who specialized in the Philosophical Radicals, were harsher in their critiques (Rossi 1970, 33–34).

Rossi also uncovers another source of the dislike of Harriet: the critic's opinion of socialism. If, like Hayek (1951), (and later Himmelfarb [1965] and even Borchard [1957]—although these commentators are not mentioned by Rossi) a critic disapproves of socialism, Harriet is seen as powerful and is thus blamed for John's move toward socialism. Critics of socialism "could then interpret Mill's socialist phase as a temporary aberration due to Harriet's influence over him." Most socialists, however, did not approve of Harriet's influence. For example, "Laski, a socialist, did not wish to view Mill's socialist thinking as a product of a woman's influence and hence followed the earlier trend toward a negative view of Harriet and of her contribution to Mill's thinking" (38). So either way, Harriet lost out. If critics didn't like socialism, it was all Harriet's fault that John leaned that way; if critics liked socialism, they weren't about to attribute it to a mere woman's influence. So Harriet was strong and evil, or weak and good. Not a happy choice.

Finally, Rossi points to the overall sexism in critics' treatment of Harriet. The history I have included here is far more extensive than the one Rossi includes, but it only reinforces the obvious bias in HTM scholarship. "Assertive women were undoubtedly an even greater irritation to Victorian men than they are to men today. Harriet Taylor was no shrinking violet, no soft and compliant woman" (Rossi 1970, 35–6). The numerous references to Harriet's masochism because she was interested in domestic violence, frigidity because she chose not to have sex with John, or the persistent attempts to portray Harriet as stupid, incompetent, or aggressive support Rossi's observation.

Looking at the history of Harriet criticism as a whole, I see a pattern that Rossi overlooked. Who are the sensitive critics of HTM? Richard Garnett and Mary Taylor in the 1910s; Diffenbaugh and Ray Strachey in the 1920s; Francis Mineka in the 1940s; Hayek in the early 1950s; Rossi, Virginia Held, and Eugene August in the 1970s. A quick comparison of these dates with a history of feminism shows a clear parallel. The 1910–1920s, 1940s, and 1970s were periods of growth for women's rights. The thirties, fifties and eighties were backlash periods. The history of criticism of Harriet is a history in miniature of women during the past one hundred years. Historians of philosophy are more influenced by the prevailing societal attitudes than most would like to admit. Philosophers like to think of themselves as "above" all that. The pattern in the critiques of Harriet demonstrates otherwise.

Even with the individual and general sexism in the history of philosophy, HTM would probably not have drawn quite so much ire if she had just "behaved herself." Historians haven't been so nasty to Jane Carlyle, Elizabeth Barrett Browning, or Sarah Austin, for example. But Harriet refused to play the role of a traditional Victorian subservient "lady." She asked questions that irritated and provoked nearly everyone but JSM.[9] Ladies don't ask such impertinent questions as, "How do you know?" "Why?" "What is the difference?" Intellectual curiosity was not an acceptable attribute in Victorian women, or in their more modern sisters. Jane Eyre wreaks havoc on others and on herself by asking dangerous questions such as, "Who is the woman in the attic?" or "What should I do?" or "What do I want?" The responses to Jane's questions—denial, subterfuge, lies, expressions of confusion and anxiety—demonstrate the danger others perceive in her questions. Questioners are always disruptive, as Socrates' death testifies, but women's questions are particularly threatening. They remind us of that source of all evil: Eve. Eve, with her unholy passion to know, to eat of the fruit of the tree of knowledge, is the mythological baggage that haunts our minds like the madwoman in the attic. Jane and Eve and Harriet don't have knowledge. They just have a passion to know. They know they don't know, so they ask. Unlike the fictional Jane Eyre, Harriet Taylor is not forced to starve or find a position as a schoolteacher, she is merely ostracized by both contemporaries and historians for her "unwise intellect."

Harriet's insistence on asking questions is the sign of her philosophizing. She wonders. Aristotle says that philosophy begins in wonder. That "radical lack which the Other cannot complete," as Le Doeuf puts it, "forms the true starting point of philosophy" (1987, 188). Men have a difficult time accepting women who cannot be completed by men's existence alone—a woman who won't give up questioning either his ideas or those of others, a woman who asks, "why, how, what for, what makes the exact difference" (Carlyle, in Diffenbaugh 1923, 204). Much of Harriet's philosophizing was verbal, not written. In her letters and in John's there are many references to their mutual desire to be together again so they can talk about the issues that concerned them. She writes, "I confess I prefer an aristocracy of men & women together to an aristocracy of men only—for I think the last is far more sure to last—but all this we have often said. . . . If you think this can be done & were to do it before Sat[y] we could talk it over together" (II/322).[10] And again, "I have so much to say to you that no one but you could understand" (L/28). And yet again,

"I have so very much to say which must wait" (L/30). Harriet writes to John, "I am ready to stand by my opinions but not to hear them travestied, & mixed up with what appears to me opinions founded on no principles & arguments so weak that I should dread for the furtherance of my anti religious opinions the imputation that they do not admit of being better defended. The fool ought to be sharply set down by *reasons*—but he is such an *excessive fool* & so lost in self sufficiency that he will cavil & prate say what you will" (original emphases). Later in the same letter she writes, "I was excessively amused by the top paragraph in the Daily News from Paris saying that Proudhon moved that the fiction of the acknowledgement of the being of a God sh^d be erased. It does one good to find one man who dares to open his mouth & say what he thinks on that subject. It did me good, & I need something for the spirits. . . . Adio caro carissimo till Sat^y when we shall talk over all these things" (L/8). This is the letter of a person who asks, challenges, critiques, and loves to talk about issues: it is the letter of a philosopher, not merely an admirer of a philosopher.

In addition to her "exasperating" questions, Harriet was strong, aggressive, and practical. She writes to her daughter about a recent journey: "The fact is we always get the last seats in the railway carriage, as I cannot run on quick, & if he goes on he never succeeds, I always find him running up and down & looking lost in astonishment, so I have given up trying to get any seats but those that are left" (LIII/12). To a man who could not clothe himself until he was ten years old, who, as an adult, was shocked to discover that the house required more coal in winter than summer, and who couldn't accomplish the difficult task of finding a seat for himself and his wife on a train by himself, Harriet was a savior. Her practical, no-nonsense ability to undertake daily life was a godsend. But to contemporaries and historians of philosophy who don't appreciate these characteristics, she was pushy, domineering, and vexatious. Harriet understood the finances of a newspaper purchase (XXVIII/174), could negotiate the details of publishing a book (XXVIII/178), and figured out that the gold rush in California might mean an increased need for the drugs her husband sold (XXVIII/225). Harriet had a type of practical knowledge that not only JSM but many "thinkers" since have lacked. These absent-minded professors are more often than not males, and each has someone, more often than not a woman, in his life who buys and prepares food, sees that the toilet is cleaned, and calls the dentist. Harriet had a practical wisdom which she asserted. I believe there is an assumption among too many philosophers that "real" philosophers, deep thinkers, are so devoted to the life of the mind that to attend to "trivial" practical affairs would take away from their intellectual pursuits. To them, being absent-minded is not a vice, but a virtue; it is proof that you are serious. Harriet's practical wisdom, conversely, is proof that she is not a serious thinker. She was a nice helper for JSM, tending to his everyday needs, but clearly not a philosopher. Real philosophers don't know how to grab a seat on the train or know who to call to catch a rat.

Furthermore, Harriet gets angry, even at the child prodigy, the famous philosopher, John Stuart Mill. She writes to him: "I am not one to 'create chimeras about nothing'—you should know enough about the effects of petty annoyances to know that they are wearing & depressing not only to body but to mind—these, on account of our relation, I have & you have not. . . . I am not a fool & I should laugh at, or very much dislike the thought, that you sh^d make your 'life obscure insignificant & useless' pour les beaux yeaux" (L/7). Historians of philosophy have not taken well to such expressions of anger against one of their own. HTM refuses to take John's reputation seriously. "Good heaven have you at last arrived at fearing to be '*obscure & insignificant*'! What *can* I say to that but 'by all means pursue your brilliant and important career'. . . . Good God what has the love of two equals to do with making obscure & insignificant. If ever you *could* be obscure & insignificant you *are* so whatever happens & certainly a person who did not feel contempt at the very idea the words create is not one to brave the world" (L/6; HTM's emphases). Sometimes her critique of him is less angry, but no less forceful, as when she chides him about his wishy-washy attitude toward Comte. She writes to him, "I now & then find a generous defect in your mind or yr method—such is your liability to take an over large *measure* of people—having to draw in afterwards—a proceeding more needful than pleasant" (II/327; HTM's emphasis). Although she is using good sense in her critique of Mill's attitude toward Comte, her lack of respect rankles historians of philosophy. As I will show below, she refuses to play the student to the "great philosopher." JSM apparently came to his senses: too many historians of philosophy have not.

To complicate matters even more, Harriet combined her potent personality with radical views about marriage, religion, and socialism. Harriet's ideas were more extreme (and more advanced) than even John's on a number of issues. She noted the discriminatory nature of the marriage contract, "the only contract ever heard of, of which a necessary condition in the contracting parties was, that one should be entirely ignorant of the nature and terms of the contract. For owing to the voting of chastity as the greatest virtue of women, the fact that a woman knew what she undertook would be considered just reason for preventing her undertaking it" (Box III/77). Harriet argues that women must be emancipated "from their present degraded slavery to the *necessity* of marriage, or to modes of earning their living which (with the sole exception of artists) consist only of poorly paid & hardly worked occupations, all the professions, mercan-

tile clerical legal & medical, as well as all government posts being mo-
nopolized by men. . . . The great practical ability of women which is now
wasted on worthless trifles or sunk in the stupidities called *love* would tell
with most 'productive' effect on the business of life" (XXVII/40; HTM's
emphases). She believed that women should be able to work outside the
home even if they were married and that if women had access to education and professions, they would choose for themselves whether or not to
have children and how many they would have. Her views on divorce were
also more revolutionary than JSM's. Both the left and the right criticized
Harriet's views and life on this subject. Those on the right thought she was
a loose woman because she abandoned her husband for a liaison with
John. Those on the left thought it unnecessary prudery on Harriet's part
not to live openly with John, not to go to bed with him, and to give in to
conventionality by marrying him only after her husband died. Furthermore, Harriet was an atheist. John was too, but an atheist woman has
been much harder for others to swallow than a man with the same beliefs.
From Henshaw in 1874 on, Harriet's religious beliefs have been a source
of irritation. Finally, her interest in the 1848 French revolution and her
pro-socialism continue, as I pointed out above, to be interpreted as part of
her seductively ruinous effect on John (according to critics on the right)
or as nothing but her insipid ineffectiveness (according to critics on the
left). Although I suspect that these ideas are the source of some of the un-
pleasantness in the HTM critiques, none of the critics attacks or even
mentions these ideas directly. They just hover like a fog behind the ad
feminam attacks.

So far I've reiterated Rossi's three reasons for the negative views of
Harriet, noted the parallel between the periods of progress and backlash
in the women's movement and periods when Harriet is treated negatively
and positively in the history of philosophy, and discussed Harriet's character traits—her penchant for asking questions, her practical wisdom,
and her radical ideas. All of these are partial answers to the question I am
pursuing. To these I now add our lack of understanding of women partners of "famous" philosophers. Michèle Le Doeuf in "Women and
Philosophy" describes a pattern of such relationships as the "Héloïse
complex." She notes that Hipparchia, Héloïse, and Elisabeth (Descartes'
correspondent) "had one thing in common: they all experienced great
passions, and their relationship with philosophy existed only through
their love for a man, a particular philosopher" (Le Doeuf 1987, 184–85).
Their love of philosophy was intertwined with their love of the man who
made philosophy available to them. This transference is not unusual
among students and teachers, but it is particularly troublesome for
women because until recently women have had no access to philosophy
except through the mediation of a man. Universities have not been open

to women until this century. "The 'godfather' relationship has opened up the whole field of philosophy to the disciple's desire, whilst women's transference relationships to the theoretical have only opened up to them the field of their idol's own philosophy" (Le Doeuf 1987, 187). Whereas the institution of the university provided support for the scholar who became disillusioned with a particular teacher or philosophical position, "the women amateurs . . . have been bound to the dual relationship, because a dual relationship does not produce the dynamics that enable one to leave it" (187).

In *Hipparchia's Choice: An Essay Concerning Women, Philosophy, Etc.,* Le Doeuf adds to her characterization of the Héloïse complex. Not only does Abelard desire the admiration of Héloïse, but he also requires the admiration of the scholarly world. He "wants not only to produce philosophy but also to be a philosopher" (Le Doeuf 1991, 164). Sartre and Beauvoir fit the general pattern, but Beauvoir may have escaped it by producing philosophy without "posing" as a philosopher (165). I believe that, like Simone de Beauvoir, Harriet may have escaped the Héloïse complex by doing philosophy without seeing herself as a philosopher. During a period in which Harriet must have felt very vulnerable, that is, during her husband's final illness, she writes to JSM, "The certainty of being really of use & quite indispensable to him (or to any one) gives me a quantity of strength and life—. . . . Take care of yourself for the world's sake" (XXIX/250–51). Although her prime reference is John Taylor, she implies that she has partially assumed the Héloïse role in regard to JSM. She wants to be of "use" to him, so that he can produce something "for the world's sake." After all, she had only written some newspaper pieces about domestic violence and some poems and reviews. And parts of books under JSM's name. But she does not remain in this role for long.

In general her letters make it clear that she acts as a partner with JSM, not as his admirer or student. In private she and John both knew she philosophized and wrote of their verbal discussions and work on manuscripts. Her few surviving letters are most often used to condemn her. Harriet's letters to her husband, John Taylor, tell of her work on manuscripts with John Mill and sometimes ask that manuscripts of her own be sent to her. About the initial work on *Principles of Political Economy*, Harriet writes to her husband, "I do certainly look more like a ghost [than] a living person, but I dare say I shall soon recover some better looks when we get to Brighton. I think I shall not be able to go before the end of next week being just now much occupied with the book" (XXVIII/170). "The book on The Principles of Political Economy which has been the work of all this winter is now nearly ready and will be published in ten days" (XXVIII/179). Harriet directs her husband to send manuscripts that she left in London because "I am very busy writing for the printers & want to get some scraps out of that"

(XXVIII/152). She is actively involved in all of their collaborative work: "I think the words which I have put the pencil through are better omitted—but they might with a little alteration be placed at the end? The *reason* I should give to Capt S. if a reason is asked, is that the way in which you are mentioned in the letters is calculated to give an erroneous impression of you. . . . The words I have added at the end do not go quite right but you will make them do so" (L/25; HTM's emphasis). Concerning a point of contention between them on an idea, JSM writes "But we shall have all these questions out together & they will all require to be entered into to a certain depth, at least in the new book which I am so glad you look forward to as I do with so much interest" (21 March 1849).[11] The text does not always reflect Harriet's suggestions; for example, John writes, "I think I agree in all your remarks & have adopted them almost all—but I do not see the possibility of bringing in the first two pages (from the preceding chapter)—I see no place which they would fit" (14 March 1854). Some revisions can be done simply by John, but meatier matters require the contribution of both. John writes, "One page I keep for consideration when I can shew it to you. It is about the qualities of English work people, & of the english generally. It is not at all as I would write it now, but I do not in reality, know how to write it" (19 February 1857).

These types of letters, and John's public proclamations that she philosophized (which no one believes no matter how many times he says it) are the evidence to show her as an uppity woman—one who pretends to do what no woman can—namely, philosophize. HTM may be more dangerous than Simone de Beauvoir, because John celebrated her philosophical activities. He openly acknowledged her philosophical contributions. He didn't pretend that he was the great philosopher and that she just wrote "feminist" (read that as "philosophically unimportant") works. Harriet got angry with some of John's ideas and revealed that in letters she did not destroy. Not Lou Salomé, not Simone de Beauvoir, not even Clotilde is treated with as much venom in the history of philosophy as Harriet was. It is Camille Claudel whose name rises to my mind. She too suffered, perhaps even more than Harriet. Again, why? Because she, like Harriet, had the audacity to move from model/supporter/helper/caregiver to sculptor? Women can't sculpt and women can't philosophize?

In addition to the peculiar relationship between women and men philosophers, our inability to penetrate the individual examples of the multiple kinds of collaboration that occurs between husbands and wives, lovers, colleagues, partners, and so on, contributes to our misreading of Harriet. We don't have a vocabulary for sharing work. We don't have enough paradigms or carefully examined particulars to show us how it is typically done, what is usual and what is not. Throughout the history of Harriet, the assumption underlying the analysis was always that someone was in control. The question was only, Who? Who controlled their lives? Who controlled their writing? The critics' understanding of collaboration, especially the collaboration of women partners of "geniuses," reminds me of a doctor's understanding of medicine in the Middle Ages—the shocking ignorance is pitiable. We are only beginning to understand and appreciate men's and women's ways of knowing (to sort out the similarities, differences, and complementaries where they exist). John was convinced that Harriet's ways of understanding complemented and furthered his own. Why doesn't anyone believe him?

One answer was pointed out by Phyllis Rose: "The world does not take kindly to a successful collaboration between a married couple. When John Lennon insisted on making records with Yoko Ono, he was accused of deifying an inferior artist, and she was accused of destroying a great artistic unit." It doesn't matter whether the star is male or female. The same incredulity occurred with Joan Sutherland and Barbra Streisand. "What is at work here seems to be a collective jealousy. The public, whose relationship with any celebrity (writer, philosopher, or film star) is partly erotic, resents another person's coming between it and the object of its attention" (Rose 1984, 132). I can't help smiling just thinking of John Stuart Mill and John Lennon in the same breath, but I believe this accounts for some of the nastiness in the comments on Harriet in JSM scholarship.

The particular problem of those in the shadows of the famous is part of the overall problem in understanding collaboration, especially collaborative writing.[12] Our acceptance of collaboration has developed since the Renaissance. Dante's Beatrice and Petrarch's Laura were merely emotional inspiration for their famous lovers, or at least that's how the story goes. Descartes and Princess Elisabeth debated his work, but he didn't claim, or she assert, a share in the work. During John and Harriet's period, women in partnership were beginning to be recognized for their contribution of ideas as well as emotional support. Comte claimed that his lover, Clotilde, was the source of his ideas. John disagrees and, according to August, "regrets only that Clotilde lacked the intellect Comte attributed to her. Were she really so perceptive . . . , she would have curbed her lover's rage for authoritarian order, as Harriet had done for [JSM] during the thirties and forties" (August 1975, 187). Eliza Flower and Sarah Austin did their own quiet work behind the lights of their husband's or lover's fame. Jane Carlyle vented her frustrated intellect in her letters.

Only after Harriet and John could biographers see a couple as truly sharing work. One couple, Sidney and Beatrice Webb (who were inspired in part by the ideas of HTM and JSM) enjoyed what Harriet and John did not: a reputation for shared ideas. This is how a biographer, Mary Agnes Hamilton, tells their story.

> Almost impossible, nowadays, to think of Sidney and Beatrice Webb
> except as a couple. It is not only that they have written, together, books
> in which no one can detach what belongs to one from what belongs to
> the other. They talk, if you meet them, in the dual, almost always. . . .
> When they say "we," the listener knows, no matter who uses it, that the
> number is right; the thinking is, somehow,—he does not know quite
> how—a joint process. . . . They are in fact, and have been, for forty
> years, the brightest example of what she has called a "double-star per-
> sonality, the light of one being indistinguishable from that of the other."
> The effective fusion of two shining minds has, indeed, worked, as he
> suggested to her in the days before it took place, not as a mere sum in
> addition . . . one and one, side by side, in a proper integrated relation-
> ship, makes not two but eleven. (Hamilton n.d., 1–2)

A double star. We still have trouble imagining such a constellation.
Albert and Mileva Maric Einstein. Simone de Beauvoir and Sartre. Hillary
and Bill Clinton. JSM and HTM assert for all couples who share the intellectual work that it doesn't matter who holds the pen, who types the page,
or who holds the office—both should share the credit. Rose describes the
relationship of Harriet and John thus:

> Both had been made lonely by exceptional intelligence, and they re-
> joiced in each other like two giants, two midgets, or any two people who
> have feared their oddness would prevent them from ever knowing close
> companionship. They were a happy couple, discussing everything,
> sharing everything. Most important, they shared his work—or what pos-
> terity called his work, despite Mill's insistence that virtually everything
> published in his name was Harriet's as much as his. Mill believed that
> when two people together probe every subject of interest, when they
> hold all thoughts and speculations in common, whatever writings may
> result are joint products. The one who has contributed the least to com-
> position may have contributed the most to thought. It is of little conse-
> quence which of them holds the pen. (Rose 1984, 127–28)

The problem of collaborative work is particularly tricky when it comes
to collaborative writing. In *Singular Texts/Plural Authors: Perspectives
on Collaborative Writing* (1990), Lisa Ede and Andrea Lunsford discuss a
number of different types and contexts of collaborative writing. The study
of collaborative writing is still quite new. It is very difficult to explain the
elaborate dance of writing, thinking, talking, arguing, discussing, rewrit-
ing, pondering, revising, writing out, writing down, and writing over which
constitutes collaboration. Each collaboration is different: each is peculiar
to those involved with that work of collaboration. Because philosophers
have rarely written collaboratively or assigned collaborative projects in

their classes, they remain embarrassingly ignorant of the silliness of asking, "who contributed what?"

Why haven't philosophers written collaboratively or acknowledged it when they did on the sly? Le Doeuf's recognition of the assumption of a pedagogy of the "master 'who knows' and the pupil 'who does not yet know'" suggests an answer. If we believe, as Socrates did, that the search for knowledge is necessarily a social enterprise, a work of collaboration, a revolution would occur. "If the subject of the enterprise is no longer a person, or better still, if each person involved in the enterprise is no longer in the position of being the subject of the enterprise but in that of being a worker, engaged in and committed to an enterprise which is seen from the outset as collective, it seems to me that the relationship to knowledge—and to gaps in knowledge—can be transformed. Here again, it is hard to describe the revolution that would be effected by a collective form of philosophical work *and* be a recognition of the fact that, in any case, the enterprise cannot be reduced to personal initiatives" (Le Doeuf 1987, 207; original emphasis).

HTM and JSM performed this revolutionary act. They created work that was "seen from the outset as collective." In the first years of their acquaintance, Harriet wrote an essay defending the necessity for collaboration in the search for truth: "We would have the Truth, and if possible all the Truth. . . . But we would never lose sight of the important fact that what is truth to one mind is often not truth to another." Language cannot capture the shades of meaning that color the truth. "To an honest mind what a lesson of tolerance is included in this knowledge." We must learn to find "something that is admirable in all, something to interest and respect in each. . . . As the study of the mind of others is the only way in which effectually to improve our own" (Box III/78).

Later, they even wrote a book defending the belief that knowledge is more likely to be gained in the interchange, debate, and struggle of those collaborating in learning. In *On Liberty* the passionate commitment to collaborative learning pours over the reader: "Truth, in the great practical concerns of life, is so much a question of the reconciling and combining of opposites that very few have minds sufficiently capacious and impartial to make the adjustment with an approach to correctness, and it has to be made by the rough process of a struggle between combatants fighting under hostile banners" (Mill 1982, 110–11). "There is always hope when people are forced to listen to both sides; it is when they attend only to one that errors harden into prejudices, and truth itself ceases to have the effect of truth by being exaggerated into falsehood" (115). Harriet Taylor Mill and John Stuart Mill recognized that they needed each other. They believed in doing philosophy the way Le Doeuf describes: "'I do not do everything on my own,' . . . I am a tributary to a collective discourse and knowledge, which have done more towards producing me than I shall contribute in continuing to produce them; and replace the mystery with a recognition of the necessarily incomplete character of all theorization" (Le Doeuf 1987, 208).

I agree with Le Doeuf that "The future of women's struggle for access to the philosophical will be played out somewhere in the field of plural work" (Le Doeuf 1987, 208). If we recognize HTM's contributions to philosophy, we will find at least one example of how philosophical work can be done. But that is a big "if."

Why is Harriet treated with so much nastiness? She asked too many questions thus challenging male assumptions of knowledge and thereby exemplifying Eve's passion to know and giving rise to those anxieties buried in the myth. Her practicality makes it easy for those with very important things on their mind, a.k.a. philosophers, to doubt her ability to think about anything other than practical matters. Her views were so radical that they were easier to ignore than to critique. Harriet's friends, the Unitarian Radicals, also got her into trouble with supporters and historians of their rivals, the Philosophical Radicals. The blatant sexism of commentators, which mirrors the sexism of the period in which the critiques were written, adds to the unfairness of the treatment of her. Her collaboration with a philosopher has been misunderstood for a number of reasons, not the least of which is that philosophers like to think of themselves as Romantic geniuses on a lonely pursuit of a type of knowledge that they have and students don't, instead of as a team of thinkers who collaborate in a search for knowledge which will never be complete. All of these reasons overlap as they contort our attempts to understand what Harriet thought.

How to tell a life? First we need to listen to Harriet. It is time to put her words together for the first time. Until now, Harriet's published works (or her published works that have been republished) have been scattered in a variety of sources.[13] Some of her letters and private manuscripts have never been published, and those that have are often buried in biographies of JSM. Next, we need to overcome our fear of the intentional fallacy and explore the intertwining of life and ideas. Furthermore, we need to compare and contrast Harriet's and John's work where it is distinct, and acknowledge collaboration when it is deserved. Finally, we need to use some of the new paradigms discovered by feminist scholars in the last twenty years so that we can properly shake hands with Harriet Taylor Mill.

NOTES

1. She lived from 1807 to 1858.

2. I will be using either the first names or initials of Harriet Taylor Mill and John Stuart Mill in contrast to the usage in all of the scholarship in which John is

regularly referred to as "Mill," while Harriet Taylor Mill is usually simply "Harriet," an unequal use of names which smacks of sexism.

3. Unless otherwise noted, all emphases in quotations have been added.

4. See also similar passages: "Perhaps, as is often the feminine way, she took a less tragic view of the affair, having a better notion than either of the men how it might be expected to turn out" (Packe 1954, 143); "During the years of Mill's activity as an editor and politician, Harriet's share in his work was commonplace and feminine. . . . Although she played no open part in the business decisions, everything was submitted to her judgment" (236); and, "Her passionate and downright sympathy with the oppressed, her robust and practical common sense, two qualities more commonly found together in women than in men, made her feel that the condition of the poor was far more miserable than she had at first supposed" (312). Other examples are abundant.

5. According to Susan Faludi, during the backlash years of the 1980s, the term masochism is associated again with women: in *Being a Woman*, "Masochism is just the naturally feminine 'desire to endure pain rather than inflict it; to relinquish control rather than seize it.' And so, [Grant] concludes, 'In this sense, certainly, most women are indeed masochistic'." Even the psychiatric community reestablishes masochistic personality disorder, almost always a problem of women, as a disease (Grant, in Faludi 1991, 344, 357).

6. It was Harriet's charms, "not the charm of common ownership to which Mill had succumbed" (Himmelfarb 1965, 26, 28–9).

7. Ellery continues the condemnation of Harriet: "Harriet Taylor seems to have had a penchant for expressing her views on the slightest provocation, and she seemingly was driven by ambitions to have them immoralized in print. . . . The force of her personality established her power over him, and she was very much aware of the fact" (Ellery 1964, 37).

8. "Harriet was a rebel not without cause. . . . Neither he nor his recent biographers have convinced us that she was the originating mind behind his work, but no one can doubt her importance in Mill's inner life, the well-springs of which had been threatened by drought" (Mineka 1963, 306).

9. See Diffenbaugh's (1923) critique above.

10. I will cite the letters by the volume and number or Box number and item number of the Mill/Taylor Collection assigned by the British Library of Political and Economic Science of the London School of Economics where they are collected.

11. This letter and the other quoted in this paragraph are located in the Sterling Library at Yale. They are included in an appendix to the *Principles of Political Economy* volume in *The Collected Works of John Stuart Mill*.

12. My unpublished "The Newspaper Writings of Harriet Taylor Mill and John Stuart Mill: The Means and Meaning of Their Collaboration," explores the importance of collaboration in the philosophizing of HTM and JSM much more thoroughly.

13. The best source of HTM's work is Hayek (1951). Hayek included the majority of letters that have been collected in the London School of Economics. Some letters not included in Hayek are found in Borchard (1957), Packe (1954), and Mazlish's (1975) biographies. Harriet's early essays on marriage and toleration appear in Hayek (1951) and in Rossi (1970). "The Enfranchisement of Women" appears in Rossi (1970). The newspaper articles appear in the *Collected Works of John Stuart Mill*, vols. 24 and 25. Harriet's chapter in the *Principles of Political Economy*, is published under JSM's name, as is *On Liberty*. I am currently working on a book that will publish all of Harriet's work for the first time.

REFERENCES

Ashworth, M. 1916. The marriage of John Stuart Mill. *Englishwoman* 30: 159–72.

Atwood, Margaret. 1989. Biographobia: Some personal reflections on the act of biography. In *Nineteenth-century lives: Essays presented to Jerome Hamilton Buckley*, ed. Lawrence S. Lockridge, John Maynard, and Donald D. Stone. Cambridge: Cambridge University Press.

August, Eugene. 1975. *John Stuart Mill: A mind at large*. New York: Charles Scribner's Sons.

Bain, Alexander, 1882. *John Stuart Mill: A criticism with personal recollections*. London: Longmans, Green & Co.

Borchard, Ruth. 1957. *John Stuart Mill: The Man*. London: Watts.

Bourne, Henry Richard Fox. 1873. John Stuart Mill: A sketch of his life. *Examiner* 17: 582–86.

Courtney, William. 1889. *The life of John Stuart Mill*. London: Walter Scott.

Cranston, Maurice. 1959. Mr. and Mrs. Mill on liberty. *The Listener* 62: 385–86.

Diffenbaugh, Guy Linton. 1923. Mrs. Taylor seen through other eyes than Mill's. *Sewanee Review* 31:198–204.

Ede, Lisa, and Andrea Lunsford. 1990. *Singular texts/plural authors: Perspectives on collaborative writing*. Carbondale: Southern Illinois University Press.

Ellery, John B. 1964. *John Stuart Mill*. New York: Twayne.

Elliot, Hugh S. R., ed. 1910. *The Letters of John Stuart Mill*. Vol. 1. New York: Longmans, Green and Co.

Faludi, Susan. 1991. *Backlash: The undeclared war against American women*. New York: Crown.

Garnett, Richard. 1910. *The life of W. J. Fox*. London: John Lane at Bodley Head.

Hagberg, Knut. 1930. *Personalities and powers*. Trans. Elizabeth Sprigge and Claude Napier. London: John Lane at Bodley Head.

Hamburger, Joseph. 1965. *Intellectuals in politics: John Stuart Mill and the philosophic radicals*. New Haven: Yale University Press.

Hamilton, Mary Agnes. N. d. [c. 1932]. *Sidney and Beatrice Webb: A study in contemporary biography*. London: Sampson Low, Marston.

Hayek, F. A. 1951. *John Stuart Mill and Harriet Taylor: Their friendship and subsequent marriage*. New York: Augustus M. Kelley.

Held, Virginia. 1971. Justice and Harriet Taylor. *The Nation* (October 25): 405–6.

Henshaw, S. E. 1874. John Stuart Mill and Mrs. Taylor. *Overland Monthly* 13: 516–23.

Himmelfarb, Gertrude. 1965. The two Mills. *The New Leader* 10 (May): 26, 28–29.

———. 1974. *On Liberty and liberalism: The case of John Stuart Mill.* New York: Alfred A. Knopf.

Kamm, Josephine. 1977. *John Stuart Mill in love.* London: Gordon & Cremonesi.

Le Doeuf, Michèle. 1987. Women and Philosophy. In *French feminist thought,* ed. Toril Moi, Oxford: Basil Blackwell.

———. 1991. *Hipparchia's choice: An essay concerning women, philosophy, etc.* Trans. Trista Selous. Oxford: Basil Blackwell.

Marston, Mansfield. 1873. *The life of John Stuart Mill: politician and philosopher, critic and metaphysician.* London: F. Farrah.

Mazlish, Bruce. 1975. *James and John Stuart Mill: Father and son in the nineteenth century.* New York: Basic Books.

Mill, John Stuart. 1982. *On Liberty.* Gertrude Himmelfarb, ed. New York: Penguin Books.

Mill-Taylor Collection. British Library of Political and Economic Science of the London School of Economics.

Mineka, Francis E. 1944. *The dissidence of dissent: "The Monthly Repository," 1806–1838.* Chapel Hill, NC: University of North Carolina Press.

———. 1963. The *Autobiography* and the lady. *University of Toronto Quarterly* 32: 301–6.

Packe, Michael St. John. 1954. *The life of John Stuart Mill.* New York: Macmillan.

Pappe, H. O. 1960. *John Stuart Mill and the Harriet Taylor myth.* Melbourne: Melbourne University Press.

Priestley, F.E.L. and J. M. Robson, eds. *The collected works of John Stuart Mill.* Toronto: University of Toronto Press.

Robbins, L. 1957. Packe on Mill. *Economics* 24 (August): 250–59. Also published in *John Stuart Mill: Critical assessments,* vol. 4, ed. John Cunningham Wood. London: Routledge, 1988.

Robson, John. 1966. Harriet Taylor and John Stuart Mill: Artist and scientist. *Queen's Quarterly* 73: 167–86.

Rose, Phyllis. 1984. *Parallel lives: Five Victorian marriages.* New York: Vintage.

Rossi, Alice S., ed. 1970. *Essays on sex equality,* by John Stuart Mill and Harriet Taylor Mill. Chicago: The University of Chicago Press.

Ryan, Alan. 1970. *John Stuart Mill.* New York: Pantheon.

———. 1991. Sense and sensibility in Mill's political thought. In *A cultivated mind: Essays on J. S. Mill presented to John M. Robson,* ed. Michael Laine. Toronto: University of Toronto Press.

Stillinger, Jack, ed. 1961. *The early draft of John Stuart Mill's "Autobiography."* Urbana: University of Illinois Press.

Strachey, Ray. 1928. *The cause: A short history of the women's movement in Great Britain.* Portway: Cedric Chivers.

Tatalovich, A. 1973. John Stuart Mill: *The subjection of women:* An analysis. *Southern Quarterly* 12 (1): 87–105. Also published in *John Stuart Mill:*

Critical assessments, vol. 4, ed. John Cunningham Wood. London: Routledge, 1988.

Taylor, Mary. 1912. Mrs. John Stuart Mill: A vindication by her granddaughter. *Nineteenth Century and after* 71: 357–63.

Trilling, Diana. 1952. Mill's intellectual beacon. *Partisan Review* 19: 115–16, 118–120.

Tulloch, Gail. 1989. *Mill and sexual equality.* Boulder, CO: Lynne Rienner.

EVOLUTIONARY THEORY IN THE
SOCIAL PHILOSOPHY OF
CHARLOTTE PERKINS GILMAN

MAUREEN L. EGAN

Charlotte Perkins Gilman has been recognized by recent scholars as one of the major feminist theorists of the period which spans the late nineteenth and early twentieth centuries. Dale Spender places Gilman's work as being at the forefront of feminist theory even today and regards her as the early feminist most closely embodying the assumptions and aims of the contemporary women's movement. For Barbara Ehrenreich and Dierdre English, Gilman's first major work, *Women and Economics,* provided "*the* theoretical breakthrough for a whole generation of feminists, [for it] appealed not to right or morality but to evolutionary theory" (Ehrenreich 1978, 67 Emphasis theirs). Gilman's biographer, Mary C. Hill, calls her life "the making of a radical feminist," because of the extensive and disciplined critique of sexual inequality which she carried out.

Regrettably, Gilman's work has yet to be recognized adequately for its contribution to American philosophy. Mary Mahowald has pointed out that "*feminist* elements are generally lacking in the canon of American philosophy" (Mahowald 1987, 411), defining feminist elements as those that challenge the subordination of women's interests to those of men. I believe that the exclusion of Gilman—whether intended or inadvertent—is a case in point. A further characteristic of the recognized American philosopher is that, ironically, while their work is marked by emphasis on the importance of experience, "none had an experience common to half the human race, that of being female" (Mahowald 1987, 410). Taking a lead from Mahowald's argument for a "majority perspective," I will try in this paper to advance the needed recognition of Gilman's contribution, by situating her philosophically in the intellectual

Hypatia vol. 4, no. 1 (Spring 1989) © by Maureen L. Egan

history of the United States as one of several influential proponents of reform Darwinism. I will indicate the main ideas which she held in common with both the Spencerians and the reform Darwinists. I will then provide a general overview of her use of the methodology of evolutionary theory for analyzing human social development and show how this methodology eventually made her arrive at conclusions both very modern and distinctly nineteenth century. Lastly, I will give some attention to what I call her "theory of the two natures" and to the role of the two sexes in social evolution.

Although these points are far from a thorough presentation of Gilman's writings which she produced over a period of forty years and which account for the greater portion of some twenty-five volumes of published work, they are representative of her work as a whole, and they give some indication of the profound and original thinking of one of the major intellectuals of the century just past. Moreover, some attention to them is greatly needed. While the merits of her psychological short story "The Yellow Wallpaper" and her utopian novels *Herland* and *With Her in Ourland* have recently received long overdue attention, her nonfiction production—in which we may see reflected the major intellectual movements of her time—has received far less. So completely did Gilman's work disappear for some five decades, until Carl Degler republished her seminal *Women and Economics* in 1966, that it is difficult for us today to grasp the influence and wide acquaintance which this work once enjoyed among an enormous audience in the United States.

A case can be made for Charlotte Perkins Gilman's inclusion in the "canon" of American philosophers defined by Max Fisch (1951). She belonged to the "classic period" which Fisch defined as beginning just after the Civil War and extending to just before World War II (Fisch 1951, 1), and her writings exhibit several of the assumptions and interests shared by the "canonical" authors, especially the ideas that would come to be understood as pragmatist, the search for a scientific explanation of culture and thought, and an evolutionary starting point for philosophy. To develop the case fully is beyond the scope of this paper. However, an analysis of Gilman's connection with the evolutionist ideas of the late nineteenth century will go some way toward placing her in the mainstream of American thought. It should be noted that one feature of her biography which accounts significantly for her exclusion from previously defined canons is the fact that she had no direct connection with Philosophy in the academy. As Fisch's work ably demonstrates, a strong network of university connections united the "canonical" American philosophers of the classic period.

Gilman was a self-taught economic theorist with a good command of the basic ideas of capitalism and a general understanding of Marxist principles. That she was also a Bellamyite is evident in, among other things, her utopian vision of the kitchenless home as the beneficiary of many technological advances. Every aspect of her social philosophy also shows the influence of Darwinian science, both in method and in substance. But perhaps above all, she was an effective popularizer of the ideas of early sociologist Lester Ward, whom she greatly admired. In her work she carried out highly suggestive refinements and developments of Ward's theory of an early matriarchic period in human history. While, therefore, the major influences on her thought overall were Ward's sociology, reform Darwinism, Edward Bellamy's socialism, and Deweyan instrumentalism, for the purposes of this paper I will concentrate primarily on reform Darwinism as it shows itself in her work.

The Social Darwinist Tradition

It would be difficult to overestimate the effects of Darwin's principle of evolution by natural selection upon virtually all areas of intellectual endeavor. The ideas of natural, gradual change over a long period; of adaptation for survival in a competitive environment; and, in humans, of the implications of "sexual selection" for the development of the species all had a profound impact upon the nineteenth century United States. As scientific thinking began to change significantly under the influence of Darwinism the resulting conflict between science and religion emerged. All of this occurred just as the social sciences were developing and opening up a fruitful avenue for application of the new science to human behavior.

Those who sought to apply the principles of Darwinism to the understanding of the human species tended to move in one of two opposite directions: some, like William Graham Sumner, who was a disciple of Herbert Spencer, looked upon human social development as a positive progression explicable by the same scientific principles as the development of other species. They disapproved of social reform movements, regarding them as artificial interferences with a natural process. Others, like Lester Ward, moved in exactly the opposite direction. They supported social reform movements on the grounds that human beings should use their intelligence and the ethical development that has resulted from their evolutionary progress, in order to modify their conditions. It is the latter direction that Charlotte Perkins Gilman took. Richard Hofstadter has observed, "Although its influence far outstripped its merits, the Spencerian system serves students of the American mind as a fossil specimen from which the intellectual body of the period may be reconstructed" (Hofstadter 1955, 32). While Gilman and other critics chose not to follow Spencer to the logical conclusions of his hard determinism, it is possible—as Hofstadter's comment indicates—to trace several intellectual trends of the nineteenth century by their relationship to Spencerianism, even through their sometimes visceral opposition to it. Reform Darwinism was one such trend.

Spencer had wished to create a unified science which would bring the natural and human worlds together, in the tradition of the eighteenth century philosophers. He found that evolutionary theory did this by showing the development from homogeneity to—within species limits—heterogeneity. It was Spencer who used the phrase "survival of the fittest," which he applied to economics, labor, business, and law. He was a strong proponent of conservatism and envisioned only a negative role for government in the process of social evolution: its purpose was to ensure that people did not overstep their natural rights. Although Spencer believed that private charity aided the inevitable evolution from egoism to altruism on the part of almsgivers, he denounced public charity, charging it with holding back progress by aiding the continued survival of the unfit. "Natural"—that is, unimpeded—growth of society was to be preferred. Carnegie, Rockefeller and others found in Spencer's ideas intellectual justification for the strong position of individualism.

William Graham Sumner's social philosophy, conservative in nature, rested upon Spencerian principles, especially those set forth in *The Study of Sociology,* and upon the ideas of Thomas Malthus. Sumner believed that the basis of society is "the man-land ratio." We cannot blame others for our tribulations, since these are but part of the struggle in nature. Unrestricted competition should be encouraged, for it promotes the selection process, which in turn leads to progress for civilization.

Sumner was skeptical of democracy and tended to regard it as a transient stage in social evolution. Leaders in industry, he felt, are entitled to amass their fortunes on the grounds of their useful function in promoting the economic progress of society. Inequality was to be valued as the result of true liberty, in which all persons are free to engage in the struggle for existence. The successful come out on top. Sumner believed in social determinism, a concept borrowed from Spencer: that is, that society is the product of gradual evolution and cannot easily be altered by legislation. He was, therefore, against reformism.

From these social Darwinists Gilman learned to see human social progress as an evolutionary process which follows the same scientifically observable patterns and principles as does animal evolution. However, she did not agree that humans are caught in a struggle for the survival of the fittest. More radically, she questioned the criteria used by Spencer and his disciples for determining fitness. Gilman rejected the deterministic assumption of the social Darwinists that the struggle for survival could not have occurred otherwise than it did. To her mind, one half of the human race had for many centuries been held at an inferior stage of evolution by the other half, with the effect that the evolutionary progress of both was jeopardized. Wishing to incorporate potentiality for change and choice into scientific explanation, she found a more satisfactory account of human development in the critics of pure social Darwinism, the so-called "reform Darwinists." In them she found her reason for optimism for the future: the modification, if not complete rejection, of social determinism.

Gilman's Debt to Reform Darwinism

One of the most outspoken of the reform Darwinists was Lester Ward. Although influenced methodologically by Spencer, Ward was opposed to what he saw as a monistic trend in sociology; namely, the practice of using the principles and laws of the natural world to explain the social. He adopted a dualistic philosophy that reflected a pragmatic bias, making a sharp distinction between physical evolution and mental evolution. Physical evolution explained the origins of the various animal species. It was purposeless in nature. Mental evolution, on the contrary, explained the purposive character of specifically human development. No other explanation, he felt, could better account for the facts of human social interaction. His physical evolution/mental evolution distinction had the further advantage that it provided theoretical support for the reform movements he advocated. Democratic sensibilities are everywhere present in Ward's writings and lectures. In an important speech to the Anthropology Society of Washington in 1881, he spoke in favor of the trend toward government intervention in social affairs, which opposed the then-current laissez-faire social theory.

Perhaps most significantly for Gilman, Ward identified two types of economics: animal economics of life and human economics of mind. According to the latter, humans transform their environment through what he called the "telic" application of intelligence: that is, through purposive behavior for both individual and social ends. Although other animals interact with their environment to more or less complex degrees, they do not alter their environment as humans do by the application of intentionality. The effect of this difference is that humans can be properly said to create their environment. For Ward there exists also a social mind, an aggregate of individual human minds. In order to explain the meliorating power of education on generations of people, he believed—as had Lamarcke, Darwin, and Spencer—in the transmission of acquired characteristics. Gilman found this a suggestive idea, which could serve as the foundation of a new social order to correct the wrongs of the past. One had only to breed into the human race the nobler sentiments and virtues which would ensure an improved society.

Although Gilman's work was most strongly influenced by the ideas of Lester Ward, elements drawn from other social Darwinists are also evident in her writings. She agreed with John Fiske on the duration of infancy as the distinguishing feature of humans, enabling and necessitating the development and passing on of culture and increasing the range of behavior later. Maternal affection and care are prolonged by long infancy and result in a deeper bond among all the family members. This idea later assumed a central significance in Gilman's analysis of sexual relationships.

With T. H. Huxley, Gilman believed that a distinction should be made between "the fittest" and "the best," and between the social process and the cosmic process. "The fittest" should never be reductionistically identified with the physically strongest, while social process—being amenable to direction by the telic application of human intelligence—is therefore in some degree distinct from cosmic processes. Advanced societies free themselves from the struggle for existence and move toward a "struggle for the means of enjoyment" (Hofstadter 1955, 96). Like Henry Drummond, she saw a *struggle for the life of others* as emerging from human evolution, out of the need for nutrition and reproduction. Drummond had asserted that this phenomenon makes the family the basis of human sympathy. His work suggests that this "higher" struggle brings spiritual perfection, an idea with which Gilman was strongly in agreement, although she sought to extricate the concept of family from its definition as an economic unit.

Prince Peter Kropotkin had proposed mutual aid among animals of the same species (including humans) as both a sign and a significant factor in their evolutionary development and recommended the elimination of competition as an indicator of a high degree of evolution. Gilman, too, believed that the same social processes which advanced the human race would eventually make competition obsolete.

While she found elements to agree with in the social Darwinists, it was with the "dissenters," therefore, that she most clearly aligned herself, especially with the movements inspired by Henry George and Edward Bellamy. These opponents of social Darwinism detested and feared the free competitive system, even though they were strongly influenced by individualism. George, in his *Progress and Poverty*, set out to disprove Malthus and to argue that Spencer's ideas were not only not radical, but on the contrary absolutely conservative in their fatalism. Gilman found George's concept of an unearned increment—that is, the value that accrues to the owner whose land increases in value by reason of the growth of society around the land, as distinct from that which occurs from the owner's work—helpful in understanding the oppression of women. The "unearned increment" which women receive in the form of "gifts" from men is theirs by reason of their powerlessness. Women are prevented from producing economic goods, but by the providence of men they are enabled to consume them.

Ward, George, Bellamy, and other "dissenters" approved of the efforts then being made to alter business practices through protective legislation, but were never fully satisfied by them. Bellamy, in *Looking Backward*, sharply attacked the fundamental principles of the competitive system and of private property. Gilman found much to admire in his vision of a society that could embody strongly communal features coexisting with a high degree of individual freedom for each of its members.

The Language of Evolution

The influence of Darwinian science is everywhere evident in the social philosophy of Charlotte Perkins Gilman. Like other evolutionists, she frequently made use of nature and of the various animal species as illustrations and examples for points she wished to make regarding human development. The gypsy moth, for instance, provided her with a model of the "absolutely stationary female" never permitted to leave the home:

> She has aborted wings, and cannot fly. She waits humbly for the winged male, lays her myriad eggs, and dies,—a fine instance of modification to sex. (Gilman, 1898, 65)

Cirripeds, bees, and spiders, on the other hand, whose males are very nearly useless and are easily discarded, offered proof that female, not male, dominance had been the pattern of nature throughout most periods of evolution. If the beehive produced literature, she suggested more than once that,

> the bee's fiction would be rich and broad, full of the complex tasks of comb-building and filling, the care and feeding of the young, the guardian-service of the queen; and far beyond that it would spread to the blue glory of the summer sky, the fresh winds, the endless beauty and sweetness of a thousand thousand flowers. It would treat of the vast fecundity of motherhood, the educative and selective processes of the group-mothers, and the passion of loyalty, of social service, which holds the hive together.
>
> But if the drones wrote fiction, it would have no subject matter save the feasting, of many; and the nuptial flight, of one. (Gilman 1911, 99)

The lesson is not difficult to draw: human relationships, under the influence of male domination, have followed the opposite pattern to that which unimpeded natural evolution would have impelled them. Since feasting and nuptial flights abound in human literature, apparently the drones have written nearly all that we possess of it!

Gilman likened the social life of humans to the biological life of individual organisms. She believed that just as there is a natural process which controls the growth of individual physical features such as arms and legs, so too a natural process would control relationships among individuals in the social body of the human species were women's growth not grotesquely distorted by economic dependency—like tumors growing without limit and without proportion (Gilman 1911, 196–7).

Gilman often noted lawlike behavior when she observed it in humans, thereby supporting her general belief that human evolution takes place in the same way as all other evolution occurs. There are "laws of brain-action" which operate to produce the effects that we experience as our ideas, feelings, and personal prejudices. One of these, the law of adaptation, brings it about that as we fit ourselves to our environment, we cease to notice the things we have become accustomed to—for example, the economic, social, and sexual domination of women by men. The things to which people are accustomed eventually appear natural and right, since they permeate the social environment. A second "law of brain-action" tends to make it easier for humans to "personalize" than to "generalize." This tendency makes it difficult for us to see our individual condition as part of a social pattern—a difficulty which has so far kept us, as a species, from abolishing the practice of male domination.

There are also sociological laws which operate like laws of physics: for example, "the strength of a current of social force is increased by the sacrifice of individuals who are willing to die in the effort to promote it" (Gilman 1898, 80). This makes social behavior among humans measurable and its underlying principles potentially discoverable by science. It is easy to see why Gilman placed great confidence in the emerging science of sociology, of which she identified herself as a practitioner. She could see its potential for discovering the principles of human social behavior.

Sociological analysis would also reveal that the law of inertia, too, "applies to the psychic as well as to the physical world: any idea, if sufficiently forced into the minds of a people, will keep going unless and until met by a sufficient opposing force, or by friction with its gradual effect" (Gilman 1911, 163). Just such an idea is the one which limits women's participation in "society" to "society page" events while extending men's participation to all areas of social life. Either slow friction over a long period of time or a strong opposing idea (such as that of women's economic freedom) would be required in order to halt this long held idea.

Social evolution, while it is affected by human telic intelligence, is every bit as natural as physical, or individual, evolution (Gilman 1898, 95). It is, however, the "fourth power" of a natural process. In the description of increasingly complex natural entities, the first power is the formation of cells; the second power of the process occurs when cells form organs; the third power is the combination of organs to form organisms; and the fourth power is the association of organisms to form society. At the level of the fourth power, organic relations among individuals are no longer based primarily on biological or sexual functions, but are instead based on "purely economic grounds;" that is, upon specialization of labor and exchange of product.

Specialization and organization are marks of evolutionary advances on a social scale (or the "fourth power" of the natural process) just as they are on an individual scale (or the "third power"). Evolutionary development in any "power" tends to increase specialization and therefore to increase interdependence. This is as true among persons in a society as among the parts of a complex physical organism. The need for competitive individual struggle, therefore, is diminished over time in an advancing society, since competition has value in inverse proportion to the degree of evolutionary development. Interdependence supplants the original competition between individuals.

One can compare and contrast individual and societal existence on a number of counts. As has been indicated above, specialization occurs in both: on the individual level a specialization of functions is exhibited by organs; on the social level it takes the form of specialization of labor on the part of organisms. Individuals experience exchange of function among their organs; societies depend upon exchange of product among the individuals that compose them. The sex relation, whether for purposes of reproduction or pleasure, is a function of the individual (that is of the "third power" of natural processes), while economic relations are social functions by their nature (that is, of the "fourth power"); the two types of relation are irreconcilable (Gilman 1898, 106). One of Gilman's most powerful and fruitful insights, unfortunately beyond the scope of this paper to explore, was that the institution of marriage conflates these two essentially separate relations: women are obliged to obtain their best economic advantage by exchanging their sexual services for financial security through marriage.

Whether we are talking about ants or humans, distinctions can be made between characteristics which belong to them as individuals and those which belong to them as members of a society. In like manner, whether they are ants or humans, social animals have two different types of functions among their kind. In the first place are those which are distinctly social—like teaching their young—in which individuals are small elements within a vast integrated social system. In the second place are functions—notably reproduction—which they carry out as individuals in a relationship with another individual. Any animal which exists in a social relation with its kind will exhibit both sorts of functions. Science had disproven the ancient idea that humans are a "special" species separated by a wide gulf from the "lower" species; on the contrary, as Gilman recognized, there are no such gaps.

The Processes of Human Social Evolution

For Gilman all the civilized States created by humans exist in organic relation with one another. This characteristic they share with all forms of animal life. The relations of human societies are industrial relations, comprised of "individual animal processes": nourishment, reproduction, socialization, mutual protection, and the like. Thus cooperative social arrangements are created, whereby the work ("industry" is the word Gilman often prefers) of one contributes to the sustenance of another. An elaborate structure of economic exchanges is built around these industrial relations. Seen in this perspective the differences among social species—birds, bears, or humans—are not differences in kind but are simply differences in the degree of complexity of the industrial relations created.

The most perfect human civilization would be marked by three characteristics: it would exhibit the highest degree of freedom, subtlety, and differentiation of labor. These characteristics, in turn, would give rise to the development of a "social spirit." The social spirit (Gilman 1898, 107), that is a sense of social duty and service, is a very advanced form of evolution. It promotes the growth of society, just as an organ of the body promotes that of the individual: "Social organized human beings tend to produce, as a gland to secrete; it is the essential nature of the relation" (Gilman 1898, 116). Gilman was not referring to biological reproduction, but to industry, the human process by which human energy is transformed into economic production. She observed with caustic humor:

> The most casual survey of social evolution shows it to be a process of growth and change, not along lines of reproductive activity, in which the rabbit is easily our leader, but in racial functions, in the trades and crafts, in art, in science, in government, in education, in religion. These are not functions of sex, nor in any way attributable to it. (Gilman 1923, 169)

While she had rejected many of the conclusions of the social Darwinists, Gilman was in agreement with them that some human behavior is instinctive. She added the refinement, however, that male and female natures explain the source of human instinctive behavior. (Fuller discussion of Gilman's theories regarding male, female, and human natures will be found later in this paper.) Among instincts which humans have developed as a race but which derive from male nature she identified a hunting and chasing instinct, which she acknowledged is present in the young of both sexes but which continues to develop in the male long after the young female has outgrown it and a "protective instinct" which serves to ensure care for wife and children. In women, two instincts remain which derive from their female nature: a maternal instinct (the result of their long "overspecialization to sex" by men) and a protective instinct, which they share with male nature, to guarantee the care and safety of their children (Gilman 1898, 56).

However, Gilman believed that these instincts emerge in women at adolescence. She felt that it was harmful to force young girls to overdevelop their instincts by having to play with dolls. "Beyond the continuous dolls and their continuous dressing," she wrote, "we provide for our little girls tea sets and kitchen sets, doll's houses, little workboxes—the imitation tools of their narrow trade" (Gilman 1911, 111). By such dangerous and limiting practices we thus contribute to the overspecialization of the female to her "lower" activities (those, like housecleaning, cooking, mending and laundering, that society has erroneously identified with her sexual nature) just at a time in her life when she should be exploring the many and varied features of her *human* nature. Moreover, it is clear that these efforts to overspecialize the female in this direction have not proven very advantageous to the race, since the "maternal instinct" has so far not prevented the existence of many sickly, undernourished children or significantly reduced the high rate of infant mortality. Indeed, "the record of untrained instinct as a maternal faculty in the human race is to be read on the rows and rows of little gravestones which crowd our cemeteries" (Gilman 1898, 198).

In the end, instincts are far less valuable to complex, higher organisms and societies than they are to simpler species. What the human species requires is more effective education of each generation, since the human is the species which creates its environment. The environment which we create is a far more significant factor in our social evolution than are the instincts which derive from our sexual nature. While instincts help to ensure survival on the individual level, it is the environment which will bring about progress on the social, or highest, level.

In all her works Gilman made certain evolutionist assumptions, some of which she articulated most fully and explicitly in her introduction to *His Religion and Hers*, one of her last works. As is already evident from the above, she took humanity to be an organic relationship among individuals in a process of social evolution. Natural law, which can be either promoted or hindered by our conscious behavior, she took to be the basis of this evolutionary process. Gilman also believed that ideas can influence human behavior and that human behavior and social conditions determine the morality of actions. A change in moral valuation, for example, comes about with a change in social conditions (Gilman 1923, 119), since ethics *is* human conduct.

The role of conscious human behavior is significant because we are the only species which is able to create its own environment (in our case a physical and a mental environment) and therefore the only species able to create itself by making use of the environment. We have the power to develop an advanced race, but we are held back by ideas such as those that religion often promotes, including and especially the idea that more emphasis should be placed on a supposed afterlife than on the present natural life of which we are part. We are also held back by the nonparticipation of the female in society generally and by the excessive influence of the male upon social evolution.

Even one generation of educated women could make a significant advance in social evolution, Gilman believed, if all would join in the effort:

> In some thirty years these aroused women could send forth a new kind of people to help the world; better born; better trained; able to discriminate and reason, to judge wisely, and strong to carry out their decisions.
>
> All this was opened to us by the perception of evolution, the law of growth. (Gilman 1923, 92)

Before considering Gilman's theory of social development and sexual relations in some detail, a summary word about her evolutionary thought in general is in order. There is much to be rejected in it. A good deal of her "science" is now outmoded, reflecting as it did the thinking of her times. Moreover, she seems to have fallen victim to a rather naive meliorism as regards the processes of biological and social evolution. Like some other social Darwinists of the period she seems to have believed that improvements in physical health and stature, as well as intellectual and moral advancement, could be literally "bred" into the human species in the space of a few generations. Lastly, in the implicit racism which pervades her cultural comparisons and her assessment of what she, along with her contemporaries, calls "savage" periods and peoples, she echoes the prejudices of her culture and class.

On the other hand, there is much in her social philosophy which is valid today. The explanation of human behavior by appeal to scientific principles, of which Gilman was an early and ardent proponent, has been vindicated. It is now the received wisdom of social scientists and philosophers of the generations which succeeded hers. Her insight that previous histories had created a skewed understanding of human nature by excessive reliance upon the description of male experience as normative is one which feminists today continue to affirm. Her confidence in the power of ideology to influence scientific "truths" could not have been more accurately placed, as the spectre of some contemporary sociobiology continues to make clear.

As both the shortcomings and the merits of Gilman's philosophy are evident in her theory of human social and sexual development, a closer look at this central piece of her evolutionary thought is now necessary.

Stages of Social Evolution and The Two Natures

According to the "Gynaecocentric Theory," which Gilman learned from Lester Ward, the earliest stage of human development was a stage of female superiority. The male at that stage represented a scattering ("katabolic") force whose function was fighting to ward off enemies and to obtain food, and the female represented a conserving force whose function was nurturing. It was maternal energy that was transformed into productive industry on behalf of the survival of the race. According to the theory, responsibility for improvement of the human race fell to women, chiefly through their selection of the best possible—in this case, the strongest and healthiest—mate. As Gilman was quick to note, the function of mate selection was in a later stage usurped by men, thus "reversing nature's order." Following upon the first stage came the androcentric stage, a period of temporary (if long) subversion of women's powers. It is the stage in which we still find ourselves as a race. According to Gilman, the second stage has had a most deleterious effect upon human social evolution, retarding the progress of the species as a whole, because in it the earlier and powerful female energy has been suppressed. A future third stage, she believed, will eventually bring about equality between the sexes, which will effectively restore the human race to its rightful pattern of evolutionary progress.

According to the Gynaecocentric Theory the male was little more than a "reproductive agent" during the first stage of social evolution. Necessary for conception, he was not involved in gestation, birth, parturition, or childrearing. Later the female gradually involved him in the rearing of the child, so that he came to have an active role in two out of the five "stages" of reproduction (conception, gestation, birth, parturition, and childrearing)—the first and the last. The family as the basic economic unit of society only came about during the second period of human social evolution, the stage of man's domination of woman. Gilman looked upon the modern family, therefore, as a "relic of the patriarchal age" (Gilman 1898, 145). It is, she argued, wholly out of place on the threshold of the era of sexual equality and is presently in process of extinction (Gilman 1898, 155).

The development of the human race through stages exhibits three laws of evolution at work. The law of self-preservation brings about race characteristics, such as industry. The law of race-preservation, or reproduction, which often takes precedence over self-preservation, brings about some race characteristics and some sex characteristics. The law of progress toward improvement of one's kind also brings about race and sex characteristics, including our intellectual characteristics and the external manufactured world that we produce (Gilman 1923, 61). In humans the third law of evolution has been carried out by the male (Gilman 1910, 88–9), who has been almost exclusively responsible for whatever cultural and social developments the human race has enjoyed, because he has so severely restricted the female's sphere of influence.

Gilman rested her version of the Gynaecological Theory on what I will call here "the theory of the two natures." In it she argued that every person has two natures, a human nature and either a female or a male nature (Gilman 1911, 165). The two natures often prompt to different actions and provide differing motivations. A woman, for example, may rebel in her human nature against a constraint which society imposes on her by reason of her female nature.

The most complete account she provided of her theory of the two natures occurs in *The Man-Made World*. "Let us begin inoffensively," she wrote, "with sheep" (Gilman 1911, 9). Gilman's aim was to identify the sex characteristics of animals, including humans, in order to distinguish them from species characteristics. Citing the principle that "function comes before organ," she hypothesized that rams, being belligerent, grow horns; while ewes, being nurturant toward their young, develop the means to feed them with milk and to guard them with their protective care. It is a sex characteristic, she suggested—here belligerency or nurturance—which brings about the physical feature. The same pattern can be observed throughout the animal kingdom. "Masculine" or "feminine," then, is that which belongs to the male or female, irrespective of species. All other characteristics are those of the animal as members of its species: bovine, feline, canine, equine—or human—characteristics.

Unfortunately for their evolutionary progress, humans have become obsessed with masculinity and femininity and very nearly ignored the common humanity of the two sexes. Furthermore, the "androcentric" culture of the patriarchal stage of social evolution has usurped qualities which are in reality human qualities and identified them falsely as male qualities or characteristics. We live, Gilman concluded, in a "masculized" world.

An individual's human nature affects social life and social development. A person can exhibit a vast array of "human processes": education, art, literature, history, and so on, quite apart form the individual's sex.

Specifically sex-identified processes are far fewer in number. Gilman regarded fatherhood as the sole purpose of the male nature, motherhood and the early education of the child as the sole purposes of the female nature. All the other myriad purposes for which human beings are "suited," she asserted, are human purposes.

According to Gilman's analysis, male and female natures are irreducibly distinct in several particulars. Male nature is characterized by three distinguishing features: Desire (for sexual activity and for other forms of self-interest), Combat (which is the origin of competition of all sorts), and Self-expression (the source of all ostentation, all the way up to that remarkable array which characterizes military trappings). Male nature expresses the centrifugal force of the universe and disposes its possessor toward the use of force. The impulse to scatter, to disseminate, and to destroy is evident in the use of many projectiles by the male at play and in sports.

Destruction has, interestingly, one constructive function in evolutionary progress: it is the male process for eliminating the unfit. Likewise, in evolutionary terms, combat, or the destructive impulse, serves two functions. It is a "subsidiary process" (like destruction) for eliminating the unfit, and it aids in the transmission of physical superiority—although it does nothing to transmit psychic and social qualities. Gilman condemned excessive destruction and combativeness, in light of the ever diminishing need for force as social development advances. Acerbically she once noted that men turned even modern forms of industry into predatory warfare. One need hardly wonder what she might think about "hostile takeovers," "forced buyouts," and other similar phenomena on the corporate battleground today.

Female nature, in evolutionary terms, expresses the centripetal force of the universe. It is the impulse to gather, to put together, and to construct. The human mother is also the first administrator and executive of the race, by reason of her authority over her children. If the male uses the destructive energy of his sexual nature to eliminate the unit, the female uses her constructive and conservative energies to select the fit. The female brings about race-improvement through heredity, of which she is the main agent, by selection of the best possible mate and by healthy childbirth. Gilman believed that the highest process in physical evolution is motherhood. Over all is the highest human process, the process through *human* nature to develop physical, intellectual, and moral "fitness."

While the differences between the sexes serve the evolution of the human race up to a point, they pale in significance to the importance of the shared human qualities that all persons possess. It is in their common human nature that men and women ought to bring about race improvement through culture. The improvement of humans as a society is no more nor less than an extension of their physical improvement through heredity. The noble task of bringing this about belongs by nature to both sexes, although throughout modern history women have been prevented from making contributions to the creation of culture.

Gilman utterly rejected any suggestion that male dominance is natural. As always she looked to evolutionary science to buttress her argument, taking as her evidence the fact that the "instinct of dominance" did not appear during the millions-of-times-longer period of natural evolution that preceded the period of human male dominance. The human species is, after all, a relatively recent evolutionary development, and—as she knew from the Gynaecological Theory—even within human history not all ages had been characterized by patriarchal structures. She found male dominance to have emerged only in the "more modern and arbitrary" relation (Gilman 1923, 180).

The theory of the two natures has implications for moral life as well as for physical and economic development. The virtues most associated with men are courage, justice, truth, loyalty to one another, generosity, patriotism, and honor. Those associated with women are the virtues of a subject class: obedience, patience, industry, kindness, cheerfulness, modesty, gratitude, thrift, and unselfishness. However, all of these, both "male" and "female" qualities, are in reality human virtues, potentially attainable in a just society by persons of both sexes. Gilman assigned to modern women the task of developing "men's" virtues and to men the task of assisting their human sisters, whose moral growth had been stunted, in their efforts.

Humans, like other living organisms, evolve in a progressive development, and it is important to recognize that their progress is vulnerable to being checked by forces in their environment. They themselves can be such forces for one another, as the oppression of women had demonstrated. To Gilman it seemed only good common sense that a healthier environment would generate a healthier population, while an unhealthy one would impede racial progress. Creating an environment in which individuals are excessively specialized to one function—for example, reproduction—is unhealthy. Thus women, who have been "modified" (that is, adapted or specialized) down through many centuries to the service of sex functions as well as to other functions incorrectly attributed to their sexual nature, while being prevented from participation in the many human functions of culture, inhibit the development of the entire species through their own thwarted human development.

An encouraging exception to the modification of women to sex, Gilman noted with pride, is the "increasing army of women wage-earners, who are changing the face of the world by their steady advance toward economic independence" (Gilman 1898, 63). These women were becoming social forces, and Gilman saw in them great cause for optimism that social evolution would benefit from their active participation in economic relations. In her eyes the woman's club movement also had enormous significance, as the focus of the "first timid steps toward social organization" on the part of previously "unsocialized" members of the race (Gilman 1898, 164) and of moral development on the part of the morally stunted.

The ultimate goal of social evolution is a Human World: an economic democracy resting on a free womanhood. Pointing to the unfortunate willingness of earlier societies to take life as a changeless fact, Gilman took encouragement from modern society's recognition of the evolutionary nature of human relationships:

> All this is giving way fast in our new knowledge of the laws of life. We find that Growth is the eternal law, and that even rocks are slowly changing. Human life is seen to be as dynamic as any other form; and the most certain thing about it is that it will change. (Gilman 1911, 258)

Our problem is that there has never been a true democracy, but only an "androcracy." Gilman does not consider a "gynaecocracy" to be ideal either, a point she made in her utopian novel *Herland* when she allowed the main characters to leave the society of women for a society of men and women governed by scientifically justified laws. Both sexes, she felt, need to share the ruling of their world.

The new age with its movements for social change (especially the labor movement and the women's movement) indicated to Charlotte Perkins Gilman that the human race is eager to exercise its natural function of production and not to be content with reproduction. This, she argued, was a measure of its social progress. The criterion she offered for assessing our degree of advancement was: How much has the progress of individuals been made available to all? It was easy for her to see that measured by this criterion only men had advanced, for all of women's energies had been spent in service of their immediate families. Men's energies, expended in the creation of culture, had turned individual progress into progress of the whole. On the other hand, women had produced people, but they were not themselves society, any more than food is a social factor just because society cannot exist without it. A cogent analogy! Directly asserting that "life means progress" (Gilman 1898, 208), she argued that all human relations—whether sexual (individual) or economic (social)—should be measured by their effects upon the progress of social evolution. The health, happiness, and increased organic development of society will testify to our success or failure.

In a single paper it has been possible only to present a small piece of Gilman's prolific work. My goals here have been modest: to place her analysis of sex roles in its context, that of the evolutionary theories of her day and, by implication, to suggest that her philosophy should be the focus of continued scholarly interest. To examine further her economic interpretation of the Gynaecocentric Theory would be a logical next step. The concept of the sexuo-economic relation between men and women—whereby women are obliged to seek their economic good through the exchange of their sexual services—is a separate project in itself, albeit one which would more than repay the effort.

A more extensive survey, which examines the influence of pragmatism on Gilman, is also needed in order to place her accurately within the history of American philosophy. The instrumentalism of John Dewey would be a suggestive place to begin. Her views on the function of human intelligence are strikingly similar to his, and she shared his belief in the originary importance of evolutionary theory to modern philosophy. She "very likely" met Dewey personally during the time in which both were involved in Jane Addams' Hull House reform campaigns (Hill 1980, 247n.), and she was in strong accord with "his demand that learning serve as a reformer's tool" (Hill 1980, 247).

It is clear that there is much in her work to disagree with a century or so later, but it is also clear that Gilman's application of the major intellectual discoveries of her day to the problem of woman's condition made a contribution that was original and powerful. Alice Rossi has noted that "there are any number of ideas in Gilman's writings that were the beginnings of an intellectually innovative view of sex differences and their origins, yet they remained undeveloped and have not yet been seized upon as significant problems in an intellectual history of human conceptions of basic sex differences" (Rossi 1973, 571). Today's socialist feminists do "seize upon" some of these ideas, especially that of the interdependence of economic and sexual oppressions in human history. The debt of Second Wave feminism to Charlotte Perkins Gilman is a profound one, one which we slowly repay as we continue to build upon her radical contributions to the First Wave.

REFERENCES

Berkin, Carol Ruth. 1979. Private woman, public woman: The contradictions of Charlotte Perkins Gilman. In *Women of America: A history.* Carol Ruth Berkin and Mary Beth Norton, eds. Boston: Houghton Mifflin.

Ehrenreich, Barbara and Deirdre English. 1978. *For her own good: 150 years of the experts' advice to women.* Garden City, NY: Doubleday.

Fisch, Max. H. 1951. *Classic American philosophers*. New York: Appleton-Century-Crofts.

Gilman, Charlotte Perkins. 1979. *Herland*. NY: Random House.

———. 1923. *His religion and hers: A study of the faith of our fathers and the work of our mothers*. NY: The Century Company.

———. 1903. *The home: Its work and influence*. NY: The Charlton Company.

———. 1911. *The man-made world or, our androcentric culture*. NY: The Charlton Company.

———. [1898.] 1966. *Women and economics: A study of the economic relation between women and men as a factor in social evolution*. Reprint, Carl N. Degler. NY: Harper & Row.

Hill, Mary A. 1980. *Charlotte Perkins Gilman: The making of a radical feminist, 1860–1986*. Philadelphia: Temple University Press.

Hofstadter, Richard. 1955. *Social Darwinism in American thought*. (Revised ed.) Boston, MA: The Beacon Press.

Lane, Ann J., ed. 1980. *The Charlotte Perkins Gilman reader: "The yellow wall-paper" and other fiction*. NY: Random House.

Mahowald, Mary B. 1987. A majority perspective: Feminine and feminist elements in American philosophy. *Cross Currents* 36(4): 410–417.

Spender, Dale. 1982. *Women of ideas and what men have done to them from Aphra Behn to Adrienne Rich*. Boston: Routledge & Kegan Paul.

Vanderpool, Harold, ed. 1973. *Darwin and Darwinism: Revolutionary insights concerning man, nature, religion and society*. Lexington, MA: D.C. Heath and Company.

EDITH STEIN'S PHILOSOPHY OF
WOMAN AND OF WOMEN'S EDUCATION

MARY CATHARINE BASEHEART, S.C.N.

Edith Stein (1891–1942) was a prominent German-Jewish philosopher, educator, lecturer, and feminist in Germany in the period between the two World Wars, at the time when Hitler was coming to power. After 1932, her public activity was halted, and she died at Auschwitz in August 1942, a victim of the Holocaust.

Her student days at the universities of Breslau, Göttingen, and Freiburg-im-Breisgau were characterized by disciplined study of phenomenology under Edmund Husserl, in company with the famous scholars who engaged him in discussion and dialogue: Max Scheler, Adolf Reinach, Fritz Kaufmann, Roman Ingarden, Hedwig Conrad-Martius, Alexandre Koyré, and Martin Heidegger, to name only a few. For several years, after achieving the Ph.D. *summa cum laude* at Freiburg in 1917, she was Husserl's assistant, transcribing and editing his voluminous works. She remained a phenomenologist, but in her efforts to construct her own body of theory, there is evidence of a strong impulse toward synthesis of phenomenology with what she found acceptable in the philosophy of other times and other schools.

Ten volumes of her works have been published by Nauwelaerts (Louvain) and Herder (Freiburg) posthumously. They could not be published in her lifetime because of the ban on works by non-Aryan writers; however, before the ban, a number of Stein's lengthy articles had appeared in Husserl's *Jahrbuch für Philosophie and phänomenlogische Forschung.* Her works deal with a wide range of philosophical subjects, but running through all her work is the thread of the investigation of the nature and structure of the human person, from her first full-length book on *Einfühlung (Empathy)* to the large work of her maturity, *Endliches und Ewiges Sein (Finite and Eternal Being)*. The circumstances that aroused

Hypatia vol. 4, no. 1 (Spring 1989) © by Mary Catharine Baseheart her feminist interests in theory and practice will be apparent in the body of the paper that follows. For a more complete account in English of her life, see Waltraud Herbstrith, *Edith Stein, A Biography* (Harper & Row, 1985).

When you read the views of Edith Stein on woman and woman's education which she expressed from the lecture platforms of European cities more than fifty years ago, you get the impression that here is a woman who could speak calmly and brilliantly on the subject today. Stein mediates the polarities of the extreme-feminism and the eternal-feminism positions in a way that is highly flexible in theory and practice, since it encompasses woman in all her dimensions: her humanity, her femininity and her individuality. Her concept of woman is rich and open, not a stereotype. By virtue of her openness to change and her active desire to stir up a revolution in education, she is a woman to turn to for further questions and insights in the present period of reform.

The question of why Edith Stein, whose work had been predominantly in speculative philosophy, spoke and wrote about the philosophy of woman and of education can be answered only in the light of conditions in German society at the time and of her own personal experiences in the role of philosopher and educator. In one of her first lectures on the subject,[1] it is evident that she was responding to the current desperate situation of German education, which she described as a shambles, calling for complete demolition and reconstruction from the ground up. She saw the problems plaguing women's education as part and parcel of the general crisis.

Her analysis found one root of the crisis in the fact that the educational system was essentially a child of the Enlightenment, with its ideal of encyclopedic knowledge and its conception of mind as a *tabula rasa* on which should be imprinted as much factual and intellectual material as possible (Stein 1959, 73–4).

The second basic difficulty, in her opinion, was the male-oriented and male-dominated educational system. Stein definitely believed that education is too important to be left to men only, that education was suffering from the lack of women's input of ideas, and that it needed their contributions in the areas of teaching, research, and administration.

Changes in education had not kept pace with the reforms effected in political and economic life after World War I; for example, the 1919 Constitution of the Reich had granted equality and full citizenship rights to women and opened the way for them to assume positions in government and professional life, but adequate programs of preparation were lacking at all educational levels.

Early in her career, Edith Stein does not appear to have been concerned with these problems. The description of her own schooling which she gives in her autobiography is very positive. Her rigorous and demanding education was quite in accord with her own interests and desires. She held her own with her fellow-students of both sexes and was held in respect by them and by her teachers, both in the lower schools and in the universities. She was usually in the company of spirited, intellectual, interesting companions in her social life as well as in the schools. It has already been noted above that she was awarded the Ph.D. degree at the University of Freiburg *summa cum laude* and became Husserl's assistant soon after, transcribing and editing his writings and giving new students preliminary instruction for his classes. Her letters to her friend Roman Ingarden in 1917 and 1918 reveal the frustrations of this work which led to her resignation in 1918: Husserl would not reread her work and tell her whether she had made a correct rendering of his texts, nor did she have any time left for her own original work. Husserl proved not to be interested in collaborating with her as a colleague—nor with any other scholars, for that matter.[2] The next step would naturally have been for her to "habilitate," that is, to become a full-scale faculty member at the university, but this was refused because the appointment of a woman would have been a major break with tradition.[3]

In the fall of 1919, when she again attempted to habilitate, this time at the University of Göttingen, the attempt met with failure for the same reason. At this point Edith wrote an appeal to the Prussian Ministry for Science, Art, and Education, and on February 21, 1921, Minister Becker issued a milestone ruling in response to her appeal, declaring for the first time that "membership in the female sex may not be seen as an obstacle to habilitation" in German universities. Her action cleared the way for women seeking a professorial career in fields other than philosophy; but it was another thirty years before the first German woman actually habilitated and took up teaching duties in philosophy at a German university. Stein herself made a final attempt to habilitate at the universities of Freiburg and Breslau in 1931; but, in spite of her eminent qualifications, she did not succeed. This time not only sexism but also anti-Semitism blocked the way.

In spring 1932, she accepted the offer to join the faculty of the German Institute of Scientific Pedagogy in Münster, where her lectures, particularly those on the philosophy of the person, attracted students from the university as well as her own students in education at the institute.

If Stein had succeeded in her habilitation attempts and had continued her career in the ranks of the philosophy faculty at Freiburg, Göttingen or Breslau, it seems doubtful that she would have probed the practical, pragmatic issues pertaining to education to the extent that appears in *Die Frau*. It is natural to suppose, however, that, given her persistent pursuance of the theme of the person in her philosophizing and her participation in the feminist movement in Germany, she might have undertaken a phenomenological inquiry into the nature and destiny of woman.

Her nine years of teaching girls at St. Magdalena's in Speyer, as well as her brief stint in Münster, and her involvement in associations intent on educational reform of both public and private schools, made it inevitable that she would follow her characteristic bent of seeking solutions by analyses of underlying philosophical foundations. The lecture tours set up for her in Germany, Switzerland, and Austria between 1928 and 1932 by Eric Przywara were an additional incentive. These lectures, assembled from subsequent publication in periodicals and from manuscripts, and edited by Lucy Gelber and Romaeus Leuven, form *Band V* of *Edith Steins Werke,* entitled *Die Frau.* This volume, published in 1959, is the principal source of knowledge of her philosophy of woman and of education.[4]

In approaching the subject of woman's nature and role, Stein does not ignore the importance of the empirical sciences of anatomy and physiology, psychology, and sociology. She outlines a total configurational approach that makes use of their methods and content, especially that of a psychology that passes beyond itself to anthropological, sociological, and cosmological considerations, thus treating woman as she exists in the life world.[5] Her analysis, however, culminates in the philosophical method, whose proper noetic function is to explore what is necessary and possible to beings (in this case, to the being of woman), according to their nature, and in the theological, which brings divine Revelation to bear on the question (Stein 1959, 125–130). Only the philosophical will be treated in this paper.

The philosophical method which she employs is, she maintains, distinct from that of the positive sciences and gives their necessary founding. In phenomenological terminology it is the *Wesensanschauung,* "intuition," which effects the cognitive grasp of concrete objects in their universal structure. She compares this *intuition* with the noetic function termed *abstraction* in traditional philosophy (Stein 1959, 126).

Stein insists on reliable method in probing the essence of woman, although she grants some value to pre-scientific experience. All of us know women by experience and think we know what a woman is, she says. But if we draw a general image from these experiences, we cannot be sure whether or not this is a faulty generalization, whether what has actually been observed in certain cases does not fail to be true for others. Individual experience has to be critically examined. Has even individual woman been properly understood? Experiences are subject to error and deception, and here the danger is, perhaps, greater than elsewhere. Or, perhaps, we are presented with an ideal image which serves as a standard by which to ascertain whether others are *genuine* women. She notes the necessity of asking the source of the ideal image and what value it has to increase our knowledge (Stein 1959, 126–127). Stein is cognizant of the difficulties of demonstrating the cognitive universality sought, of organizing the data, and of making it truly scientific.[6] In the process of effecting the *Wesensanchauung* of woman, of "bringing the essence to givenness," Stein proceeds to consider woman in the context of ontology, that is, of the science of the basic forms of being *(Sein)* and of beings *(Seienden)*. In the gradation of finite being, all lower grades (inorganic, plant, animal) are, in a sense, contained in the human structure of rational being, which occupies a unique, superior position. The structure of human being which she presents here repeats that enlarged upon in her earlier works, beginning with her dissertation on *Empathy*: material body, living body, soul, spirit, all of which belong to the human species as such. There is another simple differentiation, she adds, that cuts through the differentiation of humanity into a boundless multiplicity of individuals of unrepeatable singularity: this is the sexual differentiation *(geschlechtliche Differenzierung)*. Since her analyses of human being in general have included woman at every step, and since philosophy, as such, does not analyze the individual as individual, her analysis in *Die Frau* is directed toward woman as woman, although it encompasses her totality: her humanity, her womanhood, and her individuality (Stein 1959, 131–132).

The central question in the investigation is whether woman and man are distinct species, each having an ontologically different essence or nature.[7] Do the differences observed between man and woman involve the whole structure of the person or only the body and those psychic functions necessarily related to physical organs (Stein 1959, 133)? Scientific investigations in Germany at this time, she says, presume the difference between the sexes to be a universal fact. They try to establish the uniqueness of each through distinguishing characteristics which appear on an average or through quantitative measures of their frequency of occurrence; but she does not think they succeed in presenting a complete image of the uniqueness, and they have not yet distinguished whether the uniqueness is to be considered as variable *type* or stable *species* (Stein 1959, 122–123).[8]

In the practical order of the women's movement, there are significant implications in the question of whether woman is presented as a distinct species from man within the human species. If she is, then there are special characteristics of woman which can contribute to every area of human life and endeavor and which can complement male characteristics and service in home, school, state, and church. Edith Stein sincerely believes that this is the case.

In order to understand the question properly, Stein holds that one must understand the relationship among gender, species, type, and individual. By species she understands something fixed, which does not change.

Within the hylomorphic theory she holds that the *inner form* determines the structure of the being, its nature, which we seek to grasp in its essential features, actual and potential. The fact that the potential can become actual indicates that when Stein defines species as that which does not change, she is not using the term *change* in an absolute sense. She distinguishes *type* by stating that *type* is not unchangeable in the same sense that *species* is. In the course of development, a person may exhibit change of type and individual characteristics, but these changes take place within the limits set by the inner form or species (Stein 1959, 109, 119–121).

The basic question is, then, whether or not the different types share a uniform and unchangeable core which can be regarded as characterizing woman as a species. If there are no such species as woman and man, but only types, then the transformation of one type to another ought to be able to take place in varying conditions. If each is a species, it cannot be changed by environmental, cultural, or professional factors (Stein 1959, 109, 119–121).⁹ The positive sciences, in her opinion, can signify only that a thing is conditioned in one way or another under this or that circumstance that it may act, or possibly must act in one way or another. It remains for philosophy to reach the inner form, the ontological structure.

After a lengthy, methodical consideration of the subject, Stein arrives at the image *(Bild)* of woman. She calls it a sketching *(Skizzerung)* and uses broad strokes to present an outline, which, she says, is open to enrichment and modification. It represents progress toward giving the essence of woman its logical place in philosophical anthropology, as she expresses it. A translation of her own words may best convey her thinking about the nature of woman:

> . . . the species *human being* is actualized as a double species of *man* and *woman*; the essence of human being, in which no essential feature can be lacking in either one, is stamped in a binate way, and the entire essence-structure displays the specific stamp. It is not only the material body *(Körper)* that is structured differently: not only are there different physiological functions, but the entire living-body *(Leib)* life is something else; the relationship of soul and living-body is different, and within what pertains to the soul, the relation of spirit to sense faculty as well as the relation of spiritual powers to one another is different. The female species answers to unity and wholeness of the body-soul personality as a holistic, harmonious unfolding of the powers; the male species, to the perfecting of individual powers to the highest degree. (Stein 1959, 138)

Thus Stein believes that sexual differentiation extends beyond the somatic and psycho-somatic functions connected with the physical to the total structure and that woman's *form* must be specifically different from man's. She recognizes also that the whole problem of the body-mind relationship as it enters into sex difference needs further research, with the aid of whatever light genetics can give (Stein 1959, 133–134).[10]

Although she discovers in the nature of woman a central, unchangeable core (*Kern*), she states that there are many feminine types according to natural endowments. She describes, for example, the types given by the psychologist Else Croner: the *maternal,* the *erotic* (strongly sexual), the *romantic,* the *sedate* (sensible), and the *intellectual* types (Stein 1959, 136–137).[11] Anyone who has taught girls, she adds, recognizes students of one or other of these types, as well as of mixed types or of still other types. The types, as well as the individuals, she points out, are definitely influenced by the times and by the particular environmental circumstances of the women's lives.

In her generalizations regarding the nature of woman, she does not hesitate to make reservations, e.g., when she writes that femininity is expressed differently in different individuals. They realize the species more or less perfectly and show the various characteristics more or less pronouncedly. Man and woman have the same basic human characteristics, some of which predominate not only in one or other sex but also in individuals; therefore, some women may closely approximate the masculine nature and some men, the feminine nature (Stein 1959, 139).

In explaining further the sameness and difference of men and women, Stein begins with woman's role as paralleling man's in showing forth the image of God. Here, although it may seem that she is in the realm of religion rather than that of philosophy, her ideas may be interpreted within a philosophic theism. To be God's image both man and woman must develop their powers of *knowing,* of *enjoying,* and of *creative making* in order to image God's wisdom, goodness, and power. Woman mirrors the divine perfections in characteristic ways. Her primary role of being companion and mother (this, fulfilled not just in a physical sense) and her ways of knowing, enjoying, and creating are particularly adapted to this role as well as to her role in national and professional life. Her strength, she thinks, is in the intuitive grasp of the living, inner world of others, of entering into their aims and ways of work. Feeling *(Gemüt)* is her special gift. The principle of the womanly soul is serving love. Her special function is to nourish, shelter, and cherish (Stein 1959, 3–4, 32–34, 138–139, 171).

Stein's statement that woman's ways of knowing are characterized by the intuitive grasp of the living, the concrete, the personal does not imply a negation of her capacity for grasping the abstract. It does signify that characteristically women are not content to remain on the level of the abstract. They want the ideological, the conceptual, to be related to the world of persons and things. They want psychology, for example, to have something to do with human beings, sociology to have something to do with the concrete human situation, and physics to be related to the real world of experience.[12]

In her emphasis on the active character of woman, Stein opposes the view that predicates passivity as a characteristic disposition, either innate or acquired, in woman. Activity is the key concept in her schema for all education. If a woman is to become what she is by nature and by her calling, she should not forget herself but bring her gifts and powers to perfection. Passivity would be incompatible with the roles which Stein describes for women in marriage and motherhood, in religious life, in the professions, and in political and cultural life. "There is no profession that cannot be practiced by a woman," according to Stein. Professions which she lists as depending on special feminine gifts (though, of course, not exclusively so) include those of doctor and nurse, social worker, and scholar, especially in the sciences pertaining to the human person; but some women have the capacity for service in professions that have been regarded as typically masculine, such as those in business and industry, government, administration, law, science, and mathematics. To these, women may bring a special dimension that will benefit both men and women (Stein 1959, 7–9).

Stein's philosophy of education flows from her conviction that education should lead women to affirm and develop not only the powers which they possess in common with men but also their proper feminine nature and their individuality. Education should prepare them to fulfill their destiny to be companions and mothers, a destiny which can be fulfilled on the spiritual level in single life as well as in married life. Serving love has been given above as her idea of a characteristic of the womanly soul; however, this serving love, she says, should not find expression in a false mystique of sacrifice or in a mystique of sex. Their education should be both liberal and professional to prepare them for the work-world, whether they actually enter it or not (Stein 1959, 73–88).

Edith Stein's concept of education is simply expressed: It is the formation of human personality. It is not an external possession of knowledge but the process by which human personality takes form under various influences within and without the person. The "material" which is to be formed is the psycho-physical-spiritual predispositions which each person has at birth, as well as the raw materials which are constantly taken from the environment and built into the living being. The body draws on the material world; the soul, on the world of persons and values.

The fundamental formation happens from within. In each human being there is a unique inner form which all education from outside must respect and aid in its movement toward the determined form, the mature, fully developed personality (Stein 1959, 73–88). Although in every individual there can be distinguished the tripartite complexus of being human, being woman or man, and being this individual person, only in the abstract are these considered separately: the single form is the principle of all the person's powers and characteristics, human, feminine or masculine, and individual.

Much of what she says and writes about education is in the context of the education of women and follows from her theory of woman's nature and role. Education, she holds, should prepare women in such a way that they will be able to make free and wise choices of life roles. Because of the wide range of individual differences, women should not have to conform to a pattern. Human and female personality in some is adapted to the one choice of being wife and mother; in others, to the choice of a single life and a career; others may choose marriage *and* work outside the home. The double role had become increasingly common in Germany in Stein's day, as it has in contemporary America. She was aware of the tensions and problems involved, and the solutions she offers have much in common with those of today. She reminds husbands of their obligation not to let their wives' intellectual and spiritual lives atrophy through lack of time and opportunity for development. "Continuing education" and "life-long learning" were not phrases in her vocabulary, but the ideas are unquestionably in her educational philosophy.

It is obvious that the feminism which emerges in Edith Stein's words and actions is of a positive, non-competitive, non-combative kind, calling women to the fullness of the vocation which they share with men, but also taking cognizance of the special gifts which each sex possesses. If women are to fulfill their highest function of developing the humanity of others, she says, they must become fully-developed human beings themselves. Education is the key to women's fulfillment, just as it is for men. Each woman should be educated to her full potential, and women's specific gifts and bents should find expression in national and cultural life as well as in the home. Thus education should prepare women not only for home-making but also for professional proficiency and for political and social responsibility. In summary, it may be observed that Stein's penchant for unity and synthesis is evident in her endorsement of activity *and* receptivity in women of abstractness *and* concreteness in feminine ways of knowing; of stimulation and development of head *and* heart in the formation of personality, which is the function of education.

For both men and women, "the intellect is the key to the kingdom of the spirit. . . . The intellect must be pressed into activity. It cannot become bright and sharp enough," but purely intellectual knowing does not result in real formation of the person unless the knowledge is interiorized. The training of the intellect should not be extended at the expense of the schooling of the heart. The mean should be the target (Stein 1959, 80–83).

The educator must remember that there is not merely a speculative intellect but a practical intellect as well. It is important to train the latter proportionately through concrete tasks. Education comprises also a schooling of the will, acts of which are continually required. The abstract activity of the intellect and the concrete application should go hand in hand (Stein 1959, 171–172).

The basic curriculum in schools at all levels should include general education and should be adapted to the nature and vocational/professional goals of the student. The college curriculum, she says; should include a strong strain of liberal-arts subjects "crowned by the integrating disciplines of philosophy and theology." The liberal-arts component, she understands as including the humanities, the natural sciences and mathematics, and the social sciences; and she again emphasized that for the total education of the person, the disciplines should not be taught in a purely abstract way, but should be related to the concrete and the personal as far as possible (Stein 1959, 171–172).

In considering the "schooling of the will," referred to above, one may ask how values enter into Stein's educational schemata. In this regard, her basic principles are revealed in her philosophy of person, which comprises extensive analyses of affective acts and their relation to cognition and to the valuing activity of the person. On the ground of cognition there can and may occur the cognizing of value or non-value without affective positing of accompanying feeling toward or away from the object; but for valuing to be completely filled, the value-intuition and response-reaction must be filled. When the lively interest of the ego is lacking, there is no felt value. Since the ego-data are always present in valuing and since each individual is unique, if education is to function in bringing the student to effective valuing activity and affective response, the teacher must take into account the uniqueness of each student as well as the universal meaning-core detachable from the individual mental coloring. This involves the total structure of the person and contact with the value world in which he/she lives, the attitudes, drives, and motives which undergird the values and guide the actions. In assisting the student to change faulty values and to rise to higher values, Stein appears to hold the position that the approach is indirect, by way of appeal to reason in order to lead the student to clarify his/her values and apply the law of reason to arrive at feeling-forming, choice, and decision.

Feeling-forming is very important, since feeling (Gemüt) holds a central position in changing personal attitudes and actions, but it cannot carry out its task without the cooperation of intellect and will. Feeling, or emotion, needs the light of the intellect and the discipline of the will. If these are lacking, emotional life becomes a compulsion without direction. The teacher's very being and actions give tremendous impetus in the process of students' forming feelings, valuing, and choosing (Stein 1959, 55).

In all education, Stein states realistically, natural predispositions and the subject's freedom set limits to what can be accomplished by external educational efforts, which only provide subject matter and make it appealing. These can show the way but cannot force acceptance and imitation (Stein 1959, 57).

Stein's ultimate grounding of value education, as of her total theory of education, is to be found in religious education. Her ideas on religious education are beyond the scope of this paper on her philosophy. The fact that she considers the subject according to "nature and grace" makes it possible to separate the two and to treat only nature. It should be said, though, that her ideas yield their full significance when reviewed in the context of her unified Christian Weltanschauung, which was enriched by her Jewish heritage.

Although this chapter is focused on Stein's philosophy, it should be noted that the conceptual structure is often concertized and illuminated by literary allusions. An example in point is her comparative analysis of three women in literature: Ingunn Steinfinnsdatter from Sigrid Undset's *The Master of Hestviken*; Ibsen's Nora from *A Doll's House*; and Goethe's *Iphigenia* (Stein 1959, 46–52).[13] The differences among them are great, but in Stein's analyses they are shown to share one common characteristic; the desire to give love and receive love, and, in this respect, a longing to be lifted out of the narrowness of their actual, factual existence to higher being and acting (Stein 1959, 51–52). In another context, she gives a description of the ideal woman-soul that is charged with poetic and emotional intensity (Stein 1959, 77–80). These passages highlight woman's special nature and role.

Stein's phenomenology of woman is a good example of the way in which she takes Husserlian methodology of seeking knowledge of essence of an entity under investigation and adapts it to the complexities of the entity as it exists and operates in the world of experience. Thus she attempts to implement Husserl's idea of "concrete essence" and avoids the tendency toward over-abstraction that can plague a philosophy of essence. Stein looks at woman's humanity, femininity, and individuality from all sides as it is encountered in real life experiences and in the vicarious experiences of literature. Her view invites further exploration of its implications in present searchings into strengths and potentialities, sameness and difference of woman as woman and of each individual woman.

NOTES

1. References in this paper are made to the 1959 German edition. Translations and paraphrases are the author's own.

2. Her remarks have a touch of good-natured humor; e.g., in the letter of January 18, 1917, she wrote: "I must stay with him [Husserl] until I marry; then I must take only a husband who will likewise be his assistant, and the children too . . . ." And in a letter to Fritz Kaufmann, dated January 12 of the same year, she had written that she could not get him to look at the whole finished treatise which she made of the old material that he had lost, and so she had resolved to bring it to accessible form with him or without him. Then it could not be lost. It should be noted that she and Husserl remained devoted friends to the end of his life.

3. The following are the sources of data concerning Stein's resignation and efforts for habilitation:

Stein, Edith. 1976. *Selbstibildnis in Briefen, Edith Steins Werke*. 8: 15–48. Louvain: Nauwelaerts and Freiburg: Herder.

Basehart, Mary Catharine, Linda Lopez McAlister, with Waltrout Stein. 1995. Edith Stein. In *A history of women philosophers* Vol. 4, ed. Mary Ellen Waithe. Dordrecht, Kluwer.

Herbstrith, Waltraud. 1985. *Edith Stein, a biography*. 28, 55–57. New York and London: Harper and Row.

4. The other eight lectures or essays in *Die Frau*, all on subjects pertaining to woman and to education, were delivered or composed between 1928 and 1932, and were presented before various associations of academic women in cities such as Salzburg, Munster, Ludwigshafen, Zurich, Augsburg, etc.

5. For discussion of her method, see *Die Frau*, 122–137.

6. In Note 17, p. 127 of *Die Frau*, Stein selects one of many German works on the nature of woman to discuss: *The rhythm of being: A study on the foundation of a metaphysics of the sexes*, by Thoma Angelica Walter (Freiburg, 1932). She terms it a scientific, pioneering achievement which treats the question of the sexes in an ontological context. Her critical analysis of this work indicates both its strengths and weaknesses. In Note 21, p. 132, after an extensive analysis of Walter's schema of being, Stein questions whether male and female are really to be understood only as "rhythms of being" or whether a distinction of substantial form is the ground for different rhythms of being.

7. In her use of the terms *nature* and *essence,* Stein seems to employ them interchangeably at times, but at others to allow for the emphasis on function in the word *nature*.

8. In the course of her analyses, she refers to investigations of Mausbach, O. Lipman, Rudolf Allers, and others.

9. See also pp. 133–134, in which Stein raises questions pertaining to genetic problems which seem to relate to evolution, which she would like to investigate at another time. She raises, also, the question (which reminds one of Jungian theory) whether the nature of each individual might contain both masculine and feminine elements, with one of these predominating in each person.

10. See also M. C. Baseheart. 1966. On educating women: The relevance of Stein, in *Continuum*, (vol. 4) Illinois.

11. The work of Croner which Stein cites is *Die Psyche der weilbichen Jugend* (Langensalza, 1930).

12. Cf. Riesman (1965) would like to see more women in science not only for the sake of talented women but also for the sake of science. To his mind, prevalent "masculine" models of academic performance are inclined to favor abstraction to the point that the academic disciplines are not related to the world outside, nor to the concrete, but to each other and to their own internal development. Granted that there have been changes since Riesman expressed these ideas, they may still have some validity.

13. Stein refers also to women characters in Schiller's *Glocke*, Chamisso's *Frauenliebe und -leben*, and others which Zola, Strindberg, and Wedekind delineate.

REFERENCES

Boedeker, Elizabeth and Maria Meyer-Plath. 1987. *50 Jahre Habilitation von Frauen in Deutschland*. Boston: Martinus Nijhoff.

Riesman, David. 1965. Some Dilemmas of women's education, in *the Educational Record* 46:423–427.

Stein, Edith. 1959. *Die Frau, Edith Stein's Werke*. L. Gelber and R. Leuven, eds. Louvain: Nauwelaerts and Freiburg: Herder.

———. 1986. *Life in a Jewish family, 1981–1916*. J. Koeppel, trans. Washington, D.C.: ICS Publications.

———. 1987. *Essays on woman*. F.M. Oben, trans. Washington, D.C.: ICS Publications.

HANNAH ARENDT, FEMINISM, AND THE POLITICS OF ALTERITY
"WHAT WILL WE LOSE IF WE WIN?"

JOANNE CUTTING-GRAY

To talk about Hannah Arendt's "feminism" means admitting at the outset that she was strongly against "isms" of any kind, said little about women's issues, and sparked controversy when she did. As political philosopher, theorist, and historian, she tackled thorny issues with alacrity; as a woman she addressed gender relations indirectly. Even when her analyses reflect a personal sense of Jewish "pariahhood," and by extension a sense of female difference, she resolutely kept her private opinions hidden from the public gaze. She felt that so-called publicity, like the notoriety about her youthful love affair with Heidegger, "trivialized" politics by directing attention away from action or "world-historical" deeds.[1]

To consider Arendt's work exclusively in the context of her seeming indifference to feminism is to risk underestimating her qualities as a feminist thinker. Her largely unwritten understanding of the "female condition," gleaned from personal stories about her, was revolutionary for its time in that she implicitly understood (female) alterity as belonging to the public person, not an autonomous, private self.[2] Elisabeth Young-Bruehl, her biographer, observes that Arendt was against divorcing women's issues from broader political concerns: "Incipient in her criticism of the women's movement is the distinction she later drew between social questions and political questions—the latter, she held, should be the focus of action"(Young-Bruehl 1982, 97).[3]

However, to offer Arendt's privately held opinions about women's issues (opinions in that Arendt never presented them systematically, never offered then for public debate) as the basis of a formal feminist theory, would betray her own wish to keep her closely held thoughts in inti-

Hypatia vol. 8, no. 1 (Winter 1993) © by Joanne Cutting-Gray

mate[4]—unless a connection can be found between her personal experience and public discourse. That link is provided by her early and little-known biography on the life of Rahel Varnhagen, an eighteenth-century German-Jew.[5] Biography may be a misnomer; the heart of the work is neither history nor character but, most importantly for feminist politics, a critique of the individualistic self. As a critique, it serves the role of philosophy in carefully analyzing the human political condition, a condition not limited to a Jewish or female incarnation of it. Further, it provides us with a model or conceptual structure that aids our understanding of any political group. Because this unusual work grapples with the theoretical constitution of a female subject, it entails—more than any of Arendt's other works—a "politics of alterity" with striking applications for feminist practice.

Writing the biography enabled the youthful Arendt to distinguish the unique, distinct person from the egocentric individual, isolated, inherently private, and social. In fact, Jewish history and Varnhagen's story taught Arendt that any group linked together by personal sympathy alone does not answer to the need for a political community. It helped her to conceptualize how a community of sympathetic selves could lose its platform for action.[6] To be effective politically the distinction between *public* and *private* individual must be maintained. In other words, by making "alterity" a psychological problem rather than a unique political resource, a sympathetic sisterhood erases the historically specific differences of race, ethnicity, and gender.

The following discussion of subjectivity in the Varnhagen biography will enable us to explore the relations among difference, identity, and political community. From it we can develop the political concepts that Arendt generated and offer a constructive criticism of a sisterhood based in naturalized gender difference, shared sympathy or shared suffering. The power of the biography lies in an analogy between Jewish and female alterity, an analogy that in spite of its obvious dangers can stretch our understanding of women and politics.

I

Three anecdotes provide the context for our discussion of the Varnhagen biography by relating Jewish alterity, identity, and history to feminist politics. They serve to illustrate the essentially political concerns that Arendt developed from her study of Rahel Varnhagen—concerns pertinent not only to feminism but to any political group: the first, political judgment—to understand carefully and respectfully things quite other from ourselves; the second, the political subject—to shape our distinctness and individuality in speech and action with others rather than in eccentric displays of singular behavior; third, political practice—to test continually the adequacy of our political concepts in particular actions.

The first anecdote has to do with a note Arendt once passed to her friend Hiram Haydn during a discussion of women's liberation at the *American Scholar*'s editorial board meeting in 1972. The note quipped, "the real question to ask is, what will we lose if we win?"(Young-Bruehl 1982, 513). The view is quintessentially Arendt in that it questions the commonsense assumptions that skip over phenomena hidden by the familiar. Later, in telling Haydn that her "wisecrack" was "well-considered," she identifies what for her lies at the heart of critical thinking, namely, seeing the "doubleness of all things," openness to multiple and opposing perspectives. Elsewhere she reflects that "the experiences behind even the most worn-out concepts remain valid and must be recaptured and re-actualized if one wishes to escape certain generalizations that have proven pernicious" (Young-Bruehl 1982, 325). In this instance, her "real question" about winning and losing applies to the familiar assumption that revolution means only liberation *from* the "worn-out concepts" about gender rather than freedom *to* transform them politically.

The second anecdote illustrates Arendt's resistance to being identified as a woman exceptional to her gender. As the first woman appointed to the rank of full professor at Princeton, she evoked more than usual attention from the media. When in 1959 the university emphasized her gender in press releases, she threatened to turn down the position. To an interviewer who raised the question of woman-professor-as-exception she responded: "I am not disturbed at all about being a woman professor because I am quite used to being a woman" (Young-Bruehl 1982, 272–73). The answer effectively separates gender from accomplishment, cautions those who make a category mistake in confusing the two issues, and demonstrates her insistence that distinguishing herself in deeds of excellence does not mean being *inherently* and *essentially* different from others.

The third anecdote links the question of identity and alterity to local political conditions. In the same year Arendt went to Hamburg to accept the Lessing Prize—surely a moral victory for a German philosopher who was also a woman and a Jew. In the Lessing address, Arendt recalled with characteristic frankness the recent German past, her flight from Nazism at the age of twenty-seven, and her attitude about living "in dark times" where "honors" were no part of her birthright, and where it would not be surprising if "we were no longer capable of the openness and trustfulness that are needed simply to accept gratefully what the world offers in good faith" (1968, 17). Thus she made explicit the facticity of the identity given to her by history, telling her audience that for many years she considered the "only adequate reply to the question, Who are you? to be: A Jew" (1968,

17). She added by way of definition that a Jew was not a special human being marked for distinction by history, but a "political fact . . . which . . . outweighed all other questions of personal identity or rather had decided them in favor of anonymity, of namelessness" (1968, 18). She put forward a simple principle that underlay her attitude: "one can resist only in terms of the identity that is under attack."

These anecdotes resonate with Arendt's characteristic attention to existential and political conditions, to the concrete and particular, and suggest that the chief themes of her philosophy—human plurality, the politics of judgment, public freedom—grew out of her active engagement with the "political fact" of the question of identity, a question chosen for her by history. They also help explain why Jewishness had "outweighed all other questions of personal identity" and had posed for her a more immediate problem than what she called "the woman question."[7] It is not surprising that she found in the story of kindred spirit Rahel Varnhagen not only the solace but also the insight that enabled her to bear the burden of her own identity. The political reality of her Jewishness first confronted her within a few years of her love affair with Heidegger (1925). Stirred by their break-up and Heidegger's eventual foray into Nazism, she found consolation in the Varnhagen story of an overly introspective woman like herself a the time, one who overcame self-absorption in order to discover her "un-selfed" political identity.[8] The metaphor of Varnhagen as self-absorbed subject may be thought of a playing a hypothetical explanatory role similar to that of the chief character in a Sartrean novel: it serves to illustrate concretely some philosophical concepts. Because the biography anticipates the issues that Arendt would analyze in her later works, we can trace a "politics of alterity" in it retrospectively.

II

Rahel Levin Varnhagen (1771–1833) presided in Berlin over the most famous German intellectual salon of the late eighteenth century (1790–1806). The society comprising the salon was private and romantically individualistic, "established on the fringe of society" yet not sharing "any of its conventions or prejudices" (1974, 59). The salon formed a kind of "neutral zone" outside the realm of political action and consisted of outsiders (1974, 58). In this private society enchanted with eccentricity, Varnhagen, "not rich, not cultivated, and not beautiful" (1974, 6), symbolized otherness. Her effort was "to expose herself to life so that it could strike her 'like a storm without an umbrella'" (1974, xvi). The sheer spectacle of such an exotic and intense character drew aristocrats, intellectuals, and artists to what was only a garret. There the capacity for life and a

passionate intelligence found an outlet of expression in a cult of personality. To those attracted by Varnhagen's magnetism it came as no surprise that she single-handedly initiated the "Goethe cult" of self-absorbed,
romantic individuals and thereby significantly influenced German
Romanticism.

Varnhagen's acceptance into private society was not, as she believed,
merely a caprice of fate but, as Arendt detects, a direct result of Jewish assimilation under Enlightenment humanism. In the Prussia before that
time, only Jews who had wealth were tolerated; economic influence enabled them to enjoy business relationships with the nobility and class
identity with the bourgeoisie, though without social acceptance (1974,
xvii, 6). With the rise of Romanticism, however, intellectuals wanted
"proofs" of their own humanity and saw in the Jew a more exotic, more
alien, occasion for humanism. Jews who were accepted were to be exceptions, like Jews yet not like them, for the "exceptional" had to stand out
from *The Jew* conceived negatively as a race. With growing acceptance
Jews began to understand their identity no longer in terms of creed, faith,
and culture but as a difference in their inner nature (the psychological,
"world alienated" self) (1973, xii). In other words, Jews who assimilated
into society did so at the cost of repudiating their tradition and sacrificing
their collective political effectiveness. In this shifting social milieu, Rahel
appeared to others as an exceptional exception.

Varnhagen was one of many who felt her Jewish past to be both incom-
prehensible and personally debilitating. Ignorant of her traditions—"she
learned nothing, neither her own history nor that of the country in which
her family dwelt" (1974, 4)—she saw herself as a blank slate, her present
horribly confined by the limits of self, her future without hope. She
thought of herself as an impermeable entity whose appearance only
served to keep her "real" content hidden from view: "If only I could throw
myself open to people as a cupboard is opened, and with one gesture show
the things arranged in order in their compartments" (1974, 19). As an
effort to negate fate, assimilation seemed to promise her acceptance into
society, but at the price of extirpating her difference from others. Isolation, on the other hand, maintained Jewishness but also turned it into a
"personal" misfortune: Jewishness became a private, inner concern
(1974, 7). Under such a notion of the individual, she could understand
Jewishness only as a personal problem belonging to the self. Assimilation
versus isolation, a problem not just limited to Jews as a group, is exacer-
bated by individualism. Because this ego-centered aspect of the atomistic
individual also relates to the question of feminine identity and assimilation, we will return to it at a later point in the discussion.

Arendt particularized Varnhagen's dilemma by describing it as a choice
between the way of "pariah or of parvenu." The pariah maintains differ-

ence but at the cost of sociality and ordinary political resources, while the parvenu abandons an oppositional political agenda, direction, and desire for equal rights. In attempting to break into society and escape Jewishness, her "personal misfortune," Varnhagen learns that becoming a parvenu means not just living, but being, a lie: "Rahel's struggle against the facts, above all against the fact of having been born a Jew, very rapidly became a struggle against herself. She herself refused to consent to herself; she, born to so many disadvantages, had to deny, change, reshape by lies this self of hers, since she could not very well deny her existence out of hand" (1974, 13). Every desire, every natural affinity, every political practice had to be sacrificed to the only goal Varnhagen could have, namely, the social acceptance of one solitary individual. Arendt draws the salient political conclusion that romantic individualism severs itself from politics and turns the social group into a collection of private selves. This all-important distinction between the social and political subject becomes critical for describing political action.

Even though the society of the salon had promised limited acceptance into a group, its configuration was private and individualistic, not communal and public. "Otherness" was conceived not in terms of "others" but rather in terms of other self-contained egos. Because each "other" was autonomous, there was not opportunity for the political pluralism of many thinking voices. As a result, the inherently frail salon collapsed from the pressure of an insistent world: "The salon in which private things were given objectivity by being communicated, and in which public matters counted only insofar as they had private significance—this salon ceased to exist when the public world, the power of general misfortune, become so overwhelming that it could no longer be translated into private terms" (1974, 122).

After the breakup of the salon (1806), Varnhagen felt an even greater need to escape her Jewishness. In desperation she was baptized, changed her name to Antonie Friedericke Robert, and married a Gentile—only to be ostracized again as a pariah.[9] In the process she had sacrificed any political action for the sake of individualistic display, being the exception to a collective Jewish identity. In other words, seeing difference as a personal problem determined that both ways, pariah and parvenu, would fail. Arendt explains that Varnhagen's "unique attempt to establish a social life outside of official society" was a failure, "the way of the pariah and the parvenu equally ways of extreme solitude, and the way of conformism one of constant regret" (1974, 66). Her point is that Varnhagen's romantic sense of self—whether Jewish or female—conceived in psychological or behavioristic terms, thwarted real political action and generated her alienation: "The history of any given personality is far older than the individual as product of nature, begins long before the individual's life, and can foster or destroy the elements of nature in his heritage" (1974, 4).

Entangled in Varnhagen's sense of her Jewishness—"I can . . . derive every evil, every misfortune, every vexation from *that*" (1974, 7)—was her belief that female "otherness" compounded an already intolerable condition. While we can be cautious about an analogy between feminine and Jewish alterity, history itself conflated the two into an all-encompassing, negative otherness. The biography suggests that an extraordinary link between feminine and Jewish alterity was confirmed in German history: the changing status of Jews and women represented to the conservatives the most threatening liberal tendencies of the Enlightenment.[10] In order to protest the salons both run by and including Jews, the new nationalistic, ethnically pure German groups directed their anger at *women* in general (Hertz 1988, 253). Thus, antifeminism took the *same form* as anti-Semitism. The private salon broke up under the pressure of a public consciously united in being "intellectually against the Enlightenment, politically against France, and socially against the salons" (1974, 124).

From the description of Varnhagen, we can begin to trace some conceptual analogues between Jewish otherness and the response to it and female otherness and its relation to politics. First, to conceive everything outside oneself as a threat is to banish difference for the sake of the false comfort of an inviolate self. Such a position evacuates the messy, heterogeneous world for the unitary sameness that seeks consolation from it. The contingent world is now viewed as a hostile other. Second, the historical past is more than the collected acts of individual psyches. To conceive of it otherwise denies the real apprehension and significance of persons other than oneself, denies their boundless, indefinable substantiality. For women, choosing between pariah and parvenu, between maintaining political difference or choosing social assimilation, is a parallel dilemma.

Arendt addresses the first point in *The Human Condition* (1958) when she describes how *alteritas* or otherness belongs to everything, not just to the marginalized. Because all our definitions and concepts are distinctions—we say what something is by distinguishing it from other things—difference *is* our human condition (1958, 176). However, respect for others quite different from ourselves can only be generated in the public arena of "human plurality" when we are free from external necessity and inner compulsion. That is, "alterity" reconceived in terms of multiplicity opens the possibility for the community of plurality, a coalitional politics based on difference.

With respect to the second point about social conformism, when the marginalized relinquish the political demand of respect *for* otherness for the sake of fulfilling private desires or seeking full social assimilation, they invite discrimination. Arendt is claiming no less than that romantic individualism sows the seeds of its own rejection. Rahel learned that "pure subjectivity" which bears a world in itself is doomed because "this inner world is never able to replace what is merely given to human beings" (1974, 118). Arendt challenges that form of individualism disguised as a sympathetic sisterhood or brotherhood and consisting only of a collection of world-alienated "selves."

III

I have considered Arendt's perspective on female otherness and Jewishness in the light of her own personal interest in Varnhagen. Now I will look at her thought simply as philosophy in the sense of developing a structural or hypothetical framework that can be applied to problems inherent in any political organization. While Varnhagen's life illustrates a woman's perspective on a period of assimilation and romanticism in German-Jewish history, the heart of the biography is neither history, character, nor even Jewishness but, most importantly for feminist politics, a critique of individual subjectivity. As critique, it does what all good philosophy does: it reflects systematically upon the human condition. It provides us with a model or structure of the political group, one that serves as a powerful metaphor. It applies that model, not only or even necessarily to just an actual historical example—for example, a specific feminist theory of the subject or actual feminist political group—but to *any* group calling itself political.[11] In other words, it provides a powerful conceptual framework as an aid to understanding the political.

That critique is central to a politics of alterity and begins with the historical claim that the transformation of *alteritas* or otherness into the private selfhood—including the female selfhood—parallels the development of romantic subjectivity and a shift in the concept of the private. Varnhagen symbolizes a female stereotype when she displays the extremity of her otherness within the privacy of the salon even as she rejects all claims to public action. Arendt traces the ancient Greek roots of the private to the prepolitical space occupied by females and slaves who were considered noncitizens when the burden of necessity and reproduction thwarted their political or public distinction (1958, 32, 82–85, 119). The female, claimed by the necessity of reproduction, acquired the characteristics identified with the "otherness" belonging to the private realm and came to represent otherness *essentially*, came to occupy the "private" as both an actual and conceptual space. Because politics also became conflated with government, or worse, bureaucratic housekeeping, it was viewed as taking place somewhere other than work, home, and family. In modern times the private sphere became an *inner* space, no longer ruled, as in the past, by the necessity of survival but by inner compulsions and will.

Arendt theorizes difference nonessentially, as properly belonging to persons free from the twofold deprivation of necessity and inner compulsion.[12] Varnhagen's story reveals that the egocentric selfhood deprives one of difference, of achieved distinction and the political:

> To live an entirely private life means above all to be deprived of things essential to a truly human life: to be deprived of the reality that comes from being seen and heard by others, to be deprived of an 'objective' relationship with them that comes from being related to and separated from them through the intermediary of a common world of things, to be deprived of the possibility of achieving something more permanent than life itself. *The deprivation of privacy lies in the absence of others.* (1958, 58; italics added)

Arendt further describes this privative retreat into the selfhood as an "inner emigration," a pervasive phenomenon of the twentieth century that produces "the modern individual and his endless conflicts, his inability either to be at home in society or to live outside it altogether, his ever-changing moods and the radical subjectivism of his emotional life . . ." (1958, 39). The "flight into the self" abjures politics (1968, 19) with the result that one behaves as if she were no longer a citizen of a political order in the world.

Arendt's conclusions are sobering, for they imply no less than that the configuration of our subjectivity, how we become persons, determines the absence or presence of any real political action. Because action takes place *between* persons, it requires a preserved public space for deeds and achievements that give meaning to everyday relationships. In other words, the isolated selfhood belongs to the activity and sphere of work and labor (now the social) but *not* to that of action—the space of words and deeds.[13] While labor insures survival and work produces human artifacts, only action engages in "founding and preserving political bodies, [and] creates the condition for remembrance, that is for history" (1958, 9). Thus action does not radiate from the individual self but arises in a network of interdependent forces that prevents any act from being merely the straightforward intention of an agent toward a realizable goal. A "selfhood," on the other hand, thinks to protect her impermeability by negating history, her oppressive past, and eschewing communal relationships, her unfortunate present. When she must maintain her "individuality" at all costs, all others will appear as external threats that she must guard against or control. Paradoxically, pressed by inner necessity, seeing power as an individual possession that must be protected, and striving for the rule of the one, a form of totalitarianism, she cannot achieve political power. In this respect, Arendt implies, a female subject—if conceived autonomously as one who wishes to maintain a "naturalized" gendered alterity—perpetuates her own marginalism. She will always see the other as a menacing threat, a hostile "one" that must be controlled and subsumed or distorted by the consolation of sympathy.

What are the practical consequences for feminism of a politics and a subject conceived as antithetical to any polity? Can there be a feminist politics based on the isolated, self-contained psyche? Arendt's answer can be found in a description of how Varnhagen's "grand misconception of herself," the "fatal flaw" of introspection, corrupts political solidarity:

> Introspection accomplishes two feats: it annihilates the actual existing situation by dissolving it in mood, and at the same time it lends everything subjective an aura of objectivity, publicity, extreme interest. In mood the boundaries between what is intimate and what is public become blurred; intimacies are made public, and public matters can be experienced and expressed only in the realm of the intimate—ultimately, in gossip. (1974, 21)

Because introspection bathes everything in mood, Varnhagen's relationships were ties of affectivity with others who suffered as she did rather than bonds of communicative practice.[14]

Shared sympathy, Arendt suggests, is a form of inner compulsion, a facet of the selfhood that only seems to create the unity of a compassionate sisterhood, when in fact it does the reverse. She describes the *caritas* between persecuted peoples as "a great thing" but not sufficient for political action:

> In its full development it can breed a kindliness and sheer goodness of which human beings are otherwise scarcely capable. Frequently it is also the source of a vitality, a joy in the simple fact of being alive, rather suggesting that life comes fully into its own only among those who are, in worldly terms, the insulted and injured. But in saying this we must not forget that the charm and intensity of the atmosphere that develops is also due to the fact that the pariahs of this world enjoy the great privilege of being unburdened by care for the world. (1968, 13–14)[15]

The loss of the common world that Varnhagen experienced resulted from a sympathetic unity with other eccentric "pariahs" that shut out the world and ultimately, shut off political life. Equally tragic, the political group formed by sharing similar inner needs may spend much of its energy on deciding who is qualified to belong to it (Sawicki 1988, 187).

Without underestimating the pull of sympathy among the oppressed, Arendt suggests that the distance required for turning Varnhagen's private feelings into *political* action could not depend on an exclusive, shared suffering. The point is that neither sentiment nor any form of affective humanism can be a viable basis for politics: "The rationalism and sentimentalism of the eighteenth century are only two aspects of the same thing; both could lead equally to that enthusiastic excess in which individuals feel ties of brotherhood to all men. In any case this rationality and sentimentality were only psychological substitutes, localized in the realm of invisibility, for the loss of the common, visible world" (1968, 16). In other words, both the rational and the sentimental mask a form of apolitical behaviorism tied to feeling and radiating from the atomistic self.

In *On Revolution* (1963), Arendt extends her insights about the affective makeup of the selfhood to modern liberation movements to show that private sentiment corrupts, if not effectually subverts, the concept of freedom. In the contrast between the French and American revolutions, she charts the way sympathetic brotherhood appears among persecuted peoples who lack citizenship. When the French Revolution added fraternity to the political concepts of liberty and equality, the emphasis on public freedoms and human rights shifted to private civil liberties. Driven by internal need instead of common weal, fraternity presses for liberties at the expense of rights, private happiness over public well-being.[16] Consequently, pity for suffering becomes a legitimate political motive. By tying this understanding of fraternity to Rousseauian sentiment, Arendt reveals by implication the privative character of any sisterhood which seeks to abolish the pain and suffering of the marginalized rather than make them citizens responsible and strong enough to bear the burden of freedom.[17] A sympathetic sisterhood can breed "kindliness," "goodness," "vitality and joy," but it does not answer to the need for a feminist *political* community.

Although the biography of Varnhagen records the early nineteenth-century failure of assimilation, the rise of anti-Semitism, and the retreat from politics into individual alienation, it is not a story of a political failure nor by extension that of a failed female. Arendt describes the debilitating effects of Rahel's individualism—discrimination, exile, and despair—as fortuitous events that at last forced Varnhagen to recognize the political dimensions of life. Where Varnhagen had once found inner consolation in Goethe, now she came to discover in his works a universal description of her fate rather than a lonely platform for her solipsistic despair. She learned that otherness and suffering are *human conditions*, not just the personal misfortune of the Jew or the female. And like Lessing, she learned that thought "does not arise out of the individual and is not the manifestation of a self. Rather, the individual . . . elects such thought because he dis-

covers in thinking another mode of moving in the world in freedom"
(1968, 9). Others and otherness became related to her as more than other
selves who exact a personal price. Through public discourse (in this case,
literature), she began to see others as constitutive of her own personhood:
"She knew it was senseless to be superior to life because everything 'personal,' and the personal alone, stood for something more than itself"
(1974, 174). What changed was not merely her consciousness of a personal
conversion but also, more radical, the configuration of her personhood.

IV

How does a transformation of female subjectivity occur in one who con-
ceives of self as autonomous, otherness as personal fate, and action as behavior? Arendt's answer is startling and portentous: Varnhagen came
resolutely to apprehend the historical conditions of Jews and women—
anti-Semitism, antifeminism, and pariahhood.[18] Her extreme inner isolation, her retreat from the world into self, her repudiation of collective
history—all these efforts to negate her Jewishness had merely affirmed it
(1974, 221). The more she had refused to translate personal desires into
politically identifiable terms, to share or identify with the historical treatment of Jews, the more typically Jewish her fate had become: "She had
walked down all roads that could lead her into the alien world, and upon
all these roads she had left her track, had converted then into Jewish
roads, pariah roads; ultimately her whole life had become a segment of
Jewish history in Germany" (1974, 222).[19] She is transformed from isolated self to personhood by virtue of seeing "self" as being intertwined
with others and not by remaining singular (1974, 118).

From the perspective of her common Jewish roots forged of culture, religion, and history, Varnhagen recognized that "one does not escape
Jewishness." The one who seeks social acceptance or consensus attempts
to banish difference, for assimilation means appeasement for the sake of
sameness, or even the leveling down of difference through the most tyrannical form of egalitarianism. By extension, neither does one escape femaleness. Arendt suggests that a political agenda which obliterates women's
historical and cultural differences by surrendering history to the immediate thrill of its own suffering merely grinds difference into dust, into the
history of sameness. In contrast, seeing the difference of all things through
our *alteritas* opens us to a plurality of differences, to other perspectives.
This insight into multiplicity sharpens the political edges of our otherness.
That is, our task is one of vision, an open attention to the particular that
continually acknowledges its inexhaustible difference, without projecting
or imposing oneself so as to obscure it. To hold a clear, steady gaze toward
the particular requires concepts adequate for understanding. It means

apprehending persons other than oneself as infinitely particular, endlessly to be understood.

Arendt felt that the new understanding of otherness generated from thinking and writing the biography transformed not only Varnhagen's solitary introspection into insight but her own as well. The awareness of others and differing modes of being, the plurality between persons speaking and acting together, freed her from her isolation.

> While all aspects of the human condition are somehow related to politics, this plurality is specifically *the* condition—not only the *conditio sine qua non,* but the *conditio per quam*—of all political life. . . . Plurality is the condition of human action because we are all the same, that is human, in such a way that nobody is ever the same as anyone else who ever lived, lives, or will live. (1958, 7–8)

We are both infinite and yet particular, possessing "the paradoxical plurality of unique beings" (1958, 176). Paradoxical because we are indefinable, unrepresentable, contingent yet particular; unique but not self-made because we are shaped in concert with others. In contrast, an essentialist concept of our being (for example, "natural" or even determined gender) is really a form of identity. Identity reduces all to a false unity, the projecting and controlling self; plurality multiplies our sense of the great variety of the world and in exchange grants us our own uniqueness. In other words, if we are only the same in being different, if we have access to ourselves only through others within the public space of appearing, then the more we encounter difference as Arendt describes it, the more we have ourselves.

According to Arendt, Varnhagen affirmed her collective fate at the end of her life by saying, "The thing which all my life seemed to me the greatest shame, which was the misery and misfortune of my life—having been born a Jewess—this I should on no account now wish to have missed" (1974, 3). Her change conferred on her a historical—that is, political—identity: "Rahel had remained a Jew and pariah. Only because she clung to both conditions did she find a place in the history of European humanity" (1974, 227). She had overcome her intense subjectivism, exposed herself as a Jew and a woman to the events of history, and found a historical and therefore political identity in the very process of *failing* to escape from destiny. In other words, the biography opens Varnhagen's assumptions about her "self" to scrutiny and public debate and illuminates her more than any attempt on her part to dazzle. It illuminates her through her failures and reveals her political being. Equally important, it illuminates the critical analogues Arendt generates from her story.

Varnhagen's story provides still another political concept for analyzing feminist practice, the connection of subjectivity to ideology. Difference naturalized as the intrinsic "femaleness" of an individual selfhood destroys the communal character of women who have had their otherness forged in the crucible of history. The subjectivism of the individualistic "Varnhagen" obliterates the difference that she seeks to maintain. That is, radical subjectivism is a form of ideology, seemingly different, actually an ideology of sameness, signaling the absence of the "political" in any useful sense of the term.[20] Such an ideology banishes other differences in the interest of unanimity: "A movement . . . which does not translate ideology into concrete goals that reflect real particular changes remains alienated from concrete life" (Young-Bruehl 1982, 97). The danger of ideology—one group purporting to hold the truth about women, for example—is that "every claim in the sphere of human affairs to an absolute truth, whose validity needs no support from the side of opinion, strikes at the very roots of all politics and all governments" (Beiner 1982, 233). Truth-claims to be peremptorily acknowledged—politically correct feminisms, for example—preclude debate and wither freedom. They threaten feminist politics when they resist self-criticism; the result is that "The Woman," like "The Jew," again becomes a conceptual void, locus, dispersion, and dissemination of women.[21]

As an alternative to an ideological exclusivity of sisterhood, Arendt offers another helpful concept, "the political relevance of friendship."[22] She explains "that humaneness should be sober and cool rather than sentimental; that humanity is exemplified not in fraternity but in friendship; that friendship is not intimately personal but makes political demands and preserves reference to the world" (1968, 25). The essence of friendship she describes as *philia*, friendship among citizens in a constant exchange of thought, uniting them in a polis. *Philanthropia*, or love of humankind, "manifests itself in a readiness to share the world with other[s]" (1968, 25). The power of this concept is not in any way diminished because women have historically been denied its experience. Such an authentic political friendship based on respect rather than sentiment "comprehends" or remains "committed to 'ideas'" and dialogue (1963, 89).

Arendt offers a further principle for feminist action when she applies the politics of alterity to Nazism. Instead of limiting her action to denouncing the policies that negatively identified her as a Jew, she puts the *process of identification* itself in question, forcing the issue into the light of human debate, forcing the dark inhumanity of a single opinion into the bright scrutiny of multiple perspectives. She insists that "truth can exist only where it is humanized by discourse":

> Every truth outside of this area [human debate], no matter whether it brings men good or ill, is inhuman . . . not because it might arouse men against one another and separate them. Quite the contrary, it is because it might have the result that all men would unite in a single opinion, so that out of many opinions one would emerge, as though not men in

their infinite plurality but man in the singular, one species and its exem-
plars, were to inhabit the earth. (1968, 30, 31)

In effect, she forces the "single opinion" of Nazism, of "man in the singular," into the "area in which there are many voices" by saying to it, "Yes,
I'm a Jew; so what does it mean to be a Jew?" That question makes identity as "sameness" an issue for critical debate among feminisms even
while the most heinous and violent of deeds seem to cry out instead for a
united, immediate reaction.

The point for feminist politics is that action is both theoretical and
practical. As a form of the politics of alterity, theory clears public space of
ideology. Because theory is at its heart dialogical and *therefore* political,
serious analytical thinking always has a practical relevance. For Arendt,
theory is never an abstract and cold rationality—in fact, by directing her
own intensity of feeling toward the conceptualizing she calls "passionate
thinking," she restores theory to practice. The theoretical critique of
policy keeps debate open and creates the condition for judgment, an
ongoing evaluative understanding freely open to debate.[23] Judging, the
ability to discern the qualities of the particular without a prior subsump-
tion of them under a rule, is linked to disclosure in the public realm.
While thinking deals with invisibles, judging deals with things close at
hand. If we recognize that identities like "Jew" or "Woman" are historically constituted, then we can accept their contingency so as not to resist
them dialectically. Arendt asks whether we are prepared for the dissolu-
tion of the female as any set identity; whether we may not be more effective politically if we became more concerned with eliminating injustice
wherever it arises (1958, 188).

As a form of the politics of alterity, judgment combines theory and
practice when it analyzes the codetermination of gendered relationships
and dismantles the inhibiting polarities (alterity versus identity) of gender
in an ongoing debate. Merleau-Ponty writes in the same spirit that "true
liberty takes others as they are, tries to understand even those doctrines
which are its negation, and never allows itself to judge before understanding" (quoted in Beiner 1982, 100). The danger in subsuming particular
experiences of otherness, as, for example, in promoting a universal feminism, is that the particular loses its unique difference in the unity of consensus.

Finally, applying Arendt's political theory to the refiguration of alterity
ascribes a plurality to the female political subject, a subject who historically reflects upon otherness as contingent and no longer as a totalitarian,
hostile other. How does it accomplish such goals? First, the politics of alterity radically pluralizes otherness by recognizing that any attempt to
banish, control, or socially engineer difference implicitly bars us from

knowing ourselves and others. Second, it opens the public space to these differences even among feminisms by encouraging *disagreement* and the responsibility to understand and respect what we reject. That means understanding and bearing the burden of events, neither denying their existence nor submitting to their brutality. Third, a genuine feminist politics of alterity, because it cannot be limited to feminism, implicitly responds to all who have shared the historical condition of otherness. That is, it recognizes *female* alterity not as belonging exclusively to one special group or human being marked by history but as a political and therefore locally situated "fact" that temporally outweighs other questions of who we are. It suggests a philosophy, that is, a hypothetical structure of the political, suited for a world in which respect for rights keeps open innumerable places for the meeting of theory and practice. It enables us to test critically our political concepts for adequacy and ensures that the political group does not get sidetracked into the call for consolation or entangled in what Arendt calls the bureaucratic housekeeping assumed to be politics. This means, for example, that the relations traditionally reserved for the private, intimate, and familial can be maintained but must be freed from deprivation, from both necessity and the compulsions of the psyche. And last, the politics of alterity responds to the facticity of our condition by an ongoing questioning of it. It resists the ideology that is the negation of alterity by understanding what it must judge when it perpetually asks, what will *we* lose if we win?

NOTES

1. Arendt deplored the modern blurring of public and private in "our eagerness to see recorded, displayed and discussed in public what were once strictly private affairs and nobody's business" (as quoted in Young-Bruehl 1982, xvii). Mary Dietz says that for Arendt "the public exists in stark contrast to the private realm; it is where the revelation of individuality amidst collectivity takes place" (Dietz 1991, 236). As early as 1933 Arendt saw that the private sphere to which most women are relegated devalues their potential because it valorizes the life process and binds action to labor or production.

2. I use Arendt's term "alterity" to describe the historical human condition of being other or different. Alterity that is, diversity, otherness—is not to be confused with the terms "difference" and *"différance"* as used in deconstruction to expose the mutual determination of all hierarchical oppositions. Arendt sees *"alteritas,"* the state of being other or different, as integral to human individuality. This uniqueness, revealed in speech and action, is distinguished from the pure particularity of objects, their distinction one from another. She explains the nuances of the term as follows: "Human distinctness is not the same as otherness—the curious

quality of *alteritas* possessed by everything that is. Otherness . . . is an important aspect of plurality, the reason why all our definitions are distinctions. . . . But only man can express this distinction and distinguish himself. . . . In man, otherness, which he shares with everything that is, and distinctness, which he shares with everything alive, become uniqueness. . . . Speech and action reveal this unique distinctness. Through them, men distinguish themselves instead of being merely distinct" (Arendt 1958, 176).

3. Arendt has sometimes been misinterpreted as "hostile" to feminism or even as a misogynist. Such a view fails to handle the *concept* (rather than the *content*) of terms such as public, private, polis, gender, etc. When Arendt distinguishes between public and private, she is not simply referring to a specific historical example or commonsense understanding of the two terms but to a concept that can be used to analyze what those terms might encompass. *The Human Condition* has especially been faulted (unfairly, I think) for using a Greek *theoretical model* to help develop her concept of the polis, claiming that because the actual Greeks disenfranchised women and slaves, the concept of polis is somehow not available to women. Again, such an argument assumes that a philosophical structure or model cannot be expanded to include an actual historical condition such as the disenfranchised woman, alien male, etc., that it cannot articulate a potential experience. Margaret Canovan claims that many of Arendt's critics mistake *The Human Condition* as the summation of her political theory and disregard the way she continually developed and revised her thinking (Canovan 1992). I see Arendt as a theorist most at home with other Continental philosophers—especially Jaspers and Heidegger—who formally explore the philosophical question of subjectivity by decentering Being and human being. Nonetheless, Arendt creates a productive tension with the French (Irigaray, Kirsteva, Cixous) and postmodern feminists who also explore the problem of gender identity and its relation to subjectivity and practice. See, for example, Linda Nicholson (1990), Susan Hekman (1990), and Judith Butler (1990).

4. Even before Arendt wrote her most famous political works, she recognized that the basic unit determining women's lives, whether proletariat or bourgeois is the family (Young-Bruehl 1982, 273) and that intimate familial relations inevitably devalue women's potential. Because traditional conceptions of society had not included the family in its public, liberal thought, the family remained in the private, prepolitical space absent from the public. It is important to keep Arendt's understanding of public and private distinct from our commonsense usage of the terms: for her, the "private realm" of necessity encompassed the functions of survival, the "household sphere" where the order of rule and ruling over held sway. The "public realm" was the arena of freedom and equality where persons could distinguish themselves in speech and action (1958, 32). In other words, the "public" was not necessarily an *actual* space, the domain of politics or government as we commonly know it, but the space of plurality, any opening for communal *discourse* free from necessity and inner compulsion, hence public. According to this definition, Arendt wished to extend the public reach of free and equal discourse over the "unfree" relations of the prepolitical family. For a parallel view see Maria Markus, "Women, Success and Civil Society" (in Benhabib and Cornell 1987, 96–109).

5. *Rahel Varnhagen: The Life of a Jewish Woman* (1974) was Arendt's earliest major work after the writing and publication of her doctoral thesis on Augustine. In Germany, Varnhagen is known by her first name Rahel. Reviewer Sybille Bedford describes the biography as a "relentlessly abstract book—slow, cluttered, static, curiously oppressive; reading it feels like sitting in a hot-house with no watch. One is made to feel the subject, the waiting, distraught woman; one is made aware, almost physically, of her intense femininity, her frustration" (Bedford 1958, 24).

6. Arendt contrasted the individual as a psychological entity who reinforces her egocentrism in displays of behaviorism with the one who distinguishes herself by unique deeds of excellence and human achievement in the public world of speech and action. Jana Sawicki aligns the problem of the atomistic self with "identity politics," describing the destructive form of politics in which individuals are preoccupied with their identities more than political goals: "Such identity politics can be self-defeating insofar as it often leads to internal struggles over who really belongs to a community" (Sawicki 1988, 187). Chris Weedon speaks of the prevailing context in which feminist theory is discussed, namely "the dominant liberal discourse of the free and self-determining individual" (Weedon 1987, 5). She credits feminist post-structuralism with making explicit the theoretical implications of identity politics (Weedon, 1987, 6).

7. Iris Young cites a similar situation existing for African-American feminists who must first confront the overwhelming "fact" of their race before that of being female (Young 1990, 10–11). In the early 1930's life also forced Arendt to acknowledge that she was linked by the historical conditions of her birth with the collective fate of the Jews. She ran up against political reality and recoiled from the impact. While working on the biography she learned that the contingencies of history select our political issues for us. She too came to terms with her own alterity and accepted pariahhood by destiny *and* choice as the broadest sense of "otherness," in effect always unassimilated (Young-Bruehl 1982, xv) and therefore always politically attuned.

8. In "Hannah Arendt's *Rahel Varnhagen*" (Cutting-Gray 1991), I explore the way Arendt problematizes subjectivity and the politics of biography. Writing about Varnhagen helped Arendt to understand and combat her own introspective self-absorption, helped her to come to terms with Zionism and Nazism.

9. Varnhagen later had this to say about marriage: "I have to behave toward people as if I were nothing more than *my husband*; in the past I was *nothing*, and that is a great deal" (1974, 210).

10. "Jewish salon women provoked resentments which contributed to the downfall of their salons" (Hertz 1988, 253).

11. Arendt embodies the example of feminism that Nannerl Keohane describes when she says that "feminist theory is fundamentally experiential" (Keohane 1981, vii). Arendt provides an indissoluble link between experience and theory by bringing powerful concepts to the aid of evaluating the particular.

12. Arendt's feminist theory would find a kinship today with that of writers like Judith Butler and Druilla Cornell who distinguish between the specificity of

women as constructed by a particular context—Arendt's point about the facticity of an identity—and the ahistorical, essentialist accounts of identity. Diana Fuss qualifies the issue when cautioning that "there is no essence to essentialism" (Fuss 1989, xii), i.e., to be historical we can only speak of *essentialisms*. In this way we can flexibly respond to the particular, contingent conditions that have specifically identified us as female, Jew, African-American, etc., without using essentialism as a weapon to destroy one politics of difference or as a yardstick to measure the correctness of another.

13. Arendt presents work and labor not as constructs of class but as belonging to the human condition. I am using "social" in her sense of a private "space" for the activities of labor and necessity. Arendt insisted that only where women act together free from inner necessity and external compulsion in a public space of appearing will they generate individuality and achievment (Arendt 1958, 199–208). That is why she argued against being the "exception" woman who repudiates the context against which an individual is measured as the exception.

14. Arendt was initially attracted to a sympathetic fraternity (which she later rejected) because of the affinity she felt with Varnhagen: "My closest friend, though she has been dead for some one hundred years" (Young-Bruehl 1982, 56).

15. For a model of political empathy for a plural subject, Arendt at first turned to Augustine's concept of *caritas*, which is based upon the compassion between the oppressed: "Only galley slaves know one another," Varnhagen wrote to her friend, Heine. The Greeks recognized the affective nature of compassion, its tendency, like that of fear to immobilize us. They regarded "the most compassionate person as no more entitled to be called the best than the most fearful" because both emotions make action impossible and that is why Aristotle treated them together Arendt 1968, 15.

16. Arendt emphasizes and supports a contrasting American emphasis on the "illumination" of citizens which promotes public debate and alliances of interest and purpose rather than a liberation limited to freedom from necessity. See Arendt 1963.

17. Rousseau is an example of how every misfortune can be generalized beforehand: "By sentimentalizing memory he obliterated the contours of the remembered event. What remained were the feelings experienced in the course of those events—in other words, once more nothing but reflections within the psyche. Sentimental remembering is the best method for completely forgetting one's own destiny. It presupposes that the present itself is instantly converted into a 'sentimental' past. For Rousseau (*Confessions*) the present always first rises up out of memory, and it is immediately drawn into the inner self, where everything is eternally present and converted back into potentiality" (Arendt 1974, 11). Arendt "was concerned to preserve the distinction between private and public matters and to show how introspection can foreclose political understanding" (Young-Bruehl 1982, 88).

18. I describe the transformation in detail in Cutting-Gray (1991). Hertz (1988) takes issue with Arendt's sense of Rahel's "conversion"—the distinction is again concept versus content (see not 3 above).

19. Among fellow Jewish intellectuals in prewar Germany, Arendt observed how the desire for assimilation and escape from their backward or poorer brethren severed them from their traditions. When they refused to identify with political or revolutionary movements, anti-Semitism filled the political vacuum. In striving to understand her particular political condition in 1933, Arendt would later be able to reflect how anti-Semitism could reach its climax in Nazism, when terror was directed against people with common psychological traits abstracted from ethnic, religious and cultural differences.

20. Under the Hegelian dialectic of identity and difference. See Lacoue-Labarthe (1990, 81).

21. Alice Jardine's point about some postmodern discussions of the feminine in Jardine, 1985. The seduction of deconstruction is deterministic charm: it excludes itself from the fate of the codified and allows for sexism to be born-again.

22. Arendt describes how Lessing considered "friendship—which is as selective as compassion is egalitarian—to be the central phenomenon in which alone true humanity can prove itself" (Arendt 1968, 12). In joining the Zionist movement, in writing and thinking about fellow Jew Varnhagen, in suffering the alienation of statelessness, she rescued friendship from its psychological context, transforming it into a solidarity based on respect rather than sympathy.

23. Admittedly I am offering a version of judgment that Arendt left unarticulated at her death. She does, however, link understanding to the evaluative effort of judgment and sees criticism as "always taking sides for the world's sake, understanding and judging everything in terms of its position in the world at any given time" (Arendt 1968, 8).

REFERENCES

Arendt, Hannah. [1954]. 1977. *Between past and future.* New York: Penguin.
———. 1958. *The human condition.* Chicago: University of Chicago Press.
———. [1963], 1977. *On revolution.* New York: Penguin.
———. 1968. *Men in dark times.* New York: Harcourt Brace Jovanovich.
———. 1973. *The origins of totalitarianism.* New York: Harcourt Brace Jovanovich.
———. 1974. *Rahel Varnhagen: The Life of a Jewish woman.* Trans. Richard and Clara Winston. New York: Harcourt Brace Jovanovich.
———. 1982. *Lectures on Kant's political philosophy,* ed. Ronald Beiner. Chicago: University of Chicago Press.
Bedford, Sybille. 1958. Emancipation and destiny. *Reconstructionist* 12: 22–26.
Beiner, Ronald, ed. 1982. *Hannah Arendt: Lectures on Kant's political philosophy.* Chicago: University of Chicago Press.
Benhabib, Seyla, and Drucilla Cornell, eds. 1987. *Feminism as critique.* Minneapolis: University of Minnesota Press.
Butler, Judith. 1990. *Gender trouble: Feminism and the subversion of identity.* New York: Routledge.

Canovan, Margaret. 1992. *Hannah Arendt.* Cambridge: Cambridge University Press.

Cornell, Drucilla. 1991. *Beyond accommodation: Ethical feminism, deconstruction, and the law.* New York: Routledge.

Cutting-Gray, Joanne. 1991. Hannah Arendt's Rahel Varnhagen. *Philosophy and Literature* 15: 229–45.

Dietz, Mary G. 1991. Hannah Arendt and feminist politics. In *Feminist interpretations and political theory*, ed. Mary Lyndon Shanley and Carole Pateman. University Park: Pennsylvania State University Press.

Fuss, Diana. 1989. *Essentially speaking: Feminism, nature and difference.* New York: Routledge.

Hekman, Susan. 1990. *Gender and knowledge: Elements of a postmodern feminism.* Boston: Northeastern University Press.

Hertz, Deborah. 1988. *Jewish high society in old regime Berlin.* New Haven: Yale University Press.

Jardine, Alice. 1985. *Gynesis: configurations of woman and modernity.* Ithaca, NY: Cornell University Press.

Keohane, Nannerl, ed. 1981. *Feminist theory: a critique of ideology.* Chicago: University of Chicago Press.

Lacoue-Labarthe, Philippe. 1990. *Heidegger, art and politics.* Trans. Chris Turner. Oxford: Basil Blackwell.

Nicholson, Linda, ed. 1990. *Feminism/postmodernism.* New York: Routledge.

Sawicki, Jana. 1988. Identity politics and sexual freedom. In *Feminism and Foucault*, ed. Irene Diamond and Lee Quinby. Boston: Northeastern University Press.

Weedon, Chris. 1987. *Feminist practice and poststructuralist theory.* London: Basil Blackwell.

Young, Iris. 1990. *Throwing like a girl and other essays in feminist philosophy and social theory.* Bloomington: Indiana University Press.

Young-Bruehl, Elisabeth. 1982. *Hannah Arendt: For love of the world.* New Haven: Yale University Press.

NOTORIOUS PHILOSOPHER
THE TRANSFORMATIVE
LIFE AND WORK OF ANGELA DAVIS

JUDITH MARY GREEN AND BLANCHE RADFORD CURRY

Angela Davis notes in *Women, Culture & Politics* (1989) that if she has inspired a resurgence of campus and labor activism, then her work over the last two decades has been worthwhile. Indeed, Davis's international notoriety as a once-hunted political fugitive and symbol of resistance has given her a popular platform for speeches and magazine articles that, in addition to her scholarly audience as a philosopher, Black liberation theorist, and feminist theorist, have given her life and work a tremendous transformative impact. The brilliance of her speaking and writing reveals the depth of her analytical skills, developed through intense study of Kant, Hegel, and Marx under the tutelage of Marcuse, Adorno, and Habermas, as well as through her own extensive reading of "other voices" like Douglass, Du Bois, Fanon, Morrison, and Gilman. At the same time, her unswerving commitment to a life of activism has given her public persona mythic proportions, making her both (S)hero and Enemy to millions of people who will never read her books.

This discussion of Angela Davis's life and works will focus on three areas of her transformative contributions to late twentieth-century philosophy and beyond: Critical Theory, Black Liberation Theory, and Feminist Theory. Throughout the discussion, her contributions to a broader social transformation theory and practice will be highlighted, including her unfailing inclusiveness; her rejection of homogenizing universalisms and hierarchical dualisms that downplay the significance of the diverse elements of the complex of gender/race/class, to which she eventually added culture; her strategy of coalition-building among oppressed peoples; her awareness of the importance of popular culture; and her special commitment to aiding the incarcerated who, like her younger self, she views as political prisoners. Some theoretical problems that have at times blemished Davis's work will also be noted, including her earlier lack of attention to international cultural differences; her loyal refusal to criticize (and perhaps to realize) serious problems within quasi-Marxist socialisms in Cuba and the USSR; her lack of a post-Soviet conception of socialism, which remains her ideal goal and activist commitment; and some lingering essentialisms, though within a broader set of social and analytical categories than those she received from the complex of historical traditions she inherited.

A Mutual Transformative Impact:
Angela Davis and Critical Theory

By 1964, when Herbert Marcuse published *One-Dimensional Man*, Critical Theory had pursued to a methodological and political dead end the project of synthesizing the insights of Marx and Freud to create a transformative philosophy for twentieth-century conditions. An originating precept of Critical Theory in the 1930s had been Marx's dictum that the point of philosophy is not just to criticize the world, but to change it. Yet by the end of World War II, Theodor Adorno had become so impressed with totalizing aspects of mass society within late capitalism that he could see no way out—no way conditions could give rise to the impulse to organize a successful transformative mass struggle—and he had refocused his attention on moments of individual imaginative liberation through the arts. Though Marcuse continued to long for and search for a transformative path to a "free society," he too was pessimistic about the possibility of fundamental and lasting change because of the enormous economic, political, and cultural power of advanced capitalisms, which had drawn the working classes Marx looked to for resistance and eventual revolution into psychic complicity and passivity. In the final chapter of *One-Dimensional Man*, Marcuse wrote:

> On theoretical as well as empirical grounds, the dialectical concept pronounces its own hopelessness. The human reality is its history and, in it, contradictions do not explode by themselves. The conflict between streamlined, rewarding domination on the one hand, and its achievements that make for self-determination and pacification on the other, may become blatant beyond any possible denial, but it may well continue to be a manageable and even productive conflict, for with the growth in the technological conquest of nature grows the conquest of man by man. And this conquest reduces the freedom which is a necessary *a priori* of liberation. This is freedom of thought in the only sense in which thought can be free in the administered world—as the consciousness of its repressive productivity, and as the absolute need for breaking out of this whole. But precisely this absolute need does not prevail where

it could become the driving force of a historical practice, the effective cause of qualitative change. Without this material force, even the most acute consciousness remains powerless. (Marcuse 1964, 253)

Though he could not discover any basis for Critical Theory to become anything more than critical—no way to fulfill its original transformative purpose—Marcuse did suggest on the last pages of *One-Dimensional Man* that there might be a crack in the totality of advanced capitalism's social control that would allow change-makers to emerge. Prominent among the particular change-makers he seems to have had in mind were African Americans struggling for civil rights.

> . . . Underneath the conservative popular base is the substratum of the outcasts and outsiders, the exploited and persecuted of other races and other colors, the unemployed and the unemployable. They exist outside the democratic process; their life is the most immediate and the most real need for ending intolerable conditions and institutions. Thus their opposition is revolutionary even if their consciousness is not. Their opposition hits the system from without and is therefore not deflected by the system; it is an elementary force which violates the rules of the game and, in doing so, reveals it as a rigged game. When they get together and go out into the streets, without arms, without protection, in order to ask for the most primitive civil rights, they know that they face dogs, stones, and bombs, jail, concentration camps, even death. Their force is behind every political demonstration for the victims of law and order. The fact that they start refusing to play the game may be the fact which marks the beginning of the end of a period. (Marcuse 1964, 256–257)

Even if the Civil Rights Movement could begin to end the era of late capitalist social control, Marcuse did not expect change to come easily, nor did he see any way that Critical Theory could assist this change process in theory or in practice, having nothing to offer except solidarity in critical rejection of the status quo.

> Nothing indicates that it will be a good end. The economic and technical capabilities of the established societies are sufficiently vast to allow for adjustments and concessions to the underdog, and their armed forces sufficiently trained and equipped to take care of emergency situations. . . . But the chance is that, in this period, the historical extremes may meet again: the most advanced consciousness of humanity, and its most exploited force. It is nothing but a chance. The critical theory of society possesses no concepts which could bridge the gap between the present and its future; holding no promise and showing no success, it remains negative. Thus it wants to remain loyal to those

who, without hope, have given and give their life to the Great Refusal.
(Marcuse 1964, 257)

By "the most advanced consciousness of humanity," the social element in
this era that must bond with "its most exploited force"—African
Americans and other oppressed peoples—if change is to occur, Marcuse no
doubt meant those intellectuals who have both ethical concern and the
clarity of vision about the historical process that a good grasp of Critical
Theory expresses and confers. These two extremes were to meet in the
critical consciousness and lived experience of his student, Angela Davis.

By the time Marcuse published *An Essay on Liberation* in 1969, his
pessimism had turned to optimism, both about the possibility of social
transformation and about the contribution Critical Theory could make to
it. He began his introduction to this brief, exuberant work by calling for a
new self-conceptualization of Critical Theory to respond to the potential
for fulfillment of historical possibilities with which he believed the times
were ripe.

> Up to now, it has been one of the principal tenets of the critical theory
> of society (and particularly Marxian theory) to refrain from what might
> be reasonably called utopian speculation. Social theory is supposed to
> analyze existing societies in light of their own functions and capabilities
> and to identify demonstrable tendencies (if any) which might lead
> beyond the existing state of affairs. By logical inference from the pre-
> vailing conditions and institutions, critical theory may also be able to
> determine the basic institutional changes which are the prerequisites
> for the transition to a higher state of development: "higher" in the sense
> of a more rational and equitable use of resources, minimization of de-
> structive conflicts, and enlargement of the realm of freedom. But
> beyond these limits, critical theory did not venture for fear of losing its
> scientific character. I believe that this restrictive conception must be re-
> vised, and that the revision is suggested, and even necessitated, by the
> actual evolution of contemporary societies. (Marcuse 1969, 3)

Marcuse was now calling for the transformation of the old, gray scientific
objectivity of a purely negative, critical characterization of hopeless times
into utopian visioning moved by awareness that ideas that had "no place"
in recent history might become reality in the fast-approaching future.

In the final chapter of his *Essay on Liberation*, Marcuse sketches a
hopeful conception of the "free society" he believed was already coming
into being, including some of the new relationships resulting from discovery of what he now called "a 'biological' *solidarity* in work and purpose"
(Marcuse 1969, 88). He concluded this prophetic vision by answering the
question:

... What are the people in a free society going to do? The answer which, I believe, strikes at the heart of the matter was given by a young black girl. She said: "for the first time in our life, we shall be free to think about what we are going to do." (Marcuse 1969, 91)

Whether or not Angela Davis was the "young black girl" to whom Marcuse referred, this was Angela Davis's answer. Some of its transformative dimensions would include overcoming problems with Marcuse's conception of freedom, dissolving obstacles of essentialism and false universals within Marcuse's vision, and developing a transformative model that gave Critical Theory a concrete basis for hope arising out of activist praxis.

The experiences Angela Davis shares in her *Autobiography* (Davis 1974), "written with freedom on [her] mind," represent the beginnings of examining philosophical issues of importance to her during the formative years that made her a notorious philosopher-activist, ones she has continued to analyze and to which she has been concretely committed in the years that have followed. She tells the reader that she was influenced early on by her mother, Sallye Davis, who, as a college student, worked hard for the freedom of the Scottsboro Boys and was active with the NAACP, although it was illegal in her hometown of Birmingham, Alabama, at that time. Davis learned about racism and slavery from her grandmother (Davis 1974, 79). And her early New York experience of visiting with close family friends made her more aware of segregation and racism in Birmingham. Davis's mother responded to her anguish about racism with the philosophy of seeing white people in terms of their potential, and not so much as what they were (1974, 79). From her political work, in which she had contact with white people committed to improving race relations, Sallye Davis had learned that "it was possible for white people to walk out of their skin and respond with the integrity of human beings" (1974, 79).

While her schooling at Carrie A. Tuggle Elementary School had nurtured her self-esteem with the teaching of African American culture, Angela Davis learned that most of her New York friends were not aware of the achievements of many outstanding African Americans that were known to her. This advantage of segregated schools in the South, however, did not diminish the lack of facilities and other resources which limited the quality of education available to black children. Davis's education in Birmingham was permeated by the Booker T. Washington syndrome, work hard and you will be rewarded (1974, 92). However, Davis doubted this idea and likewise viewed its complementary idea, poverty as punishment for idleness and indolence, as a myth (1974, 89).

During her high school years at Elisabeth Irwin High School in New York City, which she attended under a program for promising Southern

Black students sponsored by the American Friends Service Committee, Davis's reading of the *Communist Manifesto* contextualized for her the African American problems of racism and poverty about which she was so concerned, and related their solution to a working-class movement that must be and ultimately would be a revolutionary communist movement to transform capitalism into socialism (1974, 109–10). She saw Marx and Engel's "scientific socialism" as offering the transformative solution she was seeking (1974, 109ff). Davis wrote:

> Of course, the most powerful impact the *Manifesto* had on me—what moved me most—was the vision of a new society, without exploiters and exploited, a society without classes, a society where no one would be permitted to own so much that he could use his possessions to exploit other human beings. After the communist revolution "we shall have an association, in which the free development of each is the condition for the free development of all." (1974, 111)

Being silent, and especially not acting, frustrated Davis tremendously, and she developed an early commitment to contributing concretely to this transformative struggle. She began to participate in meetings and action projects of Advance, a youth organization asssociated with the Communist party, and got to know other young people whose parents were successful scholars and professionals, as well as prominent Communist activists. Though she longed to return to Birmingham, where the Civil Rights Movement was once again heating up in 1961, she stayed on in New York at her parents' urging in order to finish her high school studies.

Davis further delayed her return to the South and her plunge into what she saw as the center of the Civil Rights struggle when Brandeis University offered her a full scholarship, making her one of three Black first-year students. These were important years of struggle in the North, as well, so that she had opportunities to hear both James Baldwin and Malcolm X speak on the Brandeis campus. And they were also years of expanding international awareness for her, during which she became close friends with international students at Brandeis, met revolutionary youths from other parts of the world by participating in the Eighth World Festival for Youth and Students in Helsinki, Finland, and spent her junior year in Paris, studying at the Sorbonne. But the most important event for her of these crucial years may have been the 1963 bombing deaths of four young girls at the 16th Street Baptist Church in Birmingham, all of whom were personally known to her as friends of her family. This painful event, she wrote, had a profound clarifying impact on her thinking about transformative struggle.[1]

The most important intellectual influence of these formative years was Herbert Marcuse, whose challenging 1962 work, *Eros and Civilization*, she struggled through on her own, and whom she saw for the first time when he spoke at a campus rally in response to the Cuban Missile Crisis of October 1962.[2] Davis's initial conversation with Marcuse regarding her desire to study philosophy called forth a commitment that mirrored her growing commitment to political activism. Davis relates that Marcuse asked her slowly, with emphasis on each word, "Do you really want to study philosophy?" making it sound "like an initiation into some secret society which, once you join, you can never leave" (1974, 132). She felt at that moment about the study of philosophy, as she would later feel about revolutionary activism, once committed, one cannot do otherwise. After assuring himself of young Angela Davis's seriousness, Marcuse undertook personal responsibility for guiding her philosophical development through a weekly informal independent study with her, starting with the Pre-Socratics, Plato, and Aristotle.

After graduating from Brandeis, Davis devoted two years to graduate study in philosophy through the lens of Critical Theory at Marcuse's pre–World War II intellectual home, the Institut für Sozialforschung at the University of Frankfurt, focusing on Kant, Hegel, and Marx, and studying with Jürgen Habermas and others, but especially with Theodor Adorno, who agreed to advise her Ph.D. dissertation. During this time, when her responsibilities to her studies in Frankfurt coincided with her absorption in the news of the Birmingham bombing, the metamorphosis of the Black Liberation Movement, and her developing consciousness of common struggles across different cultures, Davis relates, "[her] ability to accomplish anything was directly dependent on [her] ability to contribute something concrete to the struggle." She states that "I wanted to continue my academic work, but I knew I could not do it unless I was politically involved" (1974, 145).

Eventually, exploding conditions in Watts and elsewhere in the United States made Davis feel an irresistible longing and obligation to participate directly in the social transformation process, so she arranged with Marcuse to work once again under his guidance at the University of California at San Diego, where he had accepted a faculty position, and which was close enough to Los Angeles to allow her to immerse herself in simultaneous activist struggle there. Davis does not mention what courses she took at UCSD, though she mentions studying Spinoza, Kant, and Hegel intensively for her preliminary written exams for the Ph.D. (1974, 190). Activism was the focus of Angela Davis's life from the time she arrived in southern California, though it took her some time to find and build trust with an activist community. Simultaneously with pursuing her graduate studies, she worked successfully for the establishment of ethnic studies programs at the University of California at San Diego, ran a "liberation academy" for citizens of a poor Black community in Los Angeles, and worked through tense issues of naming, affiliation, and policy involving her own group, the Oakland-based Black Panthers, and the national Student Nonviolent Coordinating Committee.

Marx continued to be her guiding philosopher during this period, even though she found some Black activists uninterested in him as a white European, and in spite of the fact that the only Black Marxists she worked with were members of the Communist party, which she with other members of the New Left in Europe had criticized as too conservative. Eventually, after careful consideration, and influenced by the example of her activist friend Franklin Alexander, Davis made the fateful decision to become a member of the American Communist party (1974, 189). Though she mentions works by Du Bois (1974, 188) and Lenin (1974, 192), in addition to those of Marx, her lived experience of the dialectics of theorizing within movement activism in the local context of her Los Angeles political base seems to have been the most important influence in the development of her own philosophical and political vision during this period. This experience included the sexism she encountered from revolutionary Black men. They thought only men should be in leadership, that she and her close women colleagues were reinforcing "the black matriarchate" the white sociologist Daniel Patrick Moynihan had written about, and that she should be focusing her energies on home and family (1974, 181–82). As with many activist women, this experience seems to have initiated her feminism, which was to become a major focus of her later theoretical and activist work.

After passing her preliminary doctoral examinations, Davis accepted a faculty position at the University of California at Los Angeles so that she could support herself with a relatively light teaching load while finishing her dissertation and continuing her activism. However, almost immediately after the beginning of her first term at UCLA, then-governor Ronald Reagan and the University of California Board of Regents disrupted Davis's reasonable, life-balancing plans by attempting to fire her because of her membership in the Communist party. This led to a protracted, all-engulfing legal battle and a series of related political developments that consumed her time and attention for years. The doctoral dissertation fell by the wayside as she battled successfully in court against the state law that prohibited state universities from hiring communists, and then to have her contract renewed.

However, these successes in struggle gave way almost immediately to disaster as Davis became one of the Federal Bureau of Investigation's "Ten Most-Wanted Criminals," hunted nationwide on charges of conspiracy, kidnapping, and murder in connection with a failed prison escape attempt by a group of Black men incarcerated in Soledad Prison. A federal judge they were using as a hostage and shield in the ensuing gunfight that ended their escape was killed and also one of their own. Davis was charged with shared responsibility for their actions because the "Soledad Brothers" used a gun registered in her name during their escape attempt, and because she had worked actively for their release, calling them "political prisoners" instead of dangerous criminals, as they were regarded by the state. After going underground and living in terror for months, Davis was apprehended and incarcerated. During this period of deep uncertainty about her own future, Davis worked to educate and build solidarity among the women with whom she was incarcerated, as activist friends outside worked to build support for her as a political prisoner, and a worldwide "Free Angela Davis" movement sprang to life. Her first book, *If They Come in the Morning: Voices of Resistance* (Davis 1971a), an edited collection of essays written by her and by others about her and about the movement to free her and other political prisoners, was published during this time of her rise to international notoriety. In July 1972, she was finally acquitted by a jury of all three charges. Beautiful, articulate young Angela Davis with her Afro hairstyle had become through this process of struggle an international symbol of the Black Liberation Movement, hated or loved by countless people who would never meet her or read her books.[3]

Nonetheless, her notoriety created a popular demand for more information about her life and her ideas, so she was asked to write her second book, *Angela Davis: An Autobiography*, which was published a year and a half later, in 1974. For Davis, "the one extraordinary event of [her] life had nothing to do with [her] as an individual"—given a different twist of history, "another sister or brother could have easily become the political prisoner whom millions of people from throughout the world rescued from persecution and death" (Davis 1974, ix–x). Writing about her life at the unusually young age of thirty, Davis envisioned her story as a

> *political* autobiography that emphasized the people, the events and the forces in [her] life that propelled [her] to [her] present commitment. Such a book might serve a very important and practical purpose. There was the possibility that, having read it, more people would understand why so many of us have no alternative but to offer our lives—our bodies, our knowledge, our will—to the cause of our oppressed people. (1974, x)

In this sense, it was unusual in being both a relational autobiography and a group autobiography, reflecting both her relational psychology and her group-focused political ontology. Davis wrote in her *Autobiography* that her own freedom was a reflection of people's power to organize and transform their will into reality (1974, 398). Without organized struggle, she argued, hurt and rage were meaningless (1974, 170). Her own experience had confirmed the broad transformative claim she had first formulated when she read the *Communist Manifesto* in high school: it is critical to bring all liberation struggles and separate movements together, including those focusing on political prisoners, welfare rights, national liberation, labor, women, and peace (1974, 382). "Unity," she asserts from theory-shaping experience, "is the most potent weapon against racism and political persecution" (1974, 399).

Davis's *Autobiography* addresses philosophical issues of race, class, gender, revolution, political prisoners, commitment, organizing, and the transformational process. During the time when she and George Jackson were simultaneously incarcerated, she wrote him a lengthy letter about women's liberation as inseparable from the liberation of men, which was read to the jury during her trial (1974, 374). A discussion of women's work and the intersection of gender, race, and class surfaces when Mrs. Hemphill is being questioned as a potential juror (1974, 353), as well as in the course of the questioning of Mrs. Young during the trial about her work and about the comings and goings of Davis (1974, 377). Though it was written for and read by a wide audience, Davis's *Autobiography* contains patches of explicit philosophical theorizing. However, most of her theorizing in this work is implicit, including her insightful discussions of commitment, organizing, and the transformational process. Nonetheless, these are some of its major areas of original philosophical contribution, and would well repay the efforts of other scholars to make its theoretical pattern explicit.

The experiences Davis describes in her *Autobiography* have largely shaped her subsequent life, precluding any possibility of a conventional career and providing her with a perennial international platform for addressing a large audience through public speaking, magazine and journal articles, and books. Since winning her own freedom from incarceration, Davis has continued to actively participate in as many political struggles for freedom, justice, and an end to oppression as her physical and intellectual endurance allows. After her acquittal in July 1972, Davis became co-chairperson of the National Alliance against Racist and Political Repression, a nonpartisan political coalition that includes "Black, Chicano, Puerto Rican, Asian, Indian and white people, . . . Communists, Socialists, radical Democrats, and nationalists, . . . ministers and non-churchgoers, . . . workers and students" (1974, 399). In the epilogue of her *Autobiography*, she links the struggles of many other liberation-minded incarcerated people to her own as one great struggle calling for unified action.

We must ensure that the Black leader Reverend Ben Chavis is not sentenced to the 262 years in prison on the charges which that state [North Carolina] has leveled against him. We must liberate Donald Smith, sentenced at age sixteen to forty years behind bars because he participated in the movement at his high school. And we must rescue our innocent sister Marie Hill, whose death sentence, pronounced when she was sixteen, is not a sentence of living death—life without possibility of parole. Across this country, there are hundreds and thousands more like Reverend Chavis, Donald Smith and Marie Hill. We—you and I—are their only hope for life and freedom. (1974, 399)

Her experience of incarceration with other women has led to articles and political speeches addressing the ills of incarceration for women in general, as well as the difference that differences in race, class, and gender make for incarcerated women. These activities have been accompanied by efforts to implement legislation which protects women from some of the gender injustices of incarceration. A recent example includes Davis's discussions of violence against incarcerated women and calls for legislation that will impact such violence, and also require more equity regarding length of sentencing for women's crimes.

Because of her extensive opportunities and commitments as a notorious public intellectual, Davis has published only one book thus far that was intentionally created as a sustained argument, *Women, Race & Class* (Davis 1981). This book made her reputation as a serious scholar in the field of women's studies, and it makes a transformative contribution to Critical Theory, as well. To this she has added *Women, Culture & Politics* (Davis 1989), a philosophically rich collection of some of her speeches from 1984 to 1989, in which she said of her political endeavors that

the work of the political activist inevitably involves a certain tension between the requirement that positions be taken on current issues as they arise and the desire that one's contributions will somehow survive the ravages of time. In this sense the most difficult challenge facing the activist is to respond fully to need of the moment and to do so in such a way that the light one attempts to shine on the present will simultaneously illuminate the future. (Davis 1989, xiii)

Some philosophers have mourned the lack of further theoretical works of sustained argument, but others have praised her for choosing to focus her energies into more concrete and imperative arenas for her philosopher-activist commitment.[4]

Through her speaking and writing, Davis continues to participate in the stream of development and influence of Marxism and Critical Theory, a stream she has turned in a new direction.[5] In contrast with the despairing tendency of Adorno's late work and Marcuse's *One-Dimensional Man,* hope reappears in the stream of Critical Theory through Davis's work, growing not out of theoretical observation of historical events and speculation about the tendencies they express, as it did in Marcuse's 1969 *Essay on Liberation,* and not out of an ideal theory of communicative action, as it does in Habermas's work since 1969, but rather out of transformative praxis in which she has immanently lived change, both in social movements and in the minds and personalities of active participants. Hers is a philosophy of what Marcuse called "the underclass," to which she looks for leadership in the change process, rather than to the industrial working class, which Marxists and Critical Theorists had generally regarded before 1969 as the historically appointed agents of revolution, though co-opted and made passive by advanced capitalism. Class is still centrally important in her analysis, but it takes on a new, more complex meaning as it intersects with race, gender, and ethnicity as equally important theoretical and practical concepts, so that solidarities and divisions are drawn along new lines. Her analysis of class thus takes into account various historically and contemporaneously important divisions that earlier analyses had overlooked, e.g., domestic versus factory labor, slave labor and subsequent sharecropping versus free labor, and the "private" economy versus the "public" economy.

Davis treats racism and sexism as well as class bias as the supporting pillars of capitalism. Thus, cross-difference coalitions are her model of transformative agency: cross-class coalitions of black people (including interventions like the Liberation School she directed in Los Angeles), coalitions of black women and men, coalitions of women of color working together, coalitions of the free and the incarcerated, coalitions across sexual preferences, international coalitions, coalitions of those with homes and the homeless, and coalitions of living activists with past generations who struggled for freedom. As a result of this more complex social analysis, though her transformative goal is still a postcapitalist socialism (Davis 1981, 243), the lines of equity within it are differently drawn than in previous models. And the transformative issues she emphasizes are broader, including, for example, personal safety and security, health, and education, as well as jobs, income, and wealth. Davis attacks the inhumane consequences of capitalism through addressing these issues in her speaking and writing because she thinks these issues will have consciousness-altering, coalition-building revolutionary potential. Her transformative tactics focus on consciousness changing and solidarity building as necessary to deeper changes that take more time. Thus, she advocates many direct-action tactics used by the Civil Rights Movement as well as labor movements and peace movements—petitions, boycotts, marches, demonstrations, strikes, and public confrontations—that may have consciousness changing and solidarity building as their most lasting outcomes. And she emphasizes education, which, even though it takes more time, has even deeper transformative outcomes for the self-concept and the prospective social influence of those involved.

Because of her activist immersion in the change process, Davis has given up any pretense of the detached "scientific" objectivity Adorno, Marcuse, and other early Critical Theorists claimed for themselves, choosing to adopt a standpoint within the struggles that have, at the same time, shaped her life and called forth her partisan allegiance. Nonetheless, like Habermas, Davis claims ethical, historical, and factual support for her standpoint, though unlike him, her argumentative attention has been focused almost entirely on transforming particular practical situations rather than on methodological justification. Likewise, both Davis and Habermas assume and in their differing ways argue for post-Freudian psychologies in which they treat political actors as relational social beings, rather than treating them as or seeking to help them become self-sufficient autonomous individuals (Davis 1981, 242). An important difference, however, is that Davis's political actors are also richly historical beings, shaped in their standpoints, desires, and self-conceptions by particular patterns of power relations and events that must be taken fully into account in analyzing and in transforming their current situations toward a preferable though only broadly specifiable future.

In these respects, Davis's view seems closer to the pragmatism of William James, George Herbert Mead, and John Dewey, whereas Habermas's ideal theoretical approach seems closer to that of John Rawls. Like Davis, James justified his methodology and his epistemology by the lessons of experience and what "works." Like Davis's political actors, Mead's selves are richly historical relational beings, shaped by and shaping others through the interactive process. Like Davis, Dewey was a fierce critic of capitalism; unlike the young Davis, Dewey rejected Soviet-style revolutionary socialism, both because he thought it was brutally excessive and because he didn't think it could work, whereas it seems that Davis has yet to come to terms with the lessons of the Soviet experience since the collapse of the USSR. Like Dewey, nonetheless, and unlike many Marxists, Davis argues for the transformative priority of education.

The central importance of education that builds intellectual skills, teaches history, and increases the self-respect and sense of worthiness of the oppressed resounds throughout Davis's writings, as well as her career as an activist teacher.[6] The educational elements and texts she emphasizes reflect her complex social analysis and her post-Freudian social psychology, as well as her Marxist commitments. Thus, in working with poor and semiliterate black people in her Los Angeles Liberation School, she helped them work their way through essays by Lenin, building their reading skills, their sense of personal worth, and their consciousness of injustice in the process. At the University of California at San Diego, Davis participated in direct-action efforts to introduce ethnic studies into the curriculum, both for the sake of historical accuracy and inclusiveness and for the empowering potential that texts by authors like Douglass and Du Bois have for black students. In her published initial lectures on *The Life and Times of Frederick Douglass* for her course in "Recurring Philosophical Themes in Black Literature" at the University of California at Los Angeles (Davis 1971b), she revealed the transformative power of literacy for Douglass and other slaves in terms of opening up new discourses to them that could set off a series of changes in consciousness and in related life patterns. In the process, Davis suggests a new, philosophically rich conception of human freedom.

Transformative Impacts:
Angela Davis and Black Liberation Theory

The role of education in creating a consciousness that refuses to accept anything less than respect from others is one of the key ideas in Davis's lectures on *The Life and Times of Frederick Douglass*, which contain a brilliant analysis of freedom that is very different from and in many ways superior to its predecessors in the Western philosophical tradition, not only John Locke's view but also Jean-Paul Sartre's and Herbert Marcuse's.[7] These initial lectures were to be followed by others on W.E.B. Du Bois, Jean Toomer, Richard Wright, and John A. Williams, interspersed with lectures on poetry from various periods of African American history and theoretical analyses reflecting the contributions of Du Bois and Frantz Fanon, concluding with comments on related work by African writers and the Black Cuban poet Nicolas Guillen, an incalculable loss if the quality of these lectures would have been even remotely comparable to that of her reflections on Frederick Douglass. For these two initial lectures persuasively articulate a conception of the dialectical relationship between inner freedom and freedom of action that is richly born out in lived experience, ironically, not only in Douglass's life but also in the period of her own life that immediately followed them.

Davis argues that the conception of freedom contained in the history of Black literature is more insightful than that contained within all the differing Western philosophical traditions exactly because it reflects the experience of those whose freedom and whose very human existence was denied, in theory and in practice. In the course of her discussion, Davis transforms the concept of freedom from a static natural property easily taken for granted by those who feel secure in possessing it into the concept of liberation, a dynamic principle of struggle for those whose freedom has been denied. In arguing that freedom must have both an inner and an outer dimension, Davis critiques Sartre's famous claim that even a person in chains remains free because of having the choice between captivity and death. She points out that such a conception of freedom is incompatible with liberation, since in losing one's life, one loses the precondition for freedom-as-liberation. Furthermore, she argues, Sartre's conception of freedom fails to distinguish between two importantly different alternatives to accepting one's captivity, suicide or a struggle for liberation at all costs, which have very different moral and practical implications, and only one of which necessarily implies choosing death. Davis's comments on Douglass also constitute an implied critique of Marcuse's conception of freedom, which treats "freedom of thought" as a necessary precondition of liberation, and which therefore treats liberation as nearly impossible because consciousness of oppression is lacking as "the driving force of a historical practice, the effective cause of qualitative change" (Marcuse 1964, 253). For Davis, freedom is experienced as a journey with an ordered series of dialectically related stages, at the end of which the one who has been denied freedom understands and at least partially achieves its true meaning: the destruction of the master-slave relationship that binds the apparently free master as well as the slave (Davis 1971b, 5). Spurred on by both education and experience, these stages involve changes in consciousness, so that the earlier stages can be seen as inauthentic relative to the final one; these stages in consciousness also involve complementary changes in modes of action and in material circumstances within these institutional bonds.

The inner and outer voyages to freedom, Davis argues, are "mutually determinant" (Davis 1971b, 6), as shown in the life of Douglass. His journey from slavery to freedom began when he asked himself as a child why he or anyone else should be a slave. Davis suggests that such a critical attitude toward one's institutional situation, especially in the face of standard justifications, is a necessary precondition for the change in consciousness that must be a part of transforming one's condition of oppression. What Douglass had responded to, even as a child, was the contradictory nature of slavery and related forms of oppression: freedom is the essence of the human being, but the slave is a human being who is denied freedom, and even, in the attempt to resolve this paradox, denied humanity by those who would control them and who must, in the process of maintaining this system of illusion, abase their own humanity. Resistance offers the slave an alternative resolution to this paradox, which Douglass first realized when he witnessed a slave who refused to accept a whipping, offering his overseer the choice between desisting and shooting him; since he could not accept the consequences of shooting him, the overseer desisted, and thus made him, in Douglass's words, "while legally a slave virtually a free man" (Davis 1971b, 6). Davis argues that such an act of open resistance— "physical resistance, violent resistance"—signifies the first stage in the journey toward freedom, involving rejection not only of the particular oppressive act but also of the oppressive institutional relationship. The slave experiences a rudimentary form of freedom in rejecting the existence of a slave as authentic, in becoming consciously alienated from his or her own earlier unconscious alienation from freedom within an institutional definition of a human self as property. This stage is extremely painful, since it entails heightened awareness of cruelty and indignity of one's own circumstances and those of all with whom one shares ties of love and kinship.

Douglass's "owner" launched him on the path to this painful stage of alienation from his slave existence that eventually produced violent resistance when he unguardedly revealed the consciousness-transforming power of education: "'Learning will spoil the best nigger in the world. If he learns to read the Bible it will forever unfit him to be a slave'"(Davis 1971b, 8). Douglass deduced a different conclusion from this hypothetical syllogism than his "owner" had intended, and than was intended by other master-participants in the slave system by forbidding slave literacy and thereby limiting slave access to ideas critical of the system. Seeing this prohibition as a prescription for self-transformation, Douglass set out to learn to read and to gain as much knowledge of the world of ideas as he could in order to free his mind from the control of his "owner" and the whole master-slave system. Davis calls this his transformation of possibility-opening observed resistance of the slave refusing the whipping into active resistance of his own mind. "Resistance," she argues, "rejection of every level, on every front, are integral elements of the voyage towards freedom. Alienation will become conscious through the process of knowledge" (1971b, 9).

Referring to Hegel's *Phenomenology of Mind*, Davis suggests that the contradictions within the master-slave relationship illustrate a dimension of reality that makes movement, process, and activity possible. The independence of the master is always dependent upon the labor of the slave, who possesses the real, concrete power to change the relationship by resistance, and in this sense, possesses the power to become the master of the relationship. Davis illustrates this contradictory character of the master-slave relationship in her discussion of Douglass's eventual eruption into violent resistance. He had been mentally and physically broken by being driven to work to the point of collapse, and Covey had continued to beat him even as he lay on the ground. When Covey next tries to beat him, Douglass fights back, "instinctively, unconsciously" in Davis's words, because "the fighting madness had come upon me" in Douglass's words, "and I found my strong fingers attached to the throat of the tyrant, as heedless of consequences, at that very moment, as if we stood as equals before the law" (Davis 1971b, 22–23). When no slave will assist him, Covey is unable to enforce his will over Douglass, losing his identity as slave-breaker in that same moment. This same moment is also a turning point in Douglass's life, and Covey never again attempts to whip him. The slave has refused his slavery, and thereby the master has lost his mastery.

The philosophical lessons Davis finds in Douglass's experience include the following ideas. We live in a concrete, historical world, whose actual, experienced features constitute our reality, and which we call upon philosophical reflection to help us change into a world in which we can experience fully human lives. Freedom is necessary for a fully human life, but not a given, unchangeable aspect of human nature; it can be denied by external restraint and limitation of opportunities, by shaping a passive psyche that accepts restraint and limitation, by creating a social milieu in which restraint and limitation are treated as natural and appropriate, and by denying those who are restrained and whose access to knowledge of other ideas and other ways of life is limited. Freedom must be achieved through liberation from real historical relations of domination and oppression, of which the master-slave relation is paradigmatic in showing that neither oppressor nor oppressed can experience freedom until their relation is transformed into one of humane equality. The liberatory process occurs dialectically and in stages of resistance; the meaning and requirements of freedom are understood through experience of its absence as people engaged in liberatory struggle undergo interlinked changes in consciousness, objective conditions, and behavioral responses. Alienation from a fully human existence is a universal characteristic of our species, but most people are unconscious of it, instead living passively and under the influence of illusions, including those created by "normal" social expectations. Coming to consciousness of this alienation is an extremely painful but necessary step on the journey to liberation, a step that is both most possible and most painful for those whose humanity has been most fully denied. Education, including both literacy and the exposure it can bring to the ideas and experiences of others, promotes conscious awareness of their extreme alienation among the oppressed. Consciousness of such extreme alienation does and must provoke resistance, and overt, physical actions of resistance do and must accompany mental resistance. In conditions of extreme restraint and limitation, such actions may be, and may need to be, violent in order to change objective material conditions. No human being can be liberated alone because we are all interlinked within social institutions. Thus, the liberatory project of each individual must entail the liberation of all humanity. The historical experience of our forebears in the liberation struggle is inseparable from our own, as well as an invaluable guide to pitfalls and possibilities for effective transformation.

Toward the end of her first lecture on Douglass, Davis reveals her sense that his struggle and the struggle she herself is engaged in are one.

> To foreshadow Frederick Douglass' path from slavery to freedom, even when he attains his own freedom, he does not see the real goal as having been attained. It is only with the total abolition of the institution of slavery that his misery, his desolation, his alienation will be eliminated. And not even then, for there will remain remnants and there still remain in existence today the causes which gave rise to slavery (Davis 1971b, 10).

In addition to illuminating the historical and literary dimensions of Douglass's *Life and Times*, Davis aims to explore philosophical themes in the journey to liberation that reveal the dynamics of oppressive institutional and psychic structures and their liberatory transformations as an active tool for continuing and expanding the liberation process in our contemporary world, which is a continuation out of the past.

> The reasons underlying the demands for Black Studies Programs are many, but the most important one is the necessity to establish a continuum from the past to the present, to discover the genesis of problems which continue to exist today, to discover how our ancestors dealt with them. We can learn from the philosophical as well as concrete experience of the slave. We can learn what methods of coming to grips with oppression were historically successful and what methods were failures. The failures are crucial, because we do not want to be responsible for the repetition of history in its brutality. We learn what the mistakes were in order not to duplicate them. (Davis 1971b, 13).

In the process of harvesting these philosophical lessons and concrete experiences from the past, Davis redefines philosophy as a broadly human activity in which even slaves have participated, often with greater insight about central philosophical concepts like freedom than is evidenced by the great master names of the Western world, whose understanding is distorted by privilege and the illusion of independence.[8]

Tracing her view back to Socrates, Davis argues that philosophy should be understood as an active and dynamic guiding process for living well, rather than as a detached attempt to define static concepts devoid of historical and transformative implications.

> Philosophy is supposed to perform the task of generalizing aspects of experience, and not just for the sake of formulating generalizations, of dis-

covering formulas as some of my colleagues in the discipline believe. My idea of philosophy is that if it is not relevant to human problems, if it does not tell us how we can go about eradicating some of the misery in this world, then it is not worth the name of philosophy. I think that Socrates made a very profound statement when he asserted that the raison d'etre of philosophy is to teach us proper living. In this day and age "proper living" means liberation from the urgent problems of poverty, economic necessity and indoctrination, mental oppression. (Davis 1971b, 14)

Thus, Davis's conception of the raison d'etre for Black Studies in the curriculum is not simply liberal inclusiveness of another viewpoint or another variety of experience, and her claims for the significance of its philosophical dimension require more than simply valuing the views of a racial underclass. Rather, she argues that the history of the philosophical dimension of African American experience more effectively illuminates the American experience, and the larger human experience of which it is a part, than do the works of privileged white male philosophers, even those whose work she greatly admires such as Marx, Sartre, and Marcuse. Moreover, she argues that the conception of philosophy that comes out of the literature of Black experience is not merely an alternative conception, but a superior conception that should stimulate the dominant philosophical enterprise to transform itself from detachment to engagement in the struggle to change the world.

Transformative Impacts: Angela Davis and Feminist Theory

Angela Davis's subsequent writings on feminist theory closely connect to her 1969 *Lectures on Liberation,* both in her historical method of argument and as extensions of analysis of the meaning of liberation she offers there. *Women, Race & Class* (Davis 1981), *Women, Culture & Politics* (Davis 1989), and her more recent work all derive contemporary analyses from historical antecedents. The problem they address continues to be what she had earlier called liberation from interlinked "poverty, economic necessity and indoctrination, mental oppression" (Davis 1971b, 14). And they analyze the broader question of women's liberation through focusing on the experience and the transformative requirements of women of color, especially African American women who, as the descendants of slaves, continue as a Marcusian "underclass" to carry on Douglass's journey toward the liberation of all humanity. Her work in feminist theory implies and reflects her earlier work and her continuing, expanding lived experience. Thus, to feminist theory, she contributes the legacy of Marxism and Critical Theory, including class analysis, as well as the legacy of Black Liberation Theory; at the same time, her work in feminist theory contributes a unique, hopeful, and highly insightful class analysis and transformative model to Marxism and Critical Theory, an important analysis of the intersection of gender and class with race to Black Liberation Theory, and, in her latest work, culture as a category in the philosophy of liberatory transformation linking her theorizing and her activist leadership in all these fields.

One important site of Davis's contribution of class analysis to feminist theory and practice is "The Approaching Obsolescence of Housework: A Working Class Perspective" in *Women, Race & Class* (Davis 1981). Her critical concern seems to respond to Betty Friedan's white middle class presumptions in generalizing about the domestic situation of all women in *The Feminine Mystique,* and to the similar presumptions of other white middle class feminists who have followed Friedan (Friedan 1963). Davis's particular transformative suggestions echo Charlotte Perkins Gilman's turn-of-the-century call for the socialization of housework in *Women and Economics* (Gilman 1966) as well as her feminist utopian novel, *Herland* (Gilman 1979). While agreeing with other feminist theorists and activists that housework is an obstacle to women's liberation, Davis argues that it differently impacts women relative to differences in class. She argues against the proposal simply to compensate women for previously unpaid housework, and calls instead for its socialization, i.e., for all women to enter the mainstream work force and for the various elements of what is now called "housework" to be done by paid laborers, like any other valued work in the public economy.

Davis's analysis here combines some of her invaluable contributions to feminist theory with some theoretical limitations it will be her challenge to overcome in her future writings. The most striking flaw in this essay is Davis's universalizing overstatement of the oppressive character of housework. For many women today, the problem with housework lies with some of the particular tasks involved (about which women vary as to which are distasteful and which are grounding and satisfying) and overall, having too much of it, especially in combination with too many of the responsibilities outside the home Davis regards as preferable and more respect-garnering. In reality, though some middle class women are fortunate in having relatively fulfilling work outside the home, many working class women find their paid work to be drudgery within labor force conditions of insecurity and non-respect, even if in some cases they are treated equally with men doing the same jobs. While many working class women surely would be glad to have the double burden of working both inside and outside the home lightened, their choice about how to do this would not in all cases be to have their present household responsibilities covered by others through socialization of housework, so that they could focus their energies more exclusively on their present economically productive work. Nonetheless, what is so important about her discussion there is that it brings class into the analysis of women's condition, breaking down previously widespread essentialism about women based on a middle class model.

In contrast with her dismissal here of the value of housework to women, in her first chapter from the same book, "The Legacy of Slavery: Standards for a New Womanhood," Davis argues that slave women's domestic labor for their own families was crucial in maintaining their own and their family's sense of humanity, as well as their related ability to resist oppression, and that some men shared this liberatory "housework." In that context, Davis argues that black slave women's experience of the meaning of housework for their own family was entirely different than that of the emerging industrial middle class white women, in that it contributed to their positive equality with black men instead of undermining it, and in that they experienced it as fulfilling and liberatory, even though it was an arduous second set of tasks after a hard day's work in the fields that they did not experience as fulfilling (Davis 1981, 17, 23, and 29).

This essay taken with the other one suggests that the meaning and value of women's work to themselves and to others is highly contextual, that class is one important factor in understanding differences, and that a historically dynamic larger social and economic system creates highly influential but not totally determinative preconditions for alternative attitudes and experiences. Overly sharp dichotomies of housework versus economic labor, working class versus middle class, black versus white, and desirable versus distasteful may be distorting Davis's analysis somewhat in both essays; the lines are not that sharp, partly because we are all members of more than one group, and partly because individual differences always make a difference, too.

In her 1989 collection of speeches, *Women, Culture, & Politics* (Davis 1989), Davis proposes an approach to resolving "the difference problem," which was the focus of much of her historical analysis in *Women, Race & Class* (Davis 1981), and which still prevents women from effectively working as a united liberatory coalition.[9] The first section of this book, "On Women and the Pursuit of Equality and Peace," interconnects focal feminist issues of violence against women, abortion rights and freedom from involuntary sterilization, black women's health, the crisis of black families, and the struggle to prevent nuclear omnicide with what she regards as their formative and contextual issues of race, class, and the humanly warping effects of profit-oriented capitalism. In the first two essays, "Let Us All Rise Together: Radical Perspectives on Empowerment for Afro-American Women" (1987) and "Facing Our Common Foe: Women and the

Struggle against Racism" (1984), Davis places herself within the visionary framework that motivated the formation of the National Association of Colored Women's Clubs in 1896, identifying herself too as a woman wishing to work with other women "for the benefit of *all* humanity" (Davis 1989, 4). She analyzes the difficulties of forming a united women's movement as due to the same cause then as now: the tendency of relatively powerful white, middle class women to focus only on issues related to their own direct experience of oppression, and to conceptualize those issues in ways that reflect their own relatively privileged experience. Many issues that are of central importance to large numbers of Black women, she points out—such as unemployment, homelessness, racist violence—are relatively invisible to white middle class women. Other shared issues, such as homophobia, child welfare, sexism in the family and the workplace, and international peace and justice, are differently experienced and contextualized, and therefore, the solutions to such problems that seem desirable differ. This is why, Davis suggests, Black women and other women of color do not find women's organizations dominated by white middle class women appealing and responsive to their concerns. A successful women's movement, she argues, must be revolutionary, multiracial, and responsive to the issues affecting poor and working class women, "such as jobs, pay equity, paid maternity leave, federally subsidized child care, protection from sterilization abuse, and subsidized abortions" (Davis 1989, 7). It must work for an agenda that raises up all oppressed peoples (Davis 1989, 13), including an "unequivocal challenge to monopoly capitalism as a major obstacle to the achievement of equality," ultimately working "to forge a new socialist order" (Davis 1989, 14).

Creating an agenda for a united feminist movement is only one of the many interlinked issues Davis addresses in *Women, Culture & Politics* (Davis 1989). In another essay in this volume, "Women in Egypt: A Personal View," Davis confronts her own ethnocentric assumptions, making culture visible as a feminist category of analysis and a practical liberatory characteristic that must be taken into account. In an essay entitled "Brushstrokes for Social Change: The Art of Rupert Garcia" from the collection's last section, "On Education and Culture," Davis implicitly replies to Adorno's aestheticism by praising politically transformative art. And in another essay from this same section, "Imagining the Future," Davis challenges a graduating class of high school seniors to create their own utopian vision for the future that will continue the liberation struggle that had made this moment possible for them.

> Now it is your turn to imagine a more humane future—a future of justice, equality, and peace. And if you wish to fulfill your dreams, which remain the dreams of my generation as well, you must also stand up and

speak out against war, against joblessness, and against racism. (Davis 1989, 172)

It is this sense of the liberation journey and one's personal life and career path as being one that represents the nature of Angela Davis's own converging commitments to speaking, writing, teaching, and political activism. Such a lived commitment to an activist life that goes beyond theory to embrace concrete involvement with the various political struggles Davis has supported locates her in the same arena with historical and recent heroes who, like her, have transformed the liberation struggle for freedom, justice, and an end to oppressions. That Davis is counted among these was shown by her reception as keynote speaker at the historic national conference "Black Women in the Academy: Defending Our Name, 1894–1994," meeting at the Massachusetts Institute of Technology, at which 2,000 women embodying the entire spectrum of colors and cultures leaped to their feet as she stepped to the speaker's podium, let out a prolonged roar of joy, and continued to laugh, to cry, and to cheer throughout her remarks. Being counted among the heroes of liberation, especially in light of the scarcity of recent ones, and the even greater scarcity of recognizable American (S)heroes as well as African American ones, makes her an extraordinary philosopher, so beloved by those who share her ideals and her transformative vision, and so notorious among those who oppose them.

NOTES

1. Davis also writes about her experience in Cuba, the Watts Riots, and the birth of Black Power as turning points which began her concrete commitment to the liberation struggle.

2. With Horkheimer and Adorno, Marcuse had been a key participant in the development of Critical Theory within their Institut für Sozialforschung at the University of Frankfurt, before the Nazis impelled them to flee to the United States. Marcuse had remained in America when Adorno returned to Frankfurt after World War II, and Davis had heard some of his lectures during the summer of 1964, after her studies at the Sorbonne, and had begun to read the earlier works of Horkheimer, Adorno, and Marcuse in English translation.

3. In an essay written some twenty years after the events that made her notorious and her image recognizable around the world, Davis self-mockingly expresses the also-serious concern that to many young people of a later generation, she is remembered primarily for the transformative fashion influence of her Afro hairstyle. See her "Afro Images: Politics, Fashion, and Nostalgia" (Davis 1994a).

4. In reply to such a lamentation and implied criticism from Anatol Anton, Leonard Harris wrote as follows: "I do not believe that the arena of professional philosophy in America at this stage in history is the best place to pursue substantive issues arising from the reality of oppression—it is one site of struggle but not a site that makes much difference to the way the world is. And influencing my profession of philosophy to substantively take into account the reality of the oppressed by participating in that profession seems to me far less a worthy endeavor than might be supposed. The reason for this is that professional philosophy is more often influenced by events and trends outside of the profession (civil rights movement, socialist revolutions, feminism, etc.) than by its own internal dialogues. I believe that Angela is empowered to address any issue she so chooses, despite the oppressive forces that have been arrayed against her. No doubt those forces tend to sway radicals away from the field of philosophy (understanding here that philosophy is one tool in the arsenal of weapons that can be aligned on behalf of the oppressed). At the same time, the field of philosophy as currently structured is barren. Analogously, racial segregation is an evil, but assimilation into a capitalist class order is not a good. The exclusion of Angela from the professional field of philosophy is an evil, but addressing Kant and Hegel is not necessarily a good—particularly if we read Angela's work as a body of texts themselves conveying and developing a philosophy out of social analysis. Such a reading does not require addressing Marcuse, Kant, Hegel, or Marx—it requires reading Angela Davis as the central subject and broadening our conception of what's philosophically interesting." See Harris 1990.

5. Selected examples of Davis's speeches and essays since 1989 are included in the references (below).

6. After her court battles and subsequent worldwide speaking tour, Angela Davis returned to her activist work in education, teaching in various departments at a series of California universities until she developed ongoing relationships with San Francisco State University (1978–91) and the San Francisco Art Institute (1977–89). She also has been an instructor in the Education Program of the San Francisco County Jail (1990–91). She is presently Professor of the History of Consciousness at the University of California at Santa Cruz. She resumed teaching Critical Theory at Santa Cruz in 1995.

7. A revised and abbreviated version of her lectures is included as "Unfinished Lecture on Liberation—II" in Harris (1983). This version lacks some of the detail and immediacy of the original lectures. The remaining lectures in Davis's class on "Recurring Philosophical Themes in Black Literature" were never given because of Governor Ronald Reagan's and the California Board of Regents' decision to fire her from her faculty position because of her membership in the Communist party. Though she eventually was able to overturn their decision in court, the time for composing the other lectures was lost to the legal battle.

8. Davis's analysis of the master-slave relation strongly suggests the influence of Frantz Fanon, just as her analysis of the importance of education strongly reflects the influence of W.E.B. Du Bois.

9. Davis assembled this collection at her mother's suggestion as "an effort to retrospectively provide some continuity to a life that has been informed for almost two decades by local and global struggles for progressive social change," an activist life that has very little time for quiet scholarly reflection and carefully crafted book-length arguments (Davis 1989, xiii-xiv).

REFERENCES

Seyla Benhabib. 1986. *Critique, Norm, and Utopia: A Study of the Foundations of Critical Theory*. New York: Columbia University Press.

Angela Davis. 1971a. *If They Come In the Morning: Voices of Resistance*. New York: Third Press.

———. 1971b. *Lectures on Liberation*. New York: New York Committee.

———. 1974. *Angela Davis: An Autobiography*. New York: Random House.

———.1981. *Women, Race & Class*. New York: Random House.

———. 1989. *Women, Culture & Politics*. New York: Random House.

———. 1992. "Meditations on the Legacy of Malcolm X." In *Malcolm X: In Our Own Image*, ed. Joe Wood. New York: Doubleday/Anchor Books.

———. 1993a. "Keynote Address: Third National Conference on Women of Color and the Law," *Stanford Law Review* 43:6.

———. 1993b. Review of Patricia Hill Collins's *Black Feminist Thought: Knowledge, Consciousness and the Politics of Empowerment*, in *Teaching Philosophy* 16:4.

———. 1994a. "Afro Images: Politics, Fashion, and Nostalgia." *Critical Inquiry* 21 (Autumn 1994).

———. 1994b. "Black Women in the Academy." *Callaloo* 17:2.

Betty Friedan. 1963. *The Feminine Mystique*. New York: Norton.

Charlotte Perkins Gilman. [1898] 1966. *Women and Economics*. New York: Harper and Row.

———. 1979. *Herland*. New York: Pantheon Books.

Leonard Harris. 1983. *Philosophy Born of Struggle: Anthology of Afro-American Philosophy from 1917*. Dubuque: Kendall-Hunt.

———. 1990. "More About Angela Davis: Response to Anatol Anton." *Radical Philosophy Association Newsletter* 21 (Winter 1990).

Herbert Marcuse. 1964. *One-Dimensional Man*. Boston: Beacon Press.

———. 1969. *An Essay on Liberation*. Boston: Beacon Press.

CONTRIBUTORS

SISTER MARY CATHARINE BASEHEART (1910–1994) was Distinguished Professor of Philosophy at Spalding University. In 1981 she was the first winner of the Grawemeyer award for college teaching for her philosophy course "Focusing on the Person." She published numerous articles on Edith Stein and was founder and first director of the Edith Stein Center for Study and Research at Spalding.

DONALD BEGGS, Visiting Assistant Professor of Philosophy at Mills College, is working on two books, *Modernity's Navel: Historicity and Violence in Heidegger and Sartre* and *Ecological Reason: Nature and Norms after Metaphysics*.

MARTHA BRANDT BOLTON is Professor of Philosophy at Rutgers University. Her writings on early modern philosophy have appeared in *Locke's Philosophy: Content and Context, Central Themes in Early Modern Philosophy,* and *History of Philosophy Quarterly*.

JOANNE CUTTING-GRAY is the author of *Woman as "Nobody" and the Novels of Fanny Burney* as well as articles on eighteenth-century British and American literature, philosophy, and politics.

JANE DURAN is Lecturer in the Humanities and Visiting Fellow in Philosophy at the University of California, Santa Barbara. She is the author of *Toward a Feminist Epistemology* and articles on theories of knowledge and the philosophy of science.

MAUREEN L. EGAN is Professor of Philosophy at the College of Our Lady of the Elms. Her recent research has been on nineteenth-century feminist intellectual history of the United States.

LOIS FRANKEL is the author of numerous articles on topics in seventeenth-century philosophy appearing in *Journal of the History of Philosophy, History of Philosophy Quarterly*, and the edited volumes *Causation in Early Modern Philosophy* and *A History of Women Philosophers*. She is active in the politics of reproductive freedom, with a particular interest in using computer technology to empower women's groups.

JUDITH MARY GREEN teaches philosophy at Seattle University where her courses include African American Philosophy, Native American Philosophy, and Feminist Theory. She has published articles on Aristotle, feminist theory, the philosophy of Martin Luther King, Jr., American pragmatism, the philosophy of political transformation, environmental ethics, and teaching multicultural philosophy. Together with Blanche Radford Curry, Leonard Harris, and Lucius Outlaw, she is working on *Philosophy and Cultural Diversity: Motives, Methods, and Models for Curricular Transformation.*

KAREN GREEN lectures in philosophy at Monash University. She is the author of *The Woman of Reason: Feminism, Humanism, and Political Thought,* as well as articles on feminism and liberalism.

JOKE J. HERMSEN studied literature and philosophy in Amsterdam and Paris and has published two books, *Sharing the Difference Feminist Debates in Holland* (Routledge, 1991) and *Nomadisch Narcisme. Sexe, Liefde en Kunst in het werk van Lou Andreas Salome, Belle van Zuylen en Ingeborg Bachmann* (Kampen, 1993). She is a senior researcher in the Department of Philosophy at the Catholic University of Brabant in Tilburg, the Netherlands and serves on the editorial boards of several literary and philosophical reviews.

JO ELLEN JACOBS, Professor of Philosophy at Millikin University, has published articles appearing in *Journal of Aesthetics and Art Criticism, Journal of Aesthetic Education, Hypatia, Journal of Psychohistory, Teaching Philosophy,* and *Approaches to Teaching Masterpieces of World Literature.*

HELEN J. JOHN, S.N.D., is Professor of Philosophy at Trinity College, Washington, D.C. She is the author of *The Thomist Spectrum* and articles on metaphysics, personal commitment, feminism, and bioethics.

LINDA LOPEZ MCALISTER teaches feminist philosophy and theory and is Chair of the Women's Studies Department at the University of South Florida. She is editor of *Hypatia: A Journal of Feminist Philosophy* and has written numerous articles about early twentieth-century German women philosophers. She is at work on a history of feminist philosophy in the United States.

MARGARET McFADDEN teaches women's history and feminist theory in the Department of Interdisciplinary Studies at Appalachian State University. She is completing a book entitled *Mothers of the Matrix: The Development of Women's International Networks in the Atlantic Community, 1820–1880* and has published articles and reviews in such journals as *Signs, Methodist History,* and *Women's Studies International Forum.*

CATRIONA MACKENZIE is a Lecturer in Philosophy at Macquarie University. She has published articles on feminist philosophy, ethics, and applied ethics in *The Australasian Journal of Philosophy, Hypatia,* and edited collections. Her current research concerns feminist philosophy, moral psychology, and medical ethics.

URSULE MOLINARO is the author of eleven novels, most recently *Power Dreamers.* She has also published four collections of short stories and ten plays.

ANDREA NYE teaches philosophy and feminist theory at the University of Wisconsin at Whitewater. She is the author of numerous books, including *Feminist Theory and the Philosophies of Man, Words of Power, Philosophia,* and *Philosophy and Feminism: At the Border.*

BLANCHE RADFORD CURRY is an Associate Professor of Philosophy at Fayetteville State University. She received her Ph.D. in philosophy from Brown University. Her research and teaching areas include moral and social value inquiry, multicultural theory, and feminist theory. She is an assistant editor of the American Philosophical Association's *Newsletter on Philosophy and the Black Experience,* on the editorial board of *Hypatia: A Journal of Feminist Philosophy,* a Fulbright-Hayes Japan Fellow, and has done research on East Africa and China. She has published articles on feminist theory and multicultural theory. She and Judith Mary Green became collaborative writing partners when they taught at Eckerd College in St. Petersburg, Florida.

MARY ELLEN WAITHE is Professor of Philosophy at Cleveland State University. In 1981 she founded the Project on the History of Women in Philosophy, and she has edited the four-volume series *A History of Women Philosophers.*

INDEX